P9-CRX-610

THE AGE OF ABBOT DESIDERIUS

THE AGE OF ABBOT DESIDERIUS

Montecassino, the Papacy, and the Normans in the Eleventh and Early Twelfth Centuries

BY

H. E. J. COWDREY

CLARENDON PRESS · OXFORD

1983

Oxford University Press, Walton Street, Oxford OX2 6DP
London Glasgow New York Toronto
Delhi Bombay Calcutta Madras Karachi
Kuala Lumpur Singapore Hong Kong Tokyo
Nairobi Dar es Salaam Cape Town
Melbourne Auckland
and associated companies in
Beirut Berlin Ibadan Mexico City Nicosia

Oxford is a trade mark of Oxford University Press

Published in the United States
by Oxford University Press, New York

British Library Cataloguing in Publication Data

Cowdrey, H. E. J.
The age of Abbot Desiderius.
1. Desiderius 2. Abbazia di Montecassino
3. Abbots—Italy—Cassino—Biography
I. Title
255'.1'0924 BR874

ISBN 0-19-821939-3

Typeset by Joshua Associates, Oxford
Printed in Great Britain
at the University Press, Oxford
by Eric Buckley
Printer to the University

Preface

THIS book has a twofold origin. First, I wished to extend work formerly done on the abbey of Cluny in the age of the reform papacy by studying Montecassino, the oldest of western black-monk monasteries, during the same period. Secondly, it arose from work towards a book on Pope Gregory VII. The papacy of his time has been extensively investigated in the light of its dealings with North Italy and the countries to the north of the Alps. But it also demands to be viewed as it were from the south, and from this angle it is less well understood. Given the limitations of the evidence for Montecassino and South Italy especially during the critical decade of the 1080s, an attempt so to view it must be to a large extent centred upon Rome and upon papal dealings there with Henry IV of Germany and his antipope, Clement III (Archbishop Guibert of Ravenna). Hence, in the third chapter of this book I have attempted at some length to offer a fresh interpretation of those dealings. In the fourth chapter I try to look afresh at the brief but significant pontificate of Gregory's immediate successor, Victor III (Abbot Desiderius of Montecassino). These chapters form the core of the book. But the developments that they consider can be understood only against the background of the monastic institution at Montecassino that Desiderius had done much to create in its contemporary form. My earlier chapters examine its monastic life, and its personal and institutional connections with the papacy. I am aware that a full-scale interpretation of the events with which I am concerned in my central chapters would have to deal with German along with Italian affairs. But I think that the latter can usefully be considered on their own, and that such a comprehensive treatment as I hope one day to attempt would serve to confirm the tentative conclusions of this study.

While writing this book I have incurred a number of debts. I am particularly grateful to the Board of the Faculty of Modern History at Oxford University for appointing me to a five-year Special Lecturership from 1976 to 1981, without which this book could not have been written; the Board also contributed to the expense of typing my final draft. A grant from the research funds of the

British Academy enabled me to visit Montecassino and other places in South Italy. There I must especially acknowledge the kindness of Don Faustino Avagliano at Montecassino, of Don Simeone Leone at la Cava, and of Fr. Gerardo Cioffari, OP, at San Nicolà, Bari. Professor Dr Horst Fuhrmann and the Zentraldirektion of *Monumenta Germaniae Historica* most courteously acceded to my request that I might be allowed to make the citations from the new edition of the Montecassino Chronicle that appear in my Appendices; and the Department of Manuscripts at the British Library permitted me to publish material from MSS Arundel 390 and Cotton Nero C.V. A final and very great debt of which I am conscious is to two Oxford research students with whose work in the area of this book I have been concerned —Dr G. A. Loud, whose thesis I supervised, and Dr D. Whitton, of whose thesis I was an examiner. They will recognize here more of their work and of our conversations than I have specifically acknowledged; I express my gratitude once and for all.

St. Edmund Hall H. E. J. C.
Oxford

Contents

Introduction

i. MONTECASSINO AND THE REFORM PAPACY

TWENTIETH-CENTURY historians have come conventionally and appropriately to describe the eight and a half decades between 1046 and 1130 as the age of the reform papacy. It opened with the intervention at Rome of the Emperor Henry III (1039–56), when he sought to wrest control of the apostolic see from local aristocratic factions and to promote the spiritual and moral reform of the church. He inaugurated a series of praiseworthy popes drawn from Germany, Lorraine, and North Italy; the most notable of his own appointments was that of the Lotharingian, Leo IX (1048–54). Especially in the last quarter of the eleventh century, the movement for the reform of the church broadened into one for the liberty of the church through the securing of its more effective obedience to the apostolic see. It was marked by the epoch-making reigns of Popes Gregory VII (1073–85) and Urban II (1088–99), between which fell the brief pontificate of Victor III (1086–7). By contrast with their reforming predecessors since 1046, these three popes were life-long monks; and in the twelfth century the succession of monk-popes continued with Paschal II (1099–1118) and Gelasius II (1118–19). Then, with Calixtus II (1119–24) and Honorius II (1124–30), the papacy reverted to non-monks. Upon Honorius' death the Anacletan Schism (1130–8) brought to an end the reform papacy as it had emerged in the eleventh century. In 1130 a disputed election resulted in the election of Anacletus II (1130–8) by a large number of the Roman cardinals; but his rival, Innocent II (1130–43), in 1138 emerged victorious, thanks mainly to the formidable backing of St. Bernard of Clairvaux and to other support from north of the Alps: *pulsus urbe, ab orbe suscipitur.*[1] In the age of St. Bernard the papacy embarked upon a new phase of its history, in which older landmarks of reform had been overthrown and new ones were set up.

[1] Bernard of Clairvaux, *Ep.* 124, *Sancti Bernardi Opera*, vii. *Epistolae*, i, edd. J. Leclercq and H. Rochais (Rome, 1974), 305–7, at 306.

For the Anacletan Schism was not a conflict between Anacletan opponents and Innocentian sponsors of ecclesiastical reform, but between older-fashioned and more forward-looking champions of it, both of whose parties sought to enlist the loyalty of Western Christendom. Innocent found his support, not only from Bernard and the Cistercian order, but also amongst other new orders like the Carthusians and the canons regular, as well as from Abbot Peter the Venerable at Cluny. Anacletus had by contrast been a Cluniac monk of an earlier generation than Peter the Venerable's; he was favoured by the old guard at Rome who clung doggedly to an outlook formed there in the days of Pope Gregory VII, and also by many in South Italy, including Roger II of Sicily. This contrast in reforming styles and the eventual victory of the Innocentians furnish the justification for regarding the outbreak in 1130 of the Anacletan Schism as 'the end of the reform papacy'.[2]

Such an estimate of the Anacletan Schism finds confirmation in the iconography of two embellishments made during the 1120s and 1130s to the Lateran palace at Rome. The first was a series of frescos executed in Calixtus II's audience chamber. It looked back to the reform papacy's triumph over Clement III (Archbishop Guibert of Ravenna), who was antipope from 1084 to 1100. The three popes who opposed him were shown as having eventually been victorious, and a legend ran:

> Gregorius Victor Urbanus cathedram tenuerunt;
> Gibertus cum suis tandem destructi fuerunt.[3]

Calixtus also built an oratory to St. Nicholas. During his ascendancy in Rome Anacletus decorated it with a comprehensive retrospect which G. B. Ladner has described as 'the apotheosis of the reform papacy' of the past seventy years.[4] In the upper

[2] See esp. H.-W. Klewitz, 'Das Ende des Reformpapsttums', *Reformpapsttum*, pp. 207–59; Schmale, *Schisma.* For a recent appraisal of their interpretations, see E.-D. Hehl, *Kirche und Krieg im 12. Jahrhundert. Studien zu kanonischem Recht und politischer Wirklichkeit*, Monographien zur Geschichte des Mittelalters, 19 (Stuttgart, 1980), 28–38, 58–9.

[3] Details survive in drawings by Panvinio (late sixteenth cent.) in Vatican Library, MS Barb. lat. 2738, ff. 103v–105v: G. B. Ladner, *I ritratti dei papi nell'antichità e nel medioevo*, i (Vatican City, 1941), 195–201 and plate 19; C. Walter, 'Papal Imagery in the Lateran Palace', *Cahiers archéologiques*, xx (1970), 155–76, esp. 157, 162–6; xxi (1971), 109–36, esp. 109–23.

[4] The oratory was demolished in the eighteenth century; but in 1698 Gattula had made a reproduction that appears in his *Historia*, plate X, with a description on pp. 362–8. See also Ladner, op. cit. 202–18 and plate 20; Walter, art. cit., *Cahiers*

half of Anacletus' fresco, the Virgin sat crowned with Calixtus and Anacletus at her feet. (The victorious party in the Anacletan Schism naturally eliminated Anacletus from the composition.) Calixtus and Anacletus were supported by two popes of antiquity: Sylvester I, the contemporary of the Emperor Constantine, and Anacletus I, the patron of Anacletus II. In the centre of the lower half was St. Nicholas, to whom the oratory was dedicated; he was flanked by two yet more renowned popes of antiquity: St. Leo the Great and St. Gregory the Great. Outside them were depicted to Nicholas' right Popes Alexander II, Gregory VII, and Victor III; and to his left Urban II, Paschal II, and Gelasius II. They were the six reforming popes who had reigned from 1061 to 1119. In the fresco they stood as equals in esteem, mitred and making gestures of blessing; each had a halo about his head, and the adjective *sanctus* preceded his name. Such a choice and juxtaposition of ancient and latter-day popes was manifestly intended to exhibit the six as victorious restorers of the authentic Christian past who were now associated with its heroes in the roll-call of sanctity. Such was the image of the reform papacy as in Anacletus' day its conservative propagandists presented it.

Of the popes in the Lateran frescos, two—Victor III and Gelasius II—had been monks of Montecassino; so, briefly, had another reforming pope, Stephen IX (1057–8). It is not surprising that Cassinese monks should have figured in the papal succession since 1046. For while popes like Leo IX, Gregory VII, and Urban II were raising the papacy to the level of authority that it was to maintain virtually without challenge for the next two centuries, Montecassino was enjoying the golden age of its long history. This golden age was established by Abbot Desiderius (1058–87), who became Pope Victor III, and it continued if with some reduction in glory under his successor as abbot, Oderisius I (1087–1105). Under their rule Montecassino claimed and was generally allowed a primacy of age and honour amongst the major monastic centres of the western church.[5] It

archéologiques, xx (1970), 157, 160–2, fig. 3; H. Bloch, 'The Schism of Anacletus II and the Glanfeuil Forgeries of Peter the Deacon of Monte Cassino', *Traditio*, viii (1952), 159–264, esp. 180 and the plate facing; H. Toubert, 'Le renouveau paléochrétien à Rome au début du XIIe siècle', *Cahiers archéologiques*, xx (1970), 99–154, esp. 153–4.

[5] Thus, e.g., the *Liber pontificalis* described it as *monasteriorum omnium caput ac principium*: *LP* ii. 311; cf. Paschal II, *Epp.* 139, 338, Migne, *PL* clxiii. 145A, 295B.

was the foundation of St. Benedict of Nursia, the patriarch of western monasticism. He had moved there *c.*529 with a small band of followers; there, some twenty years later, he died. The very little that is known about him is preserved in the second book of the *Dialogues* of St. Gregory the Great, pope from 590 to 604.[6] It was from the *Dialogues* that men learnt how Benedict had destroyed at Montecassino the symbols of idolatrous worship and had instead set up oratories of St. Martin and St. John the Baptist. Very gradually over the succeeding centuries, the Rule that Benedict drew up for his monks *c.*530–40 won acceptance throughout the west as the basis of its monastic life. So by the eleventh century the monks of the west and all who held them in honour looked to Montecassino as the fountainhead of monasticism in their part of the Christian world. At Montecassino itself Abbot Desiderius and the monks were mindful of Benedict's promise to his sons that after his death he would work with them no less effectually than during his lifetime.[7] Montecassino enjoyed an especial prestige in its own eyes and in the church at large because Benedict's work was known from the pages of Gregory the Great, the pope who in medieval estimation was the greatest amongst the vicars of St. Peter. Rome and Montecassino, St. Peter and St. Benedict: these pairs stood together at the heart of the Christian religion as understood and practised in the Latin west.

Yet throughout the centuries that divided Abbot Desiderius from Benedict the history of Montecassino and its community was intermittent and troubled. The monastic life that Benedict established did not persist there even until Gregory the Great became pope in 590: in 581 the Lombard invasions caused it to be abandoned, and its monks fled to Rome, where they continued their way of life near the Lateran palace. Such were the vicissitudes of its history that, when its early twelfth-century historian Leo of Ostia reviewed the six centuries of its past, he picked out four high points when it was ruled by exceptional

[6] *Gregorii magni Dialogi, libri iv*, ed. U. Moricca, *Font. stor. Italia*, lvii. 71–134; for the medieval view, see *Chron. Cas.* i. 1, pp. 16–19. The conclusions of modern scholarship are summarized by G. Penco, *Storia del monachesimo in Italia delle origini alla fine del medio evo* (Rome, 1961), 47–84.

[7] 'Praesentior vobis, dilectissimi filii, carnis deposito onere vestrique per Dei gratiam cooperator existam assiduus': cited from Odo of Glanfeuil, *Vita sancti Mauri*, cap. 3, *AA SS Boll.* Jan. ii. 324, in Desiderius, *Dial.* i. 2, p. 1119; cf. *Chron. Cas.* i. 27, iv. 100, pp. 79, 561–2.

men, each of them meriting the descriptions *restaurator ac renovator*, and *fundator atque constructor*. They were Benedict himself; Petronax of Brescia (*c.*718–49/51), who revived monastic life at Montecassino after the Lombard destruction; Aligernus (948–85), who renewed it *c.*950 after the Saracen inroad of 883 which had led to its monks' exile at Teano (until 915) and then Capua; and Desiderius, who raised it to the position, fame, and glory that it enjoyed during Leo of Ostia's lifetime. Leo believed that only under Desiderius did Montecassino achieve the pre-eminence that God had of old promised to Benedict.[8] Upon such a view Montecassino came fully into its own just when the eleventh-century reform papacy was beginning to exercise its authority with renewed vigour. The succession to the papal throne during the reform period of three of its monks—two of them its abbots—points to a vital and continuing connection between them.

Montecassino therefore offers one of the most promising and instructive sources for the study of the reform papacy in relation to the monastic order. For the past seventy years or so the general problem of the relationship between them has been amongst the most energetically debated topics of medieval history. While scholars have come to no agreement, there has been a growing tendency to regard their relationship as having been close.[9] Both the papacy and the monastic order had reason to foster an association. From the monastic side, the apostolic see of Rome was acknowledged to have as its principal and ever-vigilant patron St. Peter, the prince of the apostles and the keeper of the keys of heaven. Having the sanction of his divinely conferred authority it afforded protection against the threats that conscientious monks everywhere feared—the excessive claims upon them of external powers both spiritual and temporal. When, after Pope Leo IX's accession, the papacy became more of a force in the church at large and proved its zeal by dispatching legates and letters to constrain those who were disobedient to its commands, its protection became the more to be

[8] *Chron. Cas.* iii, prol., p. 362; cf. the dedication, written in 1072, of Montecassino, Archivio capitolare, MS 99: F. Newton, 'Leo Marsicanus and the Dedicatory Text and Drawing in Monte Cassino 99', *Scriptorium*, xxxiii (1976), 181–205, at 184 and plate 20 (*b*). For Petronax, see Penco, op. cit. 136–47; for Aligernus, see T. Leccisotti, 'Aligerno', *DBI* ii. 381–2.

[9] For a summary of recent discussion, see H. E. J. Cowdrey, *The Cluniacs and the Gregorian Reform* (Oxford, 1970), pp. xiii–xxvii.

desired. If the papacy offered its protection, monasteries in return offered their obedience and service. As the eleventh century saw things, the monasteries had much to offer the papacy as well as other authorities. They held a commanding place in human society as sources of spiritual and material energy. Their ordered round of worship and almsgiving, set in a framework of magnificent buildings with ample endowments, declared them to be channels of grace and bastions of stability. Their stores of relics and treasure added to the impression of permanence and power. Above all, every grade of men, with the popes prominently among them, valued the intercessory support in life and in death which the monasteries offered to all who established a bond with them. So far as the reform papacy itself was concerned, succeeding generations of monks provided it with many of its most capable and loyal servants. Thus, for example, from Peter Damiani (1057–72) to the Montecassino chronicler Leo of Ostia (1102/7–15) himself, all five occupants of the senior Roman cardinal-bishopric—that of Ostia—were monks.[10] The reform papacy derived incalculable benefits from the prayers and services of the monastic order. Alike because of its proximity to Rome and because of its pre-eminence in the monastic order, Montecassino is of outstanding importance as a subject of study in order to determine the nature and significance of those benefits, as well as the readiness and completeness with which they were forthcoming.

ii. THE PRINCIPAL SOURCES FOR THE HISTORY OF MONTECASSINO IN ITS GOLDEN AGE

Yet twentieth-century historians have until recently paid all too little attention to Montecassino either as a centre and exemplar of the religious life or in its relationship to the reform papacy and its objectives. In large measure this is owing to the character of the surviving evidence for Montecassino, and especially to the ways in which Montecassino's official historians during and immediately after the reform period recorded its life and affairs. They concentrated very heavily indeed upon its buildings, wealth, and material acquisitions, and upon its pre-eminence in respect of cultural, literary, and artistic achievement. But they shed little light upon its concern for and standard of observance

[10] Hüls, *Kardinäle*, pp. 99–106.

in the spiritual ends of the monastic life, and they were not directly interested in its attitude to the wider concerns of the papacy or of contemporary reformers, whether monastic or secular. Thus, the most familiar sources offer a seriously unbalanced picture of Montecassino's role during the reforming period and of the contribution of individual Cassinese figures to spiritual and political life and developments.

Amongst Montecassino's official records two stand out as being of paramount importance. The first is the Montecassino Chronicle.[11] As it stands it is a composite work. It was begun by Leo, a member of the comital family of Marsia who entered the abbey in boyhood between 1060 and 1063, and who in due course served it as archivist and librarian. Because of his administrative talents he frequently acted as its agent to secure its local interests, and in Pope Gregory VII's days he pleaded its cause at Rome. However, he remained at Montecassino as a monk, attracting the notice of Pope Urban II, until at an unknown date between 1102 and 1107 Pope Paschal II recruited him for the permanent service of the Roman church as bishop of Ostia and Velletri. He died on 22 May 1115. Early in the 1090s Abbot Oderisius I had commissioned him to write a life of Abbot Desiderius; but from pressure of administrative tasks he had failed to make headway with it. In due course Oderisius gave him a wider, and essentially new, commission to write a chronicle of Montecassino from its foundation. He began work on it in or soon after 1099, and he made sufficient progress to dedicate his Chronicle to Oderisius before the abbot's death in 1105. It is first and last a monument to Montecassino itself. Its framework is the succession of abbots from the time of St. Benedict. Much of it is taken up with the record of benefactions in land and treasure, which is supported by details drawn from the abbey's archives. But it also contains narrative material about its history. The whole of Leo's contribution to the Chronicle bears the stamp of a clear, orderly, and sophisticated mind; indeed, it ranks among the most distinguished pieces of medieval historical writing. However, as a result of its plan and scope, it magnifies the abbey's power and wealth while conveying all too little about its internal monastic life and its

[11] See esp. H. Hoffmann, 'Studien zur Chronik von Montecassino', *DA* xxix (1973), 59–162, and *Chron. Cas.*, pp. vii–xxxvi. Hoffmann's edition of *Chron. Cas.*—*MGH SS* xxxiv (1980)—replaces W. Wattenbach's of 1846 in *MGH SS* vii.

external relations, save in so far as they affected its material and cultural interests.

Leo's work was not completed by him: his contribution ends with the year 1075.[12] That is to say, it stops short of the major conflict between Pope Gregory VII and the German King Henry IV, which became acute from the winter of 1075/6. A generation or so after Leo was writing, the Chronicle became the concern of another archivist and librarian of the abbey, Peter the Deacon.[13] Unfortunately, nothing more is known about Peter than can be gleaned from the large body of his own works, which he listed in *Chron. Cas.* iv. 66. He was born between 1107 and 1119; he claimed, probably with truth, that he belonged to the family of the counts of Tusculum. He said that he entered Montecassino in 1115 as a five-year-old boy. Apart from a time of exile in 1128–31 he remained there until his death at some time after 1154. He devoted his life to literary work as an author, compiler, and fabricator. His two purposes were by every means to magnify Montecassino's renown, and to advance his own interests as he saw them. But unlike Leo of Ostia he received no external promotion by way of recognition or reward.

Amongst his many endeavours was the continuation of the Chronicle. He claimed to have continued it from the point at which Leo broke off.[14] In fact, apart from the Prologue to the fourth book his only certain contribution of any length is a fairly limited section at the end.[15] It is likely, but not proven, that the chapters that follow Leo's were at first a separate work of Peter's teacher Guido.[16] Guido seems to have been a more

[12] *Chron. Cas.* iii. 33, p. 409.

[13] See esp. Caspar, *Petrus Diaconus*, and H. Hoffmann, 'Petrus Diaconus, die Herren von Tusculum und der Sturz Oderisius' II. von Montecassino', *DA* xxvii (1971), 1–109.

[14] *Chron. Cas.* iv. prol., cf. iv. 66, pp. 458, 530.

[15] i.e. the perfunctory survey of the years 1127–35 in iv. 96–7; the lengthy *Altercatio pro cenobio Casinensis* in iv. 97, 107–15 with the material concerning 1126–7 in iv. 98–106; the *Altercatio pro Romana ecclesia contra Graecum quendam*: iv. 115–16; and the narrative of the years 1137–9: iv. 117–30. These make up *Chron. Cas.*, pp. 556–607.

[16] The chapters with which Guido may have been largely concerned are iii. 34–iv. 95, pp. 409–556. W. Smidt first argued for Guido's authorship: 'Über den Verfasser der drei letzten Redaktionen der Chronik Leos von Monte Cassino', *Papsttum und Kaisertum (Festschrift P. Kehr)* (Munich, 1926), 263–86; 'Guido von Monte Cassino und die "Fortsetzung" der Chronik Leos durch Petrus Diaconus', *Festschrift Albert Brackmann*, ed. L. Santifaller (Weimar, 1931), 293–323; and 'Die vermeintliche und die wirkliche Urgestalt der Chronik Leos von Montecassino', *QFIAB* xxviii (1937/8), 286–97. For Guido, see Peter the Deacon, *DVI* cap. 41, Migne, *PL* clxxiii. 1044–5.

reliable historian than Peter, although he lacked Leo's stature; but it seems that Peter tendentiously edited, revised, and interpolated what he had written.[17] Thus, the part of the Montecassino Chronicle that records Desiderius' latter years and then his successors' reigns presents serious, intractable, and as yet—despite the recent publication of a new edition of the Chronicle—incompletely resolved problems of authorship, textual history, and historical authenticity. They compound the difficulties that arise from Leo's own work, which his continuators imitated without rising to his high standard of literary skill.

Peter the Deacon was also responsible for the second source of outstanding significance, the *Registrum Petri Diaconi*, which was compiled, probably between 1131 and 1133, as in effect a complement and companion-piece to the Chronicle.[18] Peter worked on it at the behest of Abbot Seniorect (1127-37) and with the encouragement of Prince Robert II of Capua (1127-35). In his Preface, Peter said that the abbot at first asked him to transcribe only Montecassino's papal privileges. But Seniorect later extended his commission to include the benefactions of emperors, kings, dukes, and princes, as well as those of the faithful in general. The order in which the items were referred to in the Chronicle served as a basis. Peter did not, however, follow a chronological scheme but proposed a sixfold classification based upon subject-matter—papal privileges, precepts of lay lords, oblations of other donors, leases, quitclaims, and oaths.[19] The eventual layout differed somewhat from the classification as proposed, but broadly speaking Peter fulfilled the intention

[17] To what extent is uncertain. Smidt thought that it was considerable, as did H.-W. Klewitz, 'Petrus Diaconus und die Montecassinenser Klosterchronik des Leo von Ostia', *Archiv für Urkundenforschung*, xv (1936), 414-53, repr. *Ausgewählte Aufsätze zur Kirchen- und Geistesgeschichte des Mittelalters*, ed. G. Tellenbach (Aalen, 1971), 425-64. Hoffmann's investigations have reduced it, for he has established that the recensions of the Chronicle up to iii. 33 were virtually complete before Peter's work began. Thereafter his activity was considerable. For the style of the continuation by Guido and Peter the Deacon, see also Hoffmann, 'Stilistische Tradition in der Klosterchronik von Montecassino', *MGH Mittelalterliche Textüberlieferungen und ihre kritische Aufarbeitung* (Munich, 1976), 29-41, esp. 37-40.

[18] The Register remains unedited. For descriptions and discussion, see A. Mancone, 'Il Registrum Petri Diaconi', *Bullettino dell'Archivio paleografico italiano*, NS ii-iii (1956/7), 99-126; and H. Hoffmann, 'Chronik und Urkunde in Montecassino', *QFIAB* li (1971), 93-206. The Register was largely compiled under Peter's supervision, but it was probably not written by his hand: P. Meyvaert, 'The Autograph of Peter the Deacon', *Bulletin of the John Rylands Library*, xxxviii (1955/6), 114-38.

[19] See Peter's Prologue in Gattula, *Accessiones*, p. 22, and in *MGH SS* vii. 567-8.

that he expressed in his Preface.[20] He included most of the documents to which the Chronicle referred, both in Leo of Ostia's portion and in that probably attributable to Guido; within each class of document he kept closely to the order in which they appear. Both the Chronicle and the Register contain, or refer to, a number of forged or falsified documents which were themselves calculated to enhance the abbey's standing. The two sources belong closely together as monuments of the power, wealth, and renown of Montecassino, especially in its golden age.

A third source of the utmost importance for the history of the abbey in the second and third quarters of the eleventh century is a further chronicle that was written there—the *Historia Normannorum* of Amatus.[21] Amatus began to write in 1072/3, kept pace with events until 1078, and apparently finished his work just before 1080. He was a Cassinese monk who had formerly (1047–58) been bishop of Pesto-Capaccio, to the south of Salerno, where he had been born in the 1020s. His work, which survives only in a French version—partly translation and partly paraphrase with commentary—of the early fourteenth century, is a eulogy of the Norman leaders Robert Guiscard, duke of Apulia and Calabria, and Richard, prince of Capua. Like the official Chronicle, it has much to say about Montecassino's power and wealth. But it is of more limited value as a source for the abbey's monastic life or for its external relationships, save with the Norman and Lombard rulers of South Italy.

The wealth of original material that survives in the form of charters, along with Peter the Deacon's Register, in Montecassino's archives, also tends to direct attention to the abbey's wealth and local interests rather than to its specifically monastic and spiritual concerns.[22]

iii. MONTECASSINO IN MODERN HISTORICAL STUDY

Both by their strengths and by their limitations these sources have largely determined the perspectives of modern historical

[20] See Hoffmann (as Introd. n. 18), p. 165.

[21] Amatus. For his life, see esp. A. Lentini, 'Amato di Montecassino', *DBI* ii. 682–4.

[22] Leccisotti, *Regesti*. The Introductions to the several volumes provide the best account of the Archives and their history.

study. The fullest and most lavishly documented history of the abbey of Montecassino remains that of Erasmo Gattula (1662–1734), who had charge of its archives from 1697 until his death.[23] He drew upon them to record the monastic figures who had been associated with Montecassino; he also made it a leading concern to chronicle the acquisition of dependencies and lands which by Desiderius' time made it the outstanding monastery in Italy to the south of Rome. A feature of his method is his lavish citation of original documents. In the nineteenth century L. Tosti's history, which is a less considerable work, also concentrated upon the abbey itself, its monks, and its lands.[24] Because of his use of Amatus, Tosti went somewhat more extensively than Gattula into Montecassino's external dealings. But since both of them were mainly guided by Montecassino's own sources and archives, they concentrated heavily upon its cultural, architectural, and artistic pre-eminence, and upon its enormous material wealth.

After Tosti's history, the next landmark in the study of medieval Montecassino came in 1867 with F. Hirsch's thorough monograph on Desiderius as abbot and as Pope Victor III.[25] This remains the fullest study of him. Hirsch used the full range of sources that were available to him. Unlike Gattula and Tosti he saw Montecassino's part in ecclesiastical and secular politics as demanding consideration no less than its monastic and cultural activities. But he, too, was guided by its chroniclers. He saw its political endeavours as having an overriding purpose to ensure its own independence and the unfettered control of its possessions.[26] He did not embark upon an overall assessment of its wider dealings.

For the rest of the nineteenth century there was no further major study. Since 1909 the focus of scholarly interest has tended to be Peter the Deacon; for in that year E. Caspar's monograph on Peter and his writings appeared.[27] Caspar comprehensively surveyed Peter's work and gave much attention to

[23] Gattula, *Historia* and *Accessiones*. Gattula's name is thus spelt on the title-page of the former; in the latter it appears as Gattola. I have consistently used the spelling Gattula. For the historiography of Montecassino, see esp. A. Pantoni, 'Descrizioni di Montecassino attraverso i secoli', *Benedictina*, xix (1972), 539–86, and T. Leccisotti's brief but useful summary in *Montecassino: sein Leben und seine Ausbreitung* ([Montecassino], 1949), 148–59.

[24] Tosti, *Storia*.

[25] Hirsch, 'Desiderius'.

[26] Ibid. 4.

[27] Caspar, *Petrus Diaconus*.

the problems of his complex personality and character. He emphasized Peter's personal vanity and his concern to proclaim and to enhance Montecassino's renown. Peter's hallmark was systematic forgery: to promote his two objectives he brought into play every conceivable device of literary invention, falsification, and tendentious recasting of material. Not only did he signally fail to embody the ideals of reformed monasticism, but he also continued something of the aggressive and self-interested individualism of eleventh-century Italians like Anselm of Besate and Benzo of Alba. He also foreshadowed the intense local patriotism of the Renaissance.[28] His career demonstrates how far short of the standards of contemporary reformers Montecassino had fallen by the mid-twelfth century.

It is not surprising that since Caspar's monograph appeared so busy and complex a character as Peter should have continued to concern historians, both for his own sake and also because the nature and extent of his work must be appraised before the history of Montecassino from its beginnings up to his time can be confidently appraised. To cite only some of the most notable discussions of him, H. Bloch has examined his advancing of Montecassino's claim to the obedience of the monastery of Glanfeuil, or Saint-Maur-sur-Loire (dioc. Angers), and of Glanfeuil's claim to a vicariate over the monasteries of France.[29] Building upon work by P. Meyvaert,[30] H. Hoffmann prepared the way for his edition of the Montecassino Chronicle by investigating Peter's work in it, in the Register, and in other documents. If Hoffmann has not formulated or resolved all the major problems, notably those concerning the nature, extent, and consequences of Peter's tampering with the sources for Cassinese history under Abbot Desiderius and his successors, he has shed light on his methods of working and on their effects upon Montecassino's records.[31] R. H. Rodgers has also clarified Peter's literary techniques in a new edition of his *Ortus et vita iustorum cenobii Casinensis.*[32]

Apart from the figure of Peter the Deacon, it is Montecassino's

[28] Caspar, *Petrus Diaconus*, 194–206.

[29] As Introd. n. 4.

[30] P. Meyvaert, 'Peter the Deacon and the Tomb of St. Benedict', *RB* lxv (1955), 3–70, repr. *Benedict, Gregory, Bede, and Others* (London, 1977), no. I; and as Introd. n. 18.

[31] As Introd. n. 11 and Introd. n. 18; also 'Das *Chronicon Vulturnense* und die Chronik von Montecassino', *DA* xxii (1966), 179–96.

[32] Peter the Deacon, *OV*.

cultural achievement, especially while Desiderius was abbot, that has mainly claimed the attention of twentieth-century scholars. To cite only examples, E. A. Lowe worked extensively on its manuscripts and on the Beneventan script which was used in its scriptorium.[33] The wider scholarly activities of its monks have been studied by H. Bloch and E. Kitzinger, both for their own interest and as evidence for the meeting at Montecassino of eastern and western cultural traditions.[34] L. Fabiani has published a major study of the territorial and social context of monastic life at Montecassino in the *terra sancti Benedicti.*[35] Bloch's overall survey of Montecassino in the Middle Ages is awaited.[36]

All these studies from Gattula onwards have added greatly to scholarly understanding of Cassinese monasticism in many of its aspects. But they have so far shared the perspective of the abbey's eleventh- and twelfth-century sources that they have not fully considered Montecassino and its monks in relation to the general history of these centuries: this they have discussed only secondarily or in passing. Thus, Gattula recorded with pride the reform popes' testimonials to his abbey's greatness: he noted the conferring of pontifical insignia upon its abbots, papal visits to Montecassino, and the names of the popes and cardinals with whom Montecassino provided the Roman church.[37] Tosti wrote at somewhat greater length of eleventh-century reforming currents and of Montecassino's involvement in them. He took account, not only of the problems of simony and clerical unchastity, but also of the feudalization of the episcopate and of the subjection of bishops and clergy to lay princes. He could sometimes go far towards identifying Montecassino with papal aspirations for the reform and liberty of the church. He traced the origins of reform to the world of monks and hermits. At an early date in his career Archdeacon Hildebrand—the future Pope Gregory VII—sought to promote it at

[33] E. A. Lowe (= Loew), *The Beneventan Script: a History of the South Italian Minuscule* (Oxford, 1914); *Scriptura Beneventana*, 2 vols. (Oxford, 1929).

[34] H. Bloch, *Monte Cassino, Byzantium and the West in the Early Middle Ages, DOP* iii. 163–224, and 'Monte Cassino's Teachers and Library in the High Middle Ages', *La scuola nell'occidente latino dell'alto medioevo* (Spoleto, 1972), 563–613; E. Kitzinger, 'The Gregorian Reform and the Visual Arts: a Problem of Method', *TRHS*, 5th ser., xxii (1972), 87–102.

[35] Fabiani, 'La terra di S. Benedetto'.

[36] H. Bloch, *Montecassino in the Middle Ages* (forthcoming).

[37] *Historia*, pp. 144–51, 161, 189–90, 192–5.

Montecassino through his part in the deposition of Abbot Peter and the substitution of Frederick of Lorraine. As abbot, Desiderius was sympathetic to Gregory's aspirations for the church. Desiderius sought to help him by acting as peacemaker between the papacy and the Normans. When he in turn became pope, Desiderius was the strenuous protagonist of ecclesiastical liberty. This befitted a reformer whose monks were the upholders in Italy of true religion and the builders of a more refined way of life.[38] Hirsch, on the contrary, saw little in common between Desiderius and Gregory VII. Without presenting a detailed case, he suggested that Desiderius was far from sharing Gregory's quest for papal lordship over the whole world-order; Desiderius brought peace where Gregory brought a sword. Appeasement was the keynote of his brief tenure of the papal throne.[39] In similar vein to Hirsch, F. Gregorovius went so far as to see in Desiderius a distinguished abbot, whose character, however, went utterly to pieces when he succeeded Gregory as pope.[40]

In the present century a similar division of opinion has manifested itself. Amongst Italian scholars, R. Palmarocchi recognized in Desiderius no strength of spiritual or moral purpose. If he resisted monastic abuses and vices, he had no genuine reforming zeal. Montecassino's material interests always preoccupied his attention, especially by the augmentation of the *terra sancti Benedicti* and by the pursuit of a grandiose programme of monastic building. Palmarocchi pointed out that a reformer like Cardinal Peter Damiani appeared to have hesitations about Desiderius as 'uomo di politica e di guerra', and about the Montecassino of his time. In his capacity as papal vicar having authority over the South Italian monasteries Desiderius seems to have done little to promote their well-being. At every turn he proved to be more strongly committed to his Norman neighbours and benefactors than to the reform papacy; indeed, his policy of enlisting Norman aid was indirectly the cause of Gregory VII's having to go into his last exile.[41] On the other hand, in reply to

[38] Tosti, *Storia*, i, esp. pp. 307–22, 393–4.

[39] Hirsch, 'Desiderius', p. 101.

[40] 'Der Abt Desiderius war ein grosser unsterblicher Mann, aber der Papst Victor III. eine ruhmlose Schattengestalt': *Geschichte der Stadt Rom im Mittelalter*, new edn. by W. Kampf, ii (Darmstadt, 1963), 117.

[41] R. Palmarocchi, *L'abbazia di Montecassino et la conquista normanna* (Rome, 1913), esp. pp. 85–7, 94–112, 129–38, 197–8. For a similar view of Cassinese *exclusivismo*, see L. Wollemborg, 'L'abbate Desiderio da Montecassino e i Normanni', *Samnium*, vii (1934), 5–34, 99–119, at 116–17.

Palmarocchi G. B. Borino insisted that it was precisely Desiderius' bold and far-seeing alliance with the Normans in 1058, followed by the treaty of Melfi in 1059, that facilitated the papal alliance with the Normans upon which popes like Alexander II, Gregory VII, and Urban II for so long depended. Desiderius' *Dialogues* reveal him as a man of reforming zeal, who was at one with Gregory VII in his plans to bring about the moral reform of the church and to liberate it from noxious forms of lay domination. The presence of later eleventh-century Cassinese abbots in papal company also shows that they not only shared papal aspirations for reform but also collaborated with a view to realizing them.[42]

French and German historians have similarly debated Montecassino's role. The most unfavourable of all assessments of Abbot Desiderius, and the one that has carried most weight among twentieth-century historians, has been that of the Frenchman A. Fliche. In his view, eleventh-century currents of reform largely passed Desiderius by. His single true concern was for the administration of his abbey and the renewal of its former splendours. Even so he was before else an aesthete and bibliophile. As regards the reform of the church he had no mind of his own. In the days of Gregory VII he did, indeed, for a time try to reconcile pope and emperor; but he did so with an eye to Cassinese interests. When he became pope he utterly failed to measure up to his responsibilities or to the problems that faced him. He lacked decisiveness and authority, and he was under the control of a Roman city faction. Like Gregorovius, Fliche saw him as but a shadow figure between the two great popes Gregory VII and Urban II, beside whom he was altogether unworthy to stand.[43] Among German historians, J. Haller judged Fliche's assessment to be 'highly arbitrary'. Nevertheless, he too concluded that, as pope, Desiderius did not follow Gregory's policies and that he therefore forfeited the loyalty of Gregory's partisans. He deviated from Gregory's firm, anti-imperial line by seeking peace and accommodation with Henry IV.[44] Similarly,

[42] G. B. Borino, 'Per la storia della riforma della chiesa nel sec. xi', *Arch. Soc. rom.* xxxviii (1915), 453–513.

[43] A. Fliche, 'Le pontificat de Victor III', *Revue d'histoire ecclésiastique*, xx (1924), 387–412, esp. 388, 397, 411; *La Réforme grégorienne*, 3 vols. (Paris and Louvain, 1924–37), iii. 201–5. For a more moderate French judgement, see É. Amann, 'Victor III', *Dictionnaire de théologie catholique*, xv. 2866–72.

[44] J. Haller, *Das Papsttum. Idee und Wirklichkeit*, ii (new edn., Darmstadt, 1962), 430–5, 612.

in a recent discussion of Montecassino's attitude to the lay proprietorship of churches, H. Dormeier has found that, although its acceptance from lay donors of numerous churches and monasteries proves that it shared the desire of many reformers to diminish the lay domination of lesser churches, it was far from sympathizing with the characteristic aims of papal reformers in wider respects. When Montecassino's economic interests conflicted with papal legislation the former prevailed, especially under Abbot Desiderius, but also for long after his reign.[45]

It was for long the historians of art, culture, and learning who argued most strongly for Montecassino's more or less close identification with the papal reforms of the eleventh century. H. Bloch, for example, refers to 'the glorious role which Monte Cassino had played in the Church of the Reform since the middle of the eleventh century'; it was 'a true bulwark of Rome, firmly linked with the leaders of the Church, newly reformed by the forces of Cluny'.[46] Again, E. Kitzinger, while agreeing with Haller that Desiderius did not always see eye to eye with Gregory VII, asserts that they 'shared the ideal of a reborn and inwardly purified Church establishing a new world order under the law of Christ, with the successors of St. Peter as supreme authority'.[47] E. A. Lowe considered it to be no accident that the greatest pope of the eleventh century should have been the close friend of the greatest abbot of Montecassino.[48]

But it is a French monastic historian, R. Grégoire, who has argued the most fully for the essential harmony of Montecassino and the reform papacy. In his view the abbey entered the period of reform with no cut-and-dried policies; it was associated with no particular reforming ideology. Yet its own aspirations led it to offer moral, and often material, support to the papacy in its struggles against lay investiture and simony. It was consistently a papal ally in seeking to establish Christian standards of life, especially among the clergy. The abbey's very wealth made it a sheet-anchor of the apostolic see. In the Gregorian papacy's conflict with the Empire as well as against the moral evils that disfigured the church, Montecassino followed and aided it. In

[45] Dormeier, *Montecassino*, pp. 24–106, esp. 99–100, 106.

[46] (As Introd. n. 4), p. 177; (as Introd. n. 34), p. 165.

[47] (As Introd. n. 34), p. 96.

[48] *The Beneventan Script* (as Introd. n. 33), pp. 10, 12. For similar judgements, see Caspar, *Petrus Diaconus*, p. 5; and H. Hoffmann, 'Der Kirchenstaat im hohen Mittelalter', *QFIAB* lvii (1977), 1–45, at 42, also in Dormeier, *Montecassino*, pp. 8–9.

1122 Pope Calixtus II spoke no more than the truth when, according to the Montecassino Chronicle, he applauded the abbey by declaring that 'venerabilis locus a Romanis pontificibus restauratus et Romane ecclesie filiorum unicum in adversis solacium et in prosperis infatigata requies perseverat'.[49]

As the Lateran frescos make clear, Grégoire's assessment is warranted at least in this sense: that in the second quarter of the twelfth century the old-guard Gregorians at Rome who looked back to the days of Gregory VII identified Desiderius with the reforming establishment. The object of the present study is to test how far they did so with justification. It will proceed by first making an assessment of the monastic life and political affiliations of Montecassino under Desiderius' rule, and then by examining its relationship with and contribution to the papal reform which is associated with Gregory VII and his contemporaries. It will inquire whether Desiderius' overall achievement and political stance during his long reign as abbot, and his especially close concern with the papacy between 1084 and 1087 culminating in his four-month exercise of papal authority, justified those who designed the Lateran frescos when they placed Victor III in a position of honour comparable with Gregory VII and Urban II. Did Montecassino and the reform papacy have compatible—though perhaps not identical—aims, interests, and policies? Is Montecassino, in its dealings with the papacy, to a significant extent recognizable as Calixtus II's 'in adversis solacium et in prosperis infatigata requies'?

iv. MONTECASSINO'S RELATIONS WITH OUTSIDE AUTHORITIES

An attempt to answer such questions must proceed against a background of the political and ecclesiastical pressures to which Montecassino was subject. Its abbots had repeated and grave cause for anxiety about them, and events often called for extraordinary prudence, skill, and judgement on their part.

Many pressures arose from circumstances in South Italy itself. At the beginning of the eleventh century Montecassino's nearest neighbours in political terms were, to the south-east, the

[49] R. Grégoire, 'Le Mont-Cassin dans la réforme de l'Église de 1049 à 1122', *Il monachesimo e la riforma ecclesiastica (1049–1122)* (Milan, 1971), 21–53, esp. 22, 44. For Calixtus II's words, *Chron. Cas.* iv. 78, p. 543.

three Lombard principalities of Capua, Benevento, and Salerno. To the north and west of Capua lay the lands of St. Peter which constituted the papal state, and also the duchy of Spoleto. Along the Tyrrhenian coast to the south-east of Montecassino were the tiny maritime duchies of Gaeta, Naples, Sorrento, and Amalfi, which were virtually autonomous republics. By 1000 the Saracens still controlled only the emirate of Sicily, from which Robert Guiscard and his brother Count Roger I were to expel them during the three decades after the Norman capture of Messina in 1061.

For during the early decades of the eleventh century political domination of South Italy had gradually passed to the Normans.[50] First appearing in 999 as the chance defenders of Salerno against a Saracen attack, they became of importance to Montecassino in 1018 when survivors of the battle of Cannae, in which the Byzantines defeated an insurgent force having Norman auxiliaries, settled in the abbey's vicinity. In 1030 Aversa, which lay between the cities of Capua and Naples, under the Drengot family became the first Norman lordship in South Italy. In 1050 there succeeded at Aversa Richard, the greatest of its counts. Eight years later he supplanted the Lombard dynasty of Capua and established the Norman principality. Meanwhile in Apulia and Calabria another Norman family, that of Tancred of Hauteville, pursued its fortunes no less resolutely. Its leading member was Robert Guiscard, who, after years of banditry and warfare, in 1057 became duke of Apulia and Calabria and so master of the Hauteville lands.[51] Robert remained duke until his death in 1085, while Richard reigned at Capua until his death in 1078. After Robert Guiscard's capture in the winter of 1076/7 of the Lombard principality of Salerno the Normans completely replaced the Lombard princes as Montecassino's most important local neighbours. But until that date the abbey was caught up in the strife between Lombards and Normans.

[50] Among the many histories of Italy and the Norman domination, I have mainly relied upon L. von Heinemann, *Geschichte der Normannen in Unteritalien und Sicilien*, i (Leipzig, 1894); Chalandon, *Domination*; and E. Pontieri, *I Normanni nell'Italia meridionale*, i. *La reconquista* (Naples, [1971]). For summaries, see W. Goez, *Grundzüge der Geschichte Italiens im Mittelalter und Renaissance* (Darmstadt, 1975); and G. Galasso, 'Social and Political Developments in the Eleventh and Twelfth Centuries', *The Normans in Sicily and South Italy* (London, 1977), 47–63.

[51] For his rise, see Amatus, iii. 17–18, pp. 194–8; *Chron. Cas.* iii. 15, pp. 377–9.

Greater powers than the Lombard princes and their Norman supplanters also had a stake in South Italy and added to Montecassino's political problems. At the beginning of the eleventh century the Byzantines were the nominal rulers of Apulia and Calabria. The victories of the Eastern Emperor Basil II (963–1025) led in his latter years to the renewal of an Italian catapanate under Basil Boioannes, who in 1018 destroyed the South Italian insurgents at the battle of Cannae. But the Norman penetration of the South, culminating in Robert Guiscard's capture of Bari in 1071—the year of a second Byzantine disaster in the battle of Manzikert at the hands of the Seldjuk Turks—put an end to Byzantine rule. Nevertheless, especially in Calabria the religious, cultural, and administrative traditions of Byzantium remained strong. As far north as Montecassino its memory persisted, and its abbots did not forget that the eastern emperors still regarded South Italy as properly theirs, so that one day they might again seek to assert their authority.

The western emperors, too, had claims to lordship over South Italy which affected Montecassino.[52] They stemmed from Charlemagne's assumption in 774 of the title *rex Langobardorum*, which in his eyes carried with it a claim to lordship over the *ducatus Beneventanus* as it was then constituted. Such claims were renewed in the tenth century when Otto I of Germany revived the imperial title and, in his Italian expeditions, made the Empire once more a factor in Italian politics. As a consequence he extended his protection to Montecassino.[53] Eastern and western claims upon South Italy had different results. Byzantium had the advantage of a considerable Greek population and culture there, as well as of Greek ecclesiastical and administrative institutions. In the early eleventh century it was able for long periods to wield authority through catapans. Western imperial interventions, on the other hand, took place without the advantage of a standing basis of rule. Italians must have anticipated that interventions would occur with some frequency; for the emperors necessarily came to Rome for coronation by the pope, and circumstances sometimes brought them to Italy for other reasons. But their visits were occasional and

[52] For a full discussion, see J. Deér, *Papsttum und Normannen* (Cologne and Vienna, 1972), 37–50; cf. the criticisms of H. Hoffmann, 'Langobarden, Normannen, Päpste', *QFIAB* lviii (1978), 137–80.

[53] *MGH Dipl. OI*, nos. 367, 371, 373.

transient, and they did not have lasting results once the emperors had returned to the north. After its tenth-century revival, Montecassino could hardly expect to remain unaffected by such periodic visits. The emperors came there from time to time: Otto III in 999, Henry II in 1022, Conrad II in 1038, and Henry III in 1047. In 1065 it seemed likely that Henry IV would come, and he was near at hand in 1082. Like San Vincenzo al Volturno, Montecassino ranked as an imperial abbey,[54] and its status as such was never forgotten. When emperors came there, they enjoyed a right to hospitality.[55] Lothar III, in a diploma of 1137 that Peter the Deacon drafted, could say that he came to Montecassino 'tanquam ad nostram declinantes cameram'.[56] In determining its relationship with the papacy and its attitude to papal policies, Montecassino could never be unmindful of the claims and pressures, both real and potential, of the Empires of east and west, which it must also accommodate.

The papacy, too, had claims to lordship over South Italy, or at least over large parts of it, in terms that remain a matter of controversy among historians; although they were sometimes vigorously pursued in the age of the reform papacy.[57] There were ancient precedents upon which it could, and probably did, build. Emperors of the past had used formulas which committed large areas to the Roman church. For example, in 774 Charlemagne gave *cunctum ducatum Spolitinum seu Beneventanum* —which at that time comprised most of South Italy—to St. Peter and Pope Hadrian I; and in 962 and 1020 the Emperors Otto I and Henry II respectively used similar language.[58] Behind their words lay the so-called 'Donation of Constantine' (*Constitutum Constantini*), with its alleged transference to Pope Sylvester I of 'tam palatium nostrum . . . quamque Romae urbis et omnes Italiae seu occidentalium regionum provincias, loca et

[54] *MGH Dipl. HII*, no. 483.

[55] C. Brühl, *Fodrum, Gistum, Servitium regis*, 2 vols. (Cologne and Graz, 1968), i. 472 (Henry II), 543 (Conrad II), 566–8 (Lothar III).

[56] *MGH Dipl. LIII*, no. 120; also Peter the Deacon, *Altercatio pro cenobio Casinensi*, as in *Chron. Cas.* iv. 108, 111, 112, 113, 118, pp. 572, 578, 580–2, 586, 592. See M. Inguanez, 'Montecassino *camera imperiale*', *Atti del V congresso nazionale di studi romani*, iii (1942), 34–7.

[57] Deér, op. cit. 51–106. His discussion of papal dealings with South Italy in the eleventh century usually carries conviction, and I accept it in this study; on the twelfth century his conclusions are less convincing.

[58] *LP* i. 498; *MGH Dipl. OI*, no. 235; *MGH Dipl. HII*, no. 427.

civitates'.[59] By the mid-eleventh century circumstances favoured the pressing of Petrine claims. Tusculan popes like Benedict VIII (1012–24) had become more active than their recent predecessors in South Italian affairs, and their reforming successors followed suit.[60] The breach of 1054 deepened the division between Eastern and Western Christendom, leaving the papacy less reluctant than before to assert its lordship in an erstwhile Byzantine region. Its hands were the freer after the death in 1056 of the Western Emperor Henry III, which left the German crown in the hands of a six-year-old boy and a weak regency. In 1059, by the treaty of Melfi, it entered into alliance with the Normans. Robert Guiscard of Apulia, and probably also Richard of Capua, were granted papal recognition of their lordships, so that they held their land as fiefs of St. Peter and the Roman church.[61]

Thus, both the papacy and the Western Empire claimed lordship over much, at least, of South Italy. The claims of both impinged upon Montecassino, which could anticipate that it would receive both demands and benefits from either quarter. Up to the 1070s the pressures upon South Italy in general and upon Montecassino in particular were largely offset by the virtual condominium which they were content to exercise.[62] It was based upon the complementary and collaborative character of papal and imperial relations since Carolingian times. It found expression, for example, in Pope Leo IX's dealings when, in 1050 during his South Italian travels, he 'nonnullos eo locorum principes et civitates tam sibi quam imperatori iureiurando subiecit'.[63] In 1073 Pope Gregory VII himself, when he received Prince Richard of Capua's fealty, still left room for the parallel claims of Henry IV.[64] Only with the excommunications of Henry in 1076 and 1080, and with the papal schism that threatened as from the latter year, did such reciprocity come

[59] *Das Constitutum Constantini*, ed. H. Fuhrmann, cap. 17, *MGH Font. iur. Germ.*, NS x, pp. 93–4.

[60] For recent studies of papal attitudes, see esp. K.-J. Herrmann, *Das Tuskulanerpapsttum (1012–1046)* (Stuttgart, 1973); T. Schmidt, *Alexander II. und die römische Reformgruppe seiner Zeit* (Stuttgart, 1977).

[61] *Chron. Cas.* iii. 15, pp. 377–9. For the oaths taken by Robert Guiscard, see *Le Liber censuum de l'église romaine*, edd. P. Fabre and L. Duchesne, 3 vols. (Paris, 1889–1952), i. 421–2; Ménager, *Recueil*, pp. 30–3, nos. 6–7.

[62] Deér (as Introd. n. 52), pp. 87–92.

[63] Hermann of Reichenau, *Chronicon*, *a.* 1050, *Ausgew. Quell.* xi. 692.

[64] '*Regi vero Heinrico, cum a te admonitus fuero vel a tuis successoribus*, iurabo fidelitatem, salva *tamen* fidelitate sanctae Romanae ecclesiae': *Reg.* i. 21*a*, p. 36. The words in italics are peculiar to this oath.

to an end. Then the full danger of conflict between the rival claims of the spiritual and temporal powers became apparent. As a consequence it was in the 1080s that Montecassino reached the point of crisis in its loyalties and in its association with the reforming currents of the age.

V. MONTECASSINO'S IMMUNITY AND EXEMPTION

Montecassino's relations with Empire and papacy were also affected by the large degree to which, by the mid-eleventh century, it had secured lasting benefits of immunity and exemption.[65] Such benefits do not, indeed, loom so large in Montecassino's history as they do in Cluny's. But they were nevertheless important as conferring upon it a large measure of freedom from the claims of local authorities, both secular and ecclesiastical. At the same time they gave rise to an ultimate dependence upon the imperial and papal powers which were their guarantors. This, again, particularly complicated Montecassino's problems in and after the 1080s when the estrangement of Empire and papacy was compounded by the Guibertine Schism.

Montecassino's immunity—that is, the freeing of its lands from temporal obligations to external authorities—was rooted in the grants of the Lombard princes.[66] Clear evidence for it begins in 925, when Landulf I and Atenulf II, princes of Capua, conferred upon the abbey's lands a large measure of freedom from interference by their agents, although probably not from political and military services.[67] Freedom from these came with grants such as those by Princes Landulf II and Paldulf I (952), Princes Paldulf I and Landulf III (961, 963, 967), and Prince Guaimar IV of Salerno (1040).[68] In grants of 1058 and 1080 Princes Richard and Jordan of Capua confirmed the arrangements of their Lombard predecessors.[69] Successive emperors added their sanction to this development.[70] They also augmented

[65] For the early history of immunity and exemption, see Cowdrey (as Introd. n. 9), pp. 8–36.

[66] For Montecassino's immunity, see Fabiani, 'La terra di S. Benedetto', ii. 9–45.

[67] Gattula, *Historia*, pp. 105–6; Poupardin, p. 94, no. 81; Leccisotti, *Regesti*, ii. 43.

[68] Gattula, *Accessiones*, pp. 55–6, 58–9, 61–4, 140–2; Poupardin, pp. 103–9, nos. 105, 109, 120; Leccisotti, *Regesti*, i. 38–9, 47, 71, 90.

[69] Gattula, *Accessiones*, pp. 161–3, 184–6; Leccisotti, *Regesti*, ii. 130, 131.

[70] *MGH Dipl. OII*, no. 254; *OIII*, no. 291; *HII*, no. 287.

the abbey's immunity by defining its rights of jurisdiction. It seems clear that 'low justice'—jurisdiction over lesser matters than those involving the liberty or property of individuals, or carrying a capital penalty—was in the abbey's hands by Conrad II's diploma of 1038.[71] 'High justice' was fully conceded only in 1194 by the Emperor Henry VI.[72] So Montecassino in its golden age enjoyed an immunity which was generous but not complete.

For its exemption—that is, its freedom from the spiritual jurisdiction of outside authorities—Montecassino was beholden to the papacy.[73] By the mid-eleventh century it claimed exemption from episcopal jurisdiction for itself and for its dependencies. Later Cassinese sources traced the claim to direct subjection to the apostolic see from Pope Zacharias (? 748).[74] Thereafter it had the sanction of a long sequence of papal grants and confirmations.[75] Whatever the precise historical development may have been, in the period of the reform papacy Pope Victor II's bull of 1057 guaranteed an exemption which was confirmed by Stephen IX, Nicholas II, Alexander II, Urban II, Paschal II, and Calixtus II.[76] In 1067 Archbishop Hildebrand of Capua challenged Montecassino's exemption, but Alexander II compelled him to make amends publicly at his next Lent council in Rome, and forbade him and his successors to repeat his challenge.[77] The long list of papal guarantees is a measure of Montecassino's need for the support of the apostolic see in maintaining its cherished independence of the local episcopate.

Thus, just as immunity created at Montecassino an indebtedness to princely and imperial guarantors, so exemption gave rise to obligations to the papacy. Despite all its resources the abbey did not exist in a vacuum, but was beholden to external powers of which the reform papacy in the later eleventh century was the most important.

[71] *MGH Dipl. CII*, no. 270; cf. *HIII*, no. 184.

[72] Gattula, *Accessiones*, p. 279; Leccisotti, *Regesti*, ii. 35.

[73] For Montecassino's exemption, see Fabiani, 'La terra di S. Benedetto', i. 358–63.

[74] *Chron. Cas.* i. 4, pp. 24–5, following Paul the Deacon, *Historia Langobardorum*, vi. 40, *MGH Script. rer. Lang.*, pp. 178–9. See Leccisotti, *Regesti*, i. 5–6, for a twelfth-century forged privilege.

[75] For the list, see Table 1, p. xli.

[76] For the list, see Table 2, p. xli.

[77] *Chron. Cas.* iii. 24, p. 391, on which see *IP* viii. 144, no. 100; Alexander II, *Ep.* 49 (as above, n. 76).

vi. THE PAPAL REFORM

A final matter to which attention must be paid when seeking to assess Montecassino's part in the wider concerns of the eleventh-century church is the change that has taken place since the Second World War in scholars' understanding of the papal reform movement itself, especially under Gregory VII. Undoubtedly the most influential work to appear between the two world wars was that of A. Fliche. His three-volume study of what he called, in a phrase of his own devising, 'la réforme grégorienne', remains the latest comprehensive study in any language of Gregory and his work.[78] As Fliche presented it, the Gregorian reform was a papally initiated and directed movement of moral and religious renewal. Its overriding aim was to rid the church of the two 'heresies' of simony (the sale of holy orders and ecclesiastical offices, and trafficking in them for temporal reward or advancement) and nicolaitism (the irregular sexual morality of the clergy). It was only in the course of Gregory's pontificate that the need to implement this aim by radical methods became apparent. His early experiences as pope taught Gregory that the church must also be freed root and branch from lay domination, and that the papacy must strenuously assert its leadership of Christendom. He was gradually impelled to assert the prerogatives of the apostolic see, to work for the centralization of the church, and to proclaim theocratic doctrines obliging kings and lay rulers to obey the moral and religious admonitions of the papacy. So he encountered mounting lay hostility and the papacy became involved in the conflicts that are collectively known as the 'Investiture Contest'.

Fliche believed that the way for these developments of the later eleventh century was prepared from Ottonian and Salian times. The tenth century held fast to a tradition of canon law embodying good, ancient usages which might one day be restored. So, long before any papal initiative could take place, three lines of reform emerged. One was the monastic reform that sprang up at Cluny. Its principal aim was to protect monasteries from lay interference and to build up their internal life. But if only to underline the superiority of the monastic vocation, its leaders were critical of the shortcomings of bishops and

[78] As above, Introd. n. 43; his views were also developed in *La Réforme grégorienne et la reconquête chrétienne* (Paris, 1946).

secular clergy. Secondly, there was a current of episcopal reform which was, however, only the piecemeal activity of individual bishops—notably North Italians like Atto of Vercelli (924–64) who were concerned with moral reform, and Lotharingians like Ratherius of Liège (bishop of Verona, 931–68) who also sought liberty from lay power. Thirdly, the German rulers from Otto I (936–73, emperor from 962) to Henry III instituted a period of imperial reform. At best, as under Otto I and Henry II (1002–24), it promoted the spiritual regeneration of the church. But political ambitions vitiated it. Even so generally applauded a ruler as Henry III was, as Fliche judged, in truth indifferent to the reform of the church because he was really out for temporal ends. Imperial power was a cure worse than the disease. True reform was impossible so long as the church remained subject to the caprice of lay rulers. The sole redeeming feature was that in Lorraine the tradition of Ratherius continued. In Bishop Waso of Liège (1041–8) Fliche applauded a man with the courage to denounce Henry III's abuse of his imperial power. By way of a document like the *De ordinando pontifice*[79] this tradition left evidence of a genuine reforming programme which raised hope of a better future.

With the accession of Pope Leo IX, Fliche saw the papacy coming into the centre of the picture. His councils at Rome, Reims, and Mainz attacked the moral abuses of the age. The reforming endeavours of the past hundred years with their various sponsors and programmes merged into a single movement, which was Roman in inspiration and control. But its limitations as yet were clear: however much Leo may have deprecated the emperor's 'Caesaropapism' he dared not radically oppose it. So he confined himself to moral reform, and until Gregory VII was elected pope in 1073, the tide at Rome ebbed and flowed. In the realm of ideas Cardinal Peter Damiani canvassed the themes of the tenth-century Italians, with their emphasis upon moral regeneration; while Cardinal Humbert, who came to Rome from Moyenmoutier, kept alive those of the Lotharingians. In practical policies, with Henry III's death and Henry IV's minority, Pope Nicholas II could take steps—an alliance with the South Italian Normans, the Election Decree of 1059,[80] the moral reform of the church, a decree against lay investiture—which in effect mapped out Gregory VII's

[79] *MGH Libelli*, i. 8–14.

[80] *MGH Const.* i. 539–41, no. 382.

programme. But Nicholas' early death and his replacement by the weaker Alexander II (1061–73) delayed reform by fifteen years. (The implied gap until 1076 is significant.) Nevertheless, since 1048 the cure for the church's ills had in principle been found; all that was needed was a man of action who would apply it.

Gregory in due course proved to be such a man. As pope he did not, as Fliche saw it, at once revert to Lotharingian methods. His concern was with moral reform, and initially he pursued it in the Italian tradition of Peter Damiani rather than in the Lotharingian tradition of Humbert. In 1073 he had two aims: to exercise the Roman primacy in its plenitude, and by its means to eradicate simony and nicolaitism. He entertained high hopes of securing a harmony of *sacerdotium* and *regnum* in the interests of reform. But by the end of 1074 he could see that his attempt to secure reform by 'Italian' methods had failed. So he turned to 'Lotharingian' means, the first application of which was the decree of 1075 against lay investiture.[81] In his *Dictatus papae*[82] he now spelt out the principles that had always been implicit in his rule. Reform entered a new phase that was thorough-goingly Roman. Hitherto Gregory had not emphasized the superiority of the *sacerdotium* but had merely pointed out the services that the temporal power might offer to the spiritual. Now, especially in his letters to Bishop Hermann of Metz,[83] he insisted upon the rights and active superiority of the *sacerdotium*. He vindicated *gouvernement sacerdotale*, and at Canossa in January 1077 there was displayed the apotheosis of his priestly role.

Since Fliche, no historian has offered a comparable synthesis. But it is important to remember that little of Fliche's picture now remains. It has been reasonably claimed that the stirrings of revival at Rome predated by a generation the pontificate of Leo IX, in the work of the Tusculans Benedict VIII and his successor John XIX.[84] Moreover, the movements towards reform that Fliche correctly saw in the tenth century were wider and deeper than he grasped. This is especially well illustrated by P. Toubert's survey of the structure and development of Latium,

[81] Arnulf, *Gesta archiepiscoporum Mediolanensium*, iv. 7, *MGH SS* vii. 27.

[82] *Reg.* ii. 55*a*, pp. 201–8.

[83] *Reg.* iv. 2, 25 Aug. 1076, pp. 293–7; viii. 21, 15 Mar. 1081, pp. 544–63.

[84] For a vindication of the Tusculans, see Herrmann (as Introd. n. 13). For the monastic order, see Cowdrey (as Introd. n. 9), pp. xxiv, 21–2, 38–43, 46, 63, 151–2.

the region around Rome and especially to the south-east.[85] Such a study suggests that in and after the tenth century reform was by no means only, or even mainly, a matter of clearly articulated programmes devised and enforced from above by bishops, abbots, and eventually popes, who offered authoritative spiritual guidelines that obedient subjects should follow. Instead, reforming figures were often reacting as best they could to demands that were generated from below in circles of laity, lower clergy, or quite humble monastic figures.

These demands were far from being a narrowly ecclesiastical phenomenon. They reflected economic and social, as well as mental and spiritual, changes. In Central Italy, for example, during the tenth century the process of *incastellamento*, whereby ecclesiastical and lay lords brought whole families from their scattered holdings in the countryside and settled them in nucleated settlements having at their centre walled, hill-top villages with large churches, created organic societies with a more regulated way of life. *Incastellamento* was a disciplined response to the threats of Magyars and Saracens from without, and to the disintegration of late Carolingian society from within. Such matters as land holding and tenure came to be governed by stricter rules. They involved the regulation of family and marriage arrangements. When lay people came under pressure to accept such regulation and, as a consequence, to acknowledge a heightened obligation to marital fidelity and personal chastity, it was natural for them to expect the clergy to accept a corresponding discipline in the clerical state. Changes in the social structure generated a demand, not so much for clerical celibacy in isolation, as for *castimonia* in the lay and clerical orders of society alike. Legislation for both went together.

Nor did the demand for *castimonia* stand alone. If the service of God should not be compromised by unseemly sexual behaviour, so too it should not be undermined by the traffic of the market-place in holy orders and ecclesiastical offices. Simony was, therefore, no less reprehensible than nicolaitism. Both must be rooted out in a quest to liberate the church from the corrupt, laicizing influences of a former age. Demands that they

[85] Toubert, *Latium*, and Hoffmann (as Introd. n. 52). For the concept of a 'Gregorian reform', see O. Capitani, 'La riforma gregoriana e la lotta per le investiture nella recente storiografia', *Cultura e scuola*, vi (1962/3), 108–15, and 'Esiste un' "Età Gregoriana"? Considerazioni sulle tendenze di una storiografia medievistica', *Rivista di storia e letteratura religiosa*, i (1965), 454–81.

be extirpated were not advanced only by high ecclesiastical authorities or through conciliar legislation. As Toubert has warned,

> . . . gardons-nous de schématiser. N'imaginons pas une réforme 'grégorienne' à la Fliche, un 'programme' élaboré par un homme au sommet de la hiérarchie et propagé jusqu'au bas de l'échelle par des technocrates de la théocratie. On n'impose aussi bien que ce qui peut plaire. Ce que les évêques réformateurs ont offert a leur clergé, c'est avant tout un mode concret de vie sacerdotale qui fût spirituellement attrayant. En cela, leur action était accordée aux aspirations qui s'exprimaient d'en bas en faveur d'une *vita vere apostolica.*[86]

Thus there began in eleventh-century Italy a quest for models of the Christian life, based on precedents from antiquity. The best of all these models was the life of the apostolic church as seen in the Acts of the Apostles, 2: 42-7, when the first Christians had all things in common, renouncing private possessions and living a life of prayer and simplicity that gave no handhold for the secular order to drag them down.[87] So there developed a movement for canonical reform in local churches. Clerks were to observe celibacy, to share a common table, and to avoid obligations to laymen. The movement was centred upon cathedral and other key churches. It was complemented by a developing cultus of patron saints whose virtues, martyrdoms, and miracles were zealously proclaimed and sung. Through patron saints, the demands of the apostolic life were both propagated and linked with the triumphs of the early church in its persecuted days. They became a means of spiritual renewal, welling up from below, which animated clergy and laity alike.

Everywhere in Italy reforming tendencies of this sort permeated the monastic as well as the secular church and built up links between them. Through such figures as St. Nilus and St. Romuald, the monasteries aspired to a *vita vere apostolica.* They were permeated, too, by eremitical ideals, like those of the desert fathers. Alongside them there proliferated hermits and groups of ascetics who propounded an austere standard of Christianity to monks, secular clergy, and laity alike. They did much to determine the character of reform in the eleventh-century Italian church. Besides witnessing by their manner of life, the hermits and austerer monks, with Peter Damiani as

[86] Toubert, *Latium*, ii. 791-2.

[87] See esp. G. Miccoli, *Chiesa gregoriana* (Florence, 1966), 75-100.

a conspicuous example, were the literary propagandists of reform. They articulated and canalized popular aspirations, adding to them the point and intensity of their own perceptions and discipline. By their preaching, their poetry and prose writings, and their prestige as holy men, they ministered to the aspirations of local churches and societies in an age of social change. Italian localities were finding an identity through their patron saints and the legends of dedication and martyrdom that gathered about them. So reform did not come only, or perhaps mainly, from the top downwards. It often began at local centres both small and great, both secular and monastic, each of them having its own scheme of ideas, its local pride, and very often a jealous resentment of outside interference.

It is possible up to a point to see in the revival of the papacy itself—the apostolic see of Rome which had as its patrons the martyr-princes of the apostles St. Peter and St. Paul—the greatest case in point of such a local development. Gregory VII, in particular, was dedicated to realizing in the see of Rome the lordship, rights, demands, and character of St. Peter, whose vicar and servant from youth he claimed that he was. But in the case of the Roman church this could never be the whole story. Christ had given to Peter the custody of the keys of the kingdom of heaven and the duty of bringing all mankind to salvation within its gates. So the pope's function as vicar of St. Peter must be exercised not only locally but also universally. The pope must find his own, unique means of action in order to fulfil his task. But his freedom of action was limited by the eleventh-century proliferation of reforming centres having roots of their own in local, regional, and national loyalties of the greatest intensity. To some extent men's allegiances were already pre-empted. So the popes had to come to terms with powerful currents of popular and local religion, and with ecclesiastical institutions that served and channelled them.

Montecassino in its golden age was another major example of a local centre with its own powerful and self-generated individuality of religious and corporate life. A discussion of its relations with the reform papacy must take this fully into account. Just as inquiry should not be centred exclusively upon the programmes and politics of the popes themselves, so it should not be preoccupied with the question whether Montecassino and its abbots did or did not accept and co-operate in programmes that the papacy formulated and imposed from above. The question at issue is whether Montecassino, as the institution that it became in its golden age under Abbot Desiderius, was on balance a help rather than a hindrance to papal aspirations that took shape only gradually in an age of dialogue between *sacerdotium* and *regnum.*[88] In this dialogue matters of difference were not so sharply defined from the beginning as Fliche imagined; they emerged in the heat of debate and confrontation.[89] Montecassino's serviceability to the papacy is principally to be determined by inquiring how far it came in the long run to be guided by more than local and particular interests, how far it was drawn into the dialogue of *sacerdotium* and *regnum* on the side of papal interests, and how far it committed to them its manpower and resources, both moral and material.

[88] Cf. C. Schneider, *Prophetisches Sacerdotium und heilsgeschichtliches Regnum im Dialog, 1073–1077. Zur Geschichte Gregors VII. und Heinrichs IV.* (Munich, 1972).

[89] Cf. the discussion of investiture in R. Schieffer, *Die Entstehung des päpstlichen Investiturverbots für den deutschen König* (Stuttgart, 1981).

TABLE 1 (See Introduction, p. xxxiii, n. 75)

Pope	Date	*IP* viii		Leccisotti, *Regesti*	*Reg. Pet. Diac.* no.	*Chron. Cas.*		Kehr, 'Le bolle pontificie'		Migne, *PL*	
		p.	no.			cap.	p.	p.	no.	vol.	no.
Nicholas I	858/67	125	33	i. 223–4	4	i. 24	71–2	23–6	1	—	—
John VIII	882	126	37	i. 224	5	i. 33	89	—	—	cxxvi. 950–2	356
John IX	899	121	41	—	6	i. 46	124	26–9	2	—	—
Marinus II	944	128	44	—	8	i. 56	143	—	—	cxxxiii. 867–9	4
John XII	? 962	130	49	—	14	ii. prol.	165	30–3	4	—	—
Benedict VII	977	130	51	—	12A	ii. prol.	165	—	—	cxxxvii. 326–8	9
John XV	? 985	130–1	52	i. 225	13	ii. prol.	165	34–9	6	—	—
Benedict VIII	1014	132	56	—	16	ii. 31	223	—	—	cxxxix. 1592–5	10
Benedict IX	1038	134	64	—	20	ii. 65	295	—	—	cxli. 1357–9	4
Leo IX	?1049	135	*66	—	—	ii. 79	325	—	—	—	—
Leo IX	1048/54	136–7	70	—	21	—	—	—	—	cxliii. 604–5	8

TABLE 2 (See Introduction, p. xxxiii, n. 76)

Pope	Date	*IP* viii		Leccisotti, *Regesti*	*Reg. Pet. Diac.* no.	*Chron. Cas.*		Kehr, 'Le bolle pontificie'		Migne, *PL*	
		p.	no.			cap.	p.	p.	no.	vol.	no.
Victor II	1057	138–9	79	i. 8–9	26	ii. 93	351–2	—	—	cxliii. 831–4	18
Stephen IX	1058	139–40	81	—	27	ii. 93	352	42–7	8	—	—
Nicholas II	1059	141	88	i. 223	28	iii. 12	374	—	—	cxliii. 1305–9	3
Alexander II	1067	143	96	—	29	iii. 24	391	—	—	cxlvi. 1325–9	49
Urban II	1097	154	141	i. 12–13	36	iv. 17	486	—	—	cli. 492–3	219
Paschal II	1105	158	157	i. 6–7	40	iv. 25	492	—	—	clxiii. 144–8	139
Paschal II	1112	161	170	i. 7–8	44	iv. 45	513	—	—	clxiii. 295	338
Calixtus II	1122	168	201	i. 7	46	iv. 72	538	—	—	clxiii. 1250–4	185

I

The Golden Age of Montecassino

WHEN Leo of Ostia surveyed Montecassino's history he saw in Abbot Aligernus its third *fundator et constructor*, and in Abbot Desiderius its fourth.[1] He had good reason to do so: Aligernus prepared the way for, and Desiderius brought into being, a golden age of monastic life such as Montecassino had never known before and would never know again. It largely continued under Abbot Oderisius I, who commissioned Leo's greatest work; but then it declined, so that Peter the Deacon soon afterwards looked back to the *aureum patris Desiderii seculum* as a time characterized and warranted by the 'virtutes morum ac excellentissima adque obstupescenda signa Casinensium monachorum'.[2] The golden age was in large measure the achievement of the abbots themselves. It was marked by their zeal to maintain the abbey's independence in face of both spiritual and temporal powers, and yet to stay on the best possible terms with all who impinged upon it; to defend, enlarge, and exploit the abbey's lands and possessions; to use the wealth thus derived and the benefactions of devotees to rebuild and embellish its buildings as befitted the foundation of the patriarch of western monasticism; and to make Montecassino a centre of monastic observance, culture, and learning without peer in the western church. Montecassino's effectiveness was not to stop short at the cloister wall or within the circle of its lands and monastic dependencies. It was also to permeate the monastic and secular churches of South Italy. And just as of old St. Benedict had been an inspiration of Pope Gregory the Great, so latter-day Montecassino set out to aid the reactivated papacy of the age of reform. Such in summary are the characteristics of the golden age which will be considered in this chapter under three aspects: the building up of Montecassino's resources and community life; the nature and limitations of its effectiveness as a centre of Christian life; and its relations with outside powers both ecclesiastical and lay.

[1] See Introd. n. 5. [2] *OV*, cap. 15, p. 18.

i. THE BUILDING UP OF MONTECASSINO'S RESOURCES AND MONASTIC LIFE

a. *The* terra sancti Benedicti

Situated in the frontier region between Latium and the Campania, Montecassino was well placed to develop its resources and to secure a large degree of practical autonomy. The sheer rocky eminence upon which it stood, rising to 519 metres above sea level, dominated the northern region of the principality of Capua. The city of Capua lay some fifty kilometres to the south-east, while Rome itself was some 125 kilometres to the north-west along the ancient Via Latina. The material basis of Montecassino's power was the lands of St. Benedict, a compact region surrounding the abbey itself which at its greatest extent in the central middle ages comprised more than 80,000 hectares.[3] A large proportion of these lands, in the fertile valleys of the Rivers Liri and Rapido, had first been given to Montecassino in 744 by Duke Gisulf II of Benevento, after the abbey's restoration *c.*718 by Abbot Petronax.[4] Gisulf's benefaction—an area of land of some 600 sq. km.—was the basis of the abbey's lands up to the Saracen destruction of 883. In the tenth century, Abbot Aligernus, in particular, was able to recover large tracts of them from such local lords as the *gastaldus* of Aquino and the count of Teano.[5] He fortified strongpoints like the Rocca Janula near San Germano, a castle near the church of Sant'Angelo in Theodice, and the tower of San Giorgio near Aquino. Most important of all, he repopulated Montecassino's devastated lands by attracting settlers from regions that had suffered less at Saracen hands. Aligernus enjoyed the help of Princes Landulf II and Paldulf I of Capua, whose charter of 952 set out the boundaries of its lands as by then reconstituted.[6] Soon after Aligernus died, the term *terra sancti*

[3] This section is based upon Fabiani, 'La terra di S. Benedetto'; see also Leccisotti (as Introd. n. 23), pp. 206–19. Much further light may be expected from Bloch's still unpublished study (as Introd. n. 36).

[4] *Chronica s. Benedicti Casinensis*, cap. 21, *MGH Script. rer. Lang.*, pp. 479–80, whence *Chron. Cas.* i. 5, pp. 25–8. For the original limits, see Fabiani, i. 41–5 and the map at the end; also below, Map 2.

[5] *Chron. Cas.* ii. 1–3, pp. 166–73. For the *gastaldus* of Aquino and for the group of *comites* who succeeded him, see Poupardin, pp. 42, 45.

[6] Gattula, *Accessiones*, pp. 57–8, cf. further documents at pp. 55–62; *Reg. Pet. Diac.*, nos. 214A, 312; Poupardin, pp. 100–2, 104, nos. 96–102, 107.

Benedicti began to have currency as the designation of the patrimony.[7]

During the decades that followed it suffered many vicissitudes; but with regard to its security as in other ways Abbot Richer, whom the Emperor Conrad II established at Montecassino in 1038, played a critical part in preparing the way for Desiderius, who became abbot three years after Richer's death in 1055.[8] During his troubled early years Richer was compelled to take energetic action against two especially troublesome depredators of the lands of St. Benedict—Prince Pandulf IV of Capua, from whose dependant Todinus he secured the repossession of the key Rocca d'Evandro which the Emperor Henry II had given to Montecassino in 1022;[9] and the Normans, whom Abbot Atenulf had established upon the *terra sancti Benedicti*, at first to the abbey's advantage, after the battle of Cannae in 1018. Their expulsion in 1045 gave the *terra sancti Benedicti* a security which Desiderius, in his *Dialogues*, described as lasting until the time of writing in the 1070s.[10] Throughout his abbacy, and especially after the Normans were expelled, Richer, like Aligernus before him, was concerned to strengthen and to exploit the *terra sancti Benedicti*. Himself by origin a German from the abbey of Niederaltaich, he enjoyed Conrad II's favour and protection.[11] He built castles and fortifications. Pursuing a policy of *incastellamento* he provided his peasants with strongholds to secure them against Norman raids. He built a strategically significant new bridge across the River Liri. He took steps to secure control of the Rocca d'Evandro. In 1054 he secured possession of the important castle of Saracinisco, at the north-eastern corner of the *terra sancti Benedicti*.[12] In the Montecassino Chronicle Leo of Ostia thus appraised his achievement: 'The innumerable assaults of his neighbours, which we have in part set forth, prevented him from labouring upon the monastery

[7] It first appears in a document of 982: Montecassino, Archivio capitolare, caps. XXXVI, fasc. i, no. 11, Leccisotti, *Regesti*, vii. 206 (1294); then in *MGH Dipl. OIII*, no. 333 (15 Oct. 999). It is common from the mid-eleventh century.

[8] For Richer, see W. Wühr, 'Die Wiedergeburt Montecassinos unter seinem ersten Reformabt Richer von Niederaltaich (†1055)', *SG* iii (1948), 369–450.

[9] *Chron. Cas.* ii. 67, pp. 301–2.

[10] ii. 22, p. 1139.

[11] *MGH Dipl. CII*, no. 270; *Chron. Cas.* ii. 65, p. 295.

[12] *Chron. Cas.* ii. 73–6, 87, pp. 315–20, 338; Gattula, *Accessiones*, p. 151, Leccisotti, *Regesti*, ii. 127.

itself. But he marked the true beginning and source of our present endeavours, when by his zeal and business . . . he delivered our land from the Normans' hands.'[13]

When Desiderius became abbot he speedily acknowledged the changed realities of the political situation by making the volte-face of an alliance with the new Norman rulers of South Italy—Prince Richard of Capua and Robert Guiscard, duke of Apulia. His prudence in so doing was vindicated when, in 1062, Richard completed his conquest of Capua and then, in 1063 and 1065 respectively, subdued the duchy of Gaeta and the county of Aquino. Until his death in 1078 he was Montecassino's most powerful neighbour, and to the south Robert Guiscard vied with him in political and military strength. It was Desiderius' consistent purpose as abbot both to keep the goodwill of the Normans of Capua and Apulia, and also to promote peace and collaboration between them. He used the Norman alliance, and especially Richard of Capua's friendship, to enlarge and secure the *terra sancti Benedicti*.[14] The stage for so doing was set as early as 1058, when Richard confirmed Montecassino in the possession of all its lands, including the Rocca d'Evandro.[15]

Four sources stand out as providing evidence of the abbey's holdings. Only one is contemporary with Desiderius—the still-surviving bronze doors which the merchant Maurus of Amalfi gave in 1066 for the old basilica at Montecassino and which were retained in the new, where in 1123 Abbot Oderisius II enlarged them. Their panels were inscribed with a list of the abbey's possessions, whenever acquired, both within and beyond the *terra sancti Benedicti*; it included forty-seven *castella* and 560 churches.[16] Secondly, the Montecassino Chronicle includes chapters devoted to recording accessions of monasteries, castles, churches, lands, and other property. Leo of Ostia listed donations from 1058 up to the dedication in 1071 of the new basilica; his continuators added lists covering

[13] *Chron. Cas.* ii. 89, pp. 340–1; see Hoffmann's comments in Dormeier, *Montecassino*, pp. 12–13.

[14] *Chron. Cas.* iii. 16, p. 380.

[15] Ibid. iii. 15, p. 379, Gattula, *Accessiones*, pp. 161–3, Loud, 'Calendar', p. 119, no. 2.

[16] For the list, Fabiani, 'La terra di S. Benedetto', ii. 415–23, also Gattula, *Accessiones*, pp. 172–4. A full topographical survey may be anticipated in Bloch (as Introd. n. 36).

the remainder of Desiderius' rule.[17] Thirdly, Peter the Deacon's Register incorporates texts of charters and other material, in general following the order of documents as in the Chronicle; Desiderius' reign provided him with well over a hundred items.[18] Fourthly, the Emperor Lothar III's diploma of 1137 for Montecassino, the original of which survives in its archives, lists 659 churches, monasteries, and other possessions which the abbey then held. The list was prepared by Peter the Deacon and was tendentious in matters of detail. However, it affords a striking picture of the abbey's resources in the aftermath of its golden age.[19]

As Richard of Capua extended and consolidated his conquests Desiderius was able, in his early years, to use their friendship to obtain by grant, purchase, or exchange, a number of castles and their associated lands. Among his major acquisitions from Richard were the *inclitum oppidum* of Mortola (1065) to the south-east, which safeguarded the approaches to Montecassino by way of the rivers Garigliano and Rapido; Fratte (1065)—the modern Ausonia—to the south-west on the Via Ercolanea which led northwards from the sea and the Via Appia to Montecassino itself, where there was a castle hitherto menacing to it; the monastery of San Salvatore, Cucuruzzo (1066), between Mortola and the Rocca d'Evandro; and Teramo to the west of the *terra sancti Benedicti* in the direction of Pontecorvo and Aquino.[20] Desiderius was also able to reach agreements with such vexatious neighbours as the counts of Aquino, Comino, Venafro, and Teano, whereby they surrendered claims to Cassinese lands and strongholds; by the exchange or cession of lands they enabled Desiderius to round off the *terra sancti Benedicti*. Some examples are the securing by exchange in 1067 from Count Adenulf VI of Aquino of a share in the castle of Piedemonte which covered the approach of the Via Latina to Montecassino.[21] In 1064 Desiderius was able to secure from Count Paldo of Venafro a share in the

[17] *Chron. Cas.* iii. 17, 39, 59–61, pp. 380–3, 415–17, 440–3.

[18] Hoffmann (as Introd. n. 18), pp. 110–43, 156–8.

[19] *MGH Dipl. LIII*, no. 120; cf. Caspar, *Petrus Diaconus*, pp. 189–93.

[20] *Chron. Cas.* iii. 16, 61, pp. 380, 441–3; Gattula, *Accessiones*, pp. 158, 164–7, 186, *Historia*, pp. 312–13; *Codex diplomaticus Cajetanus*, ii. 67–8, no. 226; Leccisotti, *Regesti*, ii. 128, 130, 132, 136; Loud, 'Calendar', pp. 120, 122, nos. 5–6, 13–14. For Fratte's restlessness, see *Chron. Cas.* iii. 11, p. 373.

[21] *Chron. Cas.* iii. 16, p. 380; *Reg. Pet. Diac.*, no. 345.

castles of Viticuso and Cerasuolo near the north-eastern boundaries of the *terra sancti Benedicti.*[22] He was also able to consolidate the abbey's hold on the castle of Saracinisco in the northern marches (1061/78).[23] In July 1086, and so almost at the end of his rule, he fulfilled a long-cherished aim by securing the castle of Cardito which lay between Saracinisco and Cerasuolo.[24]

Important though such acquisitions were in extending and protecting the *terra sancti Benedicti*, they did not alter its landlocked situation. It was thus of exceptional benefit that, in 1066, Prince Richard of Capua secured for Montecassino the possession of Torre a Mare, the fortification at the mouth of the River Garigliano which controlled traffic upon it.[25] The abbey thereby fulfilled its need to extend its lands to the Gulf of Gaeta and to secure a corridor to the sea. Ships could now come unimpeded up the river as far as Suio, whence their cargoes could be transported by land to Montecassino itself.[26] Desiderius sought to consolidate his abbey's hold on the vicinity of Suio, with which in 1040 Abbot Richer had already been concerned:[27] in 1078 Prince Jordan of Capua granted a charter confirming Montecassino's possession of Suio, and in 1085 the prince gave it further lands by the Garigliano.[28] The augmentation of the *terra sancti Benedicti* was completed by Abbot Oderisius I. He added to it Pontecorvo to the west (1105), and to the south of Cardito he acquired Acquafondata (1089) and obtained the full possession of Viticuso (1106).[29] He thus brought the abbey's lands to their full territorial extent during the Middle Ages.

The abbots of Montecassino took steps to exploit economically

[22] *Chron. Cas.* iii. 17, p. 382, Gattula, *Accessiones*, pp. 168–9.

[23] *Chron. Cas.* iii. 52, 61, pp. 434, 441, Gattula, *Accessiones*, pp. 189–90.

[24] *Chron. Cas.* iii. 59, p. 440, Gattula, *Accessiones*, pp. 194–5.

[25] *Chron. Cas.* iii. 16, p. 380, Gattula, *Accessiones*, p. 166, *Codex diplomaticus Cajetanus*, ii. 76–8, no. 231; and, for Jordan I's confirmation in 1085, *Chron. Cas.* iii. 61, p. 441, Gattula, *Accessiones*, p. 192, *Codex diplomaticus Cajetanus*, ii. 132–3, no. 256. See Loud, 'Calendar', pp. 121, 125, nos. 10, 32.

[26] For the importance of this route, see *Chron. Cas.* iv. 54, p. 519.

[27] Ibid. ii. 55, p. 271, Gattula, *Accessiones*, pp. 128–9, *Codex diplomaticus Cajetanus*, ii. 69–70, no. 227, Leccisotti, *Regesti*, ii. 133.

[28] *Chron. Cas.* iii. 61, p. 441, Gattula, *Accessiones*, pp. 187, 192, *Codex diplomaticus Cajetanus*, ii. 120–1, 132–3, nos. 251, 256, cf. 122–6, nos. 252–3, Leccisotti, *Regesti*, ii. 129. See Loud, 'Calendar', pp. 123, 125, nos. 21, 32.

[29] *Chron. Cas.* iv. 6, 25, pp. 471, 491–2, Gattula, *Accessiones*, pp. 222–5, Leccisotti, *Regesti*, ii. 125, 132, cf. 99, Loud, 'Calendar', p. 133, no. 79.

and to defend militarily the patrimony that they in this way developed. Advancing from Richer's policy of *incastellamento*, Desiderius began to shape the more feudalized order of the twelfth and thirteenth centuries. He conferred communal rights upon the citizens of Traetto (1061) and Suio (1079).[30] The charters by which he did so set out the services owed to the abbey, and also contain the earliest evidence from Cassinese lands of a social class superior to the peasantry whose members provided service with their horses in a region extending from Rome itself throughout the principality of Capua. At the end of his life Desiderius legislated to preserve the integrity of the abbey's lands and possessions by forbidding future abbots to alienate them and individual monks to make improper dispositions concerning them.[31] Otherwise little evidence survives for Desiderius' administration of the *terra sancti Benedicti*. But his vast programme of building and decoration testifies to the wealth and resources that became available to him. The extension, consolidation, and better exploitation of the abbey's lands must be accounted the first of his major achievements on its behalf.[32]

b. *Donations outside the* terra sancti Benedicti

Montecassino had for long accumulated possessions and benefactions outside the *terra sancta Benedicti*, and under Desiderius the process accelerated.[33] Its most regular and lavish benefactors in Desiderius' time were undoubtedly the Norman rulers of South Italy—the princes of Capua and the dukes of Apulia and Calabria. Of Prince Richard and Robert Guiscard Leo of Ostia said that before all men of their time they loved, endowed, and protected Montecassino, and that throughout Desiderius' life they were exceedingly devoted, faithful, and friendly towards him.[34] The Capuans were the earlier to make gifts on a large scale; their gifts were especially of lands and churches. Apart from donations that served to extend the *terra sancti Benedicti*, they were prominent for their donation

[30] Fabiani, 'La terra di S. Benedetto', i. 421–4, nos. 1–2; also *Codex diplomaticus Cajetanus*, ii. 37–9, 124–6, nos. 213, 253.

[31] *Chron. Cas.* iii. 73, p. 455.

[32] Cf. Amatus, iii. 52, pp. 175–6.

[33] For lists of donations to Montecassino, see Gattula, *Historia*, pp. 196–330; and Dormeier, *Montecassino*, pp. 24–106, esp. 28–52; cf. Hoffmann (as Introd. n. 18) pp. 97–163, for matter in *Reg. Pet. Diac.*

[34] *Chron. Cas.* iii. 15, p. 377.

of monasteries, for example Santa Maria in Calena (dioc. Siponto, 1059); Sant'Angelo in Formis (dioc. Capua, 1065/72), where Desiderius rebuilt the monastery and its church, establishing a community of over forty monks; Sant'Erasmo in Formis (? 1073); San Rufo, Capua (1082); and Sant' Agatha, Aversa (1085).[35] An example of a temporal grant is Prince Jordan's gift, in 1081, of extensive rights with regard to Lake Maggiore, near Aquino.[36]

Generosity of a no less outstanding order was shown to Montecassino by Robert Guiscard and his second wife Sichelgaita. It was after Robert was reconciled to Pope Gregory VII at Ceprano in June 1080 that they were to make their most lavish gifts. Although many of them were of money, movable wealth, and treasure, they included lands and churches. In the same month as the meeting at Ceprano they gave Montecassino the monastery of San Pietro Imperiale, Taranto; in the following October Robert Guiscard made two further donations, both of institutions at Troia: the monastery of San Nicandro and the churches of San Nicola and San Tommaso; and, again, he gave the monastery of Sant'Angelo and the churches of San Bartolomeo, of Sant'Angelo, and of San Giusto. In 1082 he gave Montecassino the church of San Biagio and several other properties at Amalfi. To such gifts he added mercantile donations. He gave the abbey *c.*1085 warehouse facilities (*fundicus*) at Amalfi, while in 1086 his widow Sichelgaita gave it the town and port of Cetraro in Calabria.[37] Such gifts were the more

[35] Santa Maria in Calena: *Chron. Cas.* iii. 13, pp. 374–5; Gattula, *Accessiones*, p. 161; *IP* ix. 253–5; T. Leccisotti, 'Le colonie Cassinesi in Capitanata: ii, Il Gargano', *Misc. cassin.* xv (1938), 20–4, 59–60, Loud, 'Calendar', p. 119, no. 3. Sant'Angelo in Formis: *Chron. cas.* iii. 37, pp. 413–14, Gattula, *Historia*, pp. 253–4, *Accessiones*, pp. 175–7, M. Inguanez, *Regesto di S. Angelo in Formis*, 2 vols. (Montecassino, 1925), i. 32–7, 41–5, nos. 11, 14, and ii, plates iv–v, vii; *IP* viii. 234–5; Leccisotti, *Regesti*, ii. 42, 69; Loud, 'Calendar', pp. 121–2, nos. 9, 11, 15; for the history, N. Cilento, *Italia meridionale langobarda* (2nd edn., Milan and Naples, 1971), 226–41. Sant'Erasmo in Formis: *Codex diplomaticus Cajetanus*, ii. 20–2, no. 205. San Rufo, Capua: *Chron. Cas.* iii. 47, 61, pp. 425, 441; Gattula, *Accessiones*, pp. 188–9; Inguanez, op. cit. i. 55–6, no. 19; Loud, 'Calendar', pp. 124–5, no. 27. Sant'Agatha, Aversa: *Chron. Cas.* iii. 56, 61, pp. 437, 441; Gattula, *Accessiones*, p. 191, Inguanez, op. cit. i. 62–3, no. 22, Leccisotti, *Regesti*, ii. 67–8, Loud, 'Calendar', p. 125, no. 31.

[36] *Chron. Cas.* iii. 47, 61, pp. 425, 441, Gattula, *Accessiones*, pp. 187–8, Leccisotti, *Regesti*, ii. 108–9, Loud, 'Calendar', p. 124, no. 26.

[37] For Robert's and Sichelgaita's gifts, see *Chron. Cas.* iii. 44, 58, iv. 10, pp. 421, 438–40, 474–5; Ménager, *Recueil*, pp. 101–4, 113–20, 133–6, 173–5, nos. 31, 36, 37, 42, 48. For Amalfi, see H. M. Willard, 'The *Fundicus*, a Port Facility of Montecassino

valuable because Desiderius had secured for Montecassino its corridor to the sea.

Lesser Normans followed their leaders' suit by helping to enrich Montecassino and to add to its monastic dependencies. Examples from Peter the Deacon's Register are the gift of the churches of San Constantio and of San Cristoforo near Aquino in 1068 by the Norman adventurer William of Montreuil when he was duke of Gaeta; William of Pont-Échanfray who, between 1066/7 and ? 1073, commended to Montecassino the monasteries of Santa Maria in Sorsolum and Santa Maria in Cesis, in the county of Marsia; and Geoffrey Ridel, duke of Gaeta and lord of Pontecorvo, who in 1075/6 gave Montecassino the monasteries of Sant'Erasmo at Gaeta as well as San Pietro della Foresta near Pontecorvo.[38]

Such acquisitions from Normans did not preclude others from Lombards. In 1059, for example, Prince Gisulf II of Salerno restored to Montecassino the monastery of San Benedetto, Salerno; but he met with the citizens' hostility. He therefore gave Montecassino instead the monastery of San Lorenzo.[39] Between 1065 and 1073, Duke Sergius IV of Gaeta gave the church of Santa Maria, Amalfi.[40] Most Lombard grants to Desiderius, however, were made by counts or lesser men, often because they were under pressure from the Normans and wished to prevent their property from falling into Norman hands. In 1065/6, for example, Count John Squintus of Pontecorvo gave generously to Montecassino from such a motive. The Montecassino Chronicle and Peter the Deacon's Register record many such gifts, as do some of the abbey's unpublished charters.[41]

in Medieval Amalfi', *Benedictina*, xix (1972), 253–61, and 'Abbot Desiderius and the Ties between Montecassino and Amalfi in the Eleventh Century', *Misc. cassin.* xxxvii (1973), 14–26, 29–31, 62.

[38] *Chron. Cas.* iii. 17, 41, pp. 380–2, 419; *Reg. Pet. Diac.*, nos. 461, 483; Gattula, *Historia*, p. 267; Hoffmann (as Introd. n. 18), pp. 199–201, no. 1; Dormeier, *Montecassino*, pp. 41, 68–9.

[39] *Chron. Cas.* iii. 13, p. 375; A. Mancone, 'Un diploma sconosciuto del principe Gisolfo II di Salerno a favore di Montecassino', *Bullettino dell'Archivio paleografico italiano*, new ser., iv–v (1958/9), 95–9.

[40] *Reg. Pet. Diac.*, no. 506; Willard (as Ch. I n. 37), *Misc. cassin.* xxxvii. 28–9, 62–3.

[41] See, e.g., William of Pont-Échanfray's charters, as above, Ch. 1 n. 38; and, for Count John Squintus, Gattula, *Accessiones*, pp. 169–70, and Dormeier, *Montecassino*, pp. 37, 66. For an unpublished charter, Montecassino, Archivio capitolare, caps. XXIV, fasc. i, no. 4, Leccisotti, *Regesti*, vi. 263 (651).

As in the *terra sancti Benedicti* so from Montecassino's wider possessions it is not possible to estimate how much wealth accrued to it. But it is clear that Montecassino's control over subject monasteries was close, being normally exercised through monastic *prepositi* appointed by the abbot of Montecassino. Shortly before his death Desiderius could seek to regularize annual *prandia*, or food farms, which many of its monastic and other dependencies owed to Montecassino.[42] The monks had for long collected from the peasants of their more distant possessions a tribute (*terraticum*) which included wheat; and in the famine year 1085 Desiderius could distribute relief in a wide area of Italy, at a time when he was incurring expense in providing for Gregory VII's court.[43] Of especial importance to Montecassino was its growing connection with the port of Amalfi. Besides securing the churches and harbour facilities that have been noticed, Montecassino was upon cordial terms with the leading mercantile family of Pantaleone. Pantaleone's son Maurus, who in 1066 gave the bronze doors that Desiderius had commissioned, subsequently entered Montecassino as a monk.[44] The Amalfitans seem to have had a colony near Montecassino itself.[45] The abbey thus did not lack links with the commercial world, from which substantial benefits accrued.

Under Abbot Richer Montecassino had already responded to a request from King Stephen of Hungary by sending monks to his kingdom for the reform of its monasteries, and it had received gifts in return.[46] Desiderius extended its interests outside the mainland of South Italy in several directions. He was much concerned with Sardinia, perhaps because its lead mines were important for his building plans. In 1063 he received envoys from Bareso, judge of Torres, asking for the establishment there of a monastery. Soon afterwards he determined to send as abbot his monk Aldemarius, together with twelve companions; but Pisan hostility frustrated this attempt. However, *c.*1065/6 a second mission led to Bareso's establishing a monastery at Montesanto which he endowed with two

[42] *Chron. Cas.* iii. 13, 48, 55, 73, pp. 375, 425, 436, 455–6; Dormeier, *Montecassino*, pp. 4–6, 250–2, no. 5.

[43] *Chron. Cas.* iii. 64, p. 446; cf. *Ann. Cas., a.* 1085, pp. 1422–3.

[44] *Chron. Cas.* iii. 55, p. 436; Amatus, viii. 3, pp. 341–6.

[45] This is indicated by references to Amalfitan money in *Chron. Cas.* iii. 58, iv. 13, pp. 438, 482; see Willard (as Ch. 1 n. 37), *Misc. cassin.* xxxvii. 38–9.

[46] *Chron. Cas.* ii. 65, p. 297.

churches, and to the gift by another judge, Torkitori of Cagliari, of a further six churches.[47]

Leo of Ostia recorded how, in the course of negotiations about these matters, Desiderius met Duke Godfrey of Lorraine at Pisa, where the duke reconciled the Pisans to him and to Montecassino.[48] Desiderius already had a connection with Tuscany which was to intensify with the years.[49] It began in 1056 under Abbot Peter of Montecassino, when two brothers, Roland and Henry, gave Montecassino the church of San Giorgio in Lucca. Further gifts followed in 1064, when San Giorgio became a monastic house subject to Montecassino.[50] Desiderius was thereafter at pains to develop his possessions at Lucca and elsewhere in Tuscany.[51] He thus secured a stake in a key centre of communications and reforming activity, and gained a measure of security for the Cassinese settlement in Sardinia.[52] He also forged a link with Countess Matilda of Tuscany, of which there is evidence in her charter of *c.*1080 freeing the monks of Montecassino from tolls and payments in respect of textiles passing through Pisa and Lucca.[53] The link was to matter greatly in the political developments after Pope Gregory VII's death in 1085.

Montecassino also established connections with Rome that were likewise important both economically and politically.[54] They began before Desiderius became abbot. In 1049, under

[47] Ibid. iii. 21–2, 24, pp. 387–9, 391; Gattula, *Historia*, pp. 153–5, *Accessiones*, pp. 174–5. See A. Saba, 'Montecassino e la Sardegna medioevale', *Misc. cassin.* iv (1927), esp. pp. 133–8, nos. 1–3; F. Casula, 'Barisone di Torres', *DBI* vi. 389–90; Dormeier, *Montecassino*, pp. 37, 69–70, 181–2.

[48] *Chron. Cas.* iii. 22, pp. 388–9.

[49] Ibid. iii. 61, p. 442, Gattula, *Accessiones*, p. 201, Leccisotti, *Regesti*, i. 119, and 'Riflessi Matildici sull'arce Cassinesi', *Atti e memorie della Deputazione di storia patria per le antiche provincie Modenesi*, 9th ser., iii (1963), 233–43; H.-M. Schwarzmaier, 'Das Kloster St. Georg in Lucca und der Ausgriff Montecassinos in die Toscana', *QFIAB* xlix (1969), 148–85, and *Lucca und das Reich bis zum Ende des 11. Jahrhunderts* (Tübingen, 1972), 66, 379–81, 393–4, 396, 411–12. Desiderius referred to his monks at Lucca in *Dial.* iii. 1–5, pp. 1119–20.

[50] *Chron. Cas.* iii. 61, p. 442, Gattula, *Accessiones*, pp. 195–9.

[51] Schwarzmaier, art. cit. 156–7; pp. 177–83 for the gift of San Benedetto, Arezzo.

[52] *Chron. Cas.* iii. 21, pp. 387–8.

[53] Ibid. iii. 61, p. 442; Leccisotti (as Ch. I n. 49), p. 237.

[54] See esp. H.-W. Klewitz, 'Montecassino in Rom', *QFIAB* xxviii (1937/8), 36–47, repr. *Ausgewählte Aufsätze*, pp. 465–76; D. Lohrmann, *Das Register Papst Johannes' VIII. (872–882)* (Tübingen, 1968), 102–9. For matters of Roman topography, a useful guide is R. Krautheimer, *Rome. Profile of a City, 312–1308* (Princeton, NJ, 1980), esp. pp. 231–326 with maps at 245–7.

Abbot Richer, Pope Leo IX placed the Roman monastery of Santa Croce in Gerusalemme in Montecassino's possession.[55] During Alexander II's pontificate Desiderius exchanged it for the church of Santa Maria in Pallara on the Palatine (today San Sebastiano alla Polveriera). Its abbot was to be elected by the monks, but he was to receive consecration at the hands of the pope.[56] Economic benefits to Montecassino followed these gifts. As early as 1055, under Abbot Richer, it was given the right for a ship to trade at Rome without paying dues or tolls.[57] Desiderius was able to borrow money in Rome to redeem for Montecassino the valuables that Pope Victor II had placed in pawn there.[58] When in 1066 Desiderius began to rebuild the basilica at Montecassino, it was from Rome that he obtained many of the columns, capitals, and pieces of marble that he needed for it; his newly secured use of the River Garigliano made it possible for him to transport them by water for most of the way to the abbey.[59]

The building of the new basilica and the reconstruction of the monastic buildings, which formed the most conspicuous achievement of Montecassino's golden age under Desiderius, would have been impossible without the security, extension, and wealth of the *terra sancti Benedicti*, the amassing of endowments and possessions over a very wide area, and the contacts that Desiderius established at Rome and in other centres of power.

c. *The construction and embellishment of the new basilica and the other monastic buildings*

As in so many respects, Abbot Richer anticipated and prepared the way for Desiderius' building projects by roofing with lead sheets the old basilica of St. Benedict as it had been built under Abbot Gisulf (797–817). He had also begun the construction of a range of accommodation (*palatium*) on the east side of the abbey, and he had made a curved arcade with marble

[55] Migne, *PL* cxliii. 605–6, no. 9; *Chron. Cas.* ii. 79, p. 326; Gattula, *Historia*, p. 252; *IP* i. 35, viii. 135, no. 65; Leccisotti, *Regesti*, i. 29–30.

[56] *Chron. Cas.* iii. 36, p. 413; Migne, *PL* cxlvi. 1395, no. 108; Kehr, 'Le bolle pontificie', pp. 48–9, no. 10; *IP* viii. 145–6, no. 107; Leccisotti, *Regesti*, i. 29. For Santa Maria in Pallara, see C. Huelsen, *Le chiese di Roma nel medioevo* (Florence, 1927), 353–5, no. 71; Krautheimer, op. cit. 167, 315–17, 319; M. Armellini, *Le chiese di Roma del secolo iv al xix*, 2 vols. (Rome, 1942), i. 640–2.

[57] *Chron. Cas.* ii. 84, p. 332; Migne, *PL* cxliii. 731–2, no. 85; *IP* viii. 136, no. 69.

[58] *Chron. Cas.* iii. 19, p. 384.

[59] Ibid. iii. 26, p. 394.

columns round the courtyard before the basilica.[60] When Desiderius became abbot he quickly determined to use the peace and prosperity that his own strong rule created to build more extensively and more rapidly at Montecassino than anyone had ever before attempted.[61] As Leo of Ostia put it, he found in the cramped, shapeless, and dilapidated state of the monastic buildings a stimulus to embark upon their reconstruction, despite his shortage of resources for so major an undertaking. So, as a pilot scheme, he completed Richer's *palatium* and added a small library building. Encouraged by his success in this work he proceeded to a complete rebuilding of the abbot's lodging. Next he reconstructed the monks' dormitory, using a site which he had intended for an enlargement of the cloister. Then he put up a new and richly decorated chapter house. He concluded the first phase of his rehabilitation of Montecassino's buildings by procuring, at the expense of the Amalfitan merchant Maurus, the set of bronze doors for the old basilica; they were specially cast in Constantinople in imitation of similar doors which Maurus' father Pantaleone had given to the cathedral at Amalfi.[62]

In March 1066 Desiderius judged the time to be ripe for a more ambitious undertaking. Leo of Ostia referred to the prosperity and peace that Montecassino by then enjoyed, and to the honour, obedience, and service which Desiderius could confidently anticipate from all his neighbours both great and small.[63] Despite the persistent objections of senior monks, he decided to build a small, temporary monastic church dedicated

[60] Ibid. ii. 89, pp. 340–1.

[61] Ibid. iii. 10, p. 372; cf. Peter the Deacon, *DVI*, cap. 18, Migne, *PL* clxxiii. 1029, and Alfanus' poem in Lentini and Avagliano, *Carmi*, no. 54.

[62] *Chron. Cas.* iii. 18, p. 385, and the *titulus* of the inscription on Montecassino's bronze doors: Fabiani, 'La terra di S. Benedetto', ii. 423. For Amalfi, see Willard (as Ch. I n. 37), *Misc. cassin.* xxxvii. 41–3.

[63] *Chron. Cas.* iii. 26, pp. 393–4. For the building and dedication of the new basilica, see Amatus, viii. 3, p. 343; *Chron. Cas.* iii. 26–30, pp. 393–402; Leo of Ostia, *Narratio*, pp. 219–25. For modern discussions, see K. J. Conant, *A Brief Commentary on Early Mediaeval Church Architecture* (Baltimore, 1942), 5–11, and *Carolingian and Romanesque Architecture 800–1200* (2nd integr. edn., Harmondsworth, 1978), 362–4; A. Pantoni, 'La basilica di Montecassino e quella di Salerno ai tempi di S. Gregorio VII', *Benedictina*, x (1956), 23–47, and 'Le vicende della basilica di Montecassino attraverso la documentazione archeologica', *Misc. cassin.* xxxvi (1973), esp. pp. 156–79, 210–11; G. Carbonara, *Iussu Desiderii. Montecassino e l'architettura campano-abruzzese nell'undicesimo secolo* (Rome, 1979), 47–97; Krautheimer (as Ch. 1 n. 54), pp. 178–82.

to St. Peter and to demolish the old basilica of St. Benedict.[64] He made an elaborate preparation of the site for a new basilica upon the exposed and constricted mountain top where natural hazards like storm and lightning posed a frequent threat. Much rock was blasted away by fire and worked at with iron implements, in order that the level of the building might be reduced and the sanctuary made even with the nave. Then he went to Rome and procured by purchase, or by enlisting the goodwill of his friends in the city, columns, marble, and other building material.[65] The citizens of the neighbourhood carried the first of the columns up the mountain.[66] During the levelling work, and probably in 1068, a burial was unexpectedly found beneath the floor of the old sanctuary which, according to the Montecassino Chronicle as it now stands, was declared to be St. Benedict's; although it may have included adjacent tombs of St. Benedict and St. Scholastica. Perhaps after some rearrangement Desiderius quickly ordered it to be covered again and its site decorated with precious stones; he built over it an altar of Parian marble. The plan to level the sanctuary with the nave had, as a consequence, to be abandoned. After these events Montecassino was the better able to counter the monks of Saint-Benoît-sur-Loire, who claimed to possess St. Benedict's relics. Its new basilica was now equipped to be a centre of pilgrimage and devotion without peer amongst the churches of monastic saints in the western world.[67]

Together with the rest of the monastic buildings Desiderius' basilica was largely destroyed by earthquake on 9 September 1349; later centuries saw much rebuilding; and the site was again devastated in 1944 during the Second World War: thus, little now remains of its structure and decoration.[68] In respect

[64] *Chron. Cas.* iii. 26, p. 394. Opposition persisted: iii. 33, p. 407. For the suddenness of Desiderius' decision to rebuild, iii. 18, p. 385.

[65] For Rome as a source of building materials, see J. Deér, *The Dynastic Porphyry Tombs of the Norman Period in Sicily*, *DOP* v (1959), 117–19.

[66] Thus *Chron. Cas.* iii. 26, p. 394. John of Lodi, *Vita sancti Petri Damiani*, cap. 20, Migne, *PL* cxliv. 141–2, tells of boys carrying stones.

[67] Desiderius himself claimed miracles at the rediscovered tomb: *Dial.* ii. 14–15, 17–18, pp. 1134–7. After the Lombard devastation bones believed to be St. Benedict's were taken to Fleury (Saint-Benoît-sur-Loire). For the *densum spinetum* (Baronius) of rival claims to possess the true relics, see esp. Meyvaert (as Introd. n. 30), and the contributions to *Le Culte et les reliques de Saint Benoît et de Sainte Scholastique*, *Studia monastica*, xxi (1979), esp. A. Davril, 'La tradition cassinienne', pp. 377–408, 423–8.

[68] For recent archaeological investigations, see Pantoni (as Ch. I n. 63).

of its general layout, however, Desiderius seems to have adhered to forms traditional at Montecassino which themselves had early Christian and Constantinian precedents; although for its triumphal arch he was more directly indebted to St. Peter's at Rome, the patriarchal basilica of which he was a cardinal-priest. Indeed, the exigencies of the site limited the basilica to about one-third of the size of St. Peter's. Leo of Ostia set out its dimensions—48.40 metres in length and 21.07 metres in breadth—together with details of its principal altars, including that of St. John the Baptist upon the spot where St. Benedict had built his oratory. He also described the adjacent buildings: the treasury and sacristy, the chapels of St. Nicholas and St. Bartholomew,[69] the campanile, the *atrium* or paradise in front of the church, the five pointed arches (*fornices quos spiculos dicimus*) of the porch before the church and the *atrium*,[70] the tower-like basilicas of the Archangel Michael and of St. Peter, prince of the apostles,[71] and the new marble staircase by which the whole complex of buildings was approached.

The adornment of these buildings, and especially of the basilica, impressed observers even more than did the buildings themselves. Desiderius brought from Constantinople, and also as it would seem from Alexandria, craftsmen who revived the art of mosaic, which, according to Leo of Ostia, had for long been lost in the West.[72] Leo expressed wonder at the skill of the mosaics with their lifelike figures and flowers, and also of the workmanship in gold, silver, bronze, iron, glass, ivory, wood, alabaster, and stone. He recorded the verses, composed by Alfanus of Salerno, which were written upon the apse and the main arch. They commemorated the work of Desiderius and the new law which went out from the house of St. Benedict to enlighten all lands.[73]

[69] For the consecration of the latter in 1075, see *Chron. Cas.* iii. 33, p. 408; Leo of Ostia, *Narratio*, p. 223.

[70] For similar features of the great mosque at Mahdia, see Conant (as Ch. I n. 63).

[71] Also consecrated in 1075.

[72] *Chron. Cas.* iii. 27, p. 396, refers only to Byzantines, but Amatus, iii. 52, p. 175, adds 'Saracens' from Alexandria. In his *Narratio* Leo spoke of artisans 'ex diversis orbis partibus et ab ipsa quoque regia urbe Constantinopoli': p. 219. See O. Demus, *Byzantine Art and the West* (New York, 1970), 24–8, 102–8.

[73] The apse carried the verses: 'Hec domus est similis Synai sacra iura ferentis, | Ut lex demonstrat, hic que fuit edita quondam. | Lex hinc exivit, mentes que ducit ab imis, | Et vulgata dedit lumen per clymata secli.' On the main arch was written in gold letters: 'Ut duce te patria iustis potiatur adepta, | Hinc Desiderius pater hanc

The new basilica was ready for consecration by Pope Alexander II on 1 October 1071. It was one of the great events of the eleventh century. The week of celebration was attended by an enormous concourse of people from near and far. Many came from Rome: besides the pope there were present Archdeacon Hildebrand and many cardinals and bishops of the city and its environs, together with other clerks and laity. In the Montecassino Chronicle Leo of Ostia listed, in all, ten archbishops and forty-six bishops.[74] Amongst lay magnates there attended Prince Richard of Capua, whom Leo of Ostia named first, Prince Gisulf of Salerno, Prince Landulf of Benevento, Duke Sergius of Naples, Duke Sergius of Sorrento, and the counts of Marsia and Valva, together with innumerable Normans and Lombards.[75] The relics placed under the altars were of a quantity and quality to suit the occasion, as was the display of ornaments and furnishing, which Leo of Ostia described in detail.[76] Outstanding among them was the golden altar decorated with scenes from the Gospels and from the miracles of St. Benedict, which Desiderius had commissioned in Constantinople and whose making the Byzantine emperor himself oversaw. The buildings, decoration, and furniture of the new basilica were a visible proof of the power and wealth of Montecassino in its golden age. The consecration ceremony of 1071 ensured that all who mattered at Rome and in South Italy, both clerical and lay, were duly impressed.

After its completion Desiderius' urge to build became even more compelling (*audentior iam, immo valentior*), and he was determined to extend and refurbish the whole of the monastic buildings, even where he had already made improvements. While redesigning the cloister he rebuilt and lavishly decorated the refectory, remaking the kitchen and cellar. He demolished and rebuilt the dormitory, chapter house, infirmary, and vestry. All this was the work of three years. He then had another area of ground prepared for rebuilding, and further improved the

tibi condidit aulam.' The latter inscription was modelled on one similarly placed in the Vatican basilica at Rome: 'Quod duce te mundus surrexit in astra triumphans, | Hanc Constantinus victor tibi condidit aulam': *Chron. Cas.* iii. 28, p. 397, Lentini and Avagliano, *Carmi*, no. 15. See Bloch (as Introd. n. 34), *DOP* iii. 198–9.

[74] The *Narratio*, however, lists seven archbishops and thirty-nine bishops: p. 221.

[75] A notable absentee was Robert Guiscard, who with his son Roger was at the siege of Palermo.

[76] *Chron. Cas.* iii. 32, pp. 403–5.

chapter house and the approaches to the basilica. He drastically modified Abbot Richer's *palatium* in order to provide better facilities for infirm monks, and built new novices' quarters. Having thus overhauled the monastic buildings, Desiderius turned his attention to their environs. He took much care over reconstructing Montecassino's walls and gates, and built a large new hospice for the entertainment of pilgrims. A bakery which he had constructed near the porch of the basilica was so finely designed that many mistook it for a church. Finally, he rebuilt the church of St. Martin and caused it to be decorated with his accustomed lavishness.[77]

His appetite for building was not satisfied by his work at Montecassino. When, in 1072, Prince Richard of Capua finally gave him the church of Sant'Angelo in Formis, he rebuilt it to accommodate the forty and more monks whom he purposed to establish there.[78] He ordered the rebuilding of the church of San Liberatore in the county of Teano; and at San Benedetto, Capua, he saw to the building of a new monastic church.[79] At Salerno he influenced his friend Archbishop Alfanus, who rebuilt the cathedral of St. Matthew.[80] The architecture and decoration of these buildings emphasize the character of Desiderius' reign at Montecassino as an epoch in South Italian artistic history.[81]

d. *Gifts of money and precious objects to Montecassino*

Montecassino's buildings as refashioned and embellished by Desiderius were matched in splendour by the movable riches that they contained. From his friends, patrons, and supporters, especially from the Normans, he acquired an unending succession of gifts of money and precious objects. Montecassino had already received gifts before 1058. One of the most notable

[77] Ibid. iii. 33–4, pp. 405–10. For a charter of 1076 in which a Cassinese monk named Maurus received property at Aquino for the hospital that he had established at San Germano for the reception of guests and pilgrims, see Montecassino, Archivio capitolare, caps. LXXVI, fasc. i, no. 1, Leccisotti, *Regesti*, xi. 5 (4366).

[78] Ibid. iii. 37, p. 413. Sant'Angelo affords the best surviving visual evidence for Desiderius' buildings and their decoration, but for an illuminating discussion of Santa Maria della Libera, Aquino, and San Liberatore alla Maiella, see Carbonara (as Ch. I n. 63), esp. pp. 99–187. For Sant' Angelo, see J. Wettstein, *Les Fresques de S. Angelo in Formis* (Geneva, 1960); O. Demus, *Romanesque Mural Painting* (New York, 1970), 23, 80–1, 294–8, plates 18–39.

[79] *Chron. Cas.* iii. 48, 55, pp. 427, 436.

[80] Pantoni (as Ch. I n. 63).

[81] See esp. Kitzinger (as Introd. n. 34), pp. 87–102; but cf. Demus (as Ch. I n. 72).

amongst its earlier donors was the Emperor Henry II, whose gifts included the great Gospel Book, now Vatican Library, MS Ottobonus 74.[82] But despite such largesse, Leo of Ostia could remark that, in 1058, Montecassino was somewhat poorly supplied with ecclesiastical ornaments. Desiderius' first major attempt to make good the deficiency took place at Rome. Using his own money and also loans from his Roman friends he acquired for 180 pounds the vestments that Pope Victor II was compelled to pawn in the city. Leo described seven particularly rich items. He went on to give an impressive list of other benefactions that Montecassino had received before the decision in 1066 to rebuild the basilica.[83]

Some of Desiderius' gifts were from Lombards. When Maurus of Amalfi became a monk at Montecassino, he added to his gift of bronze doors by presenting a relic of the true cross expensively set in gold and precious stones which he had brought back from Constantinople.[84] It is possible that an ivory casket, later in the possession of the abbey of Farfa, was originally also Maurus' gift to Montecassino.[85] Desiderius received generous sums of money from Cidrus, Prince Richard's *vicecomes* in the principality of Capua, who under Oderisius II became a monk at Montecassino.[86]

He also received gifts from members of the imperial houses of both west and east. A particularly open-handed donor was the Empress-mother Agnes of Poitou, widow of the Emperor Henry III and mother of Henry IV. She stayed at Montecassino from September/October 1072 until March/April 1073. Leo of Ostia recorded that she offered to St. Benedict a series of gifts, which he listed, and which were of a magnificence befitting her imperial dignity.[87] Desiderius also enjoyed the bounty of the eastern emperor. In 1076 Michael VII Ducas granted Montecassino an annual pension of twenty-three pounds of gold and four cloths (*pallia*).[88]

[82] Bloch (as Introd. n. 34), pp. 177–87.

[83] *Chron. Cas.* iii. 18, pp. 384–5.

[84] Ibid. 55, p. 436; See A. Frolow, *La Relique de la vrai croix*, Archives de l'orient chrétien, 7 (Paris, 1961), 266–8, 276, nos. 205, 227. The relic may have been brought from Constantinople after the riot of 20 Apr. 1042 against the Emperor Michael V (1041–2).

[85] Bloch (as Introd. n. 34), pp. 207–12.

[86] *Chron. Cas.* iv. 13, p. 482.

[87] Ibid. iii. 31, pp. 402–3; cf. Lentini and Avagliano, *Carmi*, no. 14, lines 388–9. See M. L. Bulst-Thiele, *Kaiserin Agnes* (Berlin and Leipzig, 1933), 95–7.

[88] *Reg. Pet. Diac.*, no. 145, Trinchera, *Syllabus*, p. 62, no. 47, Dölger, *Regesten*, no. 1006.

But of all the donors of money and treasure to the abbey the most generous by far were Robert Guiscard, duke of Apulia, and his second wife Sichelgaita. Their munificence in the form of movable wealth came to exceed even that of the princes of Capua in land and churches. As the Montecassino Chronicle put it, they were zealous above almost all other people of their time in loving, exalting, and honouring Desiderius and his monastic congregation. From the list of benefactions that follows this remark, it emerges that there was hardly a major contingency of the duke's reign when he and his wife did not offer largesse. To cite only a few examples, when Desiderius first met Robert Guiscard at Reggio in 1059, the year of the treaty of Melfi, he received 600 bezzants, five cloths (*pallia*), and a golden incense-boat. In 1071 the duke's capture of Bari prompted a gift of twelve pounds of gold. Each of his visits to Montecassino was marked by lavish generosity. Thus, when he returned from Rome in 1084 with Pope Gregory VII he placed a thousand Amalfitan pounds in the chapter house and a hundred bezzants upon the altar; on departing he gave 190 bed-coverings (*farganae*) for the monks in their dormitory. When Robert fell sick Sichelgaita sent forty-five pounds of gold and a *pallium* to Montecassino, and upon his death further gifts followed.[89]

The account of Desiderius' abbacy in the Montecassino Chronicle ends with a further long list of *ornamenta* which he left at Montecassino when he died. Almost all had been gifts which were made since the dedication of the basilica in 1071, either as presents to the abbot and community or as pledges deposited in the abbey. The final words of the Chronicle about Desiderius are a eulogy of his life and character, and of gratitude for the rebuilding and adorning of Montecassino which (as it was said) combined to assure his fame until the world should end.[90]

e. *Montecassino's pre-eminence in learning and letters*

Desiderius's work at Montecassino consisted first of all in the augmentation of its lands, buildings, and wealth. But hardly less splendid was the literary, cultural, and scientific activity in which, under his patronage, its monks were engaged. Desiderius's years as abbot witnessed the flowering of work which

[89] *Chron. Cas.* iii. 57–8, pp. 437–40.

[90] Ibid. iii. 74, pp. 456–7.

had started under Aligernus and increased under Theobald and Richer.[91] A first aspect of it was the accumulation and copying of manuscripts, which themselves formed part of the abbey's treasure. Its books served both liturgical and scholarly purposes. Often lavishly bound and decorated, they figure among Desiderius's acquisitions of precious objects and among the benefactions made to Montecassino during his rule.[92] There was also a lively current of production from Montecassino's scriptorium; E. A. Lowe judged that the manuscripts copied under Desiderius' direction were 'the highest achievement of Beneventan penmanship'. In an enumeration that is probably not exhaustive, the Montecassino Chronicle listed more than seventy codexes which Desiderius caused to be copied, to which must be added work done elsewhere, particularly at Santa Maria in Pallara at Rome. The list includes not only patristic, historical, liturgical, homiletic, and dogmatic writings, but also classical authors like Cicero, Terence, Ovid, Seneca, and Virgil, works of civil law like the *Institutes* and *Novellae* of Justinian, and the Registers of Popes Leo I (440-61) and Felix III (483-92). To Montecassino's scriptorium in the golden age and soon after, posterity owes the survival of Tacitus' later *Annals* and *Histories*, Apuleius' *Golden Ass*, Seneca's *Dialogues*, Varro's *De lingua latina*, Fontinus' *De aquis*—which survives in Peter the Deacon's hand—and part of Juvenal's sixth satire.[93]

Montecassino was also outstanding for its scholars. No other centre in Western Christendom during the eleventh century, whether monastic or otherwise, was distinguished by so accomplished and polymath a group. Once again the golden age under Desiderius had its foreshadowing, notably in Laurence of Amalfi, who was a monk at Montecassino under Abbot Theobald and from *c.*1030-49 archbishop of Amalfi; his range of learning included hagiography, biblical exegesis,

[91] For cultural life at Montecassino, see esp. Bloch (as Introd. n. 34).

[92] e.g. *Chron. Cas.* iii. 18, 31, 74, pp. 384, 403, 457.

[93] Ibid. iii. 63, pp. 444-6. For Santa Maria in Pallara, see above, Ch. I pp. 11-12. For MSS still at Montecassino, see A. Caravita, *I codici e le arti a Montecassino*, 3 vols. (Montecassino, 1869-70); Inguanez, *Catalogus*. For a discussion with examples, see Lowe, *The Beneventan Script*, pp. 11-14, 94-51, 70-5, and *Scripta Beneventana*, ii, plates lxvii-lxxiii. For the scriptorium, see F. Newton, 'The Desiderian Scriptorium at Montecassino: the Chronicle and Some Surviving Manuscripts', *DOP* xxx. 35-54. For the transmission of classical authors, L. D. Reynolds and N. Wilson, *Scribes and Scholars. A Guide to the Transmission of Greek and Latin Literature* (2nd edn., Oxford, 1974), 96-7, 231-2, with further references.

and mathematics.[94] But it was under Desiderius that Montecassino won the fame ascribed to it in the *Liber pontificalis*, where in his Life of the sometime Cassinese monk Pope Gelasius II (John of Gaeta), Pandulf praised it as the home, in *non parva copia*, of *viri ad omnia peritissimi*, and as the school in which were gathered 'diversarum regionum praeclarae indolis pueri' in order that they might be educated for the service of their generation in the liberal arts and in monastic studies.[95]

The Montecassino Chronicle, and more fully Peter the Deacon in his *De viris illustribus Casinensibus*, set out the roll-call of writers and scholars.[96] Desiderius himself was numbered among them.[97] The historian Amatus told how, at the age of about forty, the abbot began to learn grammar and rhetoric. He then composed a poem, now lost, in praise of St. Maurus. He also wrote, between 1076 and 1079, his *Dialogi de miraculis sancti Benedicti*. His model for them was the *Dialogues* of Pope Gregory the Great. They had the form of a colloquy with one Theophilus, who probably represents Desiderius' monk Alberic. In the first two books Desiderius set out to show how, over the centuries, God had given his servants at Montecassino grace to perform miracles and wonders that testified to the authenticity of its religion. In two further books, the latter of which has been lost, he showed how their work had its complement in similar marvels done elsewhere, especially (in the surviving book) amongst the circle of the reform papacy. The whole work is written in a simple and clear style: it illustrates the kind of homiletic material that Desiderius thought appropriate and

[94] W. Holtzmann, 'Laurentius von Amalfi, ein Lehrer Hildebrands', *SG* i (1947), 207–36, repr. *Beiträge*, pp. 9–33; *Laurentius monachus Casinensis archiepiscopus Amalfitanus, Opera*, ed. F. Newton, *MGH Quell. Geistesgesch.* vii (Weimar, 1973); V. Schwarz, *Amalfi im frühen Mittelalter (9.–11. Jahrhundert)* (Tübingen, 1978), 100–4.

[95] March, *Liber pontificalis*, p. 162; *LP* ii. 311.

[96] *Chron. Cas.* iii. 35, pp. 410–12. Peter the Deacon wrote his *DVI*, Migne, *PL* clxxiii. 1003–50, upon older models, notably Isidore of Seville, *Liber de viris illustribus*, Migne, *PL* lxxxiii. 1081–1106. There are discussions of Cassinese literature in M. Manitius, *Geschichte der lateinischen Literatur des Mittelalters*, 3 vols. (Munich, 1911–31), iii. 75–9, 300–5, 449–54, 546–52; F. J. E. Raby, *A History of Secular Latin Poetry in the Middle Ages*, 2 vols. (2nd edn., Oxford, 1957), i. 374–83, and *A History of Christian Latin Poetry from the Beginnings to the Close of the Middle Ages* (2nd edn., Oxford, 1953), 236–49; Wattenbach-Holtzmann, iii. 893–910; and, so far as published, *DBI* and *Repertorium fontium historiae medii aevi*, ed. A. Potthast (new edn., Rome, 1962–).

[97] Amatus, iii. 52, pp. 176–7; Peter the Deacon, *DVI*, cap. 18, Migne, *PL* clxxiii. 1028–30.

useful for the edification of his own monks, and perhaps also for a wider public.[98]

Probably the finest of the writers who were closely associated with Montecassino under Desiderius was Alfanus.[99] He was there as a monk only briefly in 1056–7, and so before Desiderius' reign. But he and Desiderius were close friends and fellow monks before Alfanus went to be abbot of San Benedetto in his native Salerno, of which city he was archbishop from 1058 to 1085. Despite the brevity of his stay at Montecassino, Alfanus always regarded himself, and others regarded him, as one of its sons. His principal literary achievement was as a poet; he composed the verses used in decorating the new basilica and an ode to celebrate its building.[100] He was also the author of a *Vita et passio sanctae Christinae* and of medical works—*De quattuor humoribus corporis humani* and *Liber de pulsibus*. He translated from the Greek Bishop Nemesius of Emesa's *Premnon physicon*, written *c.*390–400, which was a work of natural philosophy and medical theory with a widespread circulation.[101]

In medical studies Alfanus prepared the way for Constantinus Africanus, whom Peter the Deacon introduced as a *novus Hippocrates*. Born in Carthage or Tunis, he spent thirty-nine years at Baghdad and in travel to India, Ethiopia, and Egypt; his studies included grammar, dialectic, geometry, arithmetic, astronomy, and medicine. He became conversant with many languages, and as Peter the Deacon put it he became 'ad plenum

[98] *Chron. Cas.* iii. 63, p. 445. For a suggestion that Alberic was co-author, see A. Lentini, 'Alberico di Montecassino nel quadro della Riforma Gregoriana', *SG* iv (1952), 55–109, at 61–2. For the *Dial.*, see *MGH SS* xxx/2. 1111–51. They were known outside Montecassino, to Hugh of Venosa, author of the *Vitae quattuor priorum abbatum Cavensium*, ed. L. M. Cerasoli, *RIS*[2] vi/5; Hugh drew upon Desiderius' account of the first abbot, Alferius: pp. 4, 10. H.-W. Klewitz's opinion that the *Dial.* were a forgery by Peter the Deacon is untenable, as they were written before Peter was born: see Meyvaert (as Introd. n. 30), p. 21 n. 1.

[99] For Alfanus, see *Chron. Cas.* iii. 7–8, 35, pp. 368–9, 411; Peter the Deacon, *DVI*, cap. 19, Migne, *PL* clxxiii. 1030–1, and *OV* cap. 54, pp. 75–6. His poems are edited in Lentini and Avagliano, *Carmi*, and his poetry and prose in Migne, *PL* cxlvii. 1219–82; the *Vita et passio sanctae Christinae* (*BHL* 1759) is at cols. 1269–82. For Lentini's works on Alfanus, see the Select Bibliography, below. See also M. Schipa, *Alfano I, archivescovo di Salerno. Studio critico-letterario* (Salerno, 1880), and N. Acocella, *Salerno medioevale ed altri saggi* (Naples, 1971).

[100] Acocella, op. cit. 1–319, 541–59; Lentini and Avagliano, *Carmi*, no. 32. For his devotion to Montecassino, see no. 14, lines 390–9.

[101] For medical works by Cassinese monks, see Penco (as Introd. n. 6), pp. 468–71, and B. Lawn, *The Salernitan Questions* (Oxford, 1963), 17–201.

omnium gentium studiis eruditus'. When he came back to his native Africa he had to escape from fellow-countrymen who were jealous of his learning, and he took flight to Sicily. It was perhaps only subsequently that his medical studies began in earnest, after a second return to Africa. Then he travelled to the Italian mainland. Having survived shipwreck he came to Salerno, where Archbishop Alfanus seems to have taught him Latin and directed him to Montecassino, of which he became a monk. Thereafter he translated and edited an astonishing range of medical works, both theoretical and practical; in this work he was helped by Atto, a sometime chaplain of the Empress Agnes. Some of his translations, which included Galen and Hippocrates, were of works of Greek origin which came to him through Arabic; others were by Arabic authors. He dedicated to Desiderius his principal translation, that of the surgical part of the *Pantegni*, a medical encyclopaedia of the tenth-century Persian writer 'Ali ben al-'Abbās al-Madjūsī (Hali Abbas). It was Constantinus who, despite the obscurity that sometimes mars his translations, was the first to introduce Arab medicine into Europe. Between them Alfanus and Constantinus established a link between Montecassino and the nascent medical school at Salerno which served to increase the abbey's fame. Constantinus was also instrumental in reinforcing its Norman connections: when he entered Montecassino he gave it the church of Sant'Agatha, Aversa, which had been Prince Richard of Capua's present to him; and Robert Guiscard held him *in magna honorificentia*, no doubt on account of his medical skill.[102]

If Constantinus Africanus developed only Alfanus' medical work, the archbishop's other interests were shared by further highly cultivated Cassinese authors writing in poetry and prose. A poet with a high contemporary reputation was Waiferius, who was particularly learned in Virgil, and who wrote for

[102] For Constantinus, the details of whose career remain somewhat obscure, see *Chron. Cas.* iii. 35, pp. 411–12, and Peter the Deacon, *DVI*, caps. 23–4, Migne, *PL* clxxiii. 1034–5. There is no evidence that he was born a Moslem, and the date 1087 sometimes given for his death has no authentication. The Prologue to the *Pantegni* and the Dedicatory Letter to Abbot Desiderius are printed in Migne, *PL* cl. 1563–6. For an assessment of his medical works, see R. Creutz, 'Der Arzt Constantinus Africanus von Montecassino. Sein Leben, sein Werk und seine Bedeutung für die mittelalterliche medizinische Wissenschaft', *Stud. Mitt. OSB* xlvii (1929), 1–44. For a general note, B. ben Yahia, 'Constantinus Africanus', *The Encyclopaedia of Islam*, new edn. by B. Lewis *et al.*, ii (1965), 59–60.

an unnamed bishop of Troia a life of St. Secundinus whose relics were preserved in his city. He wrote, too, a life of Pope Lucius I.[103] A yet more versatile figure was Alberic. He is best known for his textbooks of rhetorical composition, and especially of letter-writing; his most notable works in this field are his *Breviarium de dictamine* and his *Flores rhetorici*. He also taught the *cursus* which his pupil John of Gaeta was to introduce into the papal curia. As a theologian he resolutely opposed Berengar's eucharistic teaching; he did so both in his treatise *De corpore Domini* and verbally before Gregory VII's Lent council at Rome in 1079.[104] He also wrote a polemical work, *Contra Heinricum imperatorem de electione Romani pontificis*. He was a prolific poet and letter-writer, and his repertoire also included music, astronomy, and hagiography. As a hagiographer he wrote lives of St. Dominicus (*c.* 1060), St. Scholastica (*c.* 1071), and St. Aspren, a *Passio sancti Caesarii*, and a *Passio sancti Modesti* (*c.* 1077). All sources agree about his great learning.[105] His pupil John of Gaeta, who became a

[103] For Waiferius (also known as Benedictus), a native of Salerno, see Amatus, iv. 43-6, pp. 214–19; *Chron. Cas.* iii. 62, p. 443; Peter the Deacon, *DVI*, cap. 29, Migne, *PL* clxxiii. 1037-8, and *OV*, cap. 48, pp. 70-1. For his poetry see A. Mirra, 'I versi di Guaiferio monaco di Montecassino nel sec. xi', and 'Guaiferio monaco poeta a Montecassino nel secolo xi', *Bull. Ist. stor. ital.* xlvi (1931), 93-107; xlvii (1932), 199-208. For the Lives of St. Secundinus (*BHL* 7556) and Pope Lucius I (*BHL* 5022), see Migne, *PL* cxlvii. 1294-1310; for other works, cols. 1283-92.

[104] See below, Chap. II pp. 92-4.

[105] For Alberic, see *Chron. Cas.* iii. 35, pp. 410-11; Peter the Deacon, *DVI*, caps. 21, 45, Migne, *PL* clxxiii. 1032-3, 1046. The *Breviarium* survives in two MSS: Munich, Bayerische Staatsbibliothek, lat. 14784, ff. 67-104, and lat. 19411, pp. 115-30; it is partly edited by L. Rockinger, 'Briefsteller und Formelbücher des eilften bis vierzehnten Jahrhunderts', *Quellen und Erörterungen zur bayerischen Geschichte*, ix (1863), 29-46; see also G. Brugnoli, 'Per il testo del *De rithmis* di Alberico di Montecassino', *Benedicina*, xiv (1967), 38-50. For the *Flores rhetorici*, see M. Inguanez and H. M. Willard, *Alberici Casinensis Flores rhetorici*, *Misc. cassin.* xiv (1938). On these treatises, see C. H. Haskins, *Studies in Mediaeval Culture* (New York, n.d.), 171-3. For Alberic's hagiographical works: *Vita s. Dominini abbatis Sorani* (*BHL* 2244, cf. 2441-6), A. Lentini, 'La "Vita s. Dominici" di Alberico Cassinese', *Benedictina*, v (1951), 57-77, text at pp. 70-7; *Vita s. Scholasticae virginis* (*BHL* 7522), Lentini, 'L'omelia e la vita di s. Scholastica di Alberico Cassinese', *Benedictina*, iii (1949), 217-38, text at pp. 231-8; *De s. Aspren Neapolitano episcopo* (*BHL* 725), Lentini (as Ch. I n. 98), text at pp. 100-8; *Passio s. Caesarii* (*BHL* 1514), *Bibl. cassin.* iii (1877), Florilegium, pp. 150-8; *Passio s. Modesti levitae et martyris* (*BHL* 5983*d*), ed. A. Poncelet, *Anal. Boll.* li (1933), 369-74. For studies, Lentini (as Select Bibliography, below); O. Engels, 'Alberich von Montecassino und sein Schüler Johannes von Gaeta', *Stud. Mitt. OSB* lxvi (1955), 35-50, in which Alberic's authorship of the *Passio s. Caesarii* is established; D. Lohrmann, 'Die Jugendwerke des Johannes von Gaeta', *QFIAB* xlvii (1967), 355-445.

monk of Montecassino under Desiderius,[106] composed, or rewrote, hagiographical works relating to Saints Eustachius, Erasmus, and Hypolistus.[107] A monk named Gerold wrote a *Passio martyrum Senatoris, Viatoris, Cassiodori, et Dominatae*, which he dedicated to Abbot Desiderius as Pope Victor III, and another eleventh-century monk, John, wrote a *Vita Iohannis episcopi Spoletini*, with an appended *Translatio* and *Miracula*.[108]

Another important group of writers is Montecassino's historians. Pandulf of Capua wrote a lost *De Agnete imperatrice*, as well as works on computation.[109] The two historians of stature whose work survives are Amatus and Leo of Ostia. Amatus' principal work was his *Historia Normannorum*, which he dedicated to Abbot Desiderius. It is a history of the Norman conquest of South Italy and Sicily up to 1078, with Richard of Capua and Robert Guiscard as its heroes.[110] Amatus' purpose in writing seems to have been to promote Lombard acceptance of Norman hegemony over South Italy. He sought to demonstrate how its society was now firmly established under the hand of divine providence upon two sure foundations—in religion upon the Montecassino of Desiderius and in politics upon the military

[106] Not under Oderisius, as incorrectly stated in the *Liber Pontificalis* (as above, Ch. I n. 95).

[107] For these works, see editions with comment by O. Engels, 'Papst Gelasius II. (Johannes von Gaeta) als Hagiograph', *QFIAB* xxxv (1955), 1-45, with the *Passio s. Eustasii* (*BHL* 2584) at pp. 16-27 and the *Passio s. Ypolisti* at pp. 28-44; 'Die Erasmuspassion des Papstes Gelasius II.', *Römische Quartalschrift*, li (1956), text at pp. 16-33; and 'Die hagiographischen Texte Papst Gelasius II. in der Uberlieferung der Eustachius-, Erasmus-, und Hypolistuslegende', *Historisches Jahrbuch*, lxxi (1956), 118-33.

[108] For Gerold, see H. Delehaye, 'Saint Cassiodore', *Mélanges P. Fabre* (Paris, 1902), 40-50, repr. *Mélanges d'hagiographie grecque et latine*, Subsidia hagiographica, 42 (1966), 179-88. For John, B. de Gaiffier, 'Les légendaires de Spolète', *Anal. Boll.* lxxiv (1956), 338, no. 43*a*, *b*. See Hoffmann's note in Dormeier, *Montecassino*, p. 16 n. 69.

[109] For Pandulf, see Peter the Deacon, *DVI*, cap. 26, Migne, *PL* clxxiii. 1035-6.

[110] For Amatus, see *Chron. Cas.* iii. 35, p. 411; Peter the Deacon, *DVI*, cap. 20, Migne, *PL* clxxiii. 1032. Modern discussions may be found in the Introduction to de Bartholomaeis's edition; W. Smidt, 'Die "Historia Normannorum" von Amatus', *SG* iii (1948), 173-231; A. Lentini, 'Amato di Montecassino', *DBI* ii. 682-4; and V. d'Alessandro, 'Lettura di Amato di Montecassino', *Bull. Ist. stor. ital.* lxxxiii (1971), 119-30, repr. *Storigrafia e politica nell'Italia normanna* (Naples, 1978), 51-98, esp. 63-77, 95-6. The *Historia Normannorum* presents problems. It survives only in an early fourteenth-century French version which is partly translation and partly paraphrase and comment. The narrative ends with the death of Prince Richard of Capua (5 Apr. 1078), and the work was probably complete before Robert Guiscard's oath to Gregory VII at Ceprano in 1080.

and political achievement of the Norman leaders. He exhibited Robert Guiscard, in particular, as a Christian hero whom God had raised up, and as an exemplar of Christian rulership and virtue. Robert's foil was the reprobate and fallen Lombard, Prince Gisulf of Salerno, whom Amatus so presented as to establish the finality of the eclipse of Lombard rule. Amatus also wrote much poetry: a long poem, dedicated to Pope Gregory VII, in honour of St. Peter; a lost eulogy of Gregory himself; and other poetry, *De duodecim lapidibus et civitate coelesti Hierusalem.*[111] But Montecassino's leading historian was Leo of Ostia, who after Desiderius' death wrote the first and best part of the Montecassino Chronicle.[112] He also wrote the *Narratio celeberrimae consecrationis et dedicationis ecclesiae Cassinensis*; a lost *Historia peregrinorum*, which was probably on account of the First Crusade; and, in hagiography, a life of St. Mennas and a trilogy of works about St. Clement which he composed after he had moved to Rome as cardinal-bishop of Ostia.[113]

A further resource of Montecassino was its arsenal of material relating to canon law. It is impossible to be certain precisely what canonical sources were available at Montecassino in the eleventh century, or what part Cassinese monks took in the

[111] See A. Lentini, 'Il poema di Amato su S. Pietro apostolo', *Misc. cassin.* xxx-xxxi (1958-9). In the Montecassino Chronicle and in *DVI* it is called *Gesta apostolorum Petri et Pauli.* In the MS—Bologna, University Library, 2843—the full title is *Liber Amati monachi Casinensis destinatus ad domnum Gregorium papam in honore beati Petri apostoli* (p. 60); but the fourth book is entitled *De passione apostolorum Petri et Pauli.* For the *De duodecim lapidibus*, see Lentini, 'Il ritmo "Cives caelestis patriae" e il "De duodecim lapidibus" di Amato', *Benedictina*, xii (1958), 15-26.

[112] For Leo, see Peter the Deacon, *DVI*, cap. 30, Migne, *PL* clxxiii. 1038-9. His career and work are best approached by way of Hoffmann's studies as noted in the Select Bibliography, below. See also Wattenbach-Holtzmann, iii. 900-1, and Hüls, *Kardinäle*, pp. 105-6.

[113] For the *Narratio*, see above, Ch. I n. 63, and for the corpus of works on St. Mennas (*BHL* 5926), B. de Gaiffier, 'Translations et miracles de S. Mennas par Léon d'Ostie et Pierre de Mont Cassin', *Anal. Boll.* lxii (1944), 5-32, and J. Orlandi, '*Vita sancti Mennatis*: opera inedita di Leone Marsicano', *Istituto lombardo, Accademia di scienze e lettere: Rendiconti, Classe di lettere e scienze morali e storiche*, xcvii (1963), 467-90. For Leo's works on St. Clement, see *Iohannis Hymmonidis et Gauderici Veliterni, Leonis Ostiensis, Excerpta ex Clementinis recognitionibus a Tyrannio Rufino translatis*, ed. I. Orlandi (Milan, 1968); and the studies by P. Meyvaert and P. Devos, 'Trois énigmes cyrillo-méthodiennes de la "Légende italique" résolues grâce à un document inédit', *Anal. Boll.* lxxiii (1955), 375-461, and 'Autour de Léon d'Ostie et de sa *Translatio s. Clementis*', ibid. lxxiv (1956), 189-240. The *Historia peregrinorum* is discussed on pp. 217-23 of the latter; also *Chron. Cas.*, pp. xxviii-xxx.

dissemination of canonical texts and teachings. Only one of the abbey's canonists, Peregrinus, is known by name. However, eight codexes which remain in the abbey's archive today contain canonical material of tenth- or eleventh-century compilation. All save one are in Beneventan script. It is likely that some, and perhaps most, were products of the abbey, and that they remained in its possession after they were written. As a group they give a fair indication of the impressive body of canonical material that was available at Montecassino in its golden age.[114] The outstanding eleventh-century texts are MS 125, a *Summa canonum* which is stated in an annotation to have been compiled by Peregrinus; and MS 216, a briefer *Institutio sanctorum patrum de qualitate culparum et de disciplina atque doctrina sanctorum.*[115] Moreover, the canon-law collection known as the *Diversorum patrum sententiae* or the *Collection in LXXIV Titles* was being copied in Cassinese circles from *c.*1076. Three early manuscripts of it are associated with Montecassino and its sphere of influence.[116] It may well reflect an outlook characteristic of many Cassinese monks in the third quarter of the eleventh century, and perhaps of the abbey itself.

Such was Montecassino's scholarly achievement. It combined with the abbey's material wealth and splendour to announce to the eleventh-century world the power, both spiritual and material, of Cassinese monasticism.

[114] The texts are listed in Fabiani, 'La terra di S. Benedetto', i. 363–5.

[115] MS 125: Inguanez, *Catalogus*, i. 206, *Bibl. casin.* iii. 130–60 and *Flor. casin.* pp. 119–30. For Peregrinus, see *Bibl. casin.* iii. 131. He cannot be certainly identified with the Peregrinus of *Chron. Cas.* iv. 42, p. 511. MS 216: Inguanez, *Catalogus*, ii. 19–20, *Bibl. casin.* iv. 197–9; see P. Fournier and G. le Bras, *Histoire des collections canoniques en occident depuis les Fausses Décretales jusqu'au Décret de Gratien*, 2 vols. (Paris, 1931–2), ii. 124–5. The *Institutio* cites Gregory VII's canon of 1078 protecting Montecassino from the Normans: *Reg.* v. 14*a* (9), p. 371. The remaining eleventh-century items are as follows. MS 1: Pseudo-Isidorian Decretals and other material, Inguanez, *Catalogus*, i. 1–3, *Bibl. casin.* i. 1–48. MS 297: includes a *Collectio canonum hibernica*, Inguanez, *Catalogus*, ii. 118–19, *Bibl. casin.* v. 70–1. MS 372: Penitential and collection of conciliar canons, Inguanez, *Catalogus*, ii. 224–8, see Fournier and le Bras, op. cit. i. 351–2. MS 384: includes a gloss on conciliar canons, Inguanez, *Catalogus*, ii. 245–7. MS 541: *Collectio canonum*, Inguanez, *Catalogus*, iii. 199–203. MS 554: *Collectio antiqua canonum poenitentialium*, Inguanez, *Catalogus*, iii. 218–19. It is not known whether the two MSS of Burchard of Worms —44–5—came into the abbey's possession at an early date: Inguanez, *Catalogus*, i. 58–9.

[116] *Diversorum patrum sententie, sive Collectio in LXXIV titulos digesta*, ed. J. T. Gilchrist (Vatican City, 1973), esp. pp. lxxxiii–lxxxviii; see below, Ch. II pp. 95–9.

ii. MONTECASSINO'S REPUTATION AND INFLUENCE AS A CENTRE OF CHRISTIAN LIFE IN SOUTH ITALY

The next matter which calls for consideration is the extent and effectiveness of Montecassino's impact upon church and society in South Italy during the eleventh century. Marked and extensive though this impact was, it was at a lower level than that of Montecassino's material, artistic, and cultural achievement.

a. *Montecassino and the monastic order*

An estimate of Montecassino's impact must depend very largely upon sources emanating from the abbey itself and from its own monastic figures. As has been shown, their presentation of it, especially in the Montecassino Chronicle, is very much in terms of Montecassino's material achievement and of its culture and scholarship. Thus, by contrast with Cluny, which is the most nearly comparable monastic centre elsewhere in Western Christendom, Montecassino yields little evidence that it was in an exceptional way dedicated to the promotion and dissemination of an exemplary monastic life through an organized body of subject and filiated houses which followed a characteristic religious style. Nor did it to the same extent as Cluny seek to draw numbers of laity into the cloister or to secure the salvation of clergy and lay people by enabling them to benefit extensively from its prayers and alms-giving.[117] Its Necrologies show that, like all contemporary monasteries, it maintained an observance of intercession for the departed. But its benefits, although offered to a limited number of great lay figures, were largely directed towards the monastic order, and Montecassino made no noteworthy innovation in the liturgical commemoration of the departed which might be compared with Cluniac developments.[118] There is also no evidence to indicate

[117] See Cowdrey (as Introd. n. 9), pp. 121–35.

[118] For Montecassino's observances, see K. Schmid and J. Wollasch, 'Societas et fraternitas, Begründung eines kommentierten Quellenwerkes zur Erforschung der Personen und Personengruppen des Mittelalters', *Frühmittelalterliche Studien*, ix (1975), 1–48, at 30. The main surviving sources are: (i) the late eleventh-century fragments containing a few lay names in M. Inguanez, 'Frammenti di un necrologio cassinese del secolo xi', *Misc. cassin.* xi. 17–24; (ii) Leo of Ostia's private work, part of a Calendar, Martyrology, and Necrology compiled *c.*1098–9: H. Hoffmann, 'Der Kalendar des Leo Marsicanus', *DA* xxi (1965), 82–140. Of 570 names in the index, 508 are of monks, fourteen of secular clergy, and forty-eight of laity; see also Hoffmann, in Dormeier, *Montecassino*, pp. 9–10; (iii) the great Necrology in Montecassino, Archivio capitolare, MS 47, begun soon after 1159 but based upon earlier

a widespread lay devotion to Montecassino beyond what was usual to a major religious house.

Similarly, the eleventh century saw at Montecassino no compilation of such monastic customaries as were made at Cluny and disseminated in and through its dependencies. Montecassino's customs remained very much what they had become during the century or so following Abbot Petronax's restoration of monastic life *c.* 718.[119] The abbey's watchword remained 'Magistram in omnibus regulam sequimur'. It regarded observances over and above the Benedictine Rule, in the form of customs distinctive of a particular house, as allowable and necessary; but it was sparing in adopting them and it insisted that they must be consistent with the Rule.[120] Thus, the stricter prescriptions about fasting that Cardinal Peter Damiani recommended might properly be recorded at Montecassino 'inter regularia mandata'.[121] If Montecassino was thus prepared occasionally to adopt practices from outside, it likewise

material, with over 6,500 names: *I Necrologi cassinesi*, i. *Il Necrologio del Cod. Cassinese 47*, ed. M. Inguanez, *Fonti stor. Italia*, lxxxiii; (iv) the *Catalogus defunctorum et benefactorum* in MS 426, pp. 125–32, from the third quarter of the eleventh century and preserved in a MS of the Cassinese dependency of Santa Maria di Albaneta: see Hoffmann's note in *DA* xxi (1965), 149, and H. Schwarzmaier, 'Der *Liber vitae* von Subiaco', *QFIAB* xlviii (1968), 80–147, at 120–3; (v) the *Liber vitae* of Subiaco, begun in 1075, which includes a list of some hundred Cassinese monks from *c.* 1000: ibid. 111–14, 124, 129–30, 134, 143–4; also Dormeier, *Montecassino*, pp. 107–98. Under Oderisius I there seems to have been a marked development of intercession for the departed, and especially for laity: ibid. 140–1, 164; Leccisotti (as Introd. n. 23), p. 46.

[119] For texts see *Conseutudines monasticae*, iii: *Antiqua monumenta maxime consuetudines Casinenses inde ab anno 716–817 illustrantia continens* (Montecassino, 1907); T. Leccisotti *et al.*, *Ordo Casinensis I dictus Ordo regularis, Ordo Casinensis II dictus Ordo officii*, J. Winandy and K. Hallinger, *Theodemari abbatis Casinensis Epistula ad Theodoricum gloriosum*, K. Hallinger and M. Wegener, *Theodemari abbatis Casinensis Epistula ad Karolum regem, Corpus consuetudinum monasticarum*, i (Siegburg, 1963), 93–175. For discussion, Leccisotti, 'A proposito di antiche consuetudini Cassinesi', *Benedictina*, x (1956), 329–38; Dormeier, *Montecassino*, pp. 139–46.

[120] Letter of the monks of Montecassino to German monks, after 1072, *Die ältere Wormser Briefsammlung*, ed. W. Bulst, *MGH Briefe*, iii. 13–16, no. 1. The correspondence involved the monasteries of Hersfeld, Fulda, and Lorsch: K. Hallinger, *Gorze-Kluny. Studien zu den monastischen Lebensformen und Gegensätze im Hochmittelalter*, Studia Anselmiana, 22–5 (Rome, 1950–1), 174–5, 450–1; J. Semmler, *Die Klosterreform von Siegburg* (Bonn, 1959), 216–19; Z. Zafarana, 'Ricerche sul' *Liber de unitate ecclesiae conservanda*', *Studi medievali*, 3rd ser., vii (1966), 617–700, at 646–8.

[121] John of Lodi, *Vita s. Petri Damiani*, cap. 19, Migne, *PL* cxliv. 139C; such action communicated them to Montecassino's dependencies: Peter Damiani, *Op.* 43, Migne, *PL* cxlv. 679A.

communicated its own usages to other places: visitors were welcome to stay, observe, and write down its customs for imitation in their own monasteries. At Subiaco in 1069, Abbot Desiderius at Pope Alexander II's prompting is known to have collaborated with Archdeacon Hildebrand in reforming a monastery that did not fall within his accredited sphere as papal vicar.[122] But Montecassino's fundamental restraint, conservatism, and reluctance to innovate are illustrated by the writings of Peter the Deacon. Its golden age left no stamp upon its monastic observance as he exhibited it. His commentary on the Rule of St. Benedict for long periods kept very closely in letter and spirit to the ninth-century work of Smaragdus and plagiarized other authors without giving signs of originality or development. Similarly, in 1112 Pope Paschal II commended with approval Montecassino's 'vetus ordinis monastici consuetudo vel disciplina'.[123] This immobility within the cloister walls had its counterpart in a lack of distinctive spiritual and devotional impact upon the church and the world at large. There is no single spiritual, devotional, or liturgical trend of the eleventh century which bears Montecassino's stamp, whether as its originator or as its disseminator.[124]

Nor does Montecassino stand out as an especially prolific nursery of saintly monks. Pope Gregory VII could boast of Cluny that since its foundation it had never been ruled by an abbot who was not a saint.[125] For its saint Montecassino in and

[122] For the general outlook, see the letter referred to above, Ch. I n. 120. For Subiaco, see *Chronicon Sublacense*, ed. R. Morghen, *RIS*[2] xxiv/6, p. 11, which states that, in order to reform Subiaco, 'cum clericis palatinis, cum Desiderio Casinensi abbate qui postea factus est papa, cum multo apparatu militum [Hildebrand] venit ad monasterium'. See H. Hoffmann, 'Zur Abtsliste von Subiaco', *QFIAB* lii (1972), 781–8.

[123] *Explanatio regulae sanctissimi patris Benedicti*, and *Explanatio brevis, Bibl. casin.* v, *Flor. casin.*, pp. 82–174, and *Disciplina Casinensis*, Migne, *PL* clxxiii. 1133–8. See P. Meyvaert, 'The Exegetical Treatises of Peter the Deacon and Eriugena's Latin Rendering of the *Ad Thalassium* of Maximus the Confessor', *Sacris erudiri*, xiv (1963), 130–48, repr. *Benedict, Gregory, Bede and Others*, no. XIII; W. Holtzmann, 'Papst-, Kaiser- und Normannenurkunden aus Unteritalien', *QFIAB* xxxv (1955), 51, no. 1.

[124] But for a devotional compilation at Montecassino, included in the *Ordo ad communicandum* from the Psalter of Abbot Oderisius (Paris, Bibliothèque Mazarin, MS 364, ff. 26^{v}–28^{v}), with parallels in other Cassinese MSS, see G. Lucchesi, 'Clavis s. Petri Damiani', *Studi su Pier Damiani in onore del card. A. G. Cicognani* (2nd edn., Faenza, 1970), 1–215, at 173–84; and for a litany of the saints and other material, A. Lentini, 'Litanie di santi e orazioni salmiche in codici cassinesi del secolo xi', *Benedictina*, xvii (1970), 13–29.

[125] *Epp. vag.*, pp. 96–9, no. 39.

after its golden age had to await the troubled abbacy of Bruno of Segni (1107-11), and his claim to sanctity had little to do with his time there.[126] Although Desiderius without doubt commanded the devotion and discipleship of most of his monks,[127] he himself became the subject of no such hagiographical tradition as gathered about the abbots of Cluny, especially his contemporary Hugh of Semur (1049-1109). That Montecassino did not fail to produce devout monks is clear from the examples of Guinizo, with his tenacity in monastic discipline, and Gebizo of Cologne, who won fame as a model of humility and honesty.[128] But, in his *Dialogues*, Desiderius told remarkably few stories of miracles in recent times;[129] nor did Peter Damiani retail such approving anecdotes of Montecassino as he brought back from Cluny after his visit in 1063.[130] In his *De ortu et vita* Peter the Deacon did not provide a very impressive list of eleventh-century Cassinese figures who were conspicuous for eminent sanctity; amongst abbots he singled out only the elderly Peter, deposed in 1055, the transient figure of Frederick of Lorraine, and Desiderius, whom he commemorated principally for his building activities; of the great literary figures he noticed for his quality of life only Waiferius; and amongst less famous men in the golden age his principal examples of especial virtue were the Empress Agnes's chaplain Theodemarius, and the monks Fortunatus, Randisius, Benedictus, Leo, another Benedictus, and Obizo.[131]

126 *Chron. Cas.* iv. 31-42, pp. 496-511; B. Gigalski, *Bruno Bischof von Segni, Abt von Montecassino. Sein Leben und seine Schriften* (Münster, 1898). But for Oderisius I, see Leccisotti (as Introd. n. 23), p. 123.

127 e.g. Amatus expressed a wish to die before Desiderius in order to have the benefit of his final absolution: iii. 52, p. 177.

128 Guinizo: *Chron. Cas.* iii. 48, pp. 425-6; Desiderius, *Dial.* i. 6-7, p. 1120; Peter the Deacon, *OV*, cap. 30, pp. 52-64. Gebizo: *Chron. Cas.* iii. 48, p. 426; Peter the Deacon, *OV*, cap. 62, pp. 80-94. Leo of Amalfi, when he died, probably late in the eleventh century, acknowledged a spiritual debt to Abbot Odilo of Cluny: Peter the Deacon, *OV*, cap. 63, p. 94.

129 Apart from Guinizo, Desiderius' main examples of recent miracles concerned John, *decanus* under Abbot Richer, who for long served at Lucca and there healed Pope Alexander II: i. 3-5, pp. 1119-20; and the eleventh-century miracles in ii. 4-21, pp. 1129-40. They bring glimpses of individual worthy monks without creating an impression of exceptional sanctity.

130 And recorded in a work addressed to Montecassino: *Op.* 34, caps. 7-10, Migne, *PL* cxlv. 581-3.

131 *OV*, caps. 47-9, pp. 70-3 (Benedictus, prior of Lucca, Waiferius, Theodemarius), cap. 53, p. 75 (Fortunatus), caps. 56-9, pp. 76-9 (Peter, Frederick, Desiderius, Randisius), caps. 68-9, pp. 95-6 (Benedictus, prior of Capua, Obizo).

Desiderius' own *Dialogues* are similarly set in a low spiritual key so far as his contemporaries at Montecassino are concerned. His aim in writing was a modest one: the miracle stories that Montecassino had accumulated were useful for edification and to show how Christ's power was still effective in his servants who worked signs and wonders; miracles had didactic value because they sometimes encouraged men in good works and a desire for heaven more effectively than did words of exhortation.[132] Latter-day miracles also proved what superhuman resources were still available to sustain the monastic life. They demonstrated Christ's own presence with his followers *usque ad consummationem seculi*, and they confirmed St. Benedict's promise to St. Maurus: 'When I have laid aside the burden of the flesh I shall be yet nearer to you, and by God's grace I shall be your constant fellow-worker.'[133] Desiderius emphasized how Benedict was active to protect his monks from lay depredations, above all those of such enemies as Prince Pandulf IV of Capua and, in early days, of the Normans.[134] He also watched over them in lesser contingencies, like fire, the hazard of insecure masonry, and the loss of property.[135] He directed his monks in their spiritual welfare, just as through miracles at his tomb he gave health to them and to others.[136] Miracles protected monks from their enemies;[137] and they also proved the worth of fasts, vigils, and prayers. They warned monks not to become fugitives from the cloister, just as they underlined the proper motives for entering the monastic state and for accepting office in the secular church. They reinforced the discipline and observances of the monastic round, keeping monks up to the mark.[138] In all these connections the *Dialogues* point to a conventional and moderate, rather than to an outstanding or heroic, level of sanctity and observance. Only occasionally did Desiderius point his monks further; he had for a time himself lived an eremetical life, and he sometimes presented it—as did the Rule of St. Benedict—as the state to which the *âmes d'élite* of

[132] pp. 1116–17; cf. Gregory the Great, *Dial.* 1. 19. 6, ed. Moricca, p. 16; also Desiderius, *Dial.* ii. 14, 21, pp. 1134, 1138.

[133] i. 1, 2, pp. 1118–19; cf. Matt. 28: 20.

[134] i. 6, 9, ii. 22, pp. 1120–1, 1123–4, 1138–9.

[135] ii. 12–13, 19–20, pp. 1132–4, 1137–8.

[136] ii. 2, 9, 14–17, pp. 1128, 1131, 1134–5.

[137] i. 10–11, 13, pp. 1124–7.

[138] i. 3, 8, 9, ii. 1, 14, pp. 1119–20, 1122–4, 1127–8, 1134.

Montecassino should and did aspire. He wished his best monks to progress towards the ideals of the desert and so to proclaim them to the generality of the brethren.[139] Yet there is nothing to suggest that such austere standards penetrated deeply into the daily round at Montecassino, as they did at Camaldoli and Vallombrosa, or that Montecassino's monastic life often rose above a moderate level of devotion and seemliness.[140]

Alfanus in his poems, and Amatus and Leo of Ostia in their historical writings, leave a similar impression when, enlarging upon the splendour of the new basilica and of the monastic buildings, they insist upon the raising of the standard of monastic observance that was made possible. Desiderius created a fitting and pleasant haven of monastic peace in which his monks could maintain a monastic round of strictness and good order.[141] The new basilica so spread Montecassino's fame throughout Christendom that from all parts many were drawn there no less by the sanctity of its monks than by its visible glories. The number of its monks rose to some two hundred, and many great men were attracted to meet Desiderius and to benefit from the prayers of his monks.[142] Again, the picture is one of conventional worthiness rather than of a distinctive excellence in the concerns of the monastic life.

External observers seem to have formed a comparable impression, noticing first and foremost the grandeur of Montecassino's buildings, and within them a decency though not a pre-eminence in the monastic life. So far as Pope Gregory VII is concerned, his letters expressed his formal esteem. The first letter in his Register is addressed to Abbot Desiderius; he thus acknowledged

[139] *Chron. Cas.* iii. 1–2, 6–7, pp. 364–5, 367–8; Peter the Deacon, *DVI*, cap. 18, Migne, *PL* clxxiii. 1028–9; *Dial.* i. 6–7, ii. 2, 11, 17, pp. 1120–2, 1128, 1132, 1135.

[140] Desiderius made a passing reference to the storage of flesh-meat (*carnes*) at Montecassino: *Dial.* i. 12, p. 1124.

[141] Alfanus, in Lentini and Avagliano, *Carmi*, no. 14, lines 390–9, 39, lines 61–5, and 54; Amatus, iii. 52, p. 175; *Chron. Cas.* iii. 33, p. 407.

[142] *Chron. Cas.* iii. 30, p. 402. The figure is confirmed by Robert Guiscard's gift in 1084 of 190 *farganas fratribus in dormitorio*: iii. 58, p. 438. That most monks were Lombards may be inferred from Leo of Ostia's remark that the assembly of visitors at the dedication ceremony in 1071 was made up of 'ceterorum . . . potentium seu nobilium tam nostratium quam Normannorum omnium circumquaque terrarum': iii. 29, p. 399. During the golden age there is little if any trace of Norman monks at Montecassino. But for monks from afar, see e.g. Desiderius, *Dial.* i. 6, p. 1120: Guinizo from Spain; Peter the Deacon, *OV*: Theodemarius from Germany, cap. 49, pp. 71–2, and Obizo from Brixen, cap. 69, p. 96; and *Chron. Cas.*: Ambrose from Milan and Gerald from Germany, iii. 24, p. 391, and Gebizo from Cologne, iii. 48, p. 426.

Montecassino's precedence over all other monasteries in the west, which by implication he reasserted in his allocution of 1080 in favour of Cluny.[143] A year earlier he wrote to its monks that their abbey was holy, famous, and held in honour throughout Christendom; it deserved the epithets *reverendissimus* and *religiosus.*[144] The Western Emperor Henry IV left behind no such expressions of regard, but in April 1076 the Eastern Emperor Michael VII Ducas wrote with a priority that is significant to declare his admiration first of the new basilica, but secondly of the worthy lives of its abbot and monks.[145]

Amongst visitors to Montecassino, Henry IV's mother, the Empress Agnes of Poitou, came—in the imagery of the Montecassino Chronicle—as a second queen of Sheba, desiring to see another Solomon and another temple. She found that Montecassino exceeded her expectations *tam secundum Deum quam secundum seculum.*[146] The Chronicle also records that Abbot Hugh of Cluny, who came in 1083, travelled *valde devote* to the home of St. Benedict. He established a monastic union (in the sense of an interchange of prayers and spiritual benefits) between the two greatest western monasteries of the age.[147] But the Chronicle's account of his visit is formal; it betrays nothing of his reaction to the monastic life that he observed.

Two decades earlier the reactions of Cardinal Peter Damiani were more fully and personally expressed. They exhibit to the full the ambiguity of reaction that many contemporaries may have felt; for he praised Montecassino's fame and magnificence while showing reserve about the spiritual standards that he found there.[148] In his letters and *Opuscula* Peter often spoke

[143] *Reg.* i. 1, 23 Apr. 1075, pp. 3–4; *Epp. vag.*, pp. 96–9, no. 39.

[144] *Epp. vag.*, pp. 74–7, nos. 28–9; cf. *Reg.* vii. 28, p. 510.

[145] Trinchera, *Syllabus*, p. 62, no. 47, Dölger, *Regesten*, no. 1006.

[146] *Chron. Cas.* iii. 31, pp. 402–3.

[147] Ibid. iii. 51, pp. 433–4.

[148] Peter Damiani's writings are listed in Lucchesi (as above, Ch. I n. 152). The principal items relating to Montecassino are:

		Addressed to	Date	Migne, *PL*
Ep.	ii. 11	Abbot Desiderius	*c.* 1061	cxliv. 275–8
	ii. 12	" "	*c.* 1061	cxliv. 278–82
	ii. 13	" "	1060/1	cxliv. 282–7
Op.	33	" "	summer 1064	cxlv. 559–72
	34. 1	" " and his monks	late 1063	cxlv. 571–84
	34. 2	Archbishop Alfanus I of Salerno	autumn 1063	cxlv. 584–90
	35	Abbot Desiderius and his monks	summer 1065	cxlv. 589–96
	36	" " " " "	summer 1067	cxlv. 595–622

warmly of Montecassino and of Desiderius personally. In his early *De natura animalium* he dedicated to Montecassino an allegory of the virtues in which the abbey was a new Noah's ark resting upon the mountains. Such a *jeu d'esprit* suggests approval and cordiality.[149] Later, too, he wrote of Montecassino as a *praestantissimum monasterium* and of Desiderius as its *venerabilis* and *religiosus abbas*, and as an *archangelus monachorum* whose prayers Peter particularly desired.[150] Truly blessed were those who lived with its monks and died in the midst of their good works. The ladder which, when St. Benedict died, was seen to rise to heaven from Montecassino was still thronged with his sons, who ascended it behind their leader like an army. A particularly praiseworthy feature of Montecassino in Peter's eyes was the absence of such a school open to boys from outside as disfigured other monasteries; its inhabitants, he wrote, were all grave elders, or disciplined young men, or youths of proven virtue.[151]

Direct observation did much to confirm Peter's estimate. Probably before the spring of 1064, Desiderius with his monks' approval promised Peter a perpetual place equal to that of an abbot of the mother house in Montecassino's commemoration of the dead. Desiderius declared that Peter loved Montecassino above all other monasteries.[152] He was anxious for him to come there in person, and as an inducement he later sent an ultimatum that, if he did not come, he would forfeit his place in the monks' intercessions. Peter's reply, in which he dwelt upon the hardship for an old and weary man of having to make the fifteen-day journey from Fonteavellana, suggests that he had indeed not yet been to Montecassino. His first visit which followed is unlikely to have occurred before the autumn of

37	Alberic of Montecassino	1065	cxlv. 621–34
43	The monks of Montecassino	after 11 Feb. 1069	cxlv. 679–86
52	Abbot Desiderius and his monks	after Oct. 1061	cxlv. 763–92

Op. 36 has been edited in Pierre Damien, *Lettre sur la toute-puissance divine*, ed. A. Cantin, Sources chrétiennes, 191 (Paris, 1972).

149 *Op.* 52.

150 *Ep.* ii. 12, col. 278B; *Op.* 19, caps. 9, 32, 34, 52, cols. 438D, 559D, 571D, 763D.

151 *Op.* 36, cap. 18, ed. Cantin, pp. 481–3.

152 *Ep.* 4, Migne, *PL* cxlv. 17–18; for the date, see G. Lucchesi, 'Per una vita di San Pier Damiani', *San Pier Damiani nel ix centenario della morte (1972–1972)*, 4 vols. (Cesena, 1972–3), ii. 61–4, no. 187.

1064.[153] Thereafter he seems to have come on several occasions; for, when, during the building of the new basilica which began in 1066 and ended in 1071 he was there and performed a healing miracle, his biographer John of Lodi said that he was visiting it *ex more.*[154] Over the years Peter found Desiderius' own conversation edifying and he profited from the society of his monks.[155] He repaid his debt to the abbey: Desiderius remained familiar with the sermons that he left there;[156] Peter's works in general were available to be copied;[157] and in the next century, the second Alberic of Montecassino perhaps drew upon Peter when compiling his visionary literature.[158] Furthermore, it is likely that at Fonteavellana Peter employed scribes who had been trained at Montecassino.[159]

And yet, for all his expressions of friendship and approval, Peter's writings reveal an undertone of criticism and anxiety. Much of it was centred upon Desiderius himself. Peter more than once exhorted him to greater zeal in the proper concerns of the monastic life. Drawing upon his own experience as cardinal-bishop of Ostia he enlarged upon the pitfalls for a monk of involvement in the business of the episcopate and of the papal palace. No one could be at once a monk and the servant of an earthly court, where a monk was a fish out of water and vulnerable to his enemies.[160] Even in early letters

[153] *Op.* 33, pref., cap. 1, cols. 559-62. For Peter's visits to Montecassino, see Lucchesi, op. cit. ii. 18-19, 61-4, 67-71, 116-20, nos. 187, 192-3, 217.

[154] 'Ipsum vero praefatum coenobium Casinense dum aliquando idem domnus Petrus ex more visitasset, cum esset ibi, beatissimi Benedicti basilica fundabatur; quae auro ac lapidibus modo adornata perspicue cernitur': John of Lodi (as Ch. I n. 121), cap. 20, col. 140.

[155] *Ep.* viii. 5, to the Roman senator Peter, ?after 1066, Migne, *PL* cxliv. 472C-3B; see Lucchesi (as Ch. I n. 124), p. 45; *Op.* 36, cap. 18, ed. Cantin, pp. 481-4.

[156] *Dial.* ii. 12, p. 1132.

[157] Two early collections of Peter's works are Montecassino, Archivio capitolare, MSS 358-9: Lucchesi, op. cit. 26-8, and 'Il Sermonario di S. Pier Damiani come monumento storico agiografico e liturgico', *SG* x (1975), esp. 12-13, 31, 36; also K. Reindel, 'Studien zur Überlieferung der Werke des Petrus Damiani', i, *DA* xv (1959), 23-102, esp. 79-88, 100-2, and iii, *DA* xviii (1962), 314-417, esp. 331-2, and 'Neue Literatur zu Petrus Damiani', *DA* xxxii (1976), 405-43, esp. 406.

[158] *Visio Alberici*, ed. M. Inguanez, *Misc. cassin.* xi. 83-103; see also A. Mirra, 'La visione di Alberico', ibid. 33-79. Alberic's work was derivative, not from Islamic sources, but from ones in the Judaeo-Christian tradition, esp. the *Visio Esdrae*: P. Dinzelbacher, 'Die Vision Alberichs und die Esdras-Apokryphe', *Stud. Mitt. OSB* lxxxvii (1976), 435-42.

[159] *Ep.* ii. 11, col. 276AB; see P. Palazzini, 'Frammenti di codici in Beneventana: amanuensi Cassinesi a Fonte Avellana?', *Aevum*, xvii (1943), 254-8.

[160] *Op.* 36, cap. 1, ed. Cantin, pp. 384-6.

Peter began to sound a warning note: Desiderius was slow to answer correspondence; more seriously, he should keep his own faults clearly before him but should not be mindful of his virtues. He should show greater readiness to judge and correct his subjects. He should himself regularly offer the holy sacrifice and take communion. In another letter, too, Peter cautioned Desiderius against relaxing his zeal in ruling his monks and against thinking too highly of himself; he should withdraw into consideration of his own soul whenever the multifariousness of business pressed too hard upon him. Again, Peter drew upon the Books of Kings in the Old Testament to caution Desiderius that those who cannot free themselves from worldly distractions cannot share in the inheritance of Jerusalem.[161] Above all in Peter's last years, when he knew the monks of Montecassino at first hand, they as well as their abbot attracted critical remarks. Perhaps during his initial visit to Montecassino, Peter induced first individual monks, and then with Desiderius' sanction the whole community, to undertake more rigorous fasting. As a devotion to the Holy Cross which Peter hoped would spread from Montecassino and its monastic dependencies into the secular church, he instituted on Fridays which were not feast-days a voluntary fast on bread and water accompanied by confession and the receiving of the discipline; and the monks were to keep a three-day fast at the beginning of Lent.[162] Upon his last visit Peter found that, prompted by Cardinal Stephen of San Grisogono, the monks' zeal for such exercises had cooled to the point of their discontinuing them. His treatise *De laude flagellorum et, ut loquitur, disciplinae* was a fervent plea to the monks for their resumption.[163]

It would be excessive to infer from Peter's writings that he increasingly expressed a criticism of Montecassino that rose to disenchantment.[164] But his warnings about preoccupation

[161] *Ep.* ii. 11-13.

[162] *Chron. Cas.* iii. 20, pp. 386-7; John of Lodi (as Ch. I n. 66), cap. 19, col. 139; Peter Damiani, *Op.* 43, prol., col. 679. See Lucchesi (as Ch. I n. 152), ii. 69-70, no. 192.

[163] *Op.* 43. For Cardinal Stephen, see Hüls, *Kardinäle*, pp. 169-70; he died on 11 Feb. 1069.

[164] No conclusion can be drawn from the absence of his name from both of Leo of Ostia's attendance lists at the dedication ceremony of 1 Oct. 1071 (as above, Ch. I n. 63); his presence is alleged only in the twelfth-century forgery, Pope Alexander II, *Ep.* 151, Migne, *PL* cxlvi. 1425-6; Kehr, *IP* viii. 144-5, no. †104; see Leccisotti, *Regesti*, i. 16, no. 20, and Lucchesi (as Ch. I n. 152), ii. 130-2. There are three

with worldly business, and his anxious admonitions about the character of the monastic life, show where, in his eyes, the weak points of Cassinese monasticism were to be found. Peter's many comments on Montecassino suggest that it owed its strengths and failings alike to its calculated blend of conservatism in monastic observance with prudence in the ways of the world.

Of these characteristics Desiderius was himself the epitome. The Montecassino chroniclers applauded his probity and wisdom: for Amatus he was 'tant saint home et de bone vie, et plein de grant sapience'; while in the Chronicle he was conspicuous for prudence and religion, as well as for standing high in the friendship of neighbouring princes.[165] Alfanus likewise praised his religion and goodness.[166] Other writers at Montecassino and elsewhere spoke of his piety and zeal.[167] In similar vein are the words that the English historian William of Malmesbury much later ascribed to the dying Pope Gregory VII as he advised about the succession: 'If they want a man powerful in the world (*in seculo potentem*) let them elect Desiderius, abbot of Montecassino, who will successfully and in due time destroy militarily the violence of the antipope Guibert.'[168]

The conclusion to which the evidence points is that as a centre of monastic life the Montecassino of Abbot Desiderius was a stabilizing and energizing, rather than an innovating and transforming, force. It directed its resources and wisdom towards upholding without substantial change or development the traditional monasticism that it had received from Carolingian times. But its exceptional resources of men and material

possibilities about Peter and the dedication, the last of which is the most likely: (i) that he attended but Leo failed to record him. This is improbable, given Leo's pains to compile an impressive list; (ii) that Peter stayed away from disapproval of the basilica and of the monks' laxity in discontinuing his austerities. But there is no confirmation that Peter took so strong a view; and (iii) that Peter, who was sixty-four years old and died on 22 Feb. 1072, was too sick to travel.

[165] Amatus, iii. 52, p. 177; *Chron. Cas.* iii. 65, p. 447, cf. iii. 30, p. 402.

[166] Lentini and Avagliano, *Carmi*, no. 54, lines 21–4: '. . . eximiae pietatis | nimiaeque fuit bonitatis.'

[167] '. . . opinione sanctitatis famosissimum': *Annales Augustani, a.* 1087, *MGH SS* iii. 132; 'probus abbas': Donizo, *Vita Matildis*, ii. 312, *MGH SS* xii. 386; 'verus Christi famulus': Frutolf of Michaelsberg, *a.* 1085, p. 102; 'Hic magnae nobilitatis et sapientiae fuit ac religionis': Orderic Vitalis, viii. 7, ed. Chibnall, iv. 166. Waiferius praised him as 'virum inter bonorum antistites operum et religione laudatum et moribus comprobatum': *Historia inventionis corporis sancti Secundini*, prol. ad episcopum Troianum, *AA SS Boll.*, Feb. ii, p. 532AB.

[168] iii. 266, ed. Stubbs, ii. 325.

riches made it a powerful and attractive centre to which monks, secular clergy, and laity all looked for the reinforcement of their own lives. In Abbot Desiderius it was ruled by an abbot *in seculo potens* who epitomized its life and represented it compellingly in the eyes of the contemporary world.

b. *Montecassino and the South Italian church*

There is much evidence to suggest that within the limits that have just been indicated, Montecassino radiated a strong spiritual and moral influence upon its neighbouring churches throughout South Italy. Circumstances were propitious for it to do so, because Desiderius' building programme and the rediscovery of St. Benedict's relics were not an isolated development. Everywhere in Italy there was a burgeoning awareness of patron saints. Cities were establishing their identity by elaborating their patrons' cultuses, by adding to their relics, and by amplifying local funds of legends, liturgies, and festival.[169] Montecassino's hagiographical literature shows how the skills of its monks were not only directed towards the cultus of St. Benedict and the saints of Montecassino, but were also available to the monks, bishops, and people of other monasteries, churches, and localities, in order to build up their own devotion and civic pride. Montecassino thus exercised a regenerative force in the South Italian church at large, secular as well as monastic.

An excellent, if rather late, example of Montecassino's fostering the cultus of an urban patron is that of St. Mennas at Caiazzo.[170] Mennas was a late sixth-century Samnian hermit. In 1094, upon advice from Abbot Madelmus of Santa Sophia, Benevento, his relics were discovered at Monte Taburno and translated to the cathedral at Caiazzo. The translation was welcomed by Count Rainulf of Alife and his son Robert, who had rebuilt the cathedral and therefore wished to find suitable relics for it. They requested Abbot Oderisius I of Montecassino

[169] See H. C. Peyer, *Stadt und Stadtpatron im mittelalterlichen Italien* (Zürich, 1955).

[170] Four sources survive in Montecassino, Archivio capitolare, MS 413, Inguanez, *Catalogus*, iii. 15–17: (i) *Vita s. Mennatis* (*BHL* 5926), ed. Orlandi (as above, Ch. I n. 113); (ii) *Sermo de translatione s. Mennatis* (*BHL* 5927), ed. de Gaiffier (as Ch. I n. 113), pp. 15–26; (iii) a second such sermon (*BHL* 5928), printed ibid. 26–8; (iv) *Miracula s. Mennatis* (*BHL* 5929), printed ibid. 28–32. Problems of date and authorship are discussed by Orlandi and de Gaiffier. For the political circumstances, see G. A. Loud, 'The Norman Counts of Caiazzo and the Abbey of Montecassino', *Misc. cassin.* xlvi. 199–217, esp. 207–8.

to commission a Life of St. Mennas from one of his monks. His choice fell upon Leo of Ostia. Leo explained in his preface why Robert looked to Montecassino, and also that he wanted the Life to be written in a form that an urban populace could readily assimilate. Robert chose Montecassino,

> not because he was unable to find in other places, or indeed at his own court, plenty of writers who were famous for learning and fluently eloquent; but rather because, being a God-fearing man and having great trust in the authority of our abbey's reputation (*auctoritate nominis loci nostri plurimum fidens*), his aim was to minister instruction to the simple folk of his neighbourhood. He thought that subjects of church history were more fittingly handled in a simple way than in the high-sounding and measured words that are appropriate for worldly learning.[171]

So Leo wrote a Life of St. Mennas that was suitable for public reading on his feast-day to the Caiazzans; it was made the more popular by the addition of hymns (*et cantus insuper aliquot et laudum suavium melodias*).[172] As a source for the Life, Leo had at his disposal only the meagre information of Pope Gregory the Great's *Dialogues.*[173] He elaborated it simply and clearly as a homily for popular edification. He presented Mennas as a *vir plane sanctissimus, ac per omnia apostolicus*, who was like John the Baptist in his life of austerity, prayer, and charity. But Leo refrained from inventing for Mennas a public martyrdom that his source did not authenticate; he sought simply to praise a patron saint and to encourage his local devotees. Montecassino's association with the cult of St. Mennas at Caiazzo continued when one of its monks recorded the further translation of his relics, at a date before 4 September 1110 and again at Count Robert's request, to the comital chapel of Sant'Agatha dei Goti, adding further miracle stories.[174]

Montecassino had promoted such urban cultuses at an earlier date. Abbot Desiderius himself recorded how during a visit to Chieti in the Abruzzi he had once encouraged its bishop and clergy in the veneration of St. Felix, a Cassinese monk whom his abbot had of old sent to be its bishop and at whose shrine miracles were being performed.[175] More significant is the cult of St. Matthew at Salerno.[176] According to Salernitan tradition, in

[171] Ed. Orlandi, p. 479. [172] Ibid. 480. No hymns survive.
[173] iii. 26, ed. Moricca, pp. 195–8.
[174] *Vita s. Mennatis*, ed. Orlandi (as Ch. I n. 113).
[175] *Dial.* ii. 3, pp. 1128–9.
[176] See N. Acocella, *La traslazione di s. Matteo* (Salerno, 1954).

954 the apostle's relics had been discovered at Paestum (Pesto) and translated to Salerno.[177] Robert Guiscard's capture of the city in the winter of 1076 led to a renewal of zeal for his cultus on the part of the Norman conquerors. Robert Guiscard planned the rebuilding of the cathedral, which Archbishop Alfanus I undertook in close touch with his friend Abbot Desiderius upon the model of the new basilica at Montecassino.[178] In 1080, during the rebuilding, the apostle's relics were recovered, an event which elicited an enthusiastic letter from Pope Gregory VII.[179] Gregory himself consecrated the new cathedral, in the presence of both Robert Guiscard and Abbot Desiderius, after his withdrawal from Rome in 1084. A poetic inscription by Alfanus proclaimed the Norman leaders' devotion to St. Matthew.[180] Alfanus' numerous hymns and poems in Matthew's honour were written with a didactic purpose which, like Leo of Ostia's in his Life of St. Mennas, was meant to communicate to members of the general public who heard them sung the virtues of the Christian life.[181] At Salerno, as later at Caiazzo, Montecassino played its part as the ally of a Norman ruler in building up the cultus of an urban patron, and in using it to foster spiritual and moral reform in the local population.

Many of Alfanus' poems in a similar way commemorate local patron saints, either because they have the form of hymns for use in liturgical offices or because they were intended for the public edification of clergy and people. At his own city of Salerno he wrote verses for the festival of its minor patrons St. Fortunatus, St. Gaius, and St. Anthes.[182] Further afield, he promoted local cultuses by writing for his friend Bishop Pandulf of Marsia poems in commemoration of St. Sabina, and of St. Rufinus and St. Cesidius; and on behalf of the church of Benevento he celebrated the Twelve Brethren.[183] He wrote verses for the Cassinese church at Sant'Angelo in Formis.[184] His interests

[177] *Chronicon Salernitanum*, cap. 165, *MGH SS* iii. 552-3; cf. *Chron. Cas.* ii. 5, p. 175.

[178] See Pantoni (as Ch. I n. 63); Kitzinger (as Introd. n. 34), pp. 92-7.

[179] *Reg.* viii. 8, 18 Sept. 1080, pp. 526-7.

[180] William of Apulia, v. 121-4, p. 242; Lentini and Avagliano, *Carmi*, no. 53. Robert Guiscard retained and carried on campaigns a relic of St. Matthew which, in 1122, was deposited at Montecassino: *Chron. Cas.* iii. 45, 57, iv. 73, pp. 423, 437-8, 539.

[181] Lentini and Avagliano, *Carmi*, nos. 7-9, 58-61, cf. 62.

[182] Ibid., nos. 10-11, cf. 8.

[183] Ibid., nos. 1-4, 55; 56; 13, 66.

[184] Ibid., no. 63.

were not only local but also served the wider authority of the papacy, since he composed a poem in honour of St. Peter as the *princeps ecclesiarum.*[185] Alfanus' poems had a manuscript circulation which gave them a currency beyond the range of their public liturgical employment.[186]

Besides Leo of Ostia's Life of St. Mennas, many of the saints' Lives by Cassinese writers which have already been noticed were written for the benefit of local churches, whether as such or for particular cathedrals or monasteries.[187] They had a similar didactic intention. Alberic's works are especially notable in this connection. His *Passio sancti Modesti*, who was a Roman deacon martyred at Benevento under Diocletian and venerated there and at Capua, was addressed to Archbishop Roffrid I of Benevento (1076–1108) and intended for the monks of San Modesto in that city. Alberic recorded the legends of the saint *fideliter festive ac sollemniter* for the benefit of hearers both present and future, and the Life is divided into nine lections for public reading. Likewise, Alberic's *Vita sancti Aspren*, who was the first bishop of Naples, was written for his successor Archbishop Peter (*c.*1094–*c.*1100), and intended for reading aloud on Aspren's feast-day. Alberic's *Vita sancti Dominici abbatis Sorani* commemorated an abbot who died in 1031 and who was venerated at Sora. It was written at the request of a certain Dodo—probably not the similarly named bishop of Roselle—upon information that Abbot Benedict of Sora, a monk named Hildebrand, and others who had known Dominicus, supplied. Alberic's *Passio sancti Caesarii* concerned a saint who was martyred and venerated at Terracina. Amongst other Cassinese hagiographers, John of Gaeta wrote his *Passio sancti Erasmi* between 1078 and 1088 for his uncle, John, about whom nothing further is known. Erasmus was the patron saint of Gaeta; he had been bishop of Antioch, where he had firmly resisted imperial power, and he had miraculously been brought thence to Formia. John's *Passio sancti Hypolisti*, who was another martyr under Diocletian, was also dedicated to Archbishop Roffrid I of Benevento. Waiferius' *Vita sancti Secundini* was written about a saint who was com-

[185] Lentini and Avagliano, *Carmi*, no. 37.

[186] e.g. Montecassino, Archivio capitolare, MS 280: ibid., pp. 7–9; Inguanez, *Catalogus*, ii. 93–5; Rome, Vatican Library, MS Urbin. lat. 585: Lentini and Avagliano, *Carmi*, pp. 17–22; P. Salmon, *Les Manuscrits liturgiques latins de la Bibliothèque Vaticane*, i, Studi e testi, 251 (Vatican City, 1968), p. 82, no. 155.

[187] See above, Ch. I pp. 22–6.

memorated at Troia, and another monk John composed a work on Bishop John of Spoleto.

These Cassinese poems and saints' Lives alike propound themes and recommend virtues which may be taken to illustrate Montecassino's message to the local churches of South Italy. In St. Aspren of Naples and St. Dominic of Sora they respectively propose for imitation an exemplary bishop and an exemplary abbot. The recurrent concern with the Christian martyrs of the pre-Constantinian church drove home the duty of a fearless confession of faith before kings and magistrates even in face of death under torture and of family pressure to relent. Such was the repeated message of Alberic, John of Gaeta, and Gerold. Leo of Ostia alluded to the same theme; but since St. Mennas was not publicly martyred his message was that those not called to martyrdom can achieve heroic sanctity in the austerity of the eremitical life. The hagiographical literature also propounds the moral virtues of everyday Christianity, with a strong emphasis upon chastity. Leo of Ostia epitomized the Cassinese message regarding patron saints as moral exemplars when he urged the Caiazzans to imitate the way of life of St. Mennas: 'Sic profecto et nos illic erimus quod est, si hic fuerimus quod fuit.'[188]

The message of Montecassino's hagiography was complemented by its propagation of canon law in collections which had a strongly pastoral and edificatory purpose directed towards the church at large.[189] The surviving compilations embody material, mostly gathered from the earliest times up to the ninth century but with a little of later date, to provide the monks with guidance to offer those outside the cloister whom they advised. There are penitentials which were intended to raise the moral standard of the clergy and laity. Other collections were more widely planned to meet pastoral needs. In the case of Montecassino, Archivio capitolare, MS 125, a splendid, large codex suited to be a work of reference, its compiler Peregrinus said that he was working at the earnest entreaty of many of Christ's servants and especially of a priest named Lupo, for the benefit of wounded souls and for the reclaiming of all who had fallen away. In his five long books he campaigned against simony and defended clerical celibacy. The clergy were urged at length and in detail to lead a common life of simplicity, prayer, and pastoral zeal. The collection contains vignettes of

[188] cap. 6, p. 489. [189] See above, Ch. I pp. 26–7.

exemplary episcopal and priestly life. The fourth and fifth books offer penitential guidance for the regulation of lay religion and morals.[190] Similar if briefer guidance is offered in the smaller, workaday *Institutio sanctorum patrum de qualitate culparum et de disciplina atque doctrina sacerdotum* (MS 216). It, too, sought to provide from the distant past a mirror of priestly life for those with cure of souls:

Institutio illa sancta quę fiebat in diebus patrum nostrorum rectas vias nunquam deseruit. . . . Nunc ergo qui voluerit auctoritatem accipere, primitus propter Deum cogitet et preparet arma eius, antequam manus episcopi tangat eius caput, id est, psalterium, lęctionarium, antiphonarium, missale, baptisterium, martyrologium, et computum cum cyclo in anni circulo. Ad praedicationem se muniat cum doctrina et bonis operibus. Hęc est lex sacerdotum. Post hęc illorum pęnitentialem . . .[191]

These collections make it apparent that, in the parts of South Italy where the Beneventan script was used, there emanated from Montecassino a body of canonical material which was designed to guide pastorally the lives of both clergy and laity. The public value of such material is shown by Archbishop Alfanus I of Salerno's reference to it in 1066 when he consecrated Bishop Risus of Sarno, and by Peter Damiani's testimony to *libri canonum* as a means of promoting the Christian life.[192] Taken with its hagiographical literature, Montecassino's canon-law collections show that the abbey had a commitment to raising the standard of Christian witness and observance among both clergy and laity in South Italy. It did much to answer the aspirations for spiritual and moral renewal that were increasingly current there.

iii. CONCLUSIONS

In the second half of the eleventh century Montecassino rose to a position of exceptional power and renown, both in the monastic order and in church and society at large. The consolidation and extension to the sea of the *terra sancti Benedicti*, and the vast accumulation of endowments in land and other forms of wealth, provided the material basis for a large

[190] See esp. *Bibl. casin.* iii. 131, 139–40, 144–5, and *Flor. casin.*, pp. 119–30. This MS is closely related to Vatican Library, MS lat. 1339, which may be derived from it.

[191] *Bibl. casin.* iv. 199.

[192] Ughelli–Coleti, vii. 571–2; Peter Damiani, *Vita sancti Romualdi*, cap. 35, Migne, *PL* cxliv. 986D–987A.

and thriving monastic community housed in buildings of splendour which many leading people admired and sought to imitate. Montecassino did not make remarkable innovations in the monastic life, nor were its spiritual standards in any way exceptional. But its many-sided scholarly and cultural achievement made it the most notable centre of learning of its age in Western Christendom, and its monks had an exceptional fund of skill in administration and affairs. Its fame was in no way limited to the monastic world. It won a high degree of influence with political authorities, and especially with the new Norman rulers of the South Italian mainland. It also made its resources available to the ecclesiastical leaders of South Italy, in order to build up the life of local churches and to encourage the aspirations after higher standards of Christian life that were widely current. In many respects it was old-fashioned and looked for guidance to a distant past. It worked in and through the many localities where demands for renewal were already stirring, and it tended to confirm and nourish pastorally what it found to be already in existence. At first independently of the papal reform and, indeed, before it began in earnest under Pope Leo IX, Montecassino was thus a powerful force in energizing ecclesiastical life. When the Roman church itself showed stirrings of reform, Montecassino was both equipped and willing to help it, no less than the churches of South Italy, even though its own position of strength enabled it to do so on its own terms and in the light of its own overriding interests.

A conspicuous feature of Montecassino's pre-eminence was the energy, activity, and success of Abbot Desiderius. The accumulation of lands and wealth, the total rebuilding of Montecassino's monastic buildings, and its high reputation with ecclesiastical and secular rulers, were largely the result of his zeal and skill. Although Desiderius' work had its apogee in 1071 when the new basilica was consecrated, it was unremitting from his accession in 1058 until his death-bed legislation of 1087. Within the monastic order at least, Desiderius was throughout the twenty-nine years of his reign a towering figure whose achievement at Montecassino in respect of its endowments, buildings, religious and cultural life, and general fame, bears comparison with that of his contemporary Abbot Hugh of Semur at Cluny.

II

Montecassino and Rome—the Pursuit of Reform

MONTECASSINO's golden age under Abbots Desiderius and Oderisius I, with its consequences for the monastic and secular church in South Italy, corresponded closely in time to the revival of the papacy after 1046 as the effective centre of the ecclesiastical government, reform, and renewal of Western Christendom. This chapter will be concerned with Montecassino's contribution in material, organizational, human, and propagandist terms to papal endeavours at Rome and more widely in the west.

With the range and richness of Montecassino's resources in mind, it is important to appreciate how favourably the abbey was situated by comparison with the reform papacy, and what a variety of benefits and services both cultural and material it was in a position to offer if it were prepared to do so. In these respects it stood in sharp contrast with a transalpine monastic centre such as Cluny. Especially because of the recurrent crises over its exemption from episcopal authority and of the pressures upon it that prelates like the archbishops of Lyons could bring to bear,[1] Cluny always stood in greater need of the papacy than the papacy stood of it. Of Montecassino the reverse seems to have been true: since it was less threatened than Cluny by its episcopal neighbours, it was less in need of papal help. Until some such major event as the Guibertine schism transpired to shock the monastic conscience, it could afford freely to prefer its own interests to those of the apostolic see whenever they came into conflict. As Desiderius' work progressed, Montecassino came to dispose of a rich, secure, and consolidated complex of lands and revenues, complemented by widespread possessions and resources outside it, with which the papacy had nothing to show that was truly comparable. Papal lands in Central Italy were, indeed, extensive. But they were and they largely remained in lay hands. The efforts of such

[1] See Cowdrey (as Introd. n. 9), pp. 32–63.

figures as Hildebrand, as archdeacon and as pope, to increase the papacy's effective resources as derived both from the lands of St. Peter and from the rest of Christendom had only the most modest results. So it had to rely upon the support of others to a very large degree, and Montecassino was a natural source to which it might look.

From 1059 the papal alliance with the Norman princes of the south made Rome's dependence on Montecassino the greater. By reason of its own position and also of the *terra sancti Benedicti*, the abbey dominated the Liri valley and a long stretch of the Via Latina. This domination gave it control of the route between Rome and the papacy's new-found allies, upon which Rome relied for the transmission of news and information and for the passage of men and military forces. The papacy required Montecassino as an intermediary, whereas it could itself maintain direct contact with the Normans, who in any case were more deeply committed to it than to the apostolic see.

In the circumstances of the late eleventh century, Montecassino was also politically less vulnerable than the papacy, which was open to challenge by factions within the city and environs of Rome. Given a figure such as Henry IV, it was no less at risk from military intervention by a German ruler who had powerful North Italian subjects and allies. In the event of his leading an Italian expedition, the simple facts of topography made it likely that the Germans would direct their attention to Rome before they turned to Montecassino. In addition, experience was repeatedly to show that, whereas Montecassino could usually count upon the Norman princes of South Italy for material aid, the papacy could not.[2] Nor did the devotion and the assistance of Countess Matilda of Tuscany sufficiently make good the papacy's needs. So it required to have Montecassino in the background as a source of help and, in the last resort, as a place of refuge. It also needed the abbey as a means of mobilizing Norman aid on its behalf, so far as was possible given the uncertainty of Norman willingness to give papal interests a high priority.

The papacy stood in no less need of Montecassino's human resources. When the number of its monks rose to some 200, many of whom were men of distinction in learning and affairs, the abbey's manpower matched its own requirements. The

[2] See below, pp. 119–21, 122–36, 143–5, 173.

reform papacy was never so nearly self-sufficient. Its increasingly active role called for a supply of human agents at Rome and for service in the church at large, which it could neither fully recruit nor sufficiently train within the city and from the papal lands. Monasteries like Montecassino were an obvious recruiting and training ground. Inevitably the reform papacy looked to them; and, as will be shown, it did not look in vain. But the very scale of Montecassino's resources in relation to the papacy's, together with its relative invulnerability to external pressures, meant that the abbey could usually choose the time, manner, and degree of its support. By reason of its own topographical position and of its close understanding with the Normans Montecassino held the trump cards. The papacy could ask but not command. It could not afford to alienate Montecassino by seeking to prescribe or to alter the abbey's policies and actions, even when there might seem to be good cause. It must commend its intentions to the astute judgement of the abbot and monks, and persuade them of their wisdom and of their consonance with the abbey's own interests.

i. THE DEVELOPMENT OF THE ROMAN CURIA AND ITS GOVERNMENT OF THE CHURCH

Much work remains to be done on the subject of the reform papacy before its development in the later eleventh and early twelfth centuries can be fully clarified. But since it is critical for the present study, an attempt must be made to summarize some of its features as currently understood, in order that what it needed and what it received from Montecassino can be appraised.[3]

[3] The literature on the growth of papal government is vast. For the curia I am especially indebted to K. Jordan, 'Die Entstehung der römischen Kurie', *ZRG KA* xxviii (1939), 97–152 (repr., with additional notes, Darmstadt, 1962); R. Elze, 'Das *sacrum palatium Lateranense* im 10. und 11. Jahrhundert', *SG* iv (1952), 27–54, repr. *Päpste–Kaiser–Könige und die mittelalterliche Herrschaftssymbolik* (London, 1982), no. I; E. Pásztor, 'San Pier Damiani, il cardinalato e la formazione della curia romana', *SG* x (1975), 319–39. For the cardinals, H.-W. Klewitz, 'Die Entstehung des Kardinalkollegiums', *ZRG KA* xxv (1936), 115–221, repr. *Reformpapsttum*, pp. 11–134; S. Kuttner, '*Cardinalis*: the History of a Canonical Concept', *Traditio*, iii (1945), 129–214, repr. *The History of Ideas and Doctrines of Canon Law in the Middle Ages* (London, 1980), no. IX, and *Retractiones*, pp. 14–18; C. G. Fürst, *Cardinalis. Prolegomena zu einer Rechtsgeschichte des römischen Kardinalkollegiums* (Munich, 1967), see reviews by F. Kempf, *AHP* vi (1968), 452–7, and K. Ganzer, *ZRG KA* lvi (1970), 152–7; G. Alberigo, 'Le origini della dottrina sullo ius divinum del cardina-

In the first place, there were significant changes in the vocabulary that was used to describe the central organs of papal administration. Over the centuries, language borrowed from the Roman imperial past had slowly been gaining currency. The papal residence on the Lateran had long since ceased to be called by its ancient names of *episcopium* or (after *c.*700) *patriarchium*, and had become the *sacrum palatium Lateranense*. This term was redolent of the *Constitutum Constantini*:[4] it proclaimed the comparability of the papal administration with the imperial government at Constantinople and, later, in the west; and it reflected western aspirations towards a *renovatio Romani imperii.*[5] Accordingly, eleventh-century writers sometimes envisaged the renewal of papal institutions upon classical models. No one gave this idiom more eloquent expression than Cardinal Peter Damiani:

Now the Roman church, the see of the apostles, should imitate the ancient court of the Romans (*antiquam . . . curiam Romanorum*). Just as of old the earthly senate strove to subdue the whole multitude of peoples to the Roman empire, so now the ministers of the apostolic see, the spiritual senators of the church universal, should make it their sole business by their laws to subdue the human race to God, the true emperor.[6]

Peter Damiani used the word *curia* of courts in general and never in particular of the papal entourage. But during the eleventh century it was increasingly applied north of the Alps to the

lato (1053-87)', *Reformata reformanda. Festgabe für H. Jedin zum 17. Juni 1965*, edd. E. Iserloh and K. Repgen, i (Münster, 1965), 39-58; E. Pásztor, 'Riforma della chiesa nel secolo xi e l'origine del collegio dei cardinali', *Studi . . . Morghen*, ii. 609-25; K. Ganzer, 'Das römische Kardinalkollegium', *Istituzioni ecclesiastiche*, i. 153-4; Hüls, *Kardinäle*. For papal finance, K. Jordan, 'Zur päpstlichen Finanzgeschichte im 11. und 12. Jahrhundert', *QFIAB* xxv (1933/4), 61-104; D. B. Zema, 'Economic Reorganization of the Roman See during the Gregorian Reform', *SG* i (1947), 137-68; M. Michaud, 'Chambre apostolique', *Dictionnaire du droit canonique*, iii (1942), 388-403; J. Sydow, 'Cluny und die Anfänge der apostolischen Kammer', *Stud. Mitt. OSB* lxiii (1951), 45-66, and 'Untersuchungen zur kurialen Verwaltungsgeschichte im Zeitalter des Reformpapsttums', *DA* xi (1954/5), 18-73. For the chancery, P. Rabikauskas, *Die römische Kuriale in der päpstlichen Kanzlei*, Miscellanea historiae pontificum, 20 (Rome, 1958). For the chapel, R. Elze, 'Die päpstliche Kapelle im 12. und 13. Jahrhundert', *ZRG KA* xxxvi (1950), 145-204, repr. *Päpste-Kaiser-Könige*, no. II; S. Haider, 'Zu den Anfängen der päpstlichen Kapelle', *MIÖG* lxxxvii (1979), 38-70.

[4] caps. 9, 13, 14, 17, ed. Fuhrmann (as Introd. n. 59), pp. 74, 84, 87, 93.

[5] See esp. P. E. Schramm, *Kaiser, Rom und Renovatio* (2nd edn., Darmstadt, 1957).

[6] *Op.* 31. 7, Migne, *PL* cxlv. 540AB. For his use of *curia* as a term for all courts, see *Op.* 36, prol., ed. Cantin (as Ch. I n. 148), p. 386.

courts of kings and lay magnates.[7] It was during the reign of Pope Urban II that it became naturalized at Rome.[8] Urban was a Frenchman well versed in the ways of the feudal world. By his time borrowings from the imperial Roman past were being blended with still newer ones from the feudal present. These borrowings from Roman and from transalpine vocabularies are symptomatic of a resolve to keep papal administration abreast of other rulers', and to equip the papacy actively to oversee the whole church.

The substantive improvements that were called for in the day-to-day functioning of papal government began well before the Emperor Henry III's intervention at Rome in 1046. Of especial importance was the emergence *c.*1000 of a papal chancellor (*cancellarius*); it illustrates how such institutions as the *palatium* at Pavia which the western emperor maintained in his capacity as king of Italy were serving as models for the *sacrum palatium Lateranese*. Alongside the chancellor there grew up from *c.*980 a circle of *notarii et scriniarii sacri Lateranensis palatii*. These officials increasingly assumed responsibility for the pope's correspondence and became his personal advisers. At the same time the ancient links between the papal entourage and the Roman city administration became more slender. It was symptomatic of openness to a wider world that papal scribes took to using parchment rather than papyrus. They also abandoned the older Roman cursive script in favour of a curial minuscule which was more readily legible in the church at large. With the accession in 1048 of the Lotharingian Pope Leo IX, albeit very gradually, a profounder transformation of papal government began. It centred upon the functions and recruitment of the Roman bishops and cardinals. As early as 1046 the Emperor Henry III's first German nominee as pope, Clement II, had recognized the especial dignity of the bishops and of the cardinal-priests and -deacons of the Roman church.[9] Up to this time all these three grades had been made up of Roman clergy who performed liturgical functions at Rome, where they were locally recruited. Under the reform papacy they also assumed

[7] Gregory VII used the term of the German court: *Reg.* i. 19, p. 32. For its recent introduction into Germany, see H. Thomas, 'Zur Neudatierung der *Ecbasis cuiusdam captivi*', *DA* xxvii (1967), 312–57, at 317–22.

[8] Pflugk-Harttung, *Acta*, ii. 145, no. 178; *Epp.* 22, 33, Migne, *PL* cli. 304C, 317A.

[9] 'Totus pene mundus noverit, quod specialissimas dignitates nostri episcopi ac cardinales presbyteri atque diacones habeant . . .': *Ep.* 2, Migne, *PL* cxlii. 580D.

administrative duties, and they were sometimes recruited from further afield. By the early twelfth century—but only by then—there had emerged a 'college' of cardinals comprising the three grades of bishops, priests, and deacons.[10]

Up to the time of its final emergence almost every aspect of the Roman cardinalate since the naturalization at Rome *c.*500 of the words *cardo* and *cardinalis* gives rise to controversy. There is an initial uncertainty about the root meaning of the word *cardinalis* itself: it is not agreed whether it expresses the 'incardination' of clerks into churches other than those in which they were at first ordained or, rather, their membership of the principal church, or *cardo*, of a diocese. But for an understanding of the term in the age of the reform papacy the second of these alternatives appears to be the more significant.[11]

To consider the three grades of cardinal in descending order, the cardinal-bishops had been the last to take their place in Roman liturgical arrangements. From the eighth century they appear as occupants of a group of seven 'suburbicarian' sees situated within some fifty kilometres of Rome, the precise list of which varied somewhat from time to time through personal or local factors. The seven bishops were responsible by rota for liturgical duties as *hebdomadarii* at the Lateran; they thus ministered at the principal altar of the leading Roman basilica. The designation *cardinales episcopi* is attested as early as the eighth century. In the eleventh it became temporarily common during the 1050s and 1060s, thereafter lapsing into only occasional use; its permanent currency dates from the end of the century. From Pope Leo IX's time some cardinal-bishops began to be recruited outside Rome, especially in prominent reforming circles. Leo himself appointed Humbert of Moyenmoutier as cardinal-bishop of Silva Candida, and in 1057 Pope Stephen IX made Peter Damiani, the hermit of Fonteavellana, cardinal-bishop of Ostia. At about this time the cardinal-bishops' liturgical functions were increasingly complemented by spiritual, administrative, and political duties undertaken on behalf of the apostolic see. Their role further developed when the breach of 1054 intensified the alienation of Rome from Constantinople.

[10] See esp. the *Descriptio sanctuarii ecclesiae Lateranensis*, in Johannes Diaconus, *Liber de ecclesia Lateranensi*, cap. 13, Migne, *PL* cxciv. 1557–8, *IP* i. 3–5; *Descriptio Lateranensis ecclesiae*, cap. 15, *Codice topografico della città di Roma*, edd. R. Valentini and G. Zucchetti, iii, *Fonti stor. Italia*, xc. 360–3.

[11] See esp. Deusdedit, *Coll. can.*, p. 17, lines 37–8, ii. 160 (130), pp. 267–8.

The patriarch of Constantinople was the senior of the four eastern patriarchs. After close relations were broken off, Rome no longer needed to remember their precedence or to consider their susceptibilities. A vacuum was left by reason of which the Roman cardinal-bishops could increase in dignity and variety of service within a more compact, Latin church where authority was uniquely concentrated upon Rome. Peter Damiani was therefore able to regard the cardinal-bishops as the eyes of the apostolic see through which it watched and guarded the whole world.[12] They became its natural agents in the church at large, and could also seem to form the inner core of the Roman church. Thus, in his Election Decree of 1059 Pope Nicholas II assigned them the leading voice in papal elections.[13] The cardinal-bishops then in office established themselves under Pope Alexander II as an effective reforming group,[14] and the cardinal-bishops were also with only one exception loyal agents of Pope Gregory VII who stood by him to the end.

In the eleventh century the cardinal-priests were twenty-eight in number. They were the senior clergy of the Roman *tituli*, or parochial churches. Of old the term *cardinales* had been used of all the clergy of the *tituli*. But from the eighth century only the *presbyter prior* of each *titulus* was deemed to belong to the bishop of Rome's *presbyterium*, and so to be the link between his *titulus* and the papal church of the Lateran. The cardinal-priests claimed the right on the greatest Christian festivals to concelebrate mass with the pope.[15] In groups of seven they by turns discharged liturgical duties in the four 'patriarchal basilicas' of Rome: St. Peter's, St. Paul's-without-the-Walls, St. Laurence's-without-the-Walls, and St. Mary Major.[16] Thus, they might be referred to not only under the names of their title-churches but also under those of the patriarchal basilicas at which they served.[17]

[12] Peter Damiani, *Epp.* 1. 7, 20, 2. 1, Migne, *PL* cxliv. 211–12, 238–9, 253–9. See M. Fois, 'I compiti e le prerogative dei cardinali vescovi secondo Pier Damiani nel quadro della sua ecclesiologia primaziale', *AHP* x (1972), 15–105.

[13] *MGH Const.* i. 537, no. 382, Krause, PWD, pp. 271–5. But see below, Ch. IV pp. 188–90.

[14] See Schmidt (as Introd. n. 60), pp. 134–49.

[15] Deusdedit, *Coll. can.* ii. 114, pp. 241–2.

[16] *Descriptio sanctuarii ecclesiae Lateranensis* (as Ch. II n. 10).

[17] Abbot Desiderius of Montecassino, cardinal-priest of Santa Cecilia, subscribed a charter as cardinal of St. Peter's; Gregory VII similarly addressed him: Alexander II, *Ep.* 27, Migne, *PL* cxlvi. 1308; *Reg.* ix. 11, p. 558; see Fürst (as Ch. II n. 3). p. 112, and R. Hüls, ' "Cardinalis sancti Petri" und "Cardinalis sancti Pauli" ', *QFIAB* lvii (1977), 332–8.

In Roman parlance they were the *cardinales* of the Roman church *par excellence*. Historically viewed they were the heart of the Roman cardinalate round whom, rather than round the bishops, the college of cardinals developed. There were, indeed, signs of tension between bishops and priests. Claims were canvassed that cardinal-priests, together with the deacons, had a special place as papal counsellors.[18] Their dignity was enhanced when, perhaps as a sop to reconcile them to the prominence of the cardinal-bishops, Pope Alexander II gave them quasi-episcopal rights of jurisdiction in their title-churches.[19] In the mid-eleventh century they, too, began to be employed by the popes for purposes other than their liturgical functions. However, the twenty-eight cardinal-priests formed too large a group for the popes to use them so readily as they used the cardinal-bishops. Only after 1088, when Pope Urban II was locked in struggle with his rival Clement III, did both sides in the papal schism bid resolutely for their support and so finally pave the way for their place in the twelfth-century college of cardinals.

As for the deacons, the Roman clergy had for long included seven regional deacons to whom the term *diaconi cardinales* was sometimes applied. In the eighth century they acquired liturgical functions in the Lateran basilica and so were known as *diaconi palatini*. By the mid-tenth century at latest the ancient, sevenfold regional division of Rome was overhauled. Primarily for military and administrative reasons the city was divided into twelve regions. So, in addition to the seven *diaconi palatini*, there emerged twelve *diaconi regionarii* with liturgical duties in the new regions. To this extent the palatine and regional deacons were the first element in the college of cardinals to begin their collective history. But, unless for reasons of individual ability or ambition, the deacons were the last element to become deeply involved in the wider administrative and political business of the apostolic see.[20] Like the priests they owed much to the manner in which, during the 1090s, Urban II and the anti-pope vied for their support.[21] Under Urban the palatine deacons, who had hitherto usually been referred to as *diaconi sanctae Romanae ecclesiae*, or simply *diaconi*, were more often called

[18] e.g. Deusdedit, *Coll. can.* iii. 160, pp. 267–8; Beno, i. 2, ix, pp. 370, 418.

[19] Pflugk-Harttung, *Acta*, ii. 120–1, no. 156.

[20] But see above, Ch. II n. 9.

[21] For Clement, see P. F. Kehr, 'Zur Geschichte Wiberts von Ravenna (Clemens III.)', *SB Berlin*, 1921, pp. 355–68, 973–88, at 987.

diaconi cardinales.[22] Under Paschal II all the deacons, both palatine and regional, came to be so described. After the merging of the office of archdeacon into one of the deaconries the *diaconi cardinales* became eighteen and no longer nineteen in number. All were assigned to a diaconal church, as the cardinal-priests were assigned to a title-church.

So by Paschal II's pontificate the college of cardinals could at last assume its permanent structure and identity, with seven bishops, twenty-eight priests, and eighteen deacons. Its international character was underlined because, since the mid-eleventh century, a number of leading personalities having offices—at first abbacies but later also bishoprics—away from Rome concurrently held cardinalates; they are the so-called 'external' cardinals of the Roman church.[23]

Nevertheless, it is of the utmost importance to notice that, despite this movement towards the formation of a threefold college, another usage for long persisted by which the term *cardinales* was also current at Rome to comprehend all the Roman clergy of the papal entourage, excluding the bishops but including clerks inferior in orders to the deacons.[24] The authentic version of the Election Decree of 1059 thus referred to *cardinales clerici* as distinct from the *reliquus clerus,*[25] and Gregory VII's electoral protocol declared his election to be by the 'sanctae Romanae . . . ecclesiae cardinales clerici, acoliti subdiaconi diaconi presbyteri'.[26] In his letters Gregory never referred to *cardinales episcopi* but, following the normal usage of his time as pope, to *episcopi et cardinales*, where the *et* is disjunctive.[27] As archdeacon he had himself subscribed documents as *Hildebrandus cardinalis subdiaconus.*[28] Thus, alongside the develop-

[22] See the papal letters cited at JL i. 657.

[23] Ganzer, *Kardinalat.*

[24] '. . . sicut cardine totum regitur ostium, ita Petro et successoribus eius totius ecclesiae disponitur emolumentum. Et sicut cardo immobilis permanens ducit et reducit ostium, sic Petrus et sui successores liberum de omni ecclesia habent iudicium, quia summa sedes a nemine iudicatur. Unde clerici eius cardinales dicuntur, cardini . . . utique illi, quo caetera moventur, vicinius adhaerentes': Leo IX, *Ep.* 100, Migne, *PL* cxliii. 765B. See also Deusdedit, *Coll. can.* ii. 160, pp. 267–8, and the claims set out in the *Constitutio de iure cardinalium*, Mansi, xvii. 247–8, Migne, *PL* cxxvi. 942–3, no. 346, on which see Kuttner (as Ch. II n. 3), pp. 193–6.

[25] As above, Ch. II n. 13.

[26] *Reg.* i. 1*, p. 2; cf. Benedict VIII, *Ep.* 22, Migne, *PL* cxxxix. 1621, and the discussion in Fürst (as Ch. II n. 3), pp. 100–2.

[27] See esp. *Reg.* i. 16, p. 26, where an interlined *et* modifies the single reference in the Register to *coepiscopis nostris cardinalibus.*

[28] Victor II, *Epp.* 1–3, 18, Migne, *PL* cxliii. 803–10, 834.

ments that led to the college of cardinals, the term *cardinales* might also be used to designate all clerks of whatever major or minor order inferior to the episcopate, who belonged to the Roman church as the *cardo* by which all other churches were moved.[29]

Notwithstanding this divergent usage, by the end of the eleventh century the way was clear for the cardinal-bishops, -priests, and -deacons—the cardinals in the dominant and familiar sense—to meet together as the core of the papal consistory. Other developments at about this time helped to reshape and to modernize the organs of papal administration. The papal chaplains (*capellani domini papae*), first attested under that name in 1026, seem to have begun their history *c.*1000, and the papal chapel (*capella*) grew in the wake of Roman contacts with the German imperial court. But for most of the eleventh century the chaplains appear in the sources but seldom. It was early in the twelfth century that they became prominent, when they and the Roman sub-deacons coalesced and enabled the chapel to become a more active and distinctive body in the liturgical and administrative work of the papal court. The emergent, threefold college of cardinals was thereby left freer to fulfil the role for which Cardinal Peter Damiani had somewhat prematurely cast the cardinal-bishops—that of forming the senate of the Roman church and acting as the eyes of the apostolic see. Under Urban II the papal entourage, which was now beginning to be called the *curia*, borrowed from across the Alps and from elsewhere outside Rome yet more ways and means of government. There emerged a papal chamber (*camera*) whose first identifiable chamberlain was a monk of Cluny who set about reordering papal finances on a Cluniac model.[30] The papal household began to include a steward (*dapifer*).[31] From a different direction the sometime Cassinese monk John of Gaeta introduced the *cursus* into the papal chancery, which itself grew in efficiency as an administrative agency.[32] In such ways as these the papal administration—for so long in evolution and yet even under Gregory VII still so conservative, so rudimentary, and so little changed—underwent a considerable development

[29] See above, Ch. II n. 24, also the use of *cardinales* in Bonizo of Sutri, vii, p. 603.

[30] Cowdrey (as Introd. n. 9), p. 170.

[31] Pflugk-Harttung, *Acta*, ii. 145, no. 178 (1089); see Jordan (as Ch. II n. 3), pp. 127–9 (= 37–9 of repr.).

[32] See below, Ch. II, pp. 69–70.

in the generation after his death. It thereby became better fitted to meet the demands of papal leadership in the church at large.

At no point in its eleventh-century development could the papacy make do with its own local resources of wealth or—more important—of men. So it was inevitably solicitous for the goodwill and aid of monasteries like Montecassino which had enough manpower and to spare to supply it with men who could take their place in the Roman church and its administration. To co-operate with their abbots and to call upon their monks for service was a recurrent papal concern.

ii. MONTECASSINO AND ROME

a. *The papacy and abbatial elections at Montecassino*

The papacy's need for the help of institutions like Montecassino was great. But during its golden age the monks of Montecassino made it clear that, although the defence of their own liberties gave them reason to maintain a close relationship with the papacy and to serve its needs, their topographical position and their superior wealth and resources enabled them to do so largely upon their own terms. Leo of Ostia's part of the Montecassino Chronicle, in particular, makes clear their absolute determination to brook no undue papal interference in abbatial elections, which were to follow inviolably the directions of the Rule of St. Benedict. This determination was the outcome of the hard experience that Leo of Ostia recorded when dealing with the abbacies which preceded Desiderius'. Montecassino had for long suffered greatly through secular intervention in elections on the part of both western emperors and Lombard princes. Particularly traumatic was the election of 1020, when Abbot Theobald was elected in the presence and at the prompting of the Emperor Henry II, with Pope Benedict VIII at his side.[33] Theobald was chosen in order to uphold western imperial interests against both the Byzantines and the princes of Capua. After Henry's death Montecassino suffered the consequences of this political appointment. In 1032 Prince Pandulf IV of Capua interned Theobald and intruded as his vice-gerent his own client Todinus, a *famulus* or lay servant of Montecassino.[34] When Theobald died, Pandulf caused a new abbot, Basil, to be elected—*indigne et seculariter* as Leo of Ostia

[33] *Chron. Cas.* ii. 42, pp. 245–7. [34] Ibid. ii. 56–7, pp. 274–9.

commented; for the election took place in his palace at Capua.[35] So in 1038, when the Emperor Conrad II came to Montecassino, he did so as a deliverer who caused Basil to flee. The new election took place under his eye; according to Leo of Ostia he insistently urged that, as the Rule demanded, the monks themselves should elect one of their own congregation. It was only at the monks' invitation that he nominated Richer of Niederaltaich.[36] It was an important demonstration of monastic liberty. There quickly followed Pope Benedict IX's privilege, which confirmed that abbatial elections were the exclusive affair of the monks themselves, although it also insisted upon the pope's right to consecrate the abbot-elect. Leo IX endorsed these provisions, as did all the reform popes in succession who issued privileges for Montecassino.[37]

As the monks thus vindicated their right to hold elections which were free from lay interference, so, following Abbot Richer's death in 1055, they were able expressly to establish their freedom from improper papal interventions as well. In that year a majority of the monks elected one of their number, Peter, who was renowned for his sanctity but who was reputed to lack talent for secular business.[38] When the news of his election reached Pope Victor II, who as Bishop Gebhard of Eichstätt and imperial chancellor had been used to the masterful ways of the royal power over the German church, he reacted strongly; for he wished to have at Montecassino a better watchdog than Peter against the growing power of the Normans. When Victor returned to Italy in 1057 after the Emperor Henry III's death he sent Cardinal Humbert, and perhaps also Cardinal Frederick of Lorraine, to Montecassino with orders if possible to effect Peter's deposition. Writing, as it must be remembered, some fifty years afterwards and so revealing a considered, long-term Cassinese view, Leo of Ostia roundly condemned as a violation of the abbey's liberty this papal initiative against a freely elected abbot:

The pope had set his mind in this way violently to bring the abbey under his yoke, although at no earlier time had any Roman pontiff presumed to

35 Amatus, i. 35, p. 47; *Chron. Cas.* ii. 61–2, pp. 285–7.

36 Desiderius, *Dial.* i. 9, pp. 1122–4; Amatus, ii. 5, pp. 61–2; *Chron. Cas.* ii. 63, pp. 288–93.

37 Unless otherwise indicated, papal privileges in this and the next two sections are as cited in Introd. nn. 75–6.

38 For Peter, see Amatus, iii. 48, p. 165; *Chron. Cas.* ii. 89–92, pp. 341–51; cf. Wühr (as Ch. I n. 8), pp. 442–7.

attempt any such thing; for from the beginning the election of an abbot had always been free, with the election itself the work of the monks while only the abbot's consecration belonged to the pope.[39]

Faced by massive resistance on the part of the monks, Humbert withdrew from the chapter. But thereafter further difficulties led to Peter's abdication. The monks assembled for a new election and they chose Frederick of Lorraine, under Humbert's presidency but also—as Leo of Ostia commented—*uno . . . consensu et unanimi voluntate*, and *de more monasterii*:[40] the proprieties of free election were observed. Frederick was consecrated by Pope Victor II, who through Humbert's agency gave Montecassino a privilege which Archdeacon Hildebrand subscribed. It once more confirmed Montecassino's claim to free abbatial elections, while also providing for the papal confirmation and consecration of whomever the monks elected. It marked the beginning of a state of equilibrium between Roman and Cassinese interests so far as elections were concerned. The papal right to consecrate the abbot went far to guarantee for the papacy a succession of amenable abbots; while from the monks' point of view their liberty to elect their own abbot without Roman no less than without secular interference in the electoral process was assured. To this day the original of Pope Victor's privilege remains at Montecassino as a Magna Carta of its liberty and of its *entente* with the papacy.

During the rest of the eleventh century, moreover, the starkness of its claim to liberty as Leo of Ostia insisted upon it was concealed by the coincidence that there were only two more abbatial elections, and that in either case the abbot happened to be nominated by a predecessor who was also pope: in 1058 Abbot Frederick of Lorraine (Pope Stephen IX) nominated Abbot Desiderius, and in 1087 Abbot Desiderius (Pope Victor III) nominated Abbot Oderisius I. The Montecassino Chronicle declared itself to be satisfied as to the canonical propriety of elections thus domestically initiated: Desiderius became abbot *ex parte fratrum omnium*, and Oderisius *iuxta quod beati Benedicti regula precipit.*[41] Indeed, the Chronicle recorded no election in which Montecassino's liberty was deemed to have

[39] *Chron. Cas.* ii. 91, p. 347.

[40] Ibid. ii. 92, pp. 350–1.

[41] Ibid. iii. 9, 73, iv. 1, pp. 370–2, 455–6, 467. For the practice whereby eleventh-century popes often retained their former sees or abbacies, see W. Goez, 'Papa qui et episcopus. Zum Selbstverständnis des Reformpapsttums im 11. Jahrhundert', *AHP* viii (1970), 27–59.

been infringed by papal actions until after what it applauded as the correctly conducted election of Abbot Oderisius II in 1125.[42]

So, throughout Montecassino's golden age its relationship with the papacy was based upon a claim to independence on the part of the monks which was expressed in their inviolable right freely to elect their abbot. But it was tempered by a papal willingness, expressed in repeated privileges, to recognize and to guarantee this claim; and it was balanced by a Cassinese recognition of the pope's right to confirm abbatial elections and to consecrate the abbot-elect. The circumstances of the elections of 1058 and 1087 made co-operation between the papacy and Montecassino particularly close and harmonious; when the times were propitious, such co-operation might readily be extended to embrace their wider interests.

b. *Papal honours conferred upon the abbots of Montecassino in their monastic capacity*

From their side the reform popes consolidated the bond between the abbots of Montecassino and the apostolic see by bestowing honours upon the abbots themselves in their monastic capacity. In or about 1049 Pope Leo IX conferred upon Abbot Richer and his successors the right of wearing at mass on major festivals the liturgical ornaments of sandals, dalmatic, and gloves.[43] This right was confirmed in their privileges for Montecassino by Popes Victor II, Stephen IX, Nicholas II, Alexander II, Urban II (implicitly), and Paschal II. Moreover, when in 1057 Victor II issued his confirmation he also accorded the abbots of Montecassino at ecclesiastical councils and tribunals a precedence over all other abbots in seating arrangements and when giving judgements. At the same time he praised Montecassino as 'monasticae normae . . . principale gymnasium et sanctae Romanae ecclesiae sedi contiguum'. Gregory VII, too, always safeguarded the abbey's precedence in the monastic order, and it was reasserted in Urban II's privilege. Urban and Paschal II gave the abbot of Montecassino an express jurisdiction over the monks and nuns of its subject houses. By such marks of favour and regard, the reform popes kept the abbots reminded of the high place that they and their abbey occupied in their perspectives.

[42] *Chron. Cas.* iv. 78, p. 542; the election happened *ut in talibus consuetudo est.*
[43] Ibid. ii. 79, pp. 325–6, *IP* viii. 135, no. *66.

c. *Material aid by Montecassino for the papacy*

As regards the services that Montecassino performed in return for such papal privileges and favours, it must first be said that, despite the abbey's great wealth, its material support for the papacy was usually slight and occasional. The major exception is in the period between Gregory VII's departure from Rome in the summer of 1084 and the death of Pope Victor III in September 1087. Then, as Pope Urban II was implicitly to acknowledge, Montecassino by its hospitality made a major contribution to the very survival of the reform papacy.[44] But the papacy seems otherwise to have upon only one occasion sought aid from Montecassino in the form of money, treasure, or military service—and then unsuccessfully. In 1058, after his election as Pope Stephen IX, Abbot Frederick of Lorraine from Rome ordered the *prepositus* of Montecassino secretly to send him his abbey's whole treasure in gold and silver, promising that he would soon recompense it with treasure yet more valuable. As it was rumoured, his object was to finance his brother Duke Godfrey of Lorraine in an attempt to secure the imperial crown; he hoped thereafter to destroy Norman power in South Italy. But according to Leo of Ostia, a vision in which St. Benedict appeared to a novice of the abbey caused him to return the treasure almost intact.[45] The incident makes clear how wrong it was thought to be for the wealth of St. Benedict to be appropriated for the purposes of St. Peter and his vicar.[46] Whatever else Montecassino might offer to Rome in the way of services, it was usually unwilling to commit its wealth and treasure.

d. *The employment of the abbots of Montecassino in the papal service*

In terms of manpower Montecassino's contribution to the papacy was larger, and it began with the services of the abbots themselves. The linchpin was the admission of its abbots to be cardinal-priests of the Roman church—a development which

[44] For the help, see below, Ch. III, pp. 172–4, Ch. IV, *passim.* Robert Guiscard's contemporary largesse should be remembered: above, Ch. I, pp. 7–8, 19. In his privilege of 1097 Urban praised Montecassino for its help: 'Is enim locus, nostrorum pauperum relevatio, fugentium refugium, fessorum sedis apostolicae filiorum requies indefessa permansit et permaneat'; see, too, his *Ep.* 247, Migne, *PL* cli. 515–17.

[45] *Chron. Cas.* ii. 97, p. 355; cf. Amatus, iii. 50–2, pp. 166–8, 170, where the treasure is said to have been brought back after Stephen's death.

[46] Cf. the Roman attitude to the pope's needs in 1082: below, Ch. III, pp. 152–3.

was made possible by the eleventh-century changes in the Roman cardinalate. It in effect complemented at Rome the liturgical honours that the abbots received at Montecassino in their strictly monastic capacity. Pope Victor II took the critical step when Frederick of Lorraine—since 1051 *bibliothecarius et cancellarius* of the Roman church and one of its deacons—journeyed to him in Tuscany for consecration as abbot. On 14 June 1057, ten days before his consecration, Victor made him cardinal-priest of the title of San Grisogono. He thus set a precedent whereby the next two abbots of Montecassino—Desiderius and Oderisius I—and many of their successors up to the thirteenth century, were cardinal-priests having the character of 'external' cardinals. As such they had a title-church at Rome and therefore membership of the papal *presbyterium* in the city; but they were under no obligation of standing personal residence there.[47]

Frederick was, indeed, the first 'external' cardinal in papal history. The second was his successor Abbot Desiderius. Early in 1059, after Desiderius' election, Pope Nicholas II summoned him to his presence in the Roman marches. On 6 May, at Osimo near Ancona, he made him cardinal-priest of the title of Santa Cecilia in Trastevere; he consecrated him abbot on the following day.[48] Desiderius' successor, Abbot Oderisius I, had first entered Montecassino in the days of Abbot Richer. In 1059 Pope Nicholas II also made him a deacon of the Lateran church, himself ordaining him at Acerra near Naples. In 1087, when he became abbot, he appears to have been senior among the deacons; a year later he became cardinal-priest of an unknown title-church.[49]

The conferring of the cardinalate upon the abbots of Montecassino led to further developments which tightened the bonds between Montecassino and Rome. When Frederick of Lorraine became a cardinal-priest, the abbey already had a papally conferred dependency in Rome—the church of Santa Croce in

[47] *Chron. Cas.* ii. 93, pp. 351–2; see Santifaller, 'Saggio', pp. 151–2, Ganzer, *Kardinalat*, pp. 15–16, Hüls, *Kardinäle*, pp. 168–9, 248.

[48] *Chron. Cas.* iii. 12, p. 374, *IP* viii. 141, no. *87; see Ganzer, pp. 17–23, Hüls, pp. 154–5.

[49] Gattula, *Historia*, p. 236; *Chron. Cas.* iii. 14, p. 376; Urban II, *Epp.* 1–2, 219, Migne, *PL* cli. 283–4, 492. Klewitz thought that Oderisius succeeded Desiderius at Santa Cecilia: *Reformpapsttum*, pp. 89, 123; but A. Ciaconius, *Vitae et res gestae pontificum Romanorum et SRE cardinalium cum notis ab Augustino Oldoino recognitae* (4th edn., Rome, 1677), i. 829, no. 6, suggested San Marcello. See Ganzer, pp. 43–5, Hüls, pp. 215–16.

Gerusalemme. Pope Alexander II exchanged it for the church of Santa Maria in Pallara.[50] This church had an earlier connection with Montecassino, for Abbot Frederick of Lorraine had a lodging there in 1057 and was taken thence for election as pope. Situated upon the Palatine near the ruins of the Septizonium, Santa Maria in Pallara was adjacent both to a stronghold of the Frangipani, a powerful urban family supporting the reform papacy, and also to the so-called *turris chartularia* in which important papal archives were kept.[51] From Alexander II's reign, besides serving as a lodging for the abbot of Montecassino when he went to Rome it housed a small community of Cassinese monks who remained at Rome in the service of both pope and abbot. From this base Desiderius built up his connections with Roman families and especially with the Frangipani.[52]

If the popes thus acquired the benefit of Cassinese services at Rome, they also sought its abbot's services in South Italy at large. After consecrating Desiderius, Pope Nicholas II appointed him to be for his lifetime papal vicar with oversight of all monasteries of monks and nuns in the Campania, the Principate, Apulia, and Calabria.[53] Desiderius is attested with some frequency, if also with some prolonged and significant intermissions, as an attender at papal councils, as a legate, and as a witness of papal documents. He attended councils at the Lateran, Melfi, and Benevento in 1059, and at the Lateran in 1073, 1079, and perhaps 1083.[54] At a date between 1077 and 1085 he acted as

[50] See above, Ch. I, pp. 11-12.

[51] *Ep.* 108, Migne, *PL* cxlvi. 1395, *Chron. Cas.* iii. 36, p. 413, *IP* viii. 145-6, no. 107. For Abbot Frederick, *Chron. Cas.* ii. 94, pp. 352-3. For the history of the church, see P. Fedele, 'Una chiesa del Palatino: S. Maria "in Pallara" ', *Arch. Soc. rom.* xxvi (1903), 343-73. For its connection with the papacy, Klewitz (as Ch. I n. 54); F. Ehrle, 'Die Frangipani und der Untergang des Archivs und der Bibliothek der Päpste am Anfang des 13. Jahrhundert', *Mélanges offerts à M. Émile Chatelain* (Paris, 1910), 448-85; Lohrmann (as Ch. I n. 54), pp. 102-17, who argues that the copy of Pope John VIII's Register, now Reg. Vat. 1, was probably taken at Santa Maria in Pallara in the 1070s for the benefit of Montecassino.

[52] *Chron. Cas.* iii. 18, 26, pp. 384, 395; see Bloch (as Introd. n. 34), pp. 215-17, and Hüls, *Kardinäle*, pp. 256-7.

[53] *Ep.* 3, Migne, *PL* cxliii. 1309; Kehr, 'Le bolle pontificie', pp. 47-8, no. 9; *Chron. Cas.* iii. 12, p. 374; *IP* viii. 141, nos. 88-9.

[54] Lateran, 1059: *MGH Const.* ii. 544, no. 383. Melfi, 1059: *Chron. Cas.* iii. 13, p. 374; *Codice diplomatico del monastero benedettino di S. Maria di Tremiti (1005-1237)*, ed. A. Petrucci, *Font. stor. Italia*, xcviii/2 (Rome, 1960), 197-8, no. 64. Benevento, 1059: Mansi, xix. 921. Lateran, 1073: *Reg.* i. 18*a*, p. 31. Lateran, Lent 1079: R. B. C. Huyghens, 'Bérenger de Tours, Lanfranc et Bernold de Constance', *Sacris erudiri*, xvi (1965), 355-403, at 400. Lateran, Nov. 1083: see below, p. 169.

papal legate in deciding a dispute between Archbishops Alfanus I of Salerno and Roffrid I of Benevento over two *castra* at Forino and Serino.[55] Such a record suggests that his cardinalate was no empty title: the practice that Pope Victor II introduced of giving the abbot of Montecassino a place in the establishment of the Roman clergy committed him to the service of the Roman church. In return the popes were occasionally visitors to Montecassino.[57] Thus, the abbey was in frequent contact with the papacy; it was kept aware of papal policies, requirements, and needs; and its abbots from time to time collaborated in giving effect to them.

e. *Cassinese monks in the papal service*

As a consequence of the place that the abbots of Montecassino were given as cardinal-priests of the Roman church, as well as of the setting up in Rome of a Cassinese house at Santa Maria in Pallara, the papacy secured help from other Cassinese monks, both at Rome itself and more widely in the church.[58] Leaving aside Desiderius' own pontificate as Pope Victor III,[59] this help can best be studied in three somewhat contrasting phases: from Frederick of Lorraine's election as abbot in 1057 up to Gregory VII's election to the papacy in 1073; during Gregory's pontificate (1073–85); and with respect to the contribution made by monks who were at Montecassino under Abbot Desiderius after Urban II's accession to the papacy in 1088.

During the period between 1057 and 1073, upon becoming Pope Stephen IX in 1057 Abbot Frederick of Lorraine set a precedent by retaining at his side a group of Cassinese monks who served him as chaplains.[60] In the next decade, figures like Cardinal Humbert and Cardinal Peter Damiani maintained close contact with Montecassino.[61] Above all, Pope Alexander II and

[55] H. Hoffmann, 'Die älteren Abtslisten von Montecassino', *QFIAB* xlvii (1967), 224–354, at 352–4.

[56] Nicholas II, *Ep.* 15, Florence, 1060, Migne, *PL* cxliii. 1330–2; F. A. Zaccaria, *Dell'antichissima badia di Leno* (Venice, 1767), 104, no. 18 (Lateran, 1060); Alexander II, *Ep.* 27, Migne, *PL* cxlvi. 1306–7 (Lateran, 1065).

[57] Stephen IX from 30 Nov. 1057 to 10 Feb. 1058: *Chron. Cas.* ii. 94, p. 353; Nicholas II, 24 June 1059, ibid. iii. 13, p. 374; Alexander II, 1071, see above, p. 16; Gregory VII, (i) July/Aug. 1073, *Chron. Cas.* iii. 36, p. 413; (ii) perhaps *c.*22 Aug. 1078, *Reg.* vi. 2–3, pp. 391–6; (iii) 1084, *Chron. Cas.* iii. 53, p. 435.

[58] A survey was made by Gattula, *Historia*, pp. 192–6.

[59] See below, Ch. IV.

[60] Amatus, iii. 52, p. 170; *Chron. Cas.* ii. 94, 98, iii. 9, pp. 353, 356, 369–70. See Haider (as Ch. II n. 3), p. 68.

[61] *Chron. Cas.* iii. 7, 20, pp. 367–8, 386; see above, pp. 34–8, 57–8.

his powerful archdeacon, Hildebrand, cultivated the favour and collaboration of Montecassino and of Abbot Desiderius. Leo of Ostia recalled Alexander's devotion to the abbey, recording how at Hildebrand's instigation he invited Desiderius to provide monks who might be his right-hand men at Rome (*quos . . . suo lateri ad ecclesiasticum ministerium sociabat*), together with others who might be employed elsewhere as bishops or as abbots.[62] Amatus said that at this time Desiderius and Hildebrand 'estoient granz amis';[63] while Alfanus of Salerno's ode to Hildebrand further testifies to the high regard in which Desiderius' circle held him.[64]

To arrive at the true extent of Cassinese service during these years it is, however, necessary to prune away some exaggerations. Two cardinal-bishops have been claimed as sometime Cassinese monks, but their profession at Montecassino is unproven. They are Bernard, cardinal-bishop of Palestrina from *c.*1061 to *c.*1065, and Mainard, cardinal-bishop of Silva Candida from 1061 to ? 1075.[65] Both had distinguished careers in the papal service, and both had associations with Montecassino: Alfanus of Salerno wrote Bernard's epitaph; Mainard was chosen by Pope Stephen IX to accompany Desiderius in 1058, while he was not yet abbot, on a mission to Byzantium, and he was with Cardinal Humbert at Montecassino during Desiderius' election.[66] But that is all. No Cassinese source, such as any of its Necrologies, offers a hint that they were monks there, and Bernard had a career in the papal service beginning from its humblest rank. Amongst the cardinal-priests a like scepticism is appropriate regarding the Cassinese connections of Peter, who became cardinal-priest of San Grisogono before 1070 and thereafter was *bibliothecarius et cancellarius* of the apostolic see.[67] Nor was Alberic of Montecassino ever a cardinal.[68]

But certainly an alumnus of the abbey was Aldemarius, first

[62] *Chron. Cas.* iii. 24, pp. 390–1.
[63] iv. 48, p. 219.
[64] Lentini and Avagliano, *Carmi*, no. 22; see below, pp. 76–7.
[65] Bernard: Klewitz, *Reformpapsttum*, pp. 35, 117, and (as Ch. I n. 54), p. 40; Santifaller, 'Saggio', pp. 173, 177, 180, 395, 396; Hüls, *Kardinäle*, pp. 109–10. Mainard: Klewitz, *Reformpapsttum*, p. 118; Ganzer, *Kardinalat*, pp. 23–6; Santifaller, pp. 164, 178–80, 196–8, 401, 303, 407; Hüls, pp. 134–6.
[66] Lentini and Avagliano, *Carmi*, no. 30; *Chron. Cas.* iii. 9, p. 370.
[67] Klewitz suggested that he might be Cassinese: *Reformpapsttum*, pp. 66, 72, 92, and (as Ch. I n. 54), pp. 41–4. See Santifaller, pp. 183–90, 197, 203–5, 398–424, 426–36, and Hüls, pp. 170–2.
[68] Lentini (as Ch. I n. 98), pp. 78–88.

known in 1058/9 as Prince Richard of Capua's notary, who entered Montecassino where he was to be Leo of Ostia's novice master. Leo praised him as *prudentissimum ac nobilem clericum.* He was chosen to lead the monks whom Desiderius planned to send to Sardinia. Thereafter he became abbot of the Roman patriarchal basilica of St. Laurence's-without-the-Walls; as a cardinal-priest his title-church is uncertain. Little is known about his service at Rome, although he died in 1076.[69] Leo also referred to Peter, son of Atenulf, a *nobilis* of Capua who, having become *c.*1063 at Prince Gisulf of Salerno's request abbot of San Benedetto, Salerno, was later made a cardinal at Rome, perhaps under Alexander II rather than Gregory VII; it is likely that he was an 'external' cardinal.[70] A Cassinese monk who figured prominently among the Roman deacons was Theodinus. He was the son of Count Berard of Marsia, and entered Alexander II's service *c.*1067. Leo of Ostia described him as a youth of great promise; under Gregory VII he appears as archdeacon at Rome. Alfanus of Salerno made him the subject of a eulogistic ode.[71]

Leo of Ostia said that Alexander II and Hildebrand also sought monks from Montecassino to fill vacant bishoprics and abbeys.[72] He cited three examples: Ambrose, a wise and learned Milanese who was archbishop of Terracina from *c.*1064 until after 1079; Gerald, of German origin and also very learned, who was archbishop of Siponto from 1063/4 to *c.*1096; and Milo, bishop of Sessa Aurunca.[73] There can be added from the

[69] Gattula, *Accessiones*, pp. 161, 163; *Chron. Cas.* iii. 21, 24, pp. 387, 391. See Hüls, pp. 211–12; Schmidt (as Introd. n. 60), pp. 168–9; Loud, 'Calendar', pp. 109, 119, nos. 2–3.

[70] *Chron. Cas.* iii. 24, p. 391. See Hüls, p. 216; Hoffmann (as Ch. I n. 118), p. 143.

[71] *Chron. Cas.* iii. 24, p. 391; Gregory VII, *Reg.* iii. 17*a*, p. 283; Lentini and Avagliano, *Carmi*, no. 24, cf. no. 1, line 61, and no. 15, line 998. See Hüls, p. 254; Schmidt, p. 168.

[72] As Ch. II n. 62. For Cassinese bishops, see A. Lentini, 'Note sui monaci-vescovi dei secoli x–xi', *Benedictina*, xxiii (1976), 8–13. Until further progress has been made towards the compilation of a new *Italia sacra* it will not be possible to make a complete list of Cassinese monks who became bishops, or to undertake the task of comparing Montecassino's contribution to the episcopate with other monasteries'. However, it seems clear that the number of Cassinese bishops was never large and that it did not compare with the Cluniacs'; but the latter were recruited from a wider-flung family of houses: J. Mehne, 'Cluniacenserbischöfe', *Frühmittelalterliche Studien*, xi (1977), 241–87. It nevertheless compared favourably with other Italian monasteries: Toubert, *Latium*, pp. 829–30.

[73] *Chron. Cas.* iii. 24, p. 391; Ughelli-Coleti, i. 1291, v. 535, vii. 823–5. Ambrose confirmed a gift to Montecassino in 1064: Gattula, *Historia*, p. 228; for him, see Schmidt, pp. 169–70. For Gerald, see T. Leccisotti, 'Due monaci Cassinesi archivescovi di Siponto', *Iapigia*, xiv (1943), 155–65; Schmidt, p. 171.

Chronicle Bishops Martin of Aquino (1060–after 1071), Peter of Venafro and Isernia, and Trasmundus of Valva, and from other sources John of Valva and Atto of Chieti.[74] Another possible Cassinese is Bishop Palumbus of Sora, attested in 1059 and 1071. Pope Nicholas II may have consulted Desiderius *c.*1058 about the vacant see of Penne;[75] while, according to Amatus, Waiferius of Montecassino refused moves to make him archbishop of Benevento.[76] In addition Desiderius' friend Alfanus was archbishop of Salerno. Thus, under Popes Stephen IX, Nicholas II, and Alexander II, Montecassino's contribution to the papacy in terms of able men who served it at Rome and in South Italy was a significant one.

During the early years of Gregory VII's pontificate relations became, by contrast, very cool. Gregory showed Montecassino little sign of favour and did not issue a privilege on its behalf;[77] for a time the evidence for the entry of Cassinese monks into papal service almost ceases. Cordiality and collaboration began to revive in the late 1070s, to become stronger only after 1080 when Gregory renewed his alliance with the Norman princes. For the initial coolness there were several reasons. The first and probably the principal reason was Gregory's displeasure at Abbot Desiderius' adherence to the Normans at a time when Robert Guiscard, in particular, was pursuing policies which were so much at variance with papal interests that they led to his repeated excommunication.[78] Secondly, and in part arising from the Norman situation, there was Gregory's sharp divergence from Desiderius over the island monastery of Tremiti in the Adriatic off the coast of the Abruzzi.[79] Thirdly, the manner of Gregory's election to the papacy seems to have created unease among the monks of Montecassino. An anecdote in the propaganda of the Guibertine cardinals during Urban II's pontificate

[74] Martin and Peter: *Chron. Cas.* iii. 14, pp. 376–7; Ughelli–Coleti, i. 396, vi. 538. Trasmundus: *Chron. Cas.* iii. 25, p. 392; Ughelli–Coleti, i. 1363–4; Gattula, *Historia*, p. 195. Atto: *I Necrologi cassinesi*, ed. Inguanez, 11 Feb., *Fonti stor. Italia*, lxxxiii; Ughelli–Coleti, vi. 676–96; Lentini and Avagliano, *Carmi*, nos. 16, 31. For Sora, P. Fedele, 'I vescovi di Sora nel secolo undecimo', *Arch. Soc. rom.* xxii (1909), 316.

[75] *Libellus querulus de miseriis ecclesiae Pennensis*, cap. 3, ed. A. Hofmeister, *MGH SS* xxx/2, p. 1464.

[76] iv. 46, p. 219.

[77] Although in his *Breviarium de dictamine* Alberic included a paradigm papal privilege of Gregory VII for Montecassino: Rockinger (as Ch. I n. 105), pp. 37–8. But see H. Bresslau, *Handbuch der Urkundenlehre für Deutschland und Italien*, i (2nd edn., Berlin and Leipzig, 1931), 248–9.

[78] See below, pp. 126–32.

[79] See below, p. 124.

told how, when Desiderius came to Rome after Gregory's election, Gregory rebuked him for his delay in coming. The abbot's riposte was: 'But you yourself have hastened overmuch! While your lord the pope was not yet buried you uncanonically usurped the apostolic see.'[80] The historicity of the exchange may be doubted. But as propaganda it may be related to an obscure passage in Amatus, which shows that at Montecassino in the mid-1070s papal elections were a sensitive subject, and that some views which were current there were not congenial at Rome.[81] Objections on the part of some at least of the monks to Gregory's election may thus have strained relations from the abbey's side.

Whatever the precise reasons may have been, contact quickly dried up. In July 1073 Gregory and Desiderius were together at Montecassino and Benevento in a vain attempt to restore relations between Rome and the Normans.[82] But it was not until about the middle of 1078 that their dealings began to be closer;[83] in the meanwhile Gregory's only recorded contact with Desiderius was in 1076, when he sought his intervention in order to save Prince Gisulf of Salerno from Robert Guiscard's attacks.[84] A result of this coolness is the striking fact that no monk of Montecassino is known to have entered the papal service at Rome during Gregory's pontificate.[85] The sole monk known to have become a bishop was John of Sora, an uncle of Leo of Ostia, whom Gregory consecrated during his first year as pope.[86] Moreover, little is heard of the already appointed Cassinese bishops, save that in 1074–5 Archbishop Gerald of Siponto was Gregory's legate in Dalmatia.[87] By contrast Gregory

[80] Beno, ii. 12, p. 380.

[81] 'Or non parlons plus de la fama et de la subcession de li pontifice de Rome, quar l'onor defailli à Rome puiz que faillirent li Thodesque. Quar, si je voill dire la costume et lo election lor, me covient mentir, et, se je di la verité, aurai je l'yre de li Romain': iii. 53, p. 177.

[82] See below, p. 124.

[83] See below, pp. 133–4.

[84] Amatus, viii. 3, p. 353.

[85] There is an isolated record in *Chron. Cas.* iii. 34, p. 410, that, apparently *c.*1075, Desiderius stood in such favour with the pope that he charged him to fill from Montecassino a number of South Italian sees and abbeys. But no details are given, and it seems to repeat iii. 24, pp. 390–1.

[86] *Chron. Cas.* iii. 33, 34, pp. 408, 410; *Reg.* i. 85*a*, p. 123; Ughelli-Coleti, i. 1244–5. Archbishop Roffrid of Benevento was never at Montecassino: D. Lohrmann, 'Roffrid von Montecassino oder Bischof Roffrid von Benevento?' *QFIAB* xlvii (1967), 30–40.

[87] *Reg.* i. 65, 30 Mar. 1074, pp. 94–5, iii. 14 (Apr. 1076), p. 276; Ughelli-Coleti, vii. 823–4.

turned to Cluny for the kinds of help, both at Rome and elsewhere, that Alexander II had sought from Montecassino.[88]

Nevertheless the Cassinese community at Santa Maria in Pallara continued to exist, and the Cassinese monks who had entered the papal service at Rome before 1073 for long remained loyal and useful to Gregory. This is illustrated by the so-called *Iudicium de regno et sacerdotio* of late 1083.[89] However, in the crisis year of 1084 the by then very small number of Cassinese who had a place in the Roman church divided in their allegiance. As senior cardinal-deacon, Oderisius remained unswervingly true to the Gregorian cause into Urban II's reign.[90] The archdeacon Theodinus, on the other hand, passed into the service of the antipope Clement III.[91]

After Urban's succession to the papacy in 1088, older levels of cordiality and co-operation with Montecassino were gradually restored. The process was more protracted than might be expected, given the extent of Cassinese involvement in Urban's election. Urban was careful to present himself as the designated successor of both Gregory VII and Victor III; at his election Oderisius, by then abbot of Montecassino, expressed the assent of the deacons of the Roman church; and Urban thereafter created him cardinal-priest.[92] Yet Urban was not swift actively to seek help from Montecassino. Oderisius' name appears in the dating clause on none of Urban II's documents and in only one of Paschal II's; although he was with Urban at Capua in 1091 and at the synod of Troia in 1093,[93] and in 1091 King Ladislaus of Hungary sought his good offices with the pope.[94] But it is not certain that, as pope, Urban ever visited Monte-

[88] Cowdrey (as Introd. n. 9), pp. 169–71, esp. 170 n. 6.

[89] See below, pp. 168–9, and Appendix V.

[90] See below, pp. 215–17.

[91] Kehr (as Ch. II n. 21), p. 978. Theodinus seems nevertheless to have been remembered in Cassinese Necrologies: Hoffmann (as Ch. I n. 118), p. 148.

[92] See below, pp. 215–17. For Urban's claim to continuity, see *Epp.* 1, 2, 4, Migne, *PL* cli. 283, 286–8; Pflugk-Harttung, *Acta,* ii. 141–2, no. 175; J. Ramackers, 'Analekten zur Geschichte des Reformpapsttums und der Cluniacenzer', *QFIAB* xxiii (1931/2), 42–4, no. 11. That Oderisius' place in the Roman church was remembered in South Italy is indicated by a charter dated at Arpino on 24 Apr. 1104 which refers to him as 'vir [vener]abile abbas Casinensis cęnobii unus de cardinalibus de sede beati Petri apostoli de urbe Roma': Montecassino, Archivio capitolare, caps. XXXVIII, fasc. v, no. 45, Leccisotti, *Regesti,* vii. 283 (1481).

[93] *Ep.* 29, Migne, *PL* clxiii. 48, at Montecassino; *Chron. Cas.* iv. 7, 9, pp. 471, 473–4.

[94] F. von Šišić, *Enchiridion fontium historiae Croaticae,* i/1 (Zagreb, 1914), 316, cited by Ganzer, *Kardinalat,* p. 44.

cassino,[95] and until his privilege of 1097 the abbey seems to have been little indebted to him for the defence of its interests.[96]

However, after 1088 Cassinese monks began once again to be taken into the papal service, and they played a part both in the college of cardinals as it took its definitive shape, and in the other organs of papal administration that emerged in a clear and settled way at about the end of the eleventh century. The survey of recruitment which follows includes only such figures as are known to have been monks at Montecassino under Abbot Desiderius.[97] No cardinal-bishop appointed under Urban had Cassinese connections, but at some date between 1102 and 1107 Leo, the author of the first part of the Montecassino Chronicle, became cardinal-bishop of Ostia, an office which he filled until his death, 22 May 1115; he also held the see of Velletri.[98] Abbot Oderisius I was the sole cardinal-priest from Montecassino;[99] but among the deacons Montecassino gave the papacy two noteworthy recruits. According to Peter the Deacon a monk named Leo wrote many of Urban II's letters and kept his (now lost) Register. Leo probably entered the papal service as a notary by late 1089, and by 1100 he was a cardinal-deacon of the title of San Vito e San Modesto. The last record of him was on 24 March 1115.[100] A more considerable figure was John of Gaeta. He was a monk of Montecassino by 1068, and under Gregory VII he perhaps spent some time in Rome at Santa Maria in Pallara. He may have entered the papal service under Victor III, thus filling the gap left by the secession to the

[95] There may be a kernel of truth in the story of a visit, perhaps in 1091, when Urban doubted whether Desiderius had discovered St. Benedict's tomb until a vision of the saint corrected him: *Chron. Cas.* iv. 5, p. 470; cf. the spurious *Ep.* 301, Migne, *PL* cli. 549–50, *IP* viii. 152, no. †136, Leccisotti, *Regesti*, i. 22–3. But the story is modelled upon *Chron. Cas.* ii. 43, pp. 247–9.

[96] See above, p. xli. After 1097 Urban supported Montecassino in disputes with Santa Maria, Capua, and Santa Sophia, Benevento: *Chron. Cas.* iv. 18, p. 487; *Ep.* 247, Migne, *PL* cli. 515–17; *IP* viii. 155–7, nos. *142–51. The only earlier evidence concerns Santa Maria, Benevento (1093, continued early in 1097): *Chron. Cas.* iv. 7, p. 471; Gattula, *Historia*, p. 54; *IP* viii. 153, nos. *137, *139.

[97] It therefore excludes Bruno of Segni, who, despite the Montecassino Chronicle, is not likely to have had contact with Montecassino before he became its abbot: *Chron. Cas.* iv. 31–42, pp. 496–511.

[98] Peter the Deacon, *DVI*, cap. 30, Migne, *PL* clxxiii. 1038–9. See Klewitz, *Reformpapsttum*, p. 119; Hüls, *Kardinäle*, pp. 105–6.

[99] See below, p. 217.

[100] Peter the Deacon, *DVI*, cap. 51, col. 1039; Paschal II, *Epp.* 18, 19, 263, 466, Migne, *PL* clxiii. 39–41, 247–8, 402–4. See Klewitz, p. 134; Hoffmann (as Introd. n. 18), pp. 201–5; Hüls, pp. 243–4.

antipope Clement III of the papal *cancellarius* Peter. From 1088 he was certainly in Urban II's entourage, and from some time after that year until his accession to the papacy in 1118 as Pope Gelasius II he was cardinal-deacon of Santa Maria in Cosmedin. As papal *cancellarius et bibliothecarius* from 1089 he left evidence of prodigious and continuous activity in the papal chancery, and under Paschal II he had care of the (lost) papal Registers. By introducing into the chancery the Leonine *cursus* he carried out a fundamental reform in papal documents. In 1116 his fidelity to traditional Gregorian principles compelled him to withdraw for a while to Montecassino.[101]

It was in the pontificate of Paschal II that Montecassino's contribution to the papal service probably reached its highest point. Its representation among the cardinals rose to six or seven: Leo was still bishop of Ostia, Amicus was priest of San Nereo e Sant'Achilleo, and another possible Cassinese was John of Sant'Eusebio; Rossemanus was deacon of San Giorgio in Velabro, Bernard of Sant'Angelo in Pescheria, Oderisius of Sant'Agatha, and John of San Vito e San Modesto.[102]

From the accession of Urban II Cassinese monks also began once more to be appointed to South Italian bishoprics. Examples from Urban's pontificate are Peter of Naples (1094–1116), Rainald of Gaeta (1098–?), Benedict and John in Sardinian sees, and Lando of Aquino. A twelfth-century example is Richard, who by 1121 became bishop of Gaeta.[103] Urban II and his successors thus once again drew upon Montecassino's resources in men and administrative skills to advance the purposes of the reform papacy, very much as the popes before Gregory VII had done.

An appraisal of Montecassino's contribution to the reform papacy must, therefore, recognize that the apostolic see made considerable use of Cassinese monks as recruits for the cardinalate

[101] March, *Liber pontificalis*, pp. 162–5; *Chron. Cas.* iv. 7, p. 471; *Annales Romani, LP* ii. 344; Peter the Deacon, *DVI*, cap. 45, col. 1046; Eadmer, *Historia novorum in Anglia*, ed. M. Rule (Rolls Series, London, 1884), p. 246. For his early life, see Lohrmann (as Ch. I n. 105) and id. (as Ch. I n. 54), pp. 87–94. See also Klewitz, p. 132; Santifaller, 'Saggio', pp. 208–14, 218, 436–73; and Hüls, pp. 231–2.

[102] Klewitz, pp. 103, 105, 119, 126–7, 132–4; Hüls, pp. 105–6, 165–7, 193–4, 221–3, 243–4.

[103] Peter of Naples, Ughelli–Coleti, vi. 92–4. Rainald of Gaeta: *Chron. Cas.* iv. 7–9, pp. 471–4; Ughelli–Coleti, i. 537. Benedict and John: *Chron. Cas.* iv. 7, p. 471; Peter the Deacon, *DVI*, cap. 47, col. 1104. Lando of Aquino: Ughelli–Coleti, i. 396. Richard of Gaeta: *Chron. Cas.* iv. 57, p. 521; Ughelli–Coleti, i. 538.

and for its administration. Both at Rome and in South Italian bishoprics it on the whole found them to be good servants. Nevertheless, apart from the career of John of Gaeta in the papal chancery, their services must be described as having been useful rather than decisive in their results. At a critical period under Gregory VII they became very attenuated. In large areas of papal affairs, for example in the sending of papal legates, Montecassino at all times lacked prominence. In terms of practical aid the great Burgundian monastery of Cluny contributed at least as much. At no point did Montecassino show such a commitment to papal ideals of liberty as was forced upon Cluny by its problems with the episcopate no less than by the aspirations of its monks. Nor, in spite of their permanent standing as cardinal-priests, did the abbots of Montecassino enjoy the long and close association with the popes that Abbot Hugh of Cluny enjoyed. Montecassino was a useful resource of the reform papacy upon which the popes could and did often draw, rather than a wholly obedient and like-minded ally.

iii. MONTECASSINO AND THE REFORM OF THE CHURCH

In turning to Montecassino's contribution to the reform of the church in the broader sense, it is necessary to bear in mind two considerations that make it easy to underestimate Montecassino's commitment to the ideals of the reform papacy, at least up to 1080. The first is that the two principal chronicles—Amatus and the Montecassino Chronicle—were written with plans and purposes that tended to leave reform on one side. Amatus wrote a history of the Normans: 'li fait de li Normant, liquel sont digne de notre memoire, ai je en .VIII. volume de livre distincte';[104] the papacy and ecclesiastical reform came into his purview seldom and incidentally. Thus, he wrote with approval of the Emperor Henry III's intervention at Rome in 1046 and he was wholeheartedly appreciative of Pope Leo IX's zeal against simony and of his reforming synods, noticing his miracles; here he reflected Desiderius' *Dialogues.*[105] But, despite the alliance of the papacy and the Normans at Melfi, Amatus made no similar observations concerning later popes, and he

[104] *Dedica*, p. 4.
[105] iii. 1, 15–16, 21, 42, pp. 116, 128–31, 134–5, 158–9.

offered no substantial judgement upon Gregory VII. No doubt his reticence reflected the cool relations between Gregory and the Normans during the years when he was writing, and also resulted from Gregory's friendship with Amatus' *bête noire* Prince Gisulf of Salerno. But it was no part of his plan to write about ecclesiastical matters in general. The Montecassino Chronicle was hardly more forthcoming. It was written within a framework of abbots' lives. Its object was to record Montecassino's monastic, material, and cultural *potentia*, and the events principally affecting it as a centre of monastic life. So like Amatus it is sparing in references to the papacy and to reform. Leo of Ostia echoed Desiderius' *Dialogues* when he wrote of the events of 1046–7 at Rome. But he dealt with Pope Leo IX almost exclusively in relation to Montecassino and not to the exercise of papal authority or to the reform of the church. He briefly praised Pope Stephen IX for his zeal against married clerks and against irregular marriages. He called Alexander II *reverentissimus et angelicus papa*, but in the context of the dedication ceremony of 1071.[106] So far as Gregory VII is concerned, the continuation of the Chronicle gave a brief and factual account of his election, and it recorded his measures against lay investiture in the context of his excommunication of Henry IV in 1076 and of the Lateran council of November 1078. But Gregory's pontificate was presented largely in relation to Cassinese affairs, and his reforming activity was not highlighted. At his death Gregory was *venerabilis et semper recolende memorie*, but no more specific or laudatory judgement occurs.[107] Since its chronicles treated Gregory in so muted a way it would be easy to conclude that Montecassino lacked sympathy with him and his objectives. Yet it will emerge in this chapter that in other writings Amatus and Leo of Ostia showed their concern for reform and especially for the struggle against simony. It is hazardous to assume that the two chronicles give a full and balanced presentation of their authors' or of the abbey's views; they must be complemented by other evidence.

Secondly, it is unfortunate in this connection that most of the literary products of Cassinese monks which bore on issues of *sacerdotum* and *regnum* have been lost. The loss has undoubtedly obscured the extent of the commitment to the

[106] ii. 77, 81, 94, iii. 29, pp. 320–9, 353, 398; cf. Leo of Ostia, *Narratio*, p. 221.
[107] iii. 36, 42, 49, 65, pp. 413, 420, 428, 446.

Gregorian cause of some, at least, of Montecassino's leading monks. Among such works are Amatus' *De laude Gregorii septimi*, Alberic's *Contra Heinricum imperatorem de electione Romani pontificis*, Pandulf of Capua's *De Agnete imperatrice*, and Guido's *Historia Heinrici imperatoris.*[108] Outside the chronicles there is, however, much that points to a considerable commitment to reform amongst Cassinese monks, if upon Montecassino's own terms and sometimes in a less than fully Gregorian way.

The following lines of inquiry into this literature appear to be the most fruitful and significant in seeking to assess the abbey's reforming outlook, commitment, and effectiveness.

a. Renovatio

Perhaps the key theme in Cassinese culture and literature so far as the reform of the church is concerned is that of a *renovatio* in the present age of the institutions and standards of the ancient Roman world.[109] In the eleventh century, *renovatio* was a widely canvassed idea with a long pedigree in Christian writers. The underlying thought was that of return, rather than of innovation. It was necessary to recover with renewed vitality what was excellent in an ideal past age, so that contemporary institutions that had lost their pristine vigour might be enabled again to fulfil their true purposes. The past age that men had in mind was above all that of pious emperors, of whom Constantine was the first and foremost. In this connection the eleventh-century view of Constantine and his legacy to the church was the reverse of that implied by Dante's outburst:

> Ahi! Constantin, di quanto mal fu matre,
> non la tua conversion, ma quella dote
> che da te prese il primo ricco patre![110]

Rather, it was Constantine who at length freed the church from the persecutions to which the pagan emperors had subjected it, because they were under the sway of Antichrist. In this sense, Constantine was the emperor who created the archetype of the *libertas ecclesiae* for which eleventh-century reformers strove.

[108] See above, pp. xviii, 24–6, but for Alberic also below, Appendix III.

[109] On *renovatio*, see esp. Schramm (as Ch. II n. 5), pp. 238–50; Kitzinger (as Introd. n. 34); Toubert (as Introd. n. 4).

[110] *Inferno*, xix. 115–17.

Constantine's conversion ushered in a golden age in which the church entered into the inheritance of ancient Rome and its universal empire. His removal of earthly sway to Constantinople and his donation of old Rome to the pope with an ample endowment enabled papal Rome to discharge its divine commission in perfect liberty under the rule of St. Peter and his vicar. The idea of *renovatio* also looked back with fervour to the great popes of the Christian west, especially those from Leo I to Gregory I; by their deeds and in their writings they had followed up the opportunity that Constantine created by appropriating for the Christian church everything in the ancient Roman order that was of permanent dignity and value. Papal Rome was thus the antithesis of ancient Rome in so far as it had been pagan and persecuting, but also its analogue and continuation in so far as it was a source of authority and order in the world.[111] Many eleventh-century figures could, therefore, find direct inspiration in the institutions of eternal Rome, both pre-Christian and Christian. Thus, Peter Damiani saw in the cardinals a *renovatio* of the senate. When true to itself Christian like pagan Rome was an exemplar of *iustitia* (righteousness), and in its decline ancient Rome paid the penalty of having abandoned it:

> Quod Roma mundo praefuit, donec legibus oboedivit.
> Praefuit urbs orbi, fuerat dum subdita legi;
> Iustitiae spretis regnum contraxit habenis.[112]

It was a lesson that Peter Damiani wished the eleventh-century church to take to heart.

At Montecassino the *renovatio* of ancient Roman institutions found visual expression in Desiderius' new church. Alfanus' Latin inscription which Desiderius set up over the central apse echoed the corresponding inscription in Constantine's Roman basilica of St. Peter.[113] Leo of Ostia wrote that, when sending to Constantinople for artisans to make his mosaics, Desiderius' concern was to revive the skills of the ancient Latin past:

[111] Apart from the *Constitutum Constantini* (as Introd. n. 59), sources for this view include Isidore of Seville, *Etymologiarum sive originum libri xx*, ed. W. M. Lindsay, 2 vols. (Oxford, 1911), 6. 16. 2-6; *Decretales Pseudo-Isidorianae et capitula Angilramni*, ed. P. Hinschius (Leipzig, 1863), 247-8; and the excerpt from the lost *De unitate fidei* of St. Boniface in Deusdedit, *Coll. can.* i. 327 (251), iv. 1, pp. 189-92, 397-401.

[112] M. Lokrantz, *L'opera poetica di s. Pier Damiani* (Stockholm, 1965), p. 69, no. 88.

[113] See above, Ch. I n. 73.

'Because the instructors of the Latin world (*magistra Latinitas*) had for five hundred years and more lost the practice of such arts, Desiderius in our day succeeded by his zeal in recovering them.'[114] St. Benedict's basilica was thus brought into relationship with Constantinian and later-antique Rome, and was a visual example of the *renovatio* of its life.

Montecassino's writers exploited the idea of *renovatio* by directing attention more widely towards Rome, both ancient and papal. When Alfanus composed an ode in praise of Abbot Desiderius' new basilica he applauded it as first of all a house of God: 'aula Dei, mons Sion altera, dux fidei'; yet it also pointed those who came to it as pilgrims to their goal at papal Rome:

Rebus in omnibus haec locuples
Indigenis, sed et hospitibus
Est locupletior; hinc etenim
Est iter urbis apostolicae,
Totius orbis adhuc dominae.

Rome was *caput mundi*. Therefore for Alberic the apostles were the twelve senators of the primitive church, and for Alfanus St. Peter could be addressed as the consul and Caesar to whom the Roman senate was obedient and whom the whole world served:

Iam cape Romanum consul Caesarque senatum;
Ecce tibi cunctus servit sub sidere mundus.[115]

In similar vein Amatus opened the fourth book of his *Liber in honore beati Petri apostoli* with a eulogy of ancient Rome in which, far from condemning it as pagan or oppressive, he celebrated it for its victories and for the law that it gave to the world:

Orbis honor, Roma, splendens decorata corona
Victorum regum, discretio maxima legum,
His simul et multis aliis redimita triumphis,
O victrix, salve, cuius super aethera palmae
Pulchrae scribuntur, et quam colit undique mundus.

According to Amatus poetic invention could not sufficiently sing Rome's praises; he went on to review at length the Latin

[114] *Chron. Cas.* iii. 27, p. 396.

[115] Lentini and Avagliano, *Carmi*, nos. 12, line 61, 32, lines 66–7, 85–9, 37, lines 25–6; Alberic, *De s. Aspren Neapolitano episcopo*, caps. 10, 33 (as Ch. I n. 98), pp. 101, 103. See Acocella (as Ch. I n. 99), pp. 287–319; also Lentini, 'Il carme di Alfano su S. Pietro', *Benedictina*, xiv (1967), 27–37.

authors of classical Rome, and also the men who had gone forth from it to subdue the world by arms and by laws:

Ex te qui cunctum meruerunt subdere mundum,
Et processerunt ex te qui iura dederunt.

But if the praises of ancient Rome were so great, those of Christian Rome were greater; the fisherman wielded a power more glorious than the emperors'. The emperors of old had seized tribute from the world; but now the peoples spontaneously brought in their gifts. Old Rome had often put its enemies to flight by stratagems and by the sword, but Christian Rome resisted the proud by the strength of words alone. The fisherman's empire was established upon earth, and it held the keys of heaven as well. Thus, Amatus placed emphasis upon St. Peter and Christ's promises to him; and when Peter was martyred at Rome he depicted him as leaving behind the assurance that he would be the patron of Christians for all time:

'Vivere me noscas, caelorum claudere portas
Nunc', ait, 'iniustis, et easdem pandere iustis.
Fratribus ista meis, o testis, pande, fidelis;
Semper namque probus vobis persisto patronus.'[116]

Leo of Ostia similarly proclaimed how, as prince of the apostles, St. Peter left a legacy to his vicars in the apostolic see by committing to his successor Clement 'omnes traditiones ecclesiasticas eiusque ordinis disciplinam seu doctrine regulas, utpote pre ceteris familiari ac sedulo auditori'.[117]

It was also by the imagery of *renovatio* that Cassinese writers praised Gregory VII, both as Archdeacon Hildebrand and as pope. The result was that they fitted him very much into their own mould, and into categories which were largely settled before he became pope and which had little in common with his presentation of himself in his letters.[118] When Alfanus wrote his ode to Hildebrand at an unknown date before 1073, he extolled his fame in imagery drawn from ancient Rome and its rule of

[116] (As Ch. I n. 111), iv. 1, lines 1–21, 24–40, iv. 22, lines 4–7, pp. 120–2, 141.

[117] Orlandi, *Excerpta* (as Ch. I n. 113), pp. 1–2.

[118] Although Gregory shared the view of Constantine that has been outlined: *Reg.* ii. 45, ix. 37, pp. 183, 631; *Epp. vag.* pp. 132–4, no. 54. For Gregory's presentation of himself, see esp. E. Caspar, 'Gregor VII. in seinen Briefen', *Historische Zeitschrift*, cxxx (1924), 1–30.

the nations. Hildebrand stood out in respect of his merits, and especially as a source of legal probity:

Omne iudicio tuo
  Ius favet . . .

Cordis eximius vigor,
  Vita nobilis, optimas
  Res sequuta, probant quidem
  Iuris ingenium, modo
  Cuius artibus uteris.

He worked in a Rome now rendered more illustrious than of old by the universal authority of Peter:

Est quibus caput urbium
  Roma iustior, et prope
  Totus orbis, eas timet
  Saeva barbaries adhuc
  Clara stemmate regio.

His et archiapostoli
  Fervido gladio Petri
  Frange robur et impetus
  Illius, vetus ut iugum
  Usque sentiat ultimum.

And so his power exceeded that of Marius and Julius Caesar: what they achieved only after wholesale slaughter, Hildebrand accomplished by his lightest word. What did Rome owe to the Scipios and the rest of the Quirites more than to Hildebrand,

Cuius est studiis suae
Nacta iura potentiae?

The ode ends with a striking eulogy:

Te quidem potioribus
  Praeditum meritis, manet
  Gloriosa perenniter
  Vita, civibus ut tuis
  Compareris apostolis.[119]

Some ten years later Amatus dedicated to Gregory his *Liber in honore sancti Petri apostoli*. He several times referred to him

[119] *Carmi*, no. 22.

in terms which reinforced his claims and policies, but always within the framework of Cassinese ideas.[120] When commenting on Christ's commission to Peter (Matt. 16: 13-19) he reflected that Gregory now held the power of the keys:

> Pastor pastori dederat quam, papa Gregori,
> Ipse potestatem gratis, tibi cessit eandem,
> Qua caelum claudis, aperis, qua vincula solvis.

Citing Luke 22: 31-2, where Christ prayed for Peter that his faith should not fail and that he should stablish his brethren, Amatus rejoiced that these words now referred to Gregory. It is possible that Amatus referred to Henry IV's submission to Gregory at Canossa in January 1077 when he spoke of 'kings who now prostrate themselves at your feet':

> Gloria sit Christo, qui talia dona magistro
> Attribuit vestro, per quem iam tramite recto
> Christicolae pergunt, et nunc vestigia sternunt
> Ad tua se reges; quas tu disponere leges
> Mavis, observant; per te sua regna gubernant.
> Hoc praeceptoris tibi ius dat, papa Gregori.

But there may be no more here than a metaphor drawn independently from such Old Testament passages as Isaiah 60: 14–16 and Proverbs 8: 15-16. When Amatus commented upon the story of Simon Magus in Acts 8: 9–23 he again addressed Gregory, stressing the identity of his work with Peter's and calling for its resolute continuance:

> Pellitur ecce foras, pro qua, pie papa, laboras,
> Symonis haec pestis; fuerat quae sordida messis,
> Iam purgata Dei defertur in horrea veri.
> Alme, manu forti gladium quo sternitur hostis
> Gestas mercator, tanti vel honoris amator.
> Ecclesia Christi laudaris in omnibus istis
> Quae, benedicte, facis, quia sunt haec dogmata pacis.[121]

Even in the 1070s, then, when political relations between Montecassino and the papacy were for some time cool, Amatus'

[120] A. Lentini, 'Gregorio VII nel *De gestis apostolorum* di Amato Cassinese', *SG* v (1956), 281–9.

[121] i. 6, lines 20–2, i. 18, lines 7–12, ii. 7, lines 9–14, pp. 65, 72–3, 84.

zeal for a *renovatio* of the past led him to plead Gregory's cause in the fight against simony.

It may be the case that, partly through such propaganda on Gregory's behalf, idiosyncratic although much of it was, Montecassino's commitment to his cause deepened and developed over the years. This is suggested by a legend which is recorded in the Chronicle. In 1087 some pilgrims to the abbey met by the way a figure who disclosed himself to be St. Peter. Asked whither he was going, he replied, 'I am going to my brother Benedict, to keep the anniversary of my death with him. For I can find no rest at Rome from the storms which are shaking my church.' The monks of Montecassino determined thereafter always to keep the feast of St. Peter with the solemnity that they by custom accorded to St. Benedict himself. The inference would seem to be that Montecassino always had an underlying bond with Rome, so that Benedict was described as Peter's brother. But it was only after the end of Gregory's reign that Montecassino felt itself so deeply committed to Peter that he was venerated in the abbey's liturgy as solemnly as was Benedict.[122]

However this may be, the idea of a *renovatio* of ancient standards of Christian life seems to have been a basis upon which Cassinese writers such as Alfanus and Amatus venerated Rome. They were thereby drawn to applaud the reforming work of the popes and not least of Gregory VII, in whom they saw the renewers of the authentic Christian past.

b. *The evidence of Abbot Desiderius'* Dialogues

Abbot Desiderius wrote his *Dialogues* between 1076 and 1079, and so before the common and testing experiences of Rome and Montecassino in face of the Guibertine Schism, and before Henry IV's Italian expeditions of 1081-4, which led to Gregory's exile. They show how Desiderius himself regarded the papacy and reform at an earlier period, when he was at the height of his power as abbot in the buildings that he had completed, and when he was gradually returning to Gregory VII's favour and counsels after a period of coolness.[123]

[122] *Chron. Cas.* iii. 69, pp. 451-2. For the liturgical offices of St. Peter at Montecassino, see F. Avagliano, 'Testi cassinesi per l'officio liturgico dei SS Pietro e Paolo', 'Monumenti del culto a San Pietro in Montecassino', and 'Altri testi della liturgia cassinese per i SS Pietro e Paolo', *Benedictina*, xiv (1967), 57-76, 161-202, xv (1968), 19-43.

[123] See below, pp. 131-6.

The third book, in particular, demonstrates his attachment to the reform papacy as the Emperor Henry III had instituted it in 1046. His strictures upon the unregenerate Rome of Pope Benedict IX were severe. He showed how, by reason of priestly negligence and especially of the failings of the Roman popes before 1046, mid-eleventh-century Italy had fallen further and further from the paths of religion into all manner of evil customs. Setting aside God's law and confusing things divine with things human, laity and clergy alike had wellnigh universally fallen victim to the sin of simony. The laity trafficked in ecclesiastical elections, as did the clergy in their powers of consecration and in the gift of the Holy Spirit. Clerical unchastity made confusion worse-confounded. Finding entry amongst the most inferior clerical levels, the custom of marriage and with it the hereditability of clerical office and goods had crept upwards through deacons and priests until some even of the bishops were also married. This evil state of affairs was particularly rife at Rome, the city which under St. Peter and his successors had once upon a time been the source from which true religion had spread. The consequence was that the popes had ceased to be popes in anything but name.

The culmination of this sad process was the conduct of Pope Benedict IX himself. When he assumed the papacy in 1032 he did so in the steps of Simon Magus rather than of Simon Peter. He polluted his office with every kind of wickedness, until in the winter of 1044–5 the Roman people expelled him in favour of Bishop John of Sabina (Pope Sylvester III). But he, too, was a simoniac whom, after a mere three months, Benedict IX violently expelled. After his restoration Benedict returned to his evil ways. He became intolerably scandalous in the eyes of the Romans; the upshot was that, 'being so given over to pleasures that he preferred to live as Epicurus rather than as pope', he simoniacally disposed of the papal office to John Gratian (Pope Gregory VI). Desiderius related with approval the sequel—the intervention at Rome in 1046 of the Emperor Henry III. But he was careful so to present it that, on the one hand, he safeguarded the electoral rights of the Roman church and, on the other, he exhibited the beneficence of imperial protection. His story ran that, when coming to Rome for the purpose of his imperial coronation, Henry summoned at Sutri a synod of many bishops, abbots, clerks, and monks. He called upon Gregory VI to attend so that church affairs might be discussed under papal presidency; especial thought would be given to the papacy, which now seemed to have three popes at once (Benedict IX, Sylvester III, and Gregory VI). But Henry had already decided with the synod's sanction to expel all three of them, and to have a new and conscientious pope elected by clergy and people. When the synod assembled Gregory accepted the situation and abdicated; thereupon the Romans elected Pope Clement II (1046–7) and, after his early death, Pope Damasus II (1047–8).[124] In thus presenting matters, Desiderius clearly had an eye to opinion at Montecassino during the 1070s.[125] His picture was that of the path to a papally led reform of the church being opened up by an emperor who had due respect for its freedom from improper lay control: the election of the pope should be in Roman hands, but in case of necessity the German emperor should exercise a wise and restrained protection over the apostolic see in order to expel wicked men and to facilitate the canonical election of reforming popes.

For Desiderius, Henry's intervention was critical because it led to the pontificate of Leo IX, in which he saw the true beginning of better things. In political terms this is somewhat surprising. For Leo inaugurated a policy of militant hostility to the Normans; after 1058 and thanks to Desiderius the Normans were Montecassino's staunchest supporters, while Leo ended his pontificate with a severe defeat at Norman hands at Civitate (1053). Yet for Desiderius, writing two decades later, Leo deserved unstinted praise and veneration. His zeal for reform and for religion had consigned his political misfortune to oblivion. Desiderius declared himself proud to have known him at first hand and to have stood by him at the altar. His was a new age:

> . . . a man in every way apostolic, born of royal stock, endowed with wisdom, pre-eminent for religion, outstandingly learned in all Christian doctrine, it was he who (in the words of scripture) 'began to call on the name of the Lord'.[126] . . . By him all ecclesiastical affairs were renewed and restored, and a new light was seen to arise in the world.

[124] iii, prol., pp. 1141–3.

[125] See above, p. 67. Thirty years after, in later recensions of his Chronicle, Leo of Ostia wrote more critically of Clement's having succeeded 'electione necessaria potius quam canonica', thus suggesting a hardening by *c*.1100 of Cassinese opinion against imperial intervention: *Chron. Cas.* ii. 77, p. 322.

[126] Gen. 4: 26, referring to the time when men began the true worship of God.

Desiderius applauded his frequent summoning of reforming councils, his replacing of evil clergy by virtuous ones, and his 'daily' sending of disciples into all the world to teach people by writing and by preaching the way of the Lord. Desiderius saw it as no wonder that a pope who always walked in the apostolic way should have further imitated apostolic men by working miracles. Leo's miracles are a feature of Desiderius' third book; and Desiderius insisted that throughout his five years in the papal office Leo exercised his priesthood with godliness and religion (*pie et religiose*).[127]

In the surviving books of the *Dialogues*, the popes who followed Leo were by contrast mentioned incidentally and without emphasis. Victor II and Alexander II appear only in passing, the former in order to underline the sanctity of Leo IX.[128] As for Gregory VII, Desiderius wrote in the 1070s after his own relations with the pope had for some years been cool and ambiguous, and he kept a prudent reserve. He could rise to tones of approval: Gregory currently occupied the highest office in the church, bringing light to it by word and by example (*nunc autem in Romana urbe culmen apostolicum tenens, ecclesiam verbis simul et exemplis illustrat*); and it was from Gregory that Desiderius had learnt some of his anecdotes about Leo IX.[129] But there is nothing in the *Dialogues* to suggest that pope and abbot had been in contact since 1073. All the stories either from or concerning Gregory that Desiderius told related to his years as archdeacon; Gregory as pope occupied no special place in Desiderius' *Dialogues*.

All in all, although Desiderius' reforming purpose is clear, he appealed above all to the early days of papal revival under Leo IX. The principal objects of Desiderius' zeal were clerical unchastity and, still more strongly, simony.[130] His zeal was genuine, but he was reticent about more recent developments and about the person and programme of Gregory VII himself. Desiderius wrote nothing to cast doubt upon his loyalty to

[127] iii, prol., pp. 1143–6; the citation is from p. 1145.

[128] Victor was said to have shown an initial disbelief in Leo's miracles that a later miracle served to dispel.

[129] iii. 1, 2, 5, pp. 1143, 1144, 1148.

[130] For anecdotes about simony, see iii. 2, p. 1144; iii. 4, pp. 1146–7 (Cardinal-bishop Peter of Albano's ordeal by fire at Florence in 1068); iii. 5, pp. 1148–9 (the Hildebrandine anecdote of the simoniacal French bishop who could not pronounce the name of the Holy Spirit when reciting the *Gloria Patri*). In his first two books, which are concerned with Montecassino, Desiderius made no reference to simony.

Leo IX's successors, but he also said little which clearly and positively registers it. Desiderius' attitudes in his *Dialogues* were shared by those of his monks and associates whose writings were concerned with these subjects, although in treating them they tended to show more warmth in their allusions to Gregory VII. They thereby suggest that Desiderius' reticence must be ascribed to the coolness that currently existed between himself and Gregory.

c. *Simony*

The surviving evidence leaves no doubt that in general Cassinese feeling against simony was intense, or that the monks' propaganda matched Desiderius' strictures. The principal source is Amatus' too-seldom-noticed poem, the *Liber in honore beati Petri apostoli*, written at Montecassino *c.*1077–9, and so at the time when Amatus was completing his *Historia Normannorum*. The poem is dedicated to Pope Gregory VII, although most of the dedicatory epistle is lost.[131] It was in four books, the first two of which dealt with St. Peter in the Gospels and in the Acts of the Apostles; in the second book Amatus included the story of Peter's encounter with Simon Magus at Samaria (Acts 8: 9–24).[132] In Book iii, Amatus covered Peter's ministry in Palestine, Syria, and Asia Minor, making direct or indirect use of a multiplicity of legendary sources. Much of his material is ultimately derived from the Pseudo-Clementine Recognitions, which were part of a body of legends originating in Syria during the early third century.[133] The Recognitions, which Rufinus (d. 410) translated into Latin, concerned Clement, a young Roman who accompanied Peter during his missionary preaching and who, in legend, was sometimes represented as his immediate successor

[131] See above, p. 26. References are to Lentini's edition.

[132] ii. 7, pp. 83–4.

[133] For the Recognitions, see *Die Pseudoklementinen*, ii, *Rekognitionen in Rufins Übersetzung*, ed. B. Rehm, Die griechischen christlichen Schriftsteller der ersten Jahrhunderte, 51 (Berlin, 1965). They are described by Rehm in 'Zur Entstehung der pseudoclementinischen Schriften', *Zeitschrift für neutestamentliche Wissenschaft*, xxxvii (1938), 77–184, and 'Clemens Romanus II (Ps. Clementinen)', *Reallexikon für Antike und Christentum*, iii (1957), 197–206. Rehm establishes the wide diffusion of the Recognitions in time and locality throughout the Middle Ages: esp. *Die Pseudoklementinen*, pp. xvii–cii. For the development in hymns of the Simon Magus theme, see J. Szövérffy, 'The Legends of St. Peter in Medieval Latin Hymns', *Traditio*, x (1954), 275–322, esp. 294–311, 319–22, and 'Der Investiturstreit und die Petrus-Hymnen des Mittelalters', *DA* xiii (1957), 228–40, esp. 235–8. Szövérffy notices the rapid growth of legends during the eleventh century.

as bishop of Rome. They said much about Peter's dealings in Palestine and Syria. A particular theme was his long-running conflict with the heresiarch Simon Magus: the incidental figure in the Acts of the Apostles became the father of all heretics who dogged Peter's footsteps at every stage of his apostolic labours. Amatus knew and used a *Vita sancti Clementi*, written in the late ninth century by John Hymmonides and Gauderic of Velletri,[134] which derived from the Recognitions an orderly presentation of Clement's life in hagiographical form. Amatus borrowed much of the material from this *Vita* about Simon Magus, representing him as the would-be subverter of all the peoples of the world; when Peter became bishop of Antioch Simon Magus bitterly but vainly opposed him.[135]

The encounter at Antioch foreshadowed a direr contest at Rome, which forms the subject of Amatus' fourth book. He incorporated in it material from many sources, including Pseudo-Marcellus, *Passio sanctorum apostolorum Petri et Pauli*, and Pseudo-Linus, *Martyrium beati Petri apostoli.*[136] He related how the Roman emperor, senate, and people were all deluded by Simon Magus' diabolical machinations and magical dealings, until they dedicated a statue to him. Simon in due course attempted to counterfeit his own resurrection from the dead after three days. There followed a long duel between Peter and Simon before Nero and the Roman people, in which Peter demonstrated his power to tame the hell-hounds that his adversary conjured up against him, and to raise from the dead a man whom Simon had failed to revive. Finally Simon's attempt to fly to heaven by angels' support from a tower which Nero built to his order brought about his humiliating death. It was this débâcle which prompted Nero to destroy Peter and Paul, whose martyrdoms Amatus narrated.[137]

Apart from Cardinal Humbert's *Adversus simoniacos,*[138] no eleventh-century source discloses so graphically as Amatus'

[134] See above, Ch. I n. 113. The *Vita sancti Clementi* survives in the early eleventh-century MS, Montecassino, Archivio capitolare, 234; for a description, see Inguanez, *Catalogus*, ii. 45.

[135] iii. 6, 27–31, pp. 100, 113–16. The former section is entitled *Ubi Symon anhelabat subvertere gentes.*

[136] For Pseudo-Marcellus (BHL 6657), see R. A. Lipsius, *Acta apostolorum apocrypha*, i (Leipzig, 1891), 119–77; for Pseudo-Linus (BHL 6655), ibid. 1–22.

[137] iv. 10–16, 23, pp. 130–5, 142.

[138] Ed. F. Thaner, *MGH Libelli*, i. 95–253. For the limited contemporary importance of Humbert's work, see Schieffer (as Introd. n. 89), pp. 41–4.

poem the contemporary detestation of the 'heresy' of simony; and Amatus probably offers a more characteristic picture than Humbert's of contemporary reasons for detesting it. Simony, as he depicts it, was no mere everyday traffic in orders and offices. It was the legacy of the father of all heretics who was, in his lifetime, the lethal opponent of St. Peter and St. Paul, the princes of the apostles. He was the cause of their martyrdom at Nero's hands. But he was no mere figure of the dead past. Just as St. Peter was vigilant and active after his death on behalf of all faithful Christians, so in every generation Simon Magus was raging about as their deadly enemy. If the pope was Peter's vicar, so all simoniacs were agents of the heresiarch, magician, and persecutor unto death, Simon Magus. As Nero had followed the bidding of Simon Magus in martyring Peter and Paul, so latter-day lay rulers who practised simony—emperors above all—were the persecutors of Christians now. Whoever joined the battle against simony was, as in duty bound, fighting the good fight which Peter himself had fought; he fought the same enemy backed by a like imperial power, and he strove for the same martyr's crown and reward. Amatus' poem powerfully communicates the urgency and immediacy of the struggle between truth and falsehood, God and the devil, which was being fought out in the eleventh-century world between reformers and simoniacs.

Such was Amatus' message in a poem that he dedicated to Gregory VII. It was in a very different key from his *Historia Normannorum*; although in the History his account of Leo IX briefly alluded to Simon Magus in a similar spirit.[139] Other Cassinese literature echoed Amatus' detestation of simony and the themes of his polemic against it. In the Chronicle, part of the account of Abbot Desiderius as Pope Victor III interpreted his struggle with the antipope Clement III in terms of a life-and-death confrontation with the heresiarch Simon Magus.[140] Again, in his ode *De sancto Petro apostolo* Alfanus of Salerno referred after the manner of Amatus to his subject's dealings at Rome with Simon Magus; he introduced the stories of Simon Magus' failure to raise the dead, of his death when trying to fly to heaven, and of Nero's putting Peter to martyrdom in consequence.[141]

[139] See above, p. 71. In his *Dial.*, Desiderius when writing of Leo did not refer to Simon Magus.

[140] *Chron. Cas.* iii. 70, pp. 452–3; see below, Appendix VIII.

[141] Lentini and Avagliano, *Carmi*, no. 37.

Further references to Simon Magus occur in the literature about St. Clement which Leo of Ostia wrote following his removal to Rome in the early years of the twelfth century. As well as being cardinal-bishop of Ostia Leo was bishop of Velletri, the see of the Bishop Gauderic who had commissioned and in part written the *Vita sancti Clementi* which Amatus had used. Dedicated to Pope John VIII, it had been written between 876 and 882, and so only a few years after St. Cyril had in 867 or 868 brought Clement's remains from Cherson in the Crimea and placed them in the Roman basilica that bore his name.[142] Leo composed a trilogy on Clement: the *De origine beati Clementi*, based on John and Gauderic's *Vita*; the *De ordinatione seu cathedra sancti Clementi*, which is almost entirely lost; and the *Translatio corporis sancti Clementi.*[143] In his preface to the first of these works Leo said that he wrote for public reading and popular edification on the vigil of Clement's feast-day.[144]

As a work written for popular instruction by a leading Cassinese writer, the *De origine beati Clementi*, in particular, is of interest. Leo wrote to tell a story, and so he both abbreviated his source and reduced the weight of doctrinal discussion. His story was that Clement's father, Faustinianus, was a Roman and a member of the emperor's family, while his mother, Mathidia, was a noble Roman lady. They had twin sons Faustinus and Faustus, and then Clement. Mathidia became the innocent object of lustful advances by her husband's brother Germanus. Wishing to avoid sowing discord between the brothers she pretended to have had a dream in which she was charged to take the twins overseas in order to forestall their violent deaths. With her husband's leave she sailed for Athens, leaving the five-year-old Clement at home with him. The mother and sons suffered shipwreck and were parted: Mathidia became a beggar on the isle of Aradus, while the twins ended up at Caesarea in Palestine. They were deceived into becoming disciples of Simon Magus. Receiving no news of his family and convinced by Germanus of

[142] For the *Vita*, see Orlandi (as Ch. I n. 113). For discussion, Meyvaert and Devos (as Ch. I n. 113); A. Lentini, 'Leone Ostiense e Gauderico', *Benedictina*, xi (1957), 131–46.

[143] The three works are printed as follows: (i) in Orlandi, op. cit.; (ii) a fragment is edited in Meyvaert and Devos, *Anal. Boll.* lxxiv (1956), 225–6; (iii) ibid. lxxiii (1955), 412–13, 455–61.

[144] Ed. Orlandi, p. 3; he also wrote the *De translatione* 'in notitiam universorum fidelium': *Anal. Boll.* lxxiii (1955), 413.

Mathidia's unchastity, Faustinianus went in search of his twin sons, leaving Clement at Rome. He too was reduced to penury and exile. Clement grew up at Rome in exemplary chastity and learnt Christianity from St. Barnabas; when he was in his thirties he travelled with Barnabas to Judaea. At Caesarea he attached himself to Peter. He was in consequence present at a confrontation of Peter with Simon Magus in which his twin brothers, now converts to Christianity, arraigned Simon Magus. Peter, the twins, and Clement afterwards left for Tripoli, where Clement was baptized. He then travelled with Peter towards Laodicea and Antioch. They landed on Aradus, where Peter encountered and identified Mathidia, and reunited her with her youngest son Clement. The twins had gone ahead to Laodicea; there, they too shed their Greek disguise and were restored to their mother, whom Peter baptized. Peter and the three sons, now themselves known to each other, thereafter met a very old man with whom they disputed about the nature and efficacy of prayer. Clement recognized him as his father Faustinianus. Peter convinced him of his wife's faithfulness, and so the whole family was restored. The story ends at Antioch, with the twins inspiring the citizens to do penance for their adherence to Simon Magus and with Peter baptizing Faustinianus.

Simon Magus came into this story incidentally;[145] but the tone and tenor of Leo's references are of a piece with Amatus' poem and with Desiderius' *Dialogues* in their detestation of simony. Cassinese writers drew deeply and with one mind on the fund of legend about St. Peter and his circle to point to its lethal nature, whether in the early days of the church or in the world of the eleventh and early twelfth centuries; and they looked to the popes for leadership in the church's struggle against it.

d. *Chastity*

If simony was incidental to Leo's story in the *De origine beati Clementi*, Desiderius' other concern in the *Dialogues*, with chastity, was near its heart and centre. Both Mathidia and her son Clement were exemplars of *inviolabilis pudicitia*; when the two were reunited Leo stated the moral of his story: it was 'quomodo innocentie ac pudicitie bonum numquam pereat apud Deum'.[146] In the work as a whole, the emphasis was on

[145] caps. 7, 21–7, 54, 86.

[146] cap. 55, ed. Orlandi, p. 96.

how Mathidia's virtue eventually found its reward in a reunited, Christian family. As an example of reformist propaganda it illustrates the association that was established between simony and unchastity as evils to be overcome. Further, its concern for chastity included lay and clerical orders of society alike: Leo's exemplars were the married laywoman Mathidia and the celibate Clement, who in Leo's view was Peter's immediate successor as bishop of Rome. Leo's advocacy of chastity was made in the context of the family, whose integrity was becoming increasingly important in social and economic life. It was the unscrupulous lust of his brother Germanus that broke up Faustinianus' family and led to twenty years of suffering; but Mathidia's chastity made possible its restoration and conversion to Christianity. Leo also referred to the subject of chastity in his *Vita sancti Mennatis*, where he insisted upon the duty of rulers to respect religious vows of chastity.[147]

Amatus, whose poem was primarily directed against simony, also insisted upon the virtue of chastity. Along with the destruction of idols the preaching of chastity was a prime concern of St. Peter at Rome.[148] With St. Paul, he won over many Roman women to zeal for it, so that they dissolved their marriages in order to live chastely. Nero's own wife was among their number. Their husbands' resentment of the conversion of Roman women compounded the activity of Simon Magus in generating hostility to Peter and his mission.[149] Alfanus' poems, which were often intended to provide public edification, likewise encouraged chastity. This was especially so in his praise of saints like Christina and Agnes, as also in his metrical exhortation to the clergy, *Sermo ad clerum in laudem Vincentii martyris*, where chastity has its place in the whole armour of God with which the Christian warfare is fought.[150]

Desiderius' zeal against simony and unchastity was thus reflected in and developed by other Cassinese writers, and was a major theme of their propaganda.

e. *Martyrdom and the eremitical life*

Another theme of the Petrine and Clementine legends upon which Amatus drew was that of martyrdom, or of fearless

[147] caps. 4–5, pp. 486–8. [148] iv. 3, p. 123.
[149] iv. 10, lines 1–15, pp. 129–30.
[150] Lentini and Avagliano, *Carmi*, nos. 35–6, 48–51.

witness before men even to death. Martyrdom was the culminating act of a Christian's witness which united him with Christ's own death and resurrection. It was the supreme earthly eventuality towards which a Christian might aspire; if he did not himself suffer it, at least he should endeavour to live a life which reflected its demand of total devotion. Amatus accordingly concluded the fourth book of his poem with an account of the martyrdom of St. Peter and St. Paul; St. Peter gave a long address proclaiming the cross as a sign of victory.[151] Leo of Ostia took up the theme of martyrdom in his *Vita sancti Mennatis*. He knew nothing of the saint's end and he refrained from inventing a martyrdom for him. Instead, he explained to his hearers that, laudable though martyrdom was, it was also meritorious sacrificially to dedicate the whole of one's life to Christ.[152] In many of Alfanus' poems praising particular saints, he too enlarged upon the glories of martyrdom, for example in the cases of Christina, Margaret, Ursula, Catharine, Lucy, and Agnes; he applauded those who had stood firm in their faith before kings and public magistrates through all the torments that they imposed.[153]

Cassinese literature also made much of the eremitical life as a standard to which Christians should aspire and as a model of the monastic life.[154] Leo of Ostia gave it extended expression in his *Vita sancti Mennatis*, which presented a popular picture of a hermit who, although not rewarded with the martyr's crown, nevertheless lived a life of devotion rooted in prayer and vigil. Mennas was a John the Baptist to all who came to him, moving the wicked to repent. He gradually won fame as a source of spiritual and material benefit to a wide region round about him. In the Montecassino Chronicle Desiderius as a young man embarked upon the eremitical life before entering Montecassino, until his health broke down under its rigours.[155] As the form of the religious life which presented its demands at their fullest intensity and as a means of raising the standard and reputation of the Christian life among the population at large, eremitism was prominent among the concerns of Montecassino and its publicists. Its qualities also had a political bearing. During the

[151] iv. 16–24, pp. 135–43.

[152] Ed. Orlandi, cap. 6, pp. 489–90.

[153] *Carmi*, nos. 1–4, 34–6, 40–4, 46, 48–50.

[154] See above, pp. 32–3.

[155] Ibid. So, too, the future Abbot Oderisius I was observed by Abbot Richer 'contemplativam vitam inianter appetere': *Chron. Cas.* iv. 1, pp. 466–7.

struggle between *sacerdotium* and *regnum* which began in earnest during the 1080s, propaganda concerning martyrdom and the rigours of the eremitical life helped to encourage those who were loyal to the Gregorian papacy by holding up the examples of those who had witnessed to the faith under the pagan emperors of pre-Constantinian times. Such a witness was called for in their own day. It seems to have been an ingredient in the attitude of Abbot Desiderius to Henry IV of Germany during their confrontation at Albano in 1082 as the Montecassino Chronicle presented it.[156] In general terms it served to direct the eyes of Cassinese monks beyond the horizons of their monastery. Like the struggle against simony and unchastity, the ideal of martyrdom was a call to the service of St. Peter against his foes wherever they might be found; for Peter was himself an exemplar of martyrdom. It therefore predisposed them to aid the papacy of their day and to play an active part in papal and Roman affairs.

Two areas of papal concern—the Berengarian controversy and the development of canon law—indicate that there was genuine growing together between Montecassino and Rome as the years went by, especially in the late 1070s and early and mid-1080s.

f. *The Berengarian controversy*

The Berengarian controversy concerned the doctrine of the eucharist. Berengar of Tours always affirmed that the eucharistic bread and wine became at the consecration the body and blood of Christ; but he argued that the manner of their so doing was figurative. He thereby followed a long tradition of western doctrine which had a spokesman in the ninth-century writer Ratramnus, upon whose work Berengar drew. But in the eleventh century this manner of thinking came under increasing challenge by those who, like Berengar's principal opponent Lanfranc, prior of Bec (*c.*1045–63), abbot of Saint-Étienne, Caen (1063–70), and archbishop of Canterbury (1070–89), held a realist view of the consecration. Lanfranc's view was destined to prevail; but in his day the concept of a substantial change in the eucharistic elements which eventually expressed the newer view was only beginning to be formulated. Many

[156] *Chron. Cas.* iii. 50, pp. 431–2; see below, pp. 158–9.

churchmen for long followed habits of thought which were not unlike Berengar's.[157]

The Berengarian controversy had two phases: from 1050 to 1059, and from 1059 to 1079. The earlier phase began in 1050 with Berengar's excommunication at Rome in his absence and then his condemnation at Vercelli by Pope Leo IX; it ended in the Lent council of 1059 with Pope Nicholas II's further condemnation at Rome. Berengar was then present, as was Alfanus of Salerno. During this phase Berengar seems to have hoped to find papal approval for a symbolist view, but in 1059 he had been made to read publicly a profession of faith drawn up by Cardinal Humbert. However, it was idiosyncratically worded, and Nicholas' condemnation was by no means decisive either in proscribing Berengar's teaching or in hindering his further career. Nothing emerges about Cassinese opinions or actions at this time, save that, probably soon after the Lateran council of 1059, an unknown friend or pupil of Berengar wrote him a letter about a visit that he subsequently paid to Alfanus at Salerno.[158] During it Alfanus referred to his friendship with Berengar. He expressed pleasure when informed of Berengar's fame, prosperity, and diligence as a teacher; indeed, Alfanus said that he had found him to be skilled in doctrine above all other learned men. As regards the opinion for which some had reproved Berengar, Alfanus admitted that fear had caused him not to stand apart from the majority which had opposed it. Yet Alfanus did not know how he could dissent from Berengar, if he wished to hold to the teaching of St. Augustine; and he sent Berengar his greetings. It is clear that in the first phase of the controversy Alfanus found nothing in Berengar's teaching against which he must take a dogmatic as distinct from a politic stand; even though in 1059 he had taken the line of least resistance by siding with Berengar's opponents.

[157] For general studies of the Berengarian controversy, see M. Cappuyns, 'Bérenger de Tours', *DHGE* viii. 385–407; J. de Montclos, *Lanfranc et Bérenger. La controverse eucharistique du XIe siècle* (Louvain, 1971); also R. W. Southern, 'Lanfranc of Bec and Berengar of Tours', *Studies in Medieval History Presented to Frederick Maurice Powicke*, edd. R. W. Hunt, W. A. Pantin, and R. W. Southern (Oxford, 1948), 27–48. Montclos offers a conspectus of recent literature: pp. ix–xiii; see also R. Somerville, 'The Case against Berengar of Tours', *SG* ix (1972), 53–75.

[158] Southern, art. cit. 48. I cannot follow later attempts, e.g. by Montclos, pp. 28, 220, to date the letter after 1079. It would have been difficult then to paint so favourable a picture of Berengar's circumstances, and opinion at Rome had gone too decisively against him for him to have been so well spoken of.

When the controversy again became active at Rome in the 1070s, Berengar was more on the defensive: he now sought the tolerance, rather than the acceptance, of his views. The crisis came with Gregory VII's Lateran councils of November 1078 and Lent 1079. Before it Berengar had spent a year or so at Rome near Gregory, and he had found both supporters and opponents.[159] According to Berengar's own account, at an assembly on 1 November 1078 Gregory himself at first looked favourably upon a profession of faith which Berengar prepared for the council, expressing his willingness to countenance his orthodoxy.[160] Up to this point it seems that, as archdeacon and as pope, Gregory had never positively associated himself with Berengar's position; but, like Alfanus of Salerno, he was nevertheless prepared to allow that it was not incompatible with traditional teachings.[161] This may have been the view of most of those at Rome who were connected with Montecassino. For when Berengar listed those who were favourably disposed towards him, he included the former Cassinese monk Archbishop Ambrose of Terracina, as well as Cardinal Deusdedit, who later dedicated his canonical collection to Desiderius as Pope Victor III and the chancellor Peter, with whom Desiderius had associations.[162] Since Gregory was disinclined to press matters against him, Berengar at this time came near to securing Roman tolerance of his teaching. However, he had powerful enemies from North Italy who were not likely to let matters rest—notably Bishops Landulf of Pisa and Ulrich of Padua. By the middle of November, when the council met, Gregory had acceded to their request that a decision be postponed until

[159] The sources of main importance for Montecassino are: (i) Berengar's memoranda of the Roman councils of 1078 and 1079: Huyghens (as Ch. II n. 54), pp. 308–403; (ii) a fragment by him from Paris, Bibliothèque nationale, MS lat. 12301, f. 3, from Subiaco: P. Meyvaert, 'Bérenger de Tours contre Albéric de Mont-Cassin', *RB* lxx (1960), 324–32, at 331–2; (iii) a fragment, from Montecassino, Archivio capitolare, MS 276, probably not by Berengar but by a disciple or partisan: M. Matronola, *Un testo inedito di Berengario e il concilio Romano del 1079* (Milan, 1936), 109–21.

[160] Huyghens, pp. 388–9, 392, 399–400; Meyvaert, p. 332. Gregory's attitude probably led to the accusations of heresy made against him at the council of Brixen (1080): Anhang C, *Ausgew. Quell.* xii. 480; Beno, i. 4, pp. 370–1.

[161] Thus, Hildebrand did not press matters to an issue at the council of Tours (1054): Berengar, *De sacra coena*, cap. 11, *Berengarii Turonensis De sacra coena adversus Lanfrancum*, ed. W. M. Beekenkamp (The Hague, 1941), 16–18; *Eusebii Brunonis Epistola ad Berengarium magistrum*, Migne, *PL* cxlvii. 1201–4. According to Berengar, Gregory allowed that his views were compatible with those of Peter Damiani.

[162] Huyghens, pp. 390–1. For Ambrose, see above, p. 65, and for Deusdedit and Peter, below, pp. 99–100 and Appendix V.

the next Lent—when, according to Berengar, his enemies from afar could be mustered.[163]

Still according to Berengar, in the interim Gregory twice employed Desiderius of Montecassino, whom Berengar described as 'summae tunc in palatio auctoritatis', as an emissary to Berengar. The first mission occurred when Berengar was preparing himself by a solemn fast on the next day to take an oath confirming the declaration of faith which he had prepared for the November council. The oath was to be supported by an ordeal by hot iron which a supporter of Berengar would undergo. But Gregory sent Desiderius with instructions that Berengar desist from his fast because the ordeal was cancelled. This cancellation was connected with Gregory's decision to reopen matters at his Lent council in 1079.[164] Secondly, Desiderius and a Cassinese monk, Petrus Neopolitanus,[165] brought Berengar private advice from Gregory that he should quickly withdraw from public controversy for so long as Gregory lived. Gregory wished thus to be spared the embarrassment of allegations that he approved of or shared Berengar's teachings.[166] Desiderius' own opinions and standpoint do not emerge from these missions. But he appears to have worked closely with a still-hesitant Gregory who was reluctant to see matters brought to a head; and in the eyes of Berengar he was an acceptable emissary.

Berengar's unpreparedness to act upon the pope's private advice that he be quiet, led to the renewed hearing of his case at the Lent council. According to Berengar's account, Gregory a few days before it summoned him and told him that he did not doubt the compatibility of his belief with holy scripture. Gregory further said that, as was his wont, he had had recourse to the Blessed Virgin: he caused one of his followers to keep a special fast, thereby securing her confirmation of his view. But at the council Gregory suddenly changed front.[167] He insisted that Berengar should confess that he had hitherto been in error; the word *substantialiter* must be included in the profession of faith that Berengar was to make about Christ's presence in the

[163] Huyghens, pp. 391–3. [164] Ibid. 400.

[165] See below, Appendix V; cf. Montclos, p. 219 n. 4, following Lentini (as Ch. I n. 98), pp. 69–70.

[166] Huyghens, p. 402.

[167] Peter the Deacon's story of a miracle demonstrating Berengar's error and winning Gregory's approval also indicates that there was a hardening of the latter's views: *OV*, cap. 49, pp. 71–2, 158.

eucharistic elements.[168] Berengar was reluctant. His persistence in pursuit of philosophical arguments which failed to clarify the issue turned both the council and Gregory against him.[169] He was compelled to make the profession as revised, and to affirm that he did so according to the council's interpretation.[170]

In his long memorial of these events Berengar made no mention of Alberic, monk of Montecassino. But it is clear that Alberic's intervention at the council was decisive in bringing about the condemnation of his views and the insistence that he accept unambiguously the adverb *substantialiter.*[171] The principal evidence is another writing of Berengar.[172] He declared himself outraged that Alberic should have shifted his ground by championing a position that he had once destroyed, when he rallied to the word *substantialiter.* The implication is that at some earlier gathering, perhaps that of 1 November 1078, Alberic had publicly agreed that Berengar's teaching was admissible. Berengar now branded him a turncoat; he was *non monachum sed daemoniacum.* Berengar's disclosure that Alberic played a critical role at the Lent council of 1079 was later confirmed by Peter the Deacon.[173] He recorded that Alberic was called in to relieve the situation when the council became deadlocked. He secured a week's adjournment to write his tract *De corpore Domini*, based upon the witness of the fathers; in it he destroyed all Berengar's assertions and consigned them to oblivion.

Alberic's views on the Berengarian question clearly underwent change. Like Alfanus he initially showed some sympathy with, or at least a tolerance of, Berengar's opinions. But faced by Berengar's intransigence Alberic in 1079 became hostile, and insisted upon an unambiguous acceptance of the word *substantialiter.* Gregory's own views and attitudes appear to have

[168] *Reg.* vi. 17*a*, pp. 42–6. The word *substantialiter* seems to have entered the debate by Nov. 1078: Matronola, p. 117.

[169] Bruno of Segni, *Expositio in Leviticum*, cap. 7, Migne, *PL* clxiv. 404.

[170] Huyghens, pp. 394, 402.

[171] Montclos suggests that Alberic formulated Berengar's profession of 1079: p. 28. But for the more likely suggestion of Guitmund of Aversa, see Somerville (as Ch. II n. 157), pp. 71, 74–5.

[172] Meyvaert (as Ch. II n. 159). It is doubtful whether the Alberic of Matronola, pp. 117–18, is Alberic of Montecassino or, if he is, whether he is correctly reported: see Montclos, p. 217.

[173] *DVI*, cap. 21, Migne, *PL* clxxiii. 1033A–B; *Chron. Cas.* iii. 35, p. 411. See Meyvaert, p. 330 n. 2.

undergone a not dissimilar development.[174] It is likely that Alberic's work helped this process. Desiderius' reactions are not known. But it would seem that the Berengarian controversy was partly responsible for bringing Desiderius and the Gregorian papacy closer together in the late 1070s. The attitudes to it of Rome and Montecassino seem to have developed on similar lines, and Alberic of Montecassino played a key part in bringing about Gregory's condemnation of Berengar. There was thus fostered a new tendency towards sympathy and collaboration which had not characterized Gregory's early years as pope, but which events were to deepen during the following decade.

g. *Canon law*

During the Berengarian controversy Montecassino and the figures associated with it seem at all times to have moved in step with Gregory VII, and in its later stages to have become actively involved as Gregory's collaborators when he turned to taking stern measures against Berengar. This represents the closest and most positive collaboration of Cassinese monks with Gregory as pope up to 1080. But the Berengarian controversy was about a specific and limited issue. The development of Montecassino's relationship with the papacy may be inferred more completely from its attitudes as suggested by canon-law texts—not now those of local, South Italian importance for pastoral purposes, but others of general significance for the church at large and for the issues of *sacerdotium* and *regnum*.

Two of the major collections of the Gregorian age bear, at least indirectly, on Montecassino's attitude and the changes that it may have undergone: the *Diversorum patrum sententiae*, and the *Collectio canonum* of Cardinal Deusdedit. That the former of these collections had a close relationship to Montecassino may be inferred from the manuscript tradition.[175] Three early manuscripts of it are certainly or possibly associated with the abbey or its sphere of influence: Montecassino, Archivio capitolare, MS 522, and Escorial, Real Biblioteca de San Lorenzo, MSS Z.III.19 and L.III.19 (incomplete). All are of late eleventh- or early twelfth-century date, and are in Beneventan script. The latest editor of the collection, J. T. Gilchrist, selected the first of the three to be the basis of his edition. In his opinion it stood

[174] See Montclos, p. 218.
[175] Gilchrist (as Ch. I n. 72), pp. xxxii–lxxxii.

at two or three removes from an exemplar that would have been found at Montecassino *c.*1076. The Cassinese recension of the *Diversorum patrum sententiae* thus represents the earliest and best textual tradition; most canonists and other writers on both sides of the Alps who used the collection up to the dissemination of Gratian's *Decretum* (*c.*1140) used manuscripts belonging to it.[176] Such a connection with Montecassino, or perhaps a daughter house like Santa Maria in Pallara at Rome, warrants the inference that the collection wherever or whenever compiled reflects a view of church and papacy which was acceptable at Montecassino in the mid-1070s.

Its provenance and date are uncertain, although there is no reason to suppose that it was compiled, as distinct from copied, by a Cassinese monk or in a Cassinese house. Arguments that the collection, at least in its original form (that is, without the so-called 'Swabian Appendix' and certain other amendments), dates from the 1050s have yielded ground to a date *c.*1074–6.[177] For supposed similarities with Cardinal Humbert's writings have proved to be inconclusive, and there is no evidence for its dissemination before the pontificate of Gregory VII. It is likely to be a product of his early years as pope. It has been seen as serving to prepare the ground for his distinctive work.[178] There is prima-facie justification for such a view. It is largely based upon papal sources, both genuine and spurious. Of its 315 *capitula* some 250 were drawn from Pseudo-Isidore, and much material in a further forty-two came, directly or indirectly, from Gregory I's Register or from his Life by John the Deacon. The collection demonstrates the coherence and consistency of papal teaching across the centuries in matters of church order and jurisdiction.[179] It strongly emphasized papal jurisdiction. Its first *sententia* was *De primatu romane ecclesie*. It upheld

[176] Gilchrist, pp. lxxxiii–lxxxvii.

[177] For recent discussions, see ibid., pp. xx–xxxi; O. Capitani, 'La figura del vescovo in alcune collezioni canoniche della seconda metà del secolo xi', *Vescovi e diocesi in Italia nel medioevo (sec. ix–xiii)*, Italia sacra, 5 (Padua, 1964), 161–91, and *Immunità vescovili ed ecclesiologia in età 'pregregoriana'* (Spoleto, 1966), 183–208; and H. Fuhrmann's (largely identical) discussions in *Einfluss und Verbreitung der pseudoisidorischen Fälschungen*, 3 vols. (Stuttgart, 1972–4), ii. 486–509, esp. 487–92, and 'Über den Reformgeist der 74-Titel-Sammlung', *Festschrift für Hermann Heimpel zum 70. Geburtstag*, 2 vols. (Göttingen, 1972), ii. 1101–20, esp. 1101–6.

[178] P. Fournier, 'Le premier manuel canonique de la réforme du XIe siècle', *Mélanges d'archéologie et d'histoire de l'École française de Rome*, xiv (1894), 147–223, 285–90; cf. Fournier and le Bras (as Ch. I n. 115), ii. 20.

[179] Gilchrist, pp. xc–cxvi; Fuhrmann, *Einfluss*, ii. 493–4, 616–17.

the duty of having recourse to Rome for judgement, since the Roman church was *caput et cardo omnium ecclesiarum* and *fundamentum et forma . . . ecclesiarum*. The collection shared many of the concerns of the papal reformers: bishops were to keep themselves from such evils as simony; clergy were bound to celibacy and chastity; laymen were not to be involved in the administration of church property; and dealings with excommunicates were prohibited. Kings and rulers were to respect the inviolability of ecclesiastical privileges.[180] In some respects, indeed, the compiler underlined papal authority more strongly than did his sources, and he balanced more carefully than they did the privileges of bishops against those of other orders in the church.[181]

In all this the *Diversorum patrum sententiae* did much to assert and to reinforce Gregory VII's aims and demands. Yet scholars have recently insisted upon its distance from them in major respects. Thus, it emphasized the jurisdiction of the apostolic see as the apex of a hierarchy, but said little about the pope's own personal, spiritual, and political authority.[182] The compiler drew upon Pseudo-Isidore most systematically, not in relation to the papal primacy and to the broader aspects of church organization, but to particular points of jurisdiction, procedure, and protocol.[183] Further, some *sententiae* were far from consistent with Gregory's principles as enunciated in such documents as the *Dictatus papae*,[184] or with his measures against disobedient clergy. The rules of *sententia* 5, *De ordine accusationis deque accusatorum personis*, are hard to square with Gregory's attempts to secure the lay accusation of simoniacal and married clerks in Germany and Italy.[185] The rules of *sententiae* 7 and 9, *Quod ordine inferiores non possint accusare pastores* and *Quod non possint oves accusare pastores*, run counter to *Dictatus papae*, cap. 24, that under papal command and licence subjects could accuse their rulers. *Sententia* 26, *Ut unusquisque suis contentus sit terminis*, left little place for Gregory's maxim that popes or their agents could override established jurisdiction and, when necessary, interfere within others' bounds.[186] There is much to warrant the judgement that in

[180] *Sentt.* 1, caps. 2, 8, 12; 15, 21; 60; 66, cap. 307; 68.

[181] Fuhrmann, ii. 501–5.

[182] Ibid. ii. 493–4.

[183] Its main borrowings are in caps. 44–110: ibid. ii. 496, 616.

[184] *Reg.* ii. 55*a*, pp. 201–8.

[185] e.g. ibid. ii. 45, pp. 182–5.

[186] e.g. *Dictatus papae*, caps. 13, 18, 20–1, 25.

essential respects the collection did not fully manifest the principles and temper of Gregory and its successors, since its 'ideal was a rigidly hierarchical church having a strong pope, unsympathetic towards lay aspirations and with little taste for devout zeal'.[187] Where a hint of warmth appears it is not for the eleventh-century papacy but for the Roman see in its earliest days, when the martyrdom of St. Peter and St. Paul by Nero established it on a basis of glory and triumph.[188] Very much of this is consistent with the outlook of Alfanus and Amatus of Montecassino, and it shows a similar reserve before the characteristic exercise of papal authority by Gregory VII.

In view of this reserve, it is of the highest significance that, from the latter years of Gregory VII's pontificate until the compilation of Gratian's *Decretum c.*1140 ushered in the *ius novum* of the medieval canon law, the circulation and use in Western Christendom of the *Diversorum patrum sententiae* became polarized. It formed part of the armoury of both Gregorian and anti-Gregorian writers. Because of its use of the Forged Decretals and of its emphasis upon the papal primacy, in its extended form it was much employed by German Gregorians, for example Manegold of Lautenbach, Bernard of Constance, Bernold of St. Blasien, the 'Swabian Annalist', and the so-called canon-law collection in Göttweig, Stiftsbibliothek, MS 56.[189] But with its insistence upon an ordered ecclesiastical hierarchy in which all distinctions of rank and all boundaries of jurisdiction were punctiliously respected no less by the papacy than by lay powers, the *Diversorum patrum sententiae* was also drawn upon by the most effective propagandist of the Henrican party in Germany—the anonymous monk of Hersfeld who wrote the *Liber de unitate ecclesiae conservanda.*[190] Twenty-five of the canonical authorities cited in the tract are derived from it.[191] The author used *sententiae* 45 and 52 when he examined Gregory's excommunication of Henry IV. *Sententiae* 5 and 26 provided grist to his mill when he further argued against the justice of Gregory's judicial proceedings against Henry, and against his invasion of the rights of the archbishop of Cologne

[187] Fuhrmann, ii. 508, 616. [188] *Sent.* 2.

[189] A. Michel, *Die Sentenzen des Kardinals Humbert, das erste Rechtsbuch der päpstlichen Reform, MGH Schriften*, vii (Leipzig, 1943), 148-54.

[190] *MGH Libelli*, ii. 173-284. For its debt to the *Diversorum patrum sententiae*, see Zafarana (as Ch. I n. 120), esp. pp. 656-66.

[191] Zafarana, art. cit. 657, 666.

when he caused Bishop Reginhard of Minden to be consecrated by Archbishop Hartwig of Magdeburg.[192] The *Diversorum patrum sententiae* exalted the papal primacy; yet it did so in essentially pre-Gregorian terms. In seeking reform it looked back to a past in the primitive church when, as Pseudo-Isidore seemed to indicate, authorities scrupulously observed the boundaries of their own and others' jurisdiction. All this reinforced the author of the *Liber de unitate ecclesiae conservanda* in his arguments against Gregory VII and his party, and also in presenting the credentials of the antipope Clement III as the true upholder of the papal primacy. The author's virulence against Abbot Desiderius after he became Pope Victor III is best explicable as expressing exasperation that, on Gregory's death, his throne should have been taken, and his stand against Henry continued, by a figure whose monastery had once been associated with such soundly conservative principles as the *Diversorum patrum sententiae* embodied, but who had now deviated from them.[193]

The fact and the extent of Montecassino's deviation are indirectly suggested by the canonical collection of Deusdedit. Deusdedit himself had no connection with Montecassino. A native of Aquitaine who had been a monk at Tulle in the Limousin, by 1078 he was cardinal-priest of the title of San Pietro in Vincoli.[194] He may have accompanied Cardinal Odo of Ostia upon his legatine travels to Saxony and Thuringia in the winter of 1084-5;[195] in any case he persisted in his loyalty to Gregory VII. His canonical collection was made between 1083 and 1087; he dedicated it in cordial terms to Desiderius as Pope Victor III: 'Beatissimo atque apostolico viro pontifici domno papae Victori tertio et omni clero sanctae Romanae ecclesiae.'[196] The date of its completion is therefore determined by the period of Victor's reign—9 May to 16 September 1087. The dedication is the first in history of a canonical collection to a reigning pope. It indicates that on the one hand Victor was a pope to whom the

[192] i. 6, 12, ii. 23-4, pp. 151, 200-1, 240-1.

[193] See below, pp. 211-12.

[194] For Deusdedit, see Fournier and le Bras (as Ch. I n. 115), ii. 37-54; C. Lefebvre, 'Deusdedit', *Dictionnaire du droit canonique*, iv (1944/9), 1186-91; W. Holtzmann, 'Kardinal Deusdedit als Dichter', *Beiträge*, pp. 35-9, esp. 46-8; Fuhrmann, *Einfluss*, ii. 522-33, 617-18; Hüls, *Kardinäle*, p. 194.

[195] H. Fuhrmann, 'Konstantinische Schenkung und abendländische Kaisertum', *DA* xxii (1966), 63-178, at 145 n. 221, commenting upon Deusdedit, *Coll. can.* iv. 420, pp. 596-7.

[196] pp. 1-5.

dedication of such a collection was deemed to be appropriate, and that on the other Victor himself by accepting the dedication approved of its contents as a proper foundation for church life. To this extent it sheds light on Victor's own standpoint by the mid-1080s.

Deusdedit's preface to Victor exhibited a view of papal power which was more amply conceived than that of the *Diversorum patrum sententiae*. He stressed its universality in theory and in practice. He began with a reference to the pope's pastoral office to feed Christ's sheep, and in due course spoke of the continuing life and work of St. Peter and St. Paul in the Roman church and of the working of Peter's faith which would never fail but would strengthen the brethren wherever they were and throughout all time. He established papal jurisdiction upon the basis of the Nicene decision that, without the Roman pontiff's ruling, councils should not be held or bishops condemned, while matters of major business should be referred to him for judgement. Deusdedit said that his collection would serve to demonstrate the *auctoritatis privilegium* of the Roman church, which gave it power over the whole Christian world. His setting out of the subject-matter of his four books concentrated upon the Roman church in its local sense: the *privilegium auctoritatis* of the Roman church; its clergy; its possessions; and lastly—since the temporal power strives to subject the church to itself—the liberty of the church, its clergy, and its goods. But Deusdedit ended his preface by telling Victor that his concern embraced all the churches: 'I have dedicated this work to your fatherhood in the belief that it will help not only the holy apostolic see but also every church and every clerk.' There can thus be no mistaking the catholicity of his intention: whatever liberty was appropriate for the papacy was a pattern for the rest of the church.

Thus, while Deusdedit's purpose was to demonstrate the authority and prerogatives of the Roman see, his collection was of general relevance.[197] The Roman church was the *fundamentum et forma . . . omnium ecclesiarum*. But it was the Roman church and its prerogatives that constituted his true concern. In

[197] See F. Hirsch, 'Die Auffassung der simonistischen und schismatischen Weihen im elften Jahrhundert, besonders bei Kardinal Deusdedit', 'Kardinal Deusdedits Stellung zur Laieninvestitur', and 'Die rechtliche Stellung der römischen Kirche und des Papstes nach Kardinal Deusdedit', *Archiv für katholisches Kirchenrecht*, lxxxvii (1907), 25–70; lxxxviii (1908), 34–49, 595–624; Fuhrmann, *Einfluss*, ii. 522–33.

the *capitulationes*, or index of cardinal propositions, with which he prefaced his work, they were defined with a terseness and an uncompromising conviction that are reminiscent of Gregory VII's *Dictatus papae*. The pope had the authority over bishops that St. Peter had over the apostles. He was exempt from all temporal judgement. Deusdedit insisted upon the pope's universal jurisdiction, not least over kings and emperors and in particular over those who disobeyed ecclesiastical canons and disregarded their censures.[198] He cited at length Gregory VII's second letter to Bishop Hermann of Metz, and followed it with Gregory's ruling at his Lent council of 1078 releasing the subjects of excommunicated rulers from their oaths of fealty.[199] Throughout his work Deusdedit took a strong stand against any subjection of the church to lay authority, notably in his fourth book *De libertate ecclesiae et rerum eius et cleri*, which in effect provides a mirror of a godly prince as papal reformers envisaged him. The pattern of a Christian emperor was Constantine, who had exalted and endowed the apostolic see, who had entrusted the whole of the west to its oversight, who had dignified it with an imperial crown and provided that the earthly empire should have no power over Rome, and who in doing all these things had bound his successors to maintain them in perpetuity. Following his example not only did the ancient and the Frankish emperors reverence Rome, but even heretical ones did so as well. Emperors should, therefore, approach the pope with requests and not with commands. The laity should have no part in papal elections; while the lay choosing of bishops, priests, and deacons was inadmissible. No grade of ecclesiastical order was subject to lay judgement. The lay power could with justice decide nothing in the church, and the emperor must not usurp the province of the *sacerdotium*. Unlike the compiler of the *Diversorum patrum sententiae*, Deusdedit called upon the godly laity to reject, by physical resistance if necessary, the ministrations of simoniacal and married clergy; in support he cited one of Gregory VII's most characteristic letters.[200] Such were the teachings of a collection which in 1087 it was deemed appropriate to dedicate to Desiderius as Pope Victor III.

During the next ten years or so Deusdedit looked back upon

[198] pp. 6, 8, 26.

[199] iv. 184–5, pp. 489–91; *Reg.* v. 14*a*, viii. 21, pp. 373, 544–63.

[200] iv. 186, pp. 491–2, cf. *Reg.* ii. 45, pp. 182–5.

Victor III as a pope who had deserved his approval. By *c.*1098 he had prepared the two recensions of his *Libellus contra invasores et symoniacos et reliquos scismaticos.*[201] He wrote this time with simony very much in mind—as he put it, 'to answer simoniacs and schismatics who say that Christ's church is subject to royal power'.[202] He looked back to Victor, no less than to Urban II, as a worthy successor of Gregory VII: both were the choice of catholics who 'protected faith and religion by the zeal of God'; Victor was *reverentissimus* and Urban *vir scientia et religione prestantissimus*. In his interpolation about the Guibertine schism Deusdedit made Guibert into a new Simon Magus and Henry a new Nero, thus employing familiar Cassinese imagery.[203] In part of its own record of Desiderius as pope, the Montecassino Chronicle borrowed Deusdedit's account, along with other material from the *Libellus* reproducing substantially his own words.[204] Retrospectively at least, Deusdedit's view of the schism and of Desiderius' place in it was acceptable to official thought at the abbey as recorded in its Chronicle. Deusdedit's approval of Desiderius in both his writings points to a similarity, or at least a compatibility, between Desiderius' ultimate outlook and Deusdedit's *Collectio canonum*. It is probably the best guide that is available to determine what may have been his standpoint when pope. It suggests that his views had developed since the days when the *Diversorum patrum sententiae* began to be disseminated from Montecassino. Under the pressure of the Guibertine schism, they were in some degree assimilated to those of his compeers among the Roman cardinal-priests who, like Deusdedit, remained loyal to Gregory VII while holding a view of the Roman church and its prerogatives which remained characteristic of the cardinal-priests. As such it did not necessarily correspond fully to that of Gregory himself or command general assent amongst his partisans. Indeed, it may be expected to have been uncongenial to some of them.

iv. CONCLUSIONS

In so far as it can thus be pieced together, the tradition of reform at Montecassino seems to have had marked peculiarities, and to deserve study in its own right as a contribution to the renewal

[201] *MGH Libelli*, ii. 292–365.
[202] Prol., p. 300.
[203] ii. 11–12, pp. 328–30.
[204] See below, Appendix VIII.

of the church in the eleventh century. The impulse to reform was not principally manifest in the internal life of the abbey, its institutions, or its spirituality; although a feature of Cassinese monasticism was its high esteem for the traditions and witness of the eremitical life. Nor did Montecassino to any exceptional degree exercise an influence outside the cloister by maintaining a round of intercessory prayers and alms for the benefit of individuals outside its walls. But this did not restrict its impact in the urban culture of South Italy. In monasteries north of the Alps such as Cluny, where intercession was made on a vast scale, the effect was to disperse monastic influence over a wide area but also to restrict it to the royal and aristocratic grades of society. With a few exceptions Montecassino impinged only locally within South Italy; but there it did so comprehensively in terms of all ranks of the populace. It touched urban monasteries and secular churches and through them all grades of clergy and laity.[205] Its homiletic material looked beyond the cloister to the task of building up the secular clergy and laity in the Christian virtues. When social and economic developments were generating from below a demand for ecclesiastical reform and revitalization, Montecassino fostered the cult of local patron saints in terms appropriate to urban churches. True to the intention of canon law to renew in the contemporary church the spirit and the letter of the primitive age, Montecassino's local canon-law collections also sought to instruct all grades of Christians in the true ways of Christianity, and to impose a salutary penitential discipline on those who went astray. Given the number of Cassinese houses and possessions in Central and South Italy, these attempts to work upon the church at large added up to a considerable impetus towards reform.

In its origin and development Montecassino's reforming work was independent of the papacy; although it was compatible with papal aspirations. Its growing concern with combating simony and incontinence, both clerical and lay, drew it near to papal reform as instituted by Pope Leo IX. It did so the more effectively because of Montecassino's deep veneration for Leo himself. Amatus' *Liber in honore beati Petri apostoli* and Leo of Ostia's Clementine writings illustrate the literary resourcefulness that were applied to this end. They also establish how

[205] For monastic austerity and popular religion, see the opening sentences of Peter Damiani, *Op.* 43, Migne, *PL* cxlv. 679AB.

strongly Cassinese writers could value the apostolic see as a source of reform, and how strongly they proclaimed the authority of St. Peter and his vicar at Rome.

It is, however, difficult to assess their degree of conviction in doing so. At worst Cassinese hagiographical writing sometimes approaches the insipid and banal; although it is usually saved by the authors' evident pastoral concern and moral fervour. Moreover, to some extent their work appears to be something of a literary exercise. Cassinese writers were imbued with the conventions of contemporary rhetoric, according to which its adepts turned their pens to the honouring of whatsoever person or cause they were charged to sponsor, with *verisimilitudo* rather than *veritas* as the criterion of what they should write.[206] The reader is bound to ask whether their elaborate propaganda against simony, and their protestations of concern for the papal cause, are not in some measure rhetorical exercises which disclose little of their authors' loyalties and commitments. So far as Amatus is concerned, his zeal in his poem for the papacy and for reform was little apparent in his history. Similarly, Alfanus of Salerno was prepared, when Gisulf II (execrated by Amatus) was still prince of Salerno, to write a eulogy of his family; with his defeat in 1077 at the hands of Robert Guiscard, Alfanus quickly turned his pen to the praise of his Norman supplanter and to the celebration of St. Matthew's patronage of him.[207]

The presence of strong rhetorical colouring, and a willingness to redirect the Muses according to political expediency, are not to be denied. Yet two considerations suggest sincerity and a genuine commitment to the papal cause. First, Amatus' zeal against simony, and his drawing upon the legends of the Pseudo-Clementine writings, have a parallel in the popular literature of the time of Gregory VII. Whether there was a direct influence or interaction is uncertain. But the propaganda that Amatus wrote had its echo in the rhythm *Adversus simoniacos* which survives among the poems of Peter Damiani.[208] It shows how deeply such ideas as those which marked Cassinese literature penetrated the urban and popular circles which Montecassino

[206] Cf. Anselm of Besate, *Rhetorimachia*, epist., ed. K. Manitius, *MGH Quell. Geistesgesch.* ii. 103. For rhetorical conventions, see I. S. Robinson, 'The "colores rhetorici" in the Investiture Contest', *Traditio*, xxxii (1976), 209-38.

[207] See above, pp. 71-2, and below, pp. 126-7, 131, 173.

[208] Lokrantz (as Cap. II n. 112), pp. 153-5, no. D7. It is preserved in Mantua, Bibl. com. MS C.II.11, f. 7^{v}. Its provenance is unknown.

set itself to instruct. The poem begins by condemning the evils of the church, including the *haeresis Simoniana*, which the pope was taking a lead in extirpating. The bishops were to show by teaching and by example how Christians should live, and they were to banish from the church simony, clerical and lay unchastity, and lay domination. Such were the commands of the embattled *gloriosus papa* Gregory VII, which had brought down upon the church the wrath of Henry IV. The poet recalled the nemesis of Simon Magus' pride when he fell to his death from the tower that he built. The warfare between Gregory and Henry was similarly a warfare of life and death. Let those who were nourished by the apostolic faith stand fast upon the rock of St. Peter and so, through their warfare, attain to total victory. This popular poem assembles virtually all the themes of reforming propaganda at Montecassino in a clarion call to the support of Gregory. It indicates that such propaganda was no mere rhetorical exercise but an effective summons which was being widely made to rally local and humble aspirations to the cause of the Gregorian papacy. It generated genuine religious enthusiasm in the urban and middle-class circles to which Gregory especially looked for allies.

Secondly, Montecassino's connections with the major canon-law collections of the late eleventh century tend to give credibility to its commitment to the papacy and to the growth of its sympathy with Roman developments. Montecassino's sponsorship of the *Diversorum patrum sententiae* suggests that, when it was compiled, probably in the early 1070s, the dominant outlook of Cassinese circles was not in complete harmony with Gregory VII's conception of papal authority and jurisdiction. But for Rome and South Italy alike, the second excommunication of Henry IV in 1080, since it led to the Guibertine schism and to Henry's attacks upon Rome, seems to have been more of a turning point than the first excommunication of 1076 and its sequel at Canossa. The year 1080 gave new force to such ideas as Amatus presented in his poem. The ensuing schism seems to have drawn Montecassino nearer to the papacy in the realm of ideas and in its appreciation of the nature of papal authority. If it did not even now fully embrace the position of Gregory VII, it advanced towards the ampler presentation of papal government which was propounded by Deusdedit. For by 1087 Abbot Desiderius was prepared to receive the dedication of Deusdedit's canonical collection; and Deusdedit's loyalty to his memory throughout the 1090s suggests an ultimate compatibility of outlook. The conclusion would seem to be that Montecassino's links with the reformed papacy by the time of Desiderius' death brought Cassinese opinion into sympathy with at least some Gregorian circles at Rome, and in particular with the loyal cardinal-priests of whom Desiderius was the senior representative.

III

Rome, Montecassino, and the Normans—the Politics of Realism and Reform

IN the age of Abbot Desiderius Montecassino not only became involved in papal administration and in eleventh-century currents of renewal and reform; it also played a part in the politics of South Italy and of the papacy. In either case the pattern of developments seems similar. Montecassino derived great strength from its favourable situation and from its ample resources and prestige. In the early years of the reform papacy it was, therefore, able to collaborate closely in the popes' political endeavours, especially because after 1059 both Montecassino and the papacy looked to the Norman princes to be their friends and allies. But in Gregory VII's early years as pope this shared alignment became strained to the limit by reason of Norman unreliability and volatility. Montecassino prudently put first its commitment to the Normans; for so long as Gregory was at odds with the most powerful of their leaders, Robert Guiscard, duke of Apulia and Calabria, Abbot Desiderius did little to help the pope in political matters. But with the struggles of Gregory's latter years against Henry IV of Germany and especially with the emergence of Guibert of Ravenna as an antipope, the Normans seemed more disposed to help the papacy, and in 1080 at Ceprano renewed their alliance. Montecassino became a strong upholder of the Gregorian papacy. It was particularly so after Gregory's departure from Rome in 1084, and it remained so after his death in 1085. In all these vicissitudes its policies were first and foremost dictated by a realistic appraisal of its own interests. But, especially in the 1080s, this opportunism was tempered by a genuine and growing desire to promote reforming interests as they had established themselves in some four decades of experience at Rome. Thus, during Desiderius' long reign as abbot, Montecassino's political attitudes showed a development which will be examined in this chapter.

i. THE PAPACY, THE NORMANS, AND MONTECASSINO TO 1061

Montecassino was situated in a region of South Italy where the claims of the papacy and of the Eastern and Western Empires overlapped. The means by which these claims were advanced in the early eleventh century have already been outlined, as have the advantages which Montecassino from time to time derived from external interventions.[1] The entry of the Normans into the pattern of relationships so created was an epoch-making development. They came into contact with the papacy at an early date. This was partly for religious reasons, since they were attracted to Italy by zeal for pilgrimage to St. Peter at Rome and St. Michael the Archangel at Monte Gargano in North Apulia. But they were primarily drawn by the prospect of reward, service, plunder, and eventual settlement. So they came to papal notice in political as well as in religious connections. Pope Benedict VIII, in particular, shared the Emperor Henry II's hostility to Byzantine overlordship of South Italy. He therefore encouraged, if he did not commission, a Norman band led by Ralph of Toeni to help Melo of Bari in the second Apulian rising of 1017–18. His attitude to the Normans was friendly, and his concern for South Italian affairs which culminated in his association with Henry II's Italian expedition of 1022 prepared the way for later papal involvement in the south.[2]

By the time of the reform papacy, and especially of Pope Leo IX, the growing numbers and political significance of the Normans in South Italy compelled the papacy to define its attitude to them more clearly. It had to decide whether they were to be recognized and recruited as allies, or treated as dangerous

[1] See above, pp. xxvii–xxxiii.

[2] For Benedict VIII's role, see the early sources Ralph Glaber, *Historiarum*, iii. 1. 3, ed. M. Prou (Paris, 1886), 52–3, and Adhemar of Chabannes: Adémar de Chabannes, *Chronique*, iii. 55, ed. J. Chavanon (Paris, 1887), 178, cf. Appendix, p. 204. But Benedict was not thus referred to by Amatus, i. 22, pp. 29–30; *Chron. Cas.* ii. 37, pp. 236–40; William of Apulia, i. 11–94, pp. 99–104; or Orderic Vitalis, iii, ed. Chibnall, ii. 56–9. The coming of the Normans to South Italy raises many problems, and Benedict's part remains controversial. E. Joranson, 'The Inception of the Career of the Normans in Italy—Legend and History', *Speculum*, xxiii (1948), 353–96, exaggerates it; it is minimized by H. Hoffmann, 'Die Anfänge der Normannen in Süditalien', *QFIAB* xlix (1969), 95–144. For a middle view, see Pontieri (as Introd. n. 50), pp. 52–3; Herrmann (as Introd. n. 60); and G. A. Loud, 'How "Norman" was the Norman Conquest of Southern Italy?' *Nottingham Medieval Studies*, xxv (1981), 13–34.

enemies to be controlled and perhaps eliminated through an alliance with their Byzantine or western opponents. For some ten years the reform papacy chose to follow the way of hostility to the Normans.[3] When Leo became pope in 1048 their depredations were particularly severe, and Lombard feeling against them was bitter. In 1050 their attacks upon Benevento prompted its citizens to seek papal lordship and help. Leo determined to rid South Italy of the Normans, and his resolve was strengthened by the papal chancellor and *bibliothecarius* Frederick, brother of Duke Godfrey of Lorraine, whom he brought to Rome.[4] Leo looked to Byzantium for help, and found an ally in Argyrus son of Melo of Bari who, although a Latin Christian, had made his peace with Byzantium and from 1051 was catapan of South Italy. Leo also set out to recover papal rights in South Italy and to extend his spiritual supervision of it. In 1049 he took the remarkable step of appointing the future Cardinal Humbert to be archbishop of Sicily although it was still in Moslem hands, and in 1050 he held reforming synods at Salerno and Siponto. In matters temporal and spiritual alike, he intended to assert papal authority. As a means to this end he sought the breaking of Norman power.

In 1052 he planned an anti-Norman campaign that came to nothing since his intended ally, Prince Guaimar V of Salerno, feared to break with the Normans. But Guaimar's assassination compelled both sides to take resolute steps in their own defence.[5] In the autumn Leo negotiated in Germany with the Emperor Henry III, who was willing to help his papal kinsman with a view to renewing the tradition of papal and imperial condominium in South Italy. Henry transferred to the papacy his rights over Benevento in return for a like transfer to himself of papal rights in Germany over the see of Bamberg and the abbey of Fulda.[6] Henry was, however, prevented from bringing Leo effective military help against the Normans by the resistance of his imperial chancellor Bishop Gebhard of Eichstätt.

[3] For the period of hostility, see esp. Heinemann (as Introd. n. 50), i. 111–52, and Chalandon, *Domination*, i. 121–66. For Leo IX's policy, see Bloch (as Introd. n. 34), pp. 189–93; Deér (as Introd. n. 52), pp. 88–90, 93–5; D'Alessandro, *Storigrafia e politica* (as Ch. I n. 110), pp. 1–50. For the problem of Benevento, see C. Vehse, 'Benevent als Territorium des Kirchenstaats bis zum Beginn der Avignonischen Epoche', *QFIAB* xxii (1930/1), 87–160.

[4] Amatus, iii. 33–4, pp. 138–40.

[5] Ibid. iii. 25–6, pp. 140–1.

[6] *Chron. Cas.* ii. 46, 81, pp. 254, 328–9; Hermann of Reichenau, *Chronicon* (as Introd. n. 63), *a.* 1053, p. 700.

A campaign upon which Leo rashly embarked in 1053 was further impeded when the Normans prevented his army from joining in North Apulia its Byzantine allies commanded by Argyrus. In June, after a humiliating defeat at Civitate, the pope found himself a Norman prisoner at Benevento. In the later Norman view he conceded that the Normans held of St. Peter *haereditali feudo* the South Italian lands that they had captured or would capture.[7] Leo's detention was, however, an honourable one, and he was able to avoid renouncing his South Italian plans. Moreover, he kept in touch with Byzantium, where, in the short term, his defeat at Civitate even helped him. For by underlining the seriousness of the Norman menace it tended to discredit Argyrus's anti-western adversary at Constantinople, the Patriarch Michael Cerularius. Byzantium perceived a need to support all who resisted Norman ambitions; and it was in response to an invitation from the Emperor Constantine IX Monomachus that the pope sent to Constantinople in January 1054 the three legates, Cardinals Humbert and Frederick of Lorraine and Archbishop Peter of Amalfi. But the patriarch's rigidity led to the breach of 1054 between Rome and Constantinople. With Constantine's death in the same year, intestine feuds and the gathering threat of the Seldjuk Turks added to the weakness of the Eastern Empire. So, in the long term, there was little serious prospect of Byzantine help for the papacy against the Normans of South Italy.

Leo IX died while the legates' mission was in progress. His successor as pope—Victor II (1054–7)—was the Bishop Gebhard of Eichstätt, who had been responsible for the withholding of German forces from the Civitate campaign. Victor was not at first disposed to continue Leo's anti-Norman policy.[8] But the rising tide of Norman violence compelled him to revert to it and, according to the Montecassino Chronicle, to regret his former opposition.[9] He accordingly resisted the election of the elderly and non-political Peter as abbot of Montecassino, in order to sponsor instead that of the strongly anti-Norman Cardinal Frederick of Lorraine.[10] The death in 1056 of the Emperor Henry III, followed by Henry IV's long and troubled minority, added to the urgency of reappraising his former policy. He

[7] Gaufredus Malaterra, i. 14, p. 15.

[8] Amatus, iii. 47, p. 163.

[9] *Chron. Cas.* ii. 86, pp. 335–6; cf. *Annales Romani, LP* ii. 334.

[10] See above, pp. 57–8.

seems to have intended to draw together the papacy, the Western Empire, and the house of Lorraine, and therefore to reconcile the German court with Duke Godfrey, whose marriage to Countess Beatrice of Tuscany had made him a powerful figure in Italy. By these means he sought to secure effective Lotharingian support for the papacy and so to confirm papal resistance to the Normans.

In 1057 Frederick of Lorraine became pope as Stephen IX. His reign of eight months was characterized by such an out-and-out hostility to the Normans as Leo IX had shown.[11] Stephen seems to have considered placing the imperial crown upon Duke Godfrey's head in order to enlist him firmly against them.[12] He also reopened negotiations with the Byzantines. He approached Argyrus, who was once again in Italy, and he determined to send as ambassadors to Constantinople Cardinal Stephen of San Grisogono, Desiderius, who was by then abbot-elect of Montecassino, and Mainard, the future cardinal-bishop of Silva Candida. But before these envoys could sail from Bari Stephen's death cut short their mission.[13]

The reign of the next pope—Nicholas II (1058–61)—brought about a revolution in papal policies. In effect, Nicholas revived the pro-Norman orientation of Benedict VIII but combined it with the fully developed religious objectives of the reform papacy. The attitude of hostility to the Normans which Leo IX, Victor II, and Stephen IX had usually maintained gave way to a quest for recognition and alliance.[14] Nicholas did not break with Duke Godfrey of Lorraine, with whom he had long-standing connections: he was a sometime canon of Liège, and Godfrey may have been responsible for his accession to his former see of Florence in Tuscany. The duke certainly played a part in his election to the papacy, which took place in the Tuscan city of Siena, and after a sharply fought military campaign it was he who secured Nicholas' enthronement at Rome. But the duke's prompt departure underlined the pope's pressing need to secure continuing and reliable support for a papacy which aspired to control its own destinies. As a first step, at his Lent council of 1059 Nicholas issued his decree on papal elections.[15] It provided

[11] Amatus, iii. 49–50, pp. 165–7; *Chron. Cas.* ii. 97, p. 355; cf. Deér (as Introd. n. 52), pp. 95–6.

[12] *Chron. Cas.* ii. 97, p. 355.

[13] Ibid. iii. 9, pp. 369–71.

[14] Deér, pp. 94–5.

[15] *MGH Const.* i. 538–41, no. 382.

that, to exclude for the future any taint of simony or of the market-place, elections were to be directed by men of ecclesiastical rank and integrity. The Roman cardinal-bishops were to take the initiative in them, but they were straightway to associate with themselves the cardinal clerks; while the consent of the remaining clergy and people of Rome was to follow. If Nicholas' decree was primarily directed against such local Roman aristocratic interference as had supported his rival the antipope Benedict X, it also set limits on the freedom of action of the German ruler: the Roman ecclesiastical electors were merely to show him due honour and reverence according to prevailing circumstances at each election, of which they were to be the judges.

During the summer, Nicholas underpinned the decree by an alliance with the Normans, who were themselves more than anxious to secure confirmation of the place in South Italy that they had recently secured with Richard of Capua's seizure of the principality of Capua and Robert Guiscard's of the duchy of Apulia and Calabria: no sanction was more to be desired than that of St. Peter and the apostolic see. So, as a preparation, the papacy's sometime foes showed themselves in May to be desirable allies, when Archdeacon Hildebrand made an agreement with Prince Richard of Capua which led to Norman hostilities against Benedict X's supporters and to the submission to the papacy of Palestrina, Tusculum, and Nomentano.[16] In August, at the council of Melfi which Richard of Capua and Robert Guiscard attended, the pope received an oath of fealty from Robert Guiscard, and probably also from Richard of Capua, together with the promise of an annual *pensio* from the Normans in recognition of their oath. The duke, whose oath alone survives, swore fealty to the Roman church; he promised to pay it an annual *census*, to uphold its rights, and to respect the *terra sancti Petri* in the sense of the lands in Central Italy which were under papal lordship and their marches with the Norman lands. The duke also guaranteed the observance of the Election Decree.[17] Henceforth the Normans were intended to be the

[16] *Annales Romani, LP* ii. 335; Bonizo of Sutri, vi, p. 593.

[17] *Le Liber censuum de l'église romaine*, caps. 162–3, edd. P. Fabre and L. Duchesne, 3 vols. (Paris, 1889–1952), i. 421–2; Ménager, *Recueil*, pp. 30–3, nos. 6–7; cf. *Chron. Cas.* iii. 15, p. 377. For the title 'duke of Apulia and Calabria', and for the phrase *terra sancti Petri*, see Deér, pp. 49–50, 68–73, 112–17. Richard of Capua's presence at Melfi is established by his charter of 23 Aug. 1059: Gattula, *Accessiones*, p. 161; Loud, 'Calendar', pp. 119–20, no. 3.

principal protectors of the apostolic see and its liberty. In return the pope recognized their legitimacy as lords in South Italy, subject to their status as papal vassals there.

Throughout the decades in which these events were taking place, the fortunes of Montecassino and of the papacy ran on lines which were at first parallel and ultimately converging. At Montecassino the reign of Abbot Richer of Niederaltaich (1038–55) marked a turning-point in the abbey's outlook and relationships which brought it into sympathy with the reform papacy under its German and Lotharingian popes after 1046. When Richer took office Montecassino had for long been perilously dependent upon whichever political authority, whether local or distant, held sway in South Italy. Thus, after the death in 986 of Abbot Aligernus, Abbot Manso (986–96) was similarly a client of the princes of Capua, while Abbot Atenulf (1011–22) was a client of Prince Pandulf IV. In 1018 Boioannes' victory at Cannae placed Montecassino under Byzantine influence, until the Western Emperor Henry II's expedition of 1022 put both Pandulf and Atenulf to flight. A new abbot, Theobald (1022–36), was installed by Henry to safeguard his interests. Prince Pandulf IV's return in 1036 and the revival of Byzantine pressure led to Theobald's exile and to the intrusion as overseer at Montecassino of Pandulf's creature Todinus. In the following year Pandulf's *familiaris* Basil was elected abbot in the prince's palace at Capua in order to suit the Capuans and Byzantines. Such was the background of the Emperor Conrad II's intervention of 1038, and to the installation of Richer as an abbot who would favour the Germans.[18]

In this respect Richer was, indeed, well chosen. But he was no mere servant of German interests. He concerned himself resolutely with Montecassino's security and independence. Above all he sought by energetic self-help to protect it and its lands against local enemies. It lay particularly open to Norman violence, not only from such colonies as Aversa but also from Normans whom Abbot Atenulf had settled upon the *terra sancti Benedicti*. Richer safeguarded Montecassino by building castles and fortifications, by constructing a new bridge over the River Rapido, and by providing the peasants with strongholds to afford security from Norman predators.[19] Furthermore, in 1045

[18] For these events see esp. the notice of the abbots in *Chron. Cas.* ii. 12–65, pp. 189–298.

[19] See above, pp. 56–9, and *Chron. Cas.* ii. 73, p. 315.

he expelled the Normans from the *terra sancti Benedicti*. Faced by the renewed attacks of Prince Pandulf IV in concert with the Normans, Richer appointed Pandulf's enemy, Count Adenulf of Aquino, as *defensor* of the abbey. This led to Adenulf's defeat of Pandulf and to the further discomfiture of the Normans. By thus dismissing them to a distance from Montecassino, Richer not only reduced their menace but also created a situation in which they could one day be safely negotiated with and recruited as allies and benefactors.[20] Both Abbot Desiderius and Leo of Ostia saw in their expulsion from the abbey's lands a turning-point in its fortunes which made possible its later prosperity.[21]

The experience of Pandulf IV's depredations, which were a byword amongst Cassinese writers, was a reminder of how menacing an ill-disposed Lombard prince might be, as well.[22] So in the last years of his abbacy Richer began to reinforce Montecassino's connections by looking towards the reform papacy. Pope Leo IX needed Montecassino's help in pursuance of his South Italian aims, at a time when Montecassino was also concerned to ward off the Normans. In 1049, during his first visit, Leo promised to do all in his power to dignify and exalt it. He returned in 1050, and also in 1053 on his way to Civitate. When he returned to Rome in 1054 he did so in Richer's company.[22] Montecassino also gained from Leo's dealings with Byzantium. In 1054, when Cardinals Humbert and Frederick were on their way to Constantinople, they visited it, and on their return they brought to it from the Emperor Constantine the promise of an annual pension of two pounds of gold.[23] Thus, in the days of Leo IX and Richer, Montecassino and the reform papacy began to be drawn together upon a basis of common interests, and leading figures at Rome became familiar with the abbey.

The link was intensified under Pope Victor II, but still with an anti-Norman purpose. In 1055 Cardinal Frederick himself entered Montecassino as a monk. In 1057 with strong papal backing he became abbot, and soon afterwards he became pope; he at first retained his office as abbot together with the papacy.[24]

[20] *Chron. Cas.* ii. 71–2, 74–5, pp. 309–18.

[21] Ibid. ii. 89, pp. 340–1; Desiderius, *Dial.* ii. 22, pp. 1138–9; see also *Ann. Cas.*, *a.* 1045, p. 1415.

[22] *Chron. Cas.* ii. 79, 81, 84, pp. 324–5, 328–9, 331–3.

[23] Ibid. ii. 85, pp. 333–4, *Reg. Pet. Diac.* no. 144, Dölger, *Regesten*, no. 915.

[24] Amatus, iii. 49, p. 166; *Chron. Cas.* ii. 93–4, iii. 9, pp. 351–3, 369–70. For the retention of former preferment, see Goez (as Ch. II n. 41).

It was also in 1055 that the future Abbot Desiderius entered Montecassino, having already become known to Pope Leo IX and his circle.[25]

Desiderius was born *c.*1027 into a branch of the Beneventan ruling house, and he was given the name of Dauferius.[26] Surmounting the bitter objections of his family, he had in 1048/9 gone to the monastery of Santissima Trinità at la Cava, but had returned to become a monk of Santa Sophia, Benevento. In 1053 he for some time retired to the island monastery of Santa Maria, Tremiti, perhaps thereby taking a deliberate step towards escaping from his Beneventan background; he also lived as a hermit on the Montagna della Maiella. However, Pope Leo IX recalled him to Benevento, and while he was there he took him into his familiarity. At first sight Desiderius' connection with the pope is surprising, for Leo's intervention at Benevento had taken place in collusion with opponents of the prince and his circle. But Desiderius may already have concluded that the princely house was no longer capable of protecting Benevento from the Normans, and that the best hope of security lay under the papal aegis.[27] Moreover, in 1047 Desiderius' father had died at Norman hands, so that he had personal grounds for adhering to their enemies. For whatever reasons he began to throw in his lot with the reformers. He was known to such members of the papal circle as Cardinals Humbert and Frederick of Lorraine, who introduced him to the pope. When Victor II succeeded Leo, it was not long before Desiderius also became known to him. It was with Victor's encouragement that, with his friend Alfanus, the future archbishop of Salerno, Desiderius in 1055 transferred to Montecassino. In 1057, when Pope Stephen IX fell ill and ordered the monks to elect an abbot-designate who might succeed him if he should die, their choice fell upon Desiderius. With Stephen's death on 29 March 1058 he became abbot of Montecassino.

On that date Desiderius had been at Bari and about to embark for Constantinople to conduct negotiations there on behalf of a pope who was still pursuing strongly anti-Norman policies.[28] But signs are not wanting that Desiderius had already perceived

[25] Desiderius, *Dial.* iii, prol., p. 1143; *Chron. Cas.* iii. 7, pp. 367–9.

[26] Amatus, iii. 52, pp. 172–4; *Chron. Cas.* iii. 1–9, pp. 364–71. For Desiderius' early life and election as abbot, see Hirsch, 'Desiderius', pp. 6–20.

[27] See Vehse (as Ch. III n. 3), p. 101.

[28] See above, pp. 110–11.

how the political future lay with the Normans, and that it would be wise to come to terms with them. In 1057 he had served for a time as prior of the Cassinese dependency of San Benedetto, Capua. He was there concerned to cultivate the favour of the Norman Count Richard of Aversa rather than that of Prince Pandulf V, whom Richard was besieging.[29] After Richard subdued the principality of Capua in 1058 he undertook a campaign against Count Adenulf of Aquino, Montecassino's protector in Abbot Richer's days but lord of a county whose rulers were often a danger to it. At the same time Richard visited Montecassino, where, in Amatus' phrase, Abbot Desiderius received him *comme roy*. The monks greeted him with a procession and with the chanting of *laudes* appropriate for a ruler, and Desiderius commended the abbey to his protection. This quasi-royal welcome had its reward. Richard gave Montecassino a charter confirming its lands and possessions. In gratitude to St. Benedict for his career of victory and good fortune Prince Richard of Capua henceforth became Montecassino's zealous supporter.[30] Desiderius was equally prompt to secure Robert Guiscard's favour; while travelling back from Bari after learning of Stephen IX's death, Desiderius paid him a friendly visit.[31]

Thus, in the months before Pope Nicholas II concluded the treaty of Melfi Desiderius also began to turn to the Normans as his potential allies. The chroniclers of Montecassino emphasized how deliberately he did so. Leo of Ostia said that from the beginning he set himself to provide Montecassino with the peace and safety that were requisite for the monastic life, securing the obedience of the fierce Norman peoples who had lately been its plunderers so that their leaders served him as father and lord. He further claimed that Robert Guiscard and Richard of Capua 'loved, enriched, and protected [Montecassino] before all men of their time, and were exceedingly friendly, loyal, and faithful to Desiderius for the whole of his life'.[32] Amatus too saw in their victories a new fulfilment of the prophecies in the book of Isaiah foretelling the rise of Cyrus the Persian: it was by divine

[29] *Chron. Cas.* iii. 8, p. 369; Hirsch conjectured that the prince of Capua may have offended Desiderius by seeking to use his abbey's treasure in support of warfare against the Normans: 'Desiderius', p. 16.

[30] Amatus, iv. 11–14, pp. 189–93, *Chron. Cas.* iii. 15, pp. 377–9, Gattula, *Accessiones*, pp. 161–3, Loud, 'Calendar', p. 119, no. 2.

[31] *Chron. Cas.* iii. 9, p. 371.

[32] *Narratio*, p. 219; *Chron. Cas.* iii. 15–16, pp. 379–80.

providence that the Norman rulers were exalted in Italy; and they used their power to show themselves devoted and generous to Montecassino.[33] Desiderius showed remarkable perception indeed by appreciating that Montecassino with its strengthened *terra sancti Benedicti* could confidently use the Normans to secure its own interests, and he showed equal foresight in perceiving from the earliest days of his abbacy that the Normans in their settled principalities would henceforth be the dominant factor in South Italian politics. At all times this perception remained the basis of Desiderius' political calculations as abbot of Montecassino.

It is clear that, fortified by such views, he was closely associated with Archdeacon Hildebrand as a promoter of the changes in papal alignments which occurred under Pope Nicholas II. The papacy seems to have taken the initiative in building up collaboration. At Eastertide 1058, when Desiderius took office as abbot, Cardinal Humbert was present and took a leading part in the ceremonies. As soon as the antipope Benedict X was defeated, Nicholas II summoned Desiderius to him. They met at Farfa. At Osimo near Ancona, on 6 and 7 March 1059, he made him cardinal-priest and consecrated him abbot. It was then that he made him papal vicar with responsibility for overseeing the monasteries of the Principate, Apulia, and Calabria. In the weeks that followed Desiderius twice visited Rome: on 14 March for his institution to his title-church of Santa Cecilia; and again, at the pope's special request, for Easter. He was in Rome during April for the council at which the Election Decree was promulgated, and he was among its subscribers. He also played a part in the taking of the oaths of the Norman rulers at Melfi. In June Nicholas came to Montecassino, whence Desiderius accompanied him on his southward journey. It was at the pope's instance that Prince Richard of Capua soon afterwards gave Montecassino the church of Santa Maria in Calena.[34] Desiderius' continuing service of the papacy is attested by his witnessing of papal charters at Florence in January 1060.[35]

During the pontificate of Nicholas II, the papacy, the Normans, and Montecassino thus drew together in an alliance based upon common interests which all parties hoped would serve to establish their security and prosperity.

[33] Amatus, dedica, iii. 52, v. 1–4, pp. 3–4, 176, 222–7.

[34] *Chron. Cas.* iii. 9, 12, 13, pp. 371–5; Loud, 'Calendar', pp. 119–20, no. 3.

[35] *Epp.* 15, 17, Migne, *PL* cxliii. 1330–2, 1334–6.

ii. POPE ALEXANDER II, THE CADALAN SCHISM, AND MONTECASSINO

Pope Nicholas II died in July 1061. The immediate sequel to his death seemed to confirm the value to the papacy of the Norman alliance and to present Montecassino with no problems. The succession to the papacy was disputed.[36] Led by Count Gerard of Galeria, who had sponsored the antipope Benedict X, a group of Romans sent the insignia of the Roman *patricius* to the German court, and requested the nomination of a new pope. The bishops of Lombardy and the imperial chancellor for Italy, Guibert, later archbishop of Ravenna, supported Gerard; but the German regency under the Empress-mother Agnes delayed a decision. Archdeacon Hildebrand and his party at Rome turned to the Normans, and Prince Richard of Capua responded as the treaty of Melfi had provided. Under his protection Bishop Anselm of Lucca was elected pope as Alexander II; he was enthroned at Rome on 1 October 1061. Abbot Desiderius of Montecassino travelled to Rome with the prince and was associated with his actions there.[37] On 2 October Prince Richard took an oath of fealty to the new pope, and it appears that in 1062 Robert Guiscard did likewise.[38]

Alexander's election prompted the opposing party to elect as antipope Bishop Cadalus of Parma, who took the name of Honorius II; thus the Cadalan Schism began. It rapidly placed Alexander in need of external help. Early in 1062 Honorius' supporters occupied most of Rome. Benzo, bishop of Alba, whom the German court sent to champion his cause, wrote of negotiations with the Byzantine Emperor Constantine X Ducas which were undertaken with a view to enthroning Honorius and defeating the Normans.[39] But it was less from the Normans than from the north that help came to Alexander: for the third time Duke Godfrey of Lorraine intervened in a papal election and its sequel by compelling both rivals to observe an armistice and to return to their bishoprics. The *coup d'état* at Kaiserwerth

[36] For the events of this section, see esp. Hirsch, 'Desiderius', pp. 26–38; Meyer von Knonau, *Jahrbücher*, i; Schmidt (as Introd. n. 60), esp. pp. 68–123.

[37] *Chron. Cas.* iii. 19, pp. 385–6; Benzo of Alba, vii. 2, p. 672.

[38] *Le Liber censuum* (as Introd. n. 61), ii. 93–4; W. Holtzmann, 'Das Privileg Alexanders II. für S. Maria Mattina', *QFIAB* xxxiv (1955), 71 n. 1; Romuald of Salerno, *a.* 1062, p. 186; Loud, 'Calendar', p. 120, no. 3*a*.

[39] ii. 7, p. 615.

in April 1062, when Archbishop Anno of Cologne seized the reins of power in Germany, worked to Alexander's advantage. In October a synod at Augsburg, for which Cardinal Peter Damiani prepared his *Disceptatio synodalis*,[40] led to the dispatch to Italy of a mission headed by Anno's nephew Bishop Burchard of Halberstadt, which was to resolve the schism by enthroning Alexander unless his election were found to be gravely irregular. In 1063 Alexander returned to Rome with the support of Godfrey of Lorraine. Although Honorius raised another army, combined action by Godfrey and the Normans eventually compelled him to withdraw to Parma;[41] while at Pentecost a synod at Mantua finally recognized Alexander as the rightful pope.

Norman troops were amongst those who established Alexander at Rome in 1063, but it was to Godfrey of Lorraine that he principally owed his victory. Throughout the schism both Richard of Capua and Robert Guiscard were preoccupied: in 1062 Richard captured the city of Capua itself, while Robert was driving the remaining Byzantines from Apulia and beginning the conquest of Sicily. It was already becoming clear that the Normans would put their own interests first and that, despite the treaty of Melfi, they could not be counted upon to promote papal interests unless it suited them to do so. Nothing is known of any part that Montecassino and its abbot may have played in the Cadalan Schism. But during and after it Desiderius kept in close contact with Richard of Capua, and a rising tide of Capuan gifts to Montecassino shows how steadily he advanced in the prince's favour.[42] It clearly emerges that Desiderius' relations with his increasingly powerful Norman neighbour were not inhibited on account of Capuan lukewarmness towards the papacy.

In the middle 1060s the situation deteriorated, since Norman activities now began to do the papacy positive harm. Robert Guiscard remained preoccupied in the south, but Richard of Capua, having occupied the city of Capua itself, pressed further

[40] Ed. L. de Heinemann, *MGH Libelli*, i. 76–94.

[41] For Norman intervention, see Benzo of Alba, ii. 15–18, pp. 618–22.

[42] Richard is said to have paid a second visit to Montecassino early in 1067: Amatus, iv. 26, p. 200. For Capuan gifts to Montecassino between 1063 and 1072, including an abbot's mitre for Desiderius, see Amatus, iv. 31, p. 205; *Chron. Cas.* iii. 15–16, pp. 379–80; *Reg. Pet. Diac.*, nos. 41, 165, 406–11, 426; Loud, 'Calendar', pp. 120–2, nos. 4–6, 10–11, 13–16.

and further northwards: after a year of successful campaigning he in 1066 captured Ceprano and raided the countryside almost to Rome itself.[43] Thus, his activities increasingly threatened papal lands. His antagonism to Pope Alexander II had intensified in the winter of 1063/4, when the pope recruited for the papal service his turbulent ex-son-in-law William of Montreuil, with whom he was at odds.[44] Richard, on the other hand, aspired to the patriciate of the city of Rome. The papacy therefore looked for help from north of the Alps. Henry IV of Germany came of age in 1065 and in that year an Italian expedition was already mooted. In 1066 Henry determined to go to Rome for imperial coronation and to check Richard. But Duke Godfrey of Lorraine forestalled him and in 1067 journeyed south as Pope Alexander's protector. Accompanied by the pope and cardinals he compelled Richard to withdraw across the River Garigliano.[45] Later in the year better relations existed between Alexander and Richard, for in October the pope stayed in Capua while returning from a journey in South Italy.[46] But by that time there was tension between the papacy and some of the family of Robert Guiscard; in August, at the synod of Melfi, Alexander excommunicated Robert's brother William of the Principate and his knights, after they had seized land belonging to Archbishop Alfanus of Salerno.[47] It was again apparent that neither Richard of Capua nor Robert Guiscard could be counted upon to consult papal interests or to refrain from attacks upon papal lands and other ecclesiastical property. By 1071 a further disquieting development took place. Hitherto the two Norman leaders had not been well disposed towards each other, but Robert Guiscard now helped Richard of Capua against the adventurer William of Montreuil, who was himself a papal vassal.[48]

In the confused politics of the late 1060s the papal policy inaugurated by Nicholas II of relying upon the alliance of

[43] *Chron. Cas.* iii. 23, p. 389; Lupus Protospatarius, p. 59.

[44] Amatus, vi. 1, pp. 262–3. For the oath embodying the title *procurator patrimonii sancti Petri* which William is likely to have taken, see Deusdedit, *Coll. can.* iii. 283 (155), pp. 392–3; *Le Liber censuum* (as Introd. n. 61), i. 421, no. 161.

[45] Amatus, vi. 9–10, pp. 270–2; *Chron. Cas.* iii. 23, pp. 389–90. For a statement that Hildebrand summoned Godfrey to Italy, see Bonizo of Sutri, vi, p. 599, cf. *Annales Altahenses maiores, a.* 1067, *MGH Script. rer. Germ.*, pp. 72–3.

[46] *Ep.* 55, Migne, *PL* cxlvi. 1337–8.

[47] *Ep.* 54, Migne, *PL* cxlvi. 1335–7.

[48] Amatus, vi. 12, p. 275. Tension between Robert and Richard was apparent soon after 1059: Amatus, iv. 20, p. 196.

a more or less united and complaisant Norman settlement in South Italy thus proved increasingly precarious. By granting the Normans the benefit that they desired of holding their lands as papal fiefs, the papacy had played its sole card. It had no further hold over them, save in so far as homage and enfeoffment would occasionally have to be renewed upon the succession of a new pope or prince of Capua or duke of Apulia.[49] Otherwise their own purposes and interests were paramount, with little regard for papal needs. Alexander had perforce to react by using William of Montreuil against Richard of Capua. The *entente* between Richard of Capua and Robert Guiscard against William was already a warning that the papacy should seek to divide these leaders from each other. Alexander therefore inaugurated the policy that the papacy was to maintain up to the end of the 1070s—that of fomenting divisions among the Normans in order to weaken and control them.

When the papacy developed this policy of *divide et impera* Abbot Desiderius at Montecassino was forced to choose between papal and Norman interests. His plans at Montecassino made it more than ever imperative that he should seek unity between his Norman neighbours and not countenance their division. He began work on his new basilica in 1066. To finance and carry out such building work as well as to provide for the security and prosperity of Montecassino's possessions and dependencies, he needed to have the goodwill and to promote the harmony of the two principal Norman leaders. It is not surprising that his relations with the papacy showed signs of strain; Amatus wrote of the *grant discorde* that Prince Gisulf of Salerno was able at this time to sow between Abbot Desiderius and Archdeacon Hildebrand.[50] It seems clear that Desiderius saw the Normans as his principal benefactors and allies, upon whose goodwill and unity his plans depended. His bond with the papacy was secondary, and he was unlikely to follow it in its policy of dividing the Norman rulers.

Nevertheless, he showed his intention so far as possible to court the favour of all the authorities that might impinge upon him. In 1065, upon first hearing of Henry IV's intended Italian expedition, he hastened to Amalfi and bought twenty silk

[49] This point is well argued by D. Whitton, 'Papal Policy in Rome, 1012–1124' (Univ. of Oxford D.Phil. thesis, 1979).
[50] Amatus, iv. 48, p. 219.

cloths dyed in three colours of a kind known as *triblatti*, so that *pro tutela . . . et honore monasterii* he might have to hand a suitable gift for the king.[51] Such a step was prudent in view of past German expeditions, when German kings had made a considerable, if short-term, impact upon Montecassino. Desiderius also kept in touch with Duke Godfrey of Lorraine, whom he met at Pisa on an unknown date during these years.[52] In spite of all the difficulties he continued to maintain a basically amicable relationship with the papacy. Alexander issued an important charter for Montecassino,[53] and in 1068 he employed Desiderius in collaboration with Archdeacon Hildebrand to depose and replace Abbot Humbald of Subiaco.[54] In 1071 Pope Alexander II not only came to Montecassino and dedicated the new basilica, but it was by means of papal letters that invitations went to the many bishops from the Campagna, the Principate, Apulia, and Calabria who thronged to one of the most illustrious gatherings of the eleventh century.[55] The political dilemmas of Alexander II's reign compelled Desiderius to put the Normans first, even when his friendship with them did not coincide with papal interests. Yet he was able to serve and to ingratiate himself with all parties, including the papacy, and thus to safeguard Montecassino's paramount interests. The proof of his skill in keeping the balance is the well-nigh universal attendance of Italian churchmen and leading laymen at the consecration ceremony of 1071, which stands as the high point of Desiderius' years as abbot.

iii. MONTECASSINO, THE NORMANS, AND POPE GREGORY VII, 1073–7

The general goodwill of the consecration ceremony did not for long persist. The early years of Gregory VII's pontificate, up to about the middle of 1077, represented the time of greatest difficulty in papal relations with the Normans, and therefore in Desiderius' purpose of retaining the favour of all his potential friends—both papal and Norman.[56] The friction between

[51] *Chron. Cas.* iii. 18, p. 385. When the likelihood of a German expedition passed Desiderius used the silk to make vestments for his church. For *triblatti*, see Peter Damiani, *Ep.* iv. 7, Migne, *PL* cxliv. 308.

[52] *Chron. Cas.* iii. 22, p. 389.

[53] See above, Introd. n. 76.

[54] See above, p. 30.

[55] *Chron. Cas.* iii. 29, pp. 398–401; *Narratio*, pp. 219–25.

[56] For another interpretation of events discussed in the remainder of this chapter,

Desiderius and Archdeacon Hildebrand that Amatus had already noted, but without citing reasons other than Prince Gisulf of Salerno's malice, became aggravated in the last years before Hildebrand became pope in April 1073. In 1071, according to the Montecassino Chronicle, Desiderius received a papal commission to reform the monastery of Santa Maria, Tremiti, which Montecassino claimed to be its own former possession by papal grant. He enlisted the help of Robert Guiscard's nephew, Count Robert I of Loritello, together with Peter, son of Count Walter of Lesina. By thus involving Robert Guiscard's relatives Desiderius was giving encouragement to Norman expansion in the direction of the Abruzzi, where Robert of Loritello's activities would become increasingly objectionable to Gregory in the next few years because of the danger that the Normans there presented to the papal states. Desiderius deposed its abbot, Adam, replacing him by Trasmundus, a monk of Montecassino who was a son of Count Oderisius of Marsia. Trasmundus disappointed Desiderius' hopes by becoming an oppressive and cruel ruler of his monks, blinding a number of them and tearing out the tongue of another. At the time of the dedication of the new basilica Desiderius recalled him to Montecassino. Thereafter, according to the Montecassino Chronicle, Hildebrand warmly espoused Trasmundus' cause, prevailing upon a reluctant Desiderius to release him so that he might become abbot of San Clemente, Casauria, and soon afterwards bishop of Valva. In 1073 Desiderius again turned to the Normans by enlisting the help of Robert Guiscard himself when he intervened once more at Tremiti against Ferro, the deputy whom Trasmundus had left there. As a result Tremiti recognized Desiderius personally during his lifetime as its *tutor et defensor* on behalf of the apostolic see;[57] he thus retained at least a foothold in its affairs.

see G. A. Loud, 'Abbot Desiderius of Montecassino and the Gregorian Papacy', *JEH* xxx (1979), 305–26.

[57] *Chron. Cas.* iii. 25, pp. 392–3; cf. *Chronicon Casauriense, a.* 1073, Muratori, *RIS* ii/2, 864–5, and *Chronica sancti Bartholomaei de Carpineto*, iv, in Ughelli–Coleti, x, Miscellanea Ughelliana, pp. 359–61. For the Abruzzi at this time, see T. Leccisotti, 'Le relazioni fra Montecassino e Tremiti e i possedimenti Cassinesi a Foggia e Nocera', *Benedectina*, iii (1949), 203–15, and L. Gatto, 'Ugo Maumouset, conte de Manoppello, normanno d'Abruzzo', *Studi . . . Morghen*, i. 355–73. At the council of Melfi in Aug. 1059 Pope Nicholas II had, in Hildebrand's presence, already disallowed Desiderius' claims to authority over Tremiti: *Codice diplomatico del monastero di Tremiti* (as Ch. II n. 54), pp. 197–8, no. 46, on which see Loud, 'Calendar', pp. 119–20, no. 3.

Whatever the exact interpretation that should be placed upon these obscure events, they were indications of more serious tension to follow between Montecassino and the papacy. Hildebrand's accession at first led to a papal bid to promote harmonious relations between the papacy, Montecassino, the Lombard princes, and the Normans, the rapid frustration of which became an exacerbating factor. Gregory sent notices of his election to Desiderius and to Prince Gisulf of Salerno, summoning them to come to Rome without delay and to consult the needs of the Roman church.[58] Almost simultaneously a false rumour reached Rome that Robert Guiscard had died at Bari. Gregory sought to use the occasion of the duke's supposed death in order to rehabilitate the papal–Norman alliance that the treaty of Melfi had envisaged. He sent a letter of condolence to Robert Guiscard's wife Sichelgaita, the gist of which Amatus has preserved. Gregory spoke warmly of the duke as 'lo karissime fil de la sainte Eglize' and invited Sichelgaita to encourage her son Roger to receive from the church's hand whatever possessions his father had held of Pope Alexander II. When Robert Guiscard, who was alive but still unwell, saw the letter he was gratified and promised to serve Gregory faithfully.[59] His motives in so promising were, no doubt, to secure his own confirmation in his fiefs by a new pope, and also to secure eventual papal support for the succession to his duchy of his younger son Roger rather than of Bohemond, his son by his former wife Alberada.

When Gregory heard of Robert Guiscard's recovery and favourable disposition, he took the initiative in seeking a meeting with him at San Germano near Montecassino. Robert showed himself cautiously willing to come; perhaps because of the size of Gregory's own military retinue he moved with a large host to Rapolla, south-west of Melfi. He secured Beneventan loyalty by concluding a treaty with Prince Landulf VI.[60] Abbot Desiderius acted as intermediary between Gregory and Robert Guiscard, but negotiations came to nothing. The reasons are uncertain. According to Amatus, Robert asked Gregory for a safe conduct to the city because he feared its rulers' malice, and

[58] *Reg.* i. 1–2, 23 Apr. 1073, pp. 3–4.

[59] Amatus, vii. 8, p. 298. The availability of the letter shows how close were relations between Montecassino and Robert Guiscard.

[60] Guy of Ferrara, i. 2, p. 534; Amatus, vii. 9, p. 298–9; *Annales Beneventani, a.* 1072 (1073), *MGH SS* iii. 181; *Reg.* i. 18*a*, 12 Aug. 1073, pp. 30–1.

there ensued discord and ill will between Robert and Gregory.[61] This sounds more like a symptom than a cause of their estrangement, which was probably attributable to Gregory's fear of Robert's northward expansion, and to Robert's dislike of Gregory's links with Gisulf of Salerno. In any case Gregory reverted to Alexander II's expedient of dividing the Normans of Apulia from those of Capua. This was not difficult, for Richard of Capua was himself uneasy about Robert Guiscard's growing power. On 14 September 1073 Richard took an oath of fealty to Gregory, who remained at Capua from 1 September to 15 November. In a letter to Erlembald, the Patarene leader at Milan, Gregory felt able to rejoice that the Normans who had lately been negotiating with each other to the jeopardy of papal interests would now agree upon peace only when Gregory willed it.[62] He implied that he controlled Norman loyalties. A papal policy of *divide et impera* was once again the order of the day.

Such a papal policy cannot have suited Desiderius. He had attested Gregory's treaty with Landulf of Benevento. But after Gregory's breach with Robert Guiscard there is for long a dearth of evidence for contact of any kind between Montecassino and the apostolic see. Gregory and Desiderius are not known to have been in touch when Gregory passed through San Germano on 20 November. Gregory's failure to confirm Montecassino's privileges at the beginning of his pontificate further indicates coolness. But when Robert Guiscard showed his strength after leaving Benevento he, for his part, was scrupulously careful not to harm the *terra sancti Benedicti* which Amatus wrote that he respected *coment temple de Dieu.*[63] He clearly meant to keep intact his friendship with Montecassino.

Throughout 1074 Gregory was energetically concerned to promote an extravagantly planned military enterprise in part directed against Robert Guiscard, which cannot but have increased Montecassino's unease with Gregory's current political concerns.[64] As Gregory at first conceived it in February, his

[61] Amatus, vii. 9, p. 299; *Chron. Cas.* iii. 36, p. 413.

[62] Amatus, vii. 10, 12, pp. 300, 303; Reg. i. 21*a*, 12 Aug. 1073, pp. 35–6, cf. i. 25, 27 Sept. 1073, p. 42.

[63] Amatus, vii. 10, p. 302; *Reg.* i. 31, 20 Nov. 1073, pp. 51–2.

[64] For fuller discussion, see H. E. J. Cowdrey, 'Pope Gregory VII's "Crusading" Plans of 1074', *Outremer. Studies in the History of the Crusading Kingdom of Jerusalem presented to Joshua Prawer*, edd. B. Z. Kedar, H. E. Mayer, and R. C. Smail (Jerusalem, 1982), 27–40.

enterprise was to involve military forces recruited from France and Tuscany, as well as from the papal lands and the principality of Salerno. By a massive show of force it would intimidate the rebellious Normans into obedience to the apostolic see. Then it would cross to Constantinople and help Eastern Christians suffering under Saracen attacks. At his Lent council Gregory also excommunicated Robert Guiscard and his accomplices.[65] In May Gregory's expedition was prepared, and by June he assembled sufficient forces from Tuscany, Salerno, and Rome to hold a council of war near Viterbo. But the expedition soon broke up, largely owing to internal strife between the Pisans and the Salernitans, whose habits of piracy they resented. Gregory had to dispatch Prince Gisulf to Rome by night in order to save him from Pisan wrath. According to Amatus, during 1074 Robert Guiscard showed his humility towards the prince of the apostles by being prepared for negotiations with Gregory at Benevento, but Gregory failed to keep an appointment.[66] Gregory was for long hesitant about what to do next with regard to the Normans;[67] in December 1074, when he revived his plan for an eastern expedition, this time in concert with Henry IV of Germany, whom he hoped to leave as protector of the Roman church, he made no reference to them. But once again his military plans were barren of success.[68]

The official reaction to Gregory's schemes of 1074 on the part of Montecassino, its abbot, and its monks does not emerge; but there are two sources from which individuals' opinions may be judged. The first, which is probably of limited significance, is the two odes which Archbishop Alfanus of Salerno wrote, probably at this time, to Prince Gisulf and his brother Guy.[69] He encouraged their participation in such an expedition as Gregory at first planned. They were exhorted to campaign against the Normans, who had settled in Lombard Italy *velut una lues pecorum*, and Guy was invited himself to seek the Byzantine crown. Written by a prelate in the service of Gregory VII's ally Prince Gisulf, they show an anti-Norman animus beyond any

[65] *Reg.* i. 46, 2 Feb. 1074, pp. 69–71; i. 85*a*, p. 123.

[66] Amatus, vii. 13–14, pp. 305–7; cf. Gregory VII's letters of 12 and 15 June, which are declared to be 'Data in expeditione': *Reg.* i. 84–5, pp. 119–23.

[67] Ibid. ii. 9, 16 Oct. 1074, pp. 138–40.

[68] Ibid. ii. 51, 7 Dec. 1074, pp. 165–8; ii. 37, 16 Dec. 1074, pp. 172–3; *Epp. vag.*, no. 5, pp. 10–13.

[69] Lentini and Avagliano, *Carmi*, nos. 17, 20.

that the pope himself felt: his objective was to secure the Normans' obedience and service, not their extirpation. The odes played upon Salernitan traditions of hostility to the Normans and to Byzantium. Such extreme anti-Norman flights of fancy are more than unlikely to have found an echo at Montecassino. They are best regarded as eccentricities of Alfanus the court poet, who was always ready to direct his muse to the service of his current political master.

A second individual reaction, that of the chronicler Amatus, was also somewhat idiosyncratic, but it was probably more representative of Montecassino. Amatus' prejudice was the reverse of Alfanus', since he was the Normans' eulogist. He mocked Gregory's plans of early 1074, dwelling upon the spectacle of a pope who, finding scant help from men, turned to women—Beatrice and Matilda of Tuscany—for military leadership:

> At that time the pope made a firm and strong friendship and league with Prince Richard [of Capua]; and Prince [Gisulf of Salerno] did likewise. They all sought how to drive Duke [Robert Guiscard] from his dukedom and from the land. The pope went to Rome and began to do what he could to complete what he had begun and planned. But, since he could find no men to help him, he sought the aid of women. He sent letters to Beatrice and her daughter Matilda, telling him why he wished them to come and talk to him. Because of their perfect faith in St. Peter and of their deep love for God's vicar, when they heard the pope's summons they did not delay to come, and they made ready to perform his will. They promised to bring 300,000 knights and, to make victory more certain, they promised that among the 300,000 there would be 500 Germans. The pope answered, 'As for the paltry Norman rabble, we can attack and conquer them with 20,000 if God pleases; for we shall have the help of Prince Richard and of those who dwell in these parts, as well as the protection of God and of the apostles.' The noble ladies replied, '. . . your holiness can leave it to us, women though we be, to bring such men as will deserve the honour of victory. We shall deliver from the enemies' hands the possessions of the prince of the Apostles.' When the pope perceived the two women's wisdom, he determined to follow their advice and counsel, committing the matter to their judgement and will.[70]

Amatus' partisanship of the Normans, and also his bitter animus against Prince Gisulf of Salerno,[71] were exaggerated. Yet he

[70] Amatus, vii. 12, pp. 303–4.

[71] Ibid. For Gisulf as Gregory's aide and counsellor, see vii. 7, 31, pp. 348, 371–2. For Amatus' denigration, iv. 33–49, viii. 2, pp. 206–20, 339. There is independent testimony to his cruelty: *Vitae quattuor priorum abbatum Cavensium*, ed. L. M. Cerasoli, *RIS*[2] vi/5, pp. 13–14.

may have written up a view that was generally held at Montecassino. Amatus dedicated his history to Abbot Desiderius, who cannot wholly have disapproved of its contents. There is no evidence that Gisulf was ever honoured at Montecassino while he was prince.[72] Amatus' view of the Norman and Salernitan leaders indicates that, as was to be expected, in 1074 Gregory and Montecassino took opposite sides. Montecassino sought to preserve good relations with the Normans and above all with Robert Guiscard. It is not known to have done anything that might prejudice his interests; while, with the exception of Alfanus of Salerno, who had his own reasons, its writers showed no sympathy with Gregory's ally and Robert Guiscard's enemy, Gisulf of Salerno.

Montecassino's overriding concerns to promote Norman unity and to secure overall Norman favour persisted into 1075. Thus, in concert with Duke Sergius V of Naples, Robert Guiscard embarked upon hostilities in the Terra di Lavoro against Gregory's other ally Prince Richard of Capua. Desiderius, whom Amatus now described as the chosen spiritual father and friend of both Norman leaders, pursued his usual policy of seeking appeasement between them. He brought them together near Aversa and they exchanged the kiss of peace. Then they negotiated a truce at Acerra. But after thirty days more of negotiations under Desiderius' eye at Apice near Benevento, Richard refused to concede that his friendship with Robert Guiscard should not be conditional upon his fealty to Gregory VII. Robert Guiscard broke off talks and the Norman leaders relapsed into hostility.[73] Desiderius' endeavours to promote his policy of Norman unity thus proved abortive, while Gregory's interest to keep the Normans divided prevailed. Gregory's own disenchantment with the Normans grew. In January 1075 he described them as being, like his other Roman and Lombard neighbours, 'worse than Jews and pagans'.[74] At his Lent council

[72] He is not on record as making any gift to Montecassino after one of *c.*1059 (the monastery of San Lorenzo 'de Monte'): *Chron. Cas.* iii. 13, p. 375; A. Mancone (as Ch. I n. 39); G. Crisci and A. Campagna, *Salerno sacra* (Salerno, 1962), 405–6. The Montecassino Chronicle referred to him as prince but seldom, and with no note of approval: ii. 82, iii. 8, 13, 15, 24, 29, 45, pp. 329, 369, 375, 378, 391, 399, 422. His death in 1091 was afterwards commemorated at Montecassino, but this may reflect his services to the papal cause after 1077: Hoffmann (as Ch. I n. 118), pp. 110, 135; Inguanez (as Ch. I n. 118), 2 June.

[73] Amatus, vii. 15–17, pp. 307–10; Bonizo of Sutri, vii, p. 604.

[74] *Reg.* ii. 49, to Abbot Hugh of Cluny, p. 189. Despite Chalandon, *Domination*,

he for a second time pronounced excommunication upon Robert Guiscard, together with Robert of Loritello, for their invasion of the property of St. Peter.[75]

Up to this point, the state of relations between Gregory, Montecassino, and the Normans had been largely determined by South Italian affairs. But during the winter of 1075/6 there supervened the first excommunication of Henry IV of Germany at Gregory's Lent council of 1076.[76] Wider political factors now began to enter the picture. Perhaps a short time before, Henry made a determined attempt to secure Robert Guiscard's alliance against Gregory. He sent to him his Italian chancellor Bishop Gregory of Vercelli and Count Eberhard of Nellenburg, with a request that he receive from himself investiture with his lands.[77] Robert returned a firm refusal, couched in masterly terms which Amatus reproduced. Ignoring ideas of condominium, he reminded Henry that he had captured his lands from the Byzantines and that his tenure of them had received papal sanction. Therefore he would not allow Henry to invest him with any of his past conquests, but he would be prepared to have him do so in respect of such fresh lands as Henry might himself in future bestow.[78] Robert Guiscard made clear his intention of remaining independent for the time being of Henry and his plans; although he left the door open for future dealings if Henry's power in Italy were to grow so that he had lands to give.

In truth, however, neither Robert Guiscard nor Richard of Capua had reason to welcome German intervention in South Italy, for if it were successful it could only threaten their own power and freedom of action. Henry's increasing hostility to Gregory therefore gave the Normans an incentive to seek agreement with each other and with Gregory in order to maintain the status quo. Gregory, too, now had good reason for promoting the reconciliation and mutual goodwill of the two Norman leaders. So times became rather more favourable for Desiderius'

i. 240, it is unlikely that, in *Reg.* ii. 51, to King Sweyn of Denmark, 25 Jan. 1075, p. 194, Gregory asked for one of Sweyn's sons to seek lands in Norman Italy; the reference is probably to lands in Croatia.

[75] *Reg.* ii. 52*a*, p. 197.

[76] Ibid. iii. 10*a*, pp. 268–71.

[77] That German claims to lordship in South Italy were alive in the 1070s is implied by the terms of Richard of Capua's oath to Gregory VII in 1073: above, p. 125.

[78] Amatus, vii. 27, pp. 320–1.

diplomacy of reconciliation between them; Amatus commented with regard to events at this time that Desiderius 'sempre estoit principe de paiz de ces dui'. There were renewed negotiations with Desiderius as mediator. They resulted in a peace which amounted to a promise of mutual aid and defence. It included a promise by Richard to help Robert capture Salerno, and another by Robert to help Richard take Naples.[79]

If Gregory knew of these terms he cannot have been gratified, for they presented a mortal threat to his ally Gisulf of Salerno. But in view of his gathering struggle with Henry IV he began to show a more conciliatory attitude towards the twice-excommunicated Robert Guiscard which, despite setbacks, began the train of events which led to Robert's renewed oath of vassalage to the pope at Ceprano in 1080. In March 1076 he instructed Archbishop Arnald of Acerenza to absolve Robert Guiscard's brother Roger and his knights, who were about to embark for Sicily, and through them to encourage Robert Guiscard himself to seek reconciliation with the church.[80] A letter which Gregory sent in April to the Milanese knight Wifred suggests that the pope was aware of Robert Guiscard's refusal to acknowledge Henry's lordship, and he expressed his confidence that negotiations then in prospect would further the interests of the Roman church by recalling the Normans to St. Peter's fealty.[81] It may have been at this time that Gregory sought to use Abbot Desiderius' good offices to reconcile Robert Guiscard with his brother-in-law Gisulf of Salerno and thus prepare for a united front of South Italian rulers in alliance with the papacy to counter the German threat.[82]

The Normans, however, showed scant solicitude for papal interests but resolutely pursued their own. Gregory kept an anxious eye on the situation,[83] which from his point of view deteriorated in the autumn and winter of 1076/7. Robert Guiscard and Richard of Capua planned an expedition into papal lands in the Roman Campagna.[84] Then they mounted the

[79] Amatus, vii. 28–9, pp. 322–3. Jordan of Capua was also reconciled to his father: ibid. vii. 33, pp. 330–3.

[80] *Reg.* iii. 11, 14 Mar. 1076, pp. 271–2.

[81] Ibid. iii. 15, (Apr.) 1076, pp. 276–7.

[82] Amatus, viii. 13, pp. 353–4; *Chron. Cas.* iii. 45, p. 422. So Chalandon, *Domination*, i. 244.

[83] *Reg.* iv. 2, to Bishop Hermann of Metz, 26 Aug. 1076, p. 293.

[84] Amatus, viii. 22, pp. 361–2.

campaign which by the spring of 1077 led to the capture of Salerno and Amalfi and in the summer to the siege of Naples. Gregory reacted with anger, telling his Milanese partisans that he would never condone the sacrilegious invasion of papal lands.[85]

Throughout these events Abbot Desiderius was as usual concerned to promote peace if possible, but above all to maintain good relations with both of the Norman leaders. According to Amatus his attempts at peacemaking between Robert Guiscard and Gisulf of Salerno were haughtily rejected by the latter.[86] When the Norman leaders were preparing to raid papal lands, both went to Montecassino, where Desiderius received them cordially and with honour; the excommunicate Robert Guiscard in particular showed piety and benevolence towards the abbey.[87] In 1076 and 1077 Desiderius still found it impossible to serve both the papacy and the Normans. In the circumstances he was ready to support the invaders of the lands of St. Peter. So, too, when Salerno was about to fall, the time-serving Archbishop Alfanus adhered to Robert Guiscard and Richard of Capua.[88]

Yet times were changing. Robert Guiscard's decisive victory over Gisulf of Salerno eliminated one source of strife in South Italy, and reduced to relative insignificance a figure about whom Montecassino and the papacy had been deeply divided.[89] Faced with the hostility of Henry IV of Germany, Gregory VII could not afford to go too far in alienating Norman sympathy. So, during the next three years, a troubled situation in South Italy eventually led to the renewal of the alliance between the papacy and the Normans which had been established at Melfi in 1059. This set the stage for Abbot Desiderius of Montecassino once more to play a role of reconciliation and gradually to associate himself more closely with papal interests.

iv. MONTECASSINO, THE NORMANS, AND POPE GREGORY VII, 1077–80

To begin with there were further setbacks. After his capture of Salerno, Robert Guiscard was above all concerned to extend

[85] *Reg.* iv. 7, 31 Oct. 1076, p. 305.

[86] Amatus, viii. 15, p. 357.

[87] Ibid. viii. 22–3, pp. 361–4; *Chron. Cas.* iii. 45, pp. 422–3.

[88] Amatus, viii. 17, pp. 357–8.

[89] Robert Guiscard allowed him to leave Salerno honourably. He passed into Gregory VII's service: Amatus, viii. 30–1, pp. 371–2; William of Apulia, iii. 457–64, p. 188.

and consolidate his own power. In accordance with his agreement with Richard of Capua, after further uneasy negotiations he left some of his forces at Naples but himself embarked upon a programme of conquest at papal expense. The death on 18 November 1077 of Prince Landulf of Benevento, who had no surviving son, gave him a pretext on 19 December to lay siege to Benevento,[90] thus challenging Gregory VII's authority over a papal city, before he departed for Calabria. Gregory was as powerless to bring military help to Benevento as he had been to Salerno, but at his Lent council in 1078 he reacted with spiritual censures. The official record did not specify names, but he excommunicated all the Normans who were trying to invade the *terra sancti Petri* (defined as the march of Fermo and the duchy of Spoleto), who were laying siege to Benevento, who were seeking to invade and plunder the Campagna, Marittima, and Sabina, and who were endeavouring to harass the city of Rome itself. By a gesture which had implications for Montecassino in view of its ties with the Normans, Gregory also threatened with perpetual exclusion from the priestly office any bishop or priest of those regions who performed divine service on the Normans' behalf.[91]

However, the late 1070s also saw a tendency, which had first become manifest during the winter of 1076 in connection with Henry IV's fruitless seeking of Robert Guiscard's alliance, for Norman horizons to be extended beyond South Italy in ways which at least indirectly helped to draw Robert Guiscard and the papacy together. Robert Guiscard made marriage plans for his numerous daughters which in every case involved families in good standing with Gregory. In the west, the duke's occupation of Amalfi led in the spring of 1078 to a splendid marriage ceremony at Troia, when a daughter of unknown name was married to Hugh, son of Albert Azzo II, marquis of Este; according to Lampert of Hersfeld Henry IV at Canossa had chosen the marquis, along with Abbot Hugh of Cluny, to stand surety with Gregory because he was confident of his probity in Gregory's eyes.[92] In a double marriage at Salerno in 1080,

[90] For events in the rest of this paragraph, see Amatus, viii. 32-5, pp. 372-4; *Chron. Cas.* iii. 45, p. 423; *Ann. Cas., aa.* 1077-8, pp. 1420-1; *Annales Beneventani, a.* 1077, *MGH SS* iii. 181.

[91] *Reg.* v. 14*a*, caps. 9, 11, 27 Feb.-3 Mar. 1078, p. 371. Amatus said that Duke Robert was himself excommunicated.

[92] William of Apulia, iii. 488-501, p. 190, cf. pp. 305-6; Amatus, viii. 34, pp. 373-4; Lampert of Hersfeld, *a.* 1077, pp. 404, 408-10.

Robert Guiscard gave his daughter Matilda to Count Raymond Berengar II of Barcelona, who was important to Gregory in view of the Spanish Reconquest, and his daughter Sybilla to Count Ebolus II of Roucy, who had for long stood high in Gregory's estimation as a fighter in Spain for the honour of St. Peter.[93]

Of still greater effect in tending to draw Robert Guiscard and Gregory together was the marriage into the Byzantine royal family, which had formed one of the duke's devices for penetrating the Byzantine Empire. Papal and ducal policies with regard to Byzantium had for long run on parallel lines. As early as 1073 Gregory had entered negotiations with the Emperor Michael VII Ducas (1071–8) with a view to promoting the unity of the eastern and western churches;[94] his 'Crusading' plans of 1074 had included this amongst its objectives.[95] Robert Guiscard, for his part, had found himself impeded by the asylum that rebels against his authority were finding in the Illyrian provinces of the Byzantine Empire. Furthermore, he increasingly aspired to win the Empire for himself. In 1074 he secured a foothold by negotiating with Michael VII a marriage alliance by which he agreed to dispatch to Constantinople his infant daughter, who was betrothed to a son of the emperor.[96] Both Gregory and Robert were, therefore, adversely affected when in October 1078 Michael VII was deposed and succeeded by Nicephorus III Botaniates (1078–81); at his November council Gregory excommunicated Nicephorus,[97] and Robert Guiscard remained Michael's champion. Their interests thus tended to converge in Michael's support.

During 1078 and 1079 the course of relations between the

[93] William of Apulia, iv. 8–15, p. 204, cf. p. 311; Anna Comnena, 1. 12. 11, ed. Leib, i. 46–7. For Raymond Berengar, see *Reg.* vi. 16, 2 Jan. 1079, pp. 421–2; and for Ebolus, ibid. i. 6, 30 Apr. 1073, pp. 9–10, vi. 3, 22 Aug. 1078, p. 395, viii. 18, 27 Dec. 1080, pp. 539–40. Robert Guiscard also sought unsuccessfully to conclude a marriage alliance with King William I of England: *Vita Simonis comitis Crespeiensis*, cap. 7, *MGH SS* xv. 908.

[94] *Reg.* i. 18, 9 July 1073, pp. 29–30.

[95] For fuller discussion, see Cowdrey (as Ch. III n. 64).

[96] For the alliance, see William of Apulia, iii. 501–2, p. 190, cf. p. 306; Amatus, vii. 26, pp. 318–20; Anna Comnena, 1. 10. 3, 12. 2, ed. Leib, i. 27, 43, 171; John Scylitzes, Continuation of George Cedrenus, *Synopsis historiarum*, ed. I. Bekker, *Corp. Bonn.* ii (Bonn, 1839), ii. 720, 724; John Zonaras, *Epitomae historiarum*, 18. 17. 7, ed. T. Büttner-Wobst, *Corp. Bonn.* xlix (Bonn, 1897), 714. The Greek text of the treaty is printed by P. Bezobrazov, 'Chrisovul imperatora Michaila VII Duki', *Vizantiiskii Vremennik*, vi (1899), 140–3, with corrections by E. Kurtz in *Byzantinische Zeitschrift*, ix (1900), 280; see Dölger, *Regesten*, no. 1003.

[97] *Reg.* vi. 5*b*, 19 Nov. 1078, p. 400.

Norman rulers of South Italy also served gradually to bring Gregory and Robert Guiscard closer together. The death on 5 April 1078 of Prince Richard of Capua marked the first change of a major Norman ruler since the treaty of Melfi. Papal interests had latterly been threatened by the Normans of Capua as well as by those of Apulia. But, in the circumstances of Prince Richard's illness, Gregory's excommunication of Lent 1078 produced the result that Gregory had always sought—that of dividing the Normans. No doubt desirous of securing a smooth succession upon his father's death, which excommunication might have placed at risk, Prince Jordan of Capua hastened to Rome in the company of his uncle Count Rainulf of Caiazzo and secured absolution.[98] Before Prince Richard died he restored to St. Peter his own conquests in the Campagna, as a step towards also receiving absolution—in his case from Guitmund of Aversa. Robert Guiscard was put at a disadvantage. Not only did Jordan connive in a widespread revolt of his Apulian and Calabrian vassals, but he abandoned the siege of Naples and compelled Apulian troops to leave Benevento. The longer consequence was to make Robert Guiscard less of a threat to papal interests, and thus to ease the way for a *rapprochement* between Gregory and Robert Guiscard.

Two factors in South Italy combined with the consequences of the duke's marriage alliances to bring about such a *rapprochement*. First, Gregory's anxiety about the situation following Richard of Capua's death led him to be more concerned to secure the goodwill of Montecassino and its abbot. His presence at Capua on 1 July 1078 is an indication of this concern, and since on 22 August he was at San Germano he may have been in touch with the abbey.[99] Berengar of Tours yields evidence that soon after this time Abbot Desiderius had once again become a major figure in Gregory's counsels (*summae tunc in palatio auctoritatis*).[100] Gregory now championed Desiderius' interests, for at the November council of 1078 he decreed that Montecassino was to be defended *ab omnibus Normannis*, laying down that Normans and others who persistently invaded or robbed it should suffer excommunication. Further, he upheld its possession of the monastery of Sant'Angelo in Formis against the claims of Archbishop Hildebrand of Capua, and he

[98] The sources for the following developments are as in Ch. III n. 90.

[99] *Reg.* vi. 1–3, pp. 389–96.

[100] See above, p. 93.

vindicated its rights at San Benedetto, Salerno. Also in 1078, he recognized Desiderius' position as *tutor et defensor* of the monastery of Santa Maria, Tremiti.[101] Far more than in Gregory's earlier years Montecassino was now associated with papal actions and interests, and it also became a recipient of his favour.

Secondly, despite his politic reconciliation with Gregory when his father's death was in prospect, Prince Jordan of Capua quickly established himself as a violent and unreliable figure who presented a danger both to Montecassino and to Rome. On 21 April 1079 Gregory expressed his disenchantment with him in an outraged letter naming three causes of offence: Jordan had compelled his stepmother to remarry against her will; he had recently (*nuper*) hindered and robbed an unnamed bishop who was on his way to visit Rome; and still more recently (*novissime*) he had entered, plundered, and violated Montecassino.[102] Gregory followed this letter with two more which referred only to the last of these offences. He rebuked Desiderius for his lack of resolution in failing to punish so great an outrage, placing the abbey under an interdict but also committing himself to further steps on the abbey's behalf. He quickly lifted the interdict because the feast of the Ascension was approaching, and urged the monks to pray for Jordan's repentance. The Montecassino Chronicle gave the substance of the last two letters, but identified the plunder, as Gregory's letters did not, with money deposited by Bishop Dudo of Grosseto (Roselle); it seems to have conflated incidents which in Gregory's letters were unconnected.[103] Whatever the precise nature of these obscure happenings, the effect of Gregory's anger was to isolate

[101] *Reg.* vi. 5*b*, cap. 7, decr. 2, 19 Nov. 1078, pp. 401, 403; *Chron. Cas.* iii. 42, 46, pp. 420, 424; *Regesto di S. Angelo in Formis* (as Ch. I n. 35), i. 6–8, no. 3. For Tremiti, Santifaller, *QF* i. 162, no. 147; see above, p. 123.

[102] *Reg.* vi. 37, 21 Apr. 1079, pp. 453–4. For the following, see V. Tirelli, 'Osservazioni sui rapporti tra sede apostolica, Capua e Napoli durante i pontificati di Gregorio VII e di Urbano II', *Studi . . . Morghen*, ii. 961–1010, at 999–1001; H. Hoffmann, 'Zum Register und zu den Briefen Papst Gregors VII.', *DA* xxxii (1976), 86–130, at 104.

[103] *Epp. vag.*, pp. 72–7, nos. 28–9, from *Reg. Pet. Diac.* nos. 34–5; *Chron. Cas.* iii. 46, p. 424. The explanatory note in *Reg. Pet. Diac.* is based on this chapter but adds details, notably about Jordan's blindness. Dudo, bishop of Grosseto (*c.*1060–*c.*1079), had long-standing connections with Montecassino and its region. In 1061 he was papal vicar of Benevento: Ughelli-Coleti, viii. 81–2, x. 507–8. According to *Chron. Cas.* iii. 29, p. 399, he was at the dedication ceremony of 1071, although he is not listed in the *Narratio* (p. 221). He is not necessarily the Dodo to whom Alberic of Montecassino dedicated his Life of St. Dominic of Sora: Lentini (as Ch. I n. 105), pp. 68, 70.

Jordan of Capua. Robert Guiscard returned from Calabria and prepared to attack him on the River Sarno between Salerno and Aversa. Jordan sought to open peace talks, thus providing Abbot Desiderius with an opportunity to resume his attempts to reconcile all parties in South Italy. He hastened to meet the duke and secured his agreement. Thus safeguarded in the north, the duke spent the winter of 1079/80 in finally subjugating the Apulian rebels.[104]

The years 1077 to 1080 had thus seen the elimination of Prince Gisulf of Salerno as an independent papal ally and as a cause of friction between Gregory VII and Robert Guiscard. Prince Richard of Capua had been superseded by the weak and volatile Jordan, who was predatory by nature but bowed to an effective show of military strength. Both Gregory and Montecassino needed Robert Guiscard as a stabilizing factor. In Byzantium, Gregory and Robert Guiscard had a converging interest in their common hostility to the Emperor Nicephorus III Botaniates. And in Italy Robert Guiscard had no reason to welcome intervention by Henry IV of Germany, whose claims to lordship over him he had denied, and whose excommunication and deposition Gregory again proclaimed at Rome on 7 March 1080 during his Lent council.[105] Circumstances seemed to have become uniquely favourable for Abbot Desiderius of Montecassino—once more in a position of trust with Gregory—to bring about Robert Guiscard's reconciliation to the apostolic see after his three excommunications. Desiderius could hope to rehabilitate the arrangements of the treaty of Melfi whereby the duke of Apulia and the prince of Capua were set up as allies and protectors of the apostolic see, while both were also patrons of Montecassino.

v. MONTECASSINO AND POPE GREGORY VII IN A WIDER CONFLICT, 1080–5

So far as South Italian affairs are concerned, the second excommunication of Henry IV was a turning-point in a way that the first excommunication was not. The drama culminating in

[104] *Chron. Cas.* iii. 45, pp. 423–4; William of Apulia, iii. 617–87, pp. 198–202; E. Cuozzo, 'Il "Breve Chronicon Northmannicum" ', *Bull. Ist. stor. ital.* lxxxiii (1971), 131–232, at pp. 171, 223–8.

[105] *Reg.* vii. 14*a*, pp. 483–7.

Gregory's absolution of Henry at Canossa in January 1077 had been enacted in Germany and Lombardy. South Italian and even Roman sources suggest that it made relatively little lasting impression in their regions. At Montecassino Amatus paid little heed to the struggle of Gregory and Henry. If it be objected that his subject was the Normans, it may be rejoined that his History reflects what one of its monks in the late 1070s thought to be worth recording, and that in his *Liber in honore beati Petri apostoli* he made only one, far from certain, reference to Canossa.[106] In the Montecassino Chronicle the summary of relations between Gregory and Henry between 1076 and 1080 is little more than a confused travesty.[107] Other South Italian sources, whether contemporary or later, show little awareness or recollection of the wider events of these years.[108] Only in the 1080s did horizons significantly widen. They did so for two reasons: first, the spectre of ecclesiastical schism was added to the struggle of pope and king; and secondly, Henry now made a number of expeditions to Italy and to Rome. The result for Montecassino was that it became directly caught up in developments that called into question fundamental ecclesiastical loyalties. At the same time, the activities of the Normans on both sides of the Adriatic Sea became part of a struggle more completely involving the Christian world, both Latin and Byzantine, and its chief rulers in both Germany and Constantinople. Henceforth South Italian affairs must be studied as part of the universal struggles within Christendom between *sacerdotium* and *regnum*, Gregorian and Guibertine, Norman and Byzantine, east and west.

The nature of the evidence, too, requires the South Italian scene to be understood as part of these wider and interlocking struggles. At Montecassino Amatus is no longer available as a source. The Montecassino Chronicle, although offering more evidence for the early 1080s than for the later 1070s, is made difficult to interpret by the historical and literary deficiencies of Leo of Ostia's continuators. A study of South Italian affairs is possible only as part of a general interpretation of Gregory VII's latter years. Unfortunately this is itself the least well

[106] See above, p. 78; cf. Gregory's reference to the attitude of the *Latini* in *Reg.* vii. 3, 1 Oct. 1079, p. 462.

[107] *Chron. Cas.* iii. 49, pp. 427–9.

[108] e.g. William of Apulia referred to Henry only from the beginning of his fourth book, when he reached the winter of 1080: iv. 31–68, pp. 204–6.

documented, studied, and understood stage of his pontificate. A key to understanding it is that, rather as in his early years as pope, he was engaged in a wide-ranging dialogue between papacy and German kingdom, into which other ecclesiastical institutions were drawn, and with regard to which such powers as the Normans had to determine their policies.[109]

An attempt to explore and to understand this renewed dialogue may conveniently proceed from year to year.

a. *1080*

The year 1080 was one in which both Gregory VII and Henry IV took up positions which were extreme, and difficult to exploit with any degree of tactical success. The record of Gregory's Lent council shows that he proclaimed for a second time Henry's excommunication and deposition, in the confidence that he was depriving him and his supporters of their power to secure military and temporal prosperity. The blessing that God conferred upon the righteous but withheld from the wicked would certainly devolve upon Henry's rival for the German crown, Rudolf of Swabia, whom the German princes had elected king at Forchheim in March 1077. St. Peter and St. Paul, the princes of the apostles, would now prove that, just as they could bind and loose in heaven, so upon earth they could confer and take away earthly dignities according to the merits or demerits of those who held them. Against the reprobate Henry their sentence would be swift and decisive.[110]

Thus fortified—as he believed—by heavenly aid, Gregory saw in Robert Guiscard and Jordan of Capua his necessary allies and agents upon earth.[111] He proceeded with determination to cement their alliance with the apostolic see. At his Lent council his anti-Norman decrees were more conciliatory than those of the 1070s. The Normans were again adjured under threat of excommunication to refrain from invading or plundering the *terra sancti Petri*—express mention being made of the still intact part of the march of Fermo, Spoleto, Marittima, Sabina, and the county of Tivoli—together with Montecassino and its lands, and Benevento. But Gregory now also promised legal redress from himself or his agents for Normans who were

[109] See Schneider (as Introd. n. 88).
[110] *Reg.* vii. 14*a* (7), pp. 483–7.
[111] Ibid. viii. 7, summer 1080, pp. 524–5; ix. 4, Feb. 1081, pp. 577–9.

aggrieved by inhabitants of those regions. If redress should fail the Normans might take the law into their own hands, although with moderation and as became Christians.[112] Abbot Desiderius, for his part, was anxious to secure the release from excommunication of Robert Guiscard, his friend and supporter. Probably before the Lent council took place he went to Rome in order to seek this release.[113] Little is known of the negotiations that followed, although one figure involved was Count Simon of Crépy; his *Vita* indicates that Gregory took the initiative in dispatching him to Robert.[114] The negotiations were successful, and according to the Montecassino Chronicle it was Desiderius himself, *pacis amator et conservator*, who with other cardinals went to the duke and restored him to communion.[115] Early in June Gregory thought the time ripe himself to travel south. At Ceprano on 6 June he invested Robert Guiscard with the lands that Popes Nicholas II and Alexander II had granted him. The deed of investiture also referred to lands like Salerno, Amalfi, and part of the march of Fermo which the duke was holding unjustly. These he was clearly unprepared to relinquish; Gregory could only say with regard to them that he trusted him to act well for the future.[116] On 10 June he took an oath of fealty from Prince Jordan of Capua.[117] On 29 June Robert Guiscard took a similar oath.[118] In effect, as the price of renewing the Norman alliance Gregory recognized or at least tolerated all of Robert Guiscard's conquests. As for Desiderius, he reaped his reward. He stood well in the pope's favour.[119] From Jordan of Capua he secured a general precept guaranteeing all his lands, and from Robert Guiscard he received the

[112] Ibid. vii. 14*a* (7), p. 481.

[113] *Chron. Cas.* iii. 45, p. 424.

[114] *Vita Simonis comitis Crespeiensis*, caps. 20–1, *MGH SS* xv. 906. Simon had gone to Rome *c.*1079 and lived an eremitical life near the church of Santa Thecla: cap. 19, pp. 905–6.

[115] *Chron. Cas.* iii. 45, p. 424.

[116] William of Apulia, iv. 16–32, 69–70, pp. 204, 206, 311–12; Anna Comnena, 1. 13. 6–7, ed. Leib, i. 48–9; Bonizo of Sutri, ix. p. 612; Romuald of Salerno, *a.* 1080, p. 191. For Robert Guiscard's investiture, *Reg.* viii. 1*b*, pp. 515–16.

[117] Deusdedit, *Coll. can.* iii. 289 (159), p. 396.

[118] *Reg.* viii. 1*a*, *c*, pp. 514–17, Ménager, *Recueil*, pp. 98–101, nos. 29–30. A variant text of 1*a* is preserved in a Bible of the Roman monastery of St. Paul's-without-the-Walls: Pitra, *Anal. noviss.* i. 478–9, whence J. Deér, *Das Papsttum und die süditalienischen Normannenstaaten* (Göttingen, 1969), p. 32, no. 18*b*. See also Cuozzo (as Ch. III n. 104), p. 171.

[119] *Reg.* vii. 28, (1080), pp. 509–10.

monastery of San Pietro at Taranto with the promise of further largesse.[120]

While Gregory, Desiderius, and the two Norman rulers were thus drawing closer together, Henry IV was also acting with determination. At Whitsun (31 May) a meeting of German bishops decreed that Hildebrand, the guileful invader of the apostolic see, should be deposed and a worthier man substituted.[121] There followed the synod of Brixen which on 25 June —four days before Robert Guiscard's fealty to Gregory at Ceprano—reiterated the demand that Gregory be canonically deposed.[122] To implement it Henry took the first step of choosing Guibert, archbishop of Ravenna since 1073, to be pope in Gregory's stead. It is important to establish what Henry thereby did. Although Guibert's election had the synod's concurrence,[123] it was Henry's own act, approved by imperial prelates at a place far from Rome. As such it could only be a preparatory, not a definitive, step to get rid of Gregory. For the events of 1076 had made it clear that only the Roman church could effect a papal deposition. Not until he had been elected, enthroned, and acclaimed at Rome and by the Roman church itself could Guibert of Ravenna be regarded as pope, even by his own partisans.[124] At Brixen he was immantled and honoured; but he did

[120] For Jordan, *Reg. Pet. Diac.*, no. 412, 19 Sept. 1080, Gattula, *Accessiones*, pp. 184–6, Loud, 'Calendar', p. 124, no. 24; cf. *Chron. Cas.* iii. 47, pp. 424–5. In 1080 Robert Guiscard gave Montecassino the following monasteries:

	Reg. Pet. Diac., no.	*Chron. Cas.*		Ménager, *Recueil*	
		cap.	p.	pp.	no.
June:					
San Pietro Imperiale, Taranto	420	iii. 44	421	101–4	31
October:					
San Nicandro, Monte Maggiore, and other churches	422	iii. 58	439	116–20	37
Sant'Angelo, Troia, and other churches	423	iii. 58	439	113–16	36

[121] Letter of Bishop Huzmann of Speyer to the Lombards, *Codex Udalrici*, no. 60, Jaffé, *Bibl.* v. 126–7.

[122] Anhang C, ed. C. Erdmann, *Ausgew. Quell.* xii. 476–82.

[123] *Vita Bennonis II episcopi Osnabrugensis auctore Nortberto abbate Iburgensi*, cap. 18, ed. H. Bresslau, *MGH Script. rer. Germ.*, pp. 24–5.

[124] I accept the interpretation of the events of 1076 by H. Zimmermann, 'Wurde Gregor VII. 1076 in Worms abgesetzt?', *MIÖG* lxxviii (1970), 121–31.

not assume the name Clement III, nor did he perform papal functions, until after his enthronement at Rome in March 1084.[125] In the meantime his position was far from secure, even within the Henrician camp. Should Henry's interests so dictate, he was readily dispensable.

In 1080 and for some time after it was by no means unthinkable that he might be dispensed with. Henry was committed to a march to Rome, partly because it was only there that Gregory's deposition and Guibert's election as pope, if persisted with, could be put into effect; but still more because it was only in Rome and at the hands of a duly constituted pope that Henry could receive his long-desired imperial coronation. There was still a possibility that Henry might find a *rapprochement* with Gregory an easier way to imperial coronation than persistence in his sponsorship of Guibert.

Gregory, too, took up a hard-line position at his Lent council, but was likely to experience tactical vulnerability and a need to seek freedom of manœuvre. Events were to prove his confidence in the material effectiveness of the sentence of St. Peter and St. Paul to be exaggerated, and the Normans had never in the past for long at a time been reliable as papal allies. It was therefore possible that, should his position become weakened, Gregory might feel that he must once again meet a penitent or a conciliatory Henry half way, conceding imperial coronation in return for Henry's abandoning Guibert and returning to the church. So long as Gregory was not deposed by the Roman church and so long as Guibert was not established by that church in his stead, there was room for dialogue and for diplomatic as well as military interplay between Gregory and Henry. That there was such dialogue and diplomatic manœuvre right up to March 1084 will be argued in the remainder of this section.

A move towards a possible accommodation did not, however, take place in 1080, at least from Gregory's side; for he felt sufficiently confident to maintain a hard-line stance. As he saw the events of that year, they heralded the swift vindication of God's righteousness upon all the enemies whatsoever who opposed him.[126] His reactions were correspondingly extravagant. The summer saw him threatening and organizing military

[125] See below, Appendix I. Twelfth-century sources gave a different, but distorted, picture: e.g. *Vita Heinrici IV*, cap. 6, *Ausgew. Quell.* xii. 430.

[126] *Reg.* viii. 9, to the faithful in Germany, 22 Sept. 1080, pp. 527–8.

campaigns upon a scale and with a boldness that far exceeded even his bizarre enough 'Crusading' plans of 1074. He began his menaces at Ceprano while negotiating with Robert Guiscard, by threatening King Alphonso VI of León-Castile that in view of a sudden crisis in his kingdom he would come to Spain in person and lead a military campaign (*dura et aspera moliri*) against the king as an enemy of the Christian religion.[127] Other, no less sweeping, proposals for military action followed. Upon hearing news of Guibert of Ravenna's election at Brixen Gregory quickly planned warfare against him, as well. On 21 July he wrote to the bishops of the Principate, Apulia, and Calabria—that is, of the lands of his allies Jordan of Capua and Robert Guiscard. In his address to a South Italian public Gregory drew upon the legends about Simon Magus which figured so strongly in Cassinese reforming literature. He described the Guibertines as slaves of the Simon Magus whom St. Peter had of old marvellously overthrown when he climbed after things too high. A similar nemesis for their own madness would not be long delayed. Gregory called on the South Italian bishops to help the Roman church by their prayers and by all other means (*orationibus aliisque modis*); in his idiom this meant by procuring military and political support.[128] He followed this letter with a summons to all the clerical and lay *fideles sancti Petri* to join the princes of Southern and Central Italy in a campaign for the recovery of Ravenna *armata manu*. He referred to his conference at Ceprano with the Normans, upon whose support he evidently counted, together with that of the vassals in the papal states and in Tuscany.[129] In October he called upon his partisans in the marches of Tuscany and Fermo and in the exarchate of Ravenna to see to the election of a new archbishop. By December a certain Richard had been chosen; Gregory urged that he be given every assistance.[130]

Nor was this all. In addition to his plans for Spain and Ravenna Gregory sought to promote military intervention in

[127] *Reg.* viii. 2–4, 27 June 1080, pp. 517–21; see Cowdrey (as Introd. n. 9), pp. 230–9.

[128] *Reg.* viii. 5, pp. 521–3, cf. Gregory's *Vita* in *LP* ii. 289. For his vocabulary see C. Erdmann, *Die Entstehung des Kreuzzugsgedankens* (Stuttgart, 1935), 147–8, trans. M. W. Baldwin and W. Goffart, *The Origin of the Idea of Crusade* (Princeton, NJ, 1977), 162–3.

[129] *Reg.* viii. 7, pp. 524–5.

[130] Ibid. xiii. 12–14, 11–15 Oct. 1080, pp. 531–5. Richard is not elsewhere referred to.

the Byzantine Empire. He was prompted by the appearance at Bari of a Greek who, according to Anna Comnena, gave himself out to be the Emperor Michael VII, deposed in 1078, whom Robert Guiscard and Gregory had both regarded with favour.[131] Robert Guiscard took his claim at its face value. Gregory, too, accepted his story and sent a letter in his favour to the Apulian and Calabrian bishops; he urged them to back Robert Guiscard's military measures in support of 'Michael''s right to the imperial throne.[132]

From Gregory's point of view his community of interest with Robert Guiscard seemed the more genuine because the autumn of 1080 saw the implementation of the duke's plans, formed after his capture of Salerno in 1077, to begin the rebuilding of the city's cathedral.[133] Furthermore, in September 1080 Gregory was able to congratulate Archbishop Alfanus, who had quickly become a staunch Norman ally, upon the uncovering of the body of St. Matthew, the city's patron saint.[134] The next few years saw the rebuilding of the cathedral in imitation of Desiderius' new basilica at Montecassino, and probably by workmen trained there. Robert Guiscard intended the cathedral to express his prestige and authority as a ruler.[135] In his letter to Alfanus Gregory declared that he, too, saw in the relics of St. Matthew a pledge of the victory of his own plans for the church at large, which he hoped to accomplish with Norman help.

The apparent coincidence of papal and Norman interests did not, however, persist. During the winter of 1080/1 Robert Guiscard began to reassess the situation in Byzantium. He sent an envoy there, ostensibly to seek redress for the injury done to the daughter whom he had betrothed to Michael VII's son by placing her in a convent, but in fact to secure the alliance of the rising figure of Alexius Comnenus, at this time grand domestic and exarch of the west.[136] It was apparent that the duke would

131 Anna Comnena, 1. 12. 6–10, ed. Leib, i. 44–6; Lupus Protospatarius, *a.* 1080, p. 60; William of Apulia, iv. 162–70, p. 212; Romuald of Salerno, *a.* 1080, p. 191.

132 *Reg.* viii. 6, 25 July 1080, pp. 523–4; Cuozzo (as Ch. III n. 104), pp. 171–2, 229–32.

133 *Chron. Cas.* iii. 45, p. 423.

134 *Reg.* viii. 8, 18 Sept. 1080, pp. 526–7. The relics of St. Matthew had first been recovered in 954: *Chronicon Salernitanum*, cap. 165, *MGH SS* iii. 552–3; *Chron. Cas.* ii. 5, p. 175. See Acocella (as Ch. I n. 176), and Crisci and Campagna (as Ch. III n. 72), pp. 119–20.

135 William of Apulia, iv. 70–2, v. 280–1, pp. 206–9, 250.

136 Anna Comnena, 1. 15. 2, ed. Leib, i. 53–4.

assist Gregory's plans only to the degree that suited himself. There is unfortunately no direct evidence for Abbot Desiderius' attitude to or part in the events of the second half of 1080. But he appears to have been in close touch with Robert Guiscard, with whom he was associating at Melfi in December.[137] On the other hand Gregory's letter of 12 December 1080, in which he ordered Bishop Trasmundus of Valva to retire to Montecassino and remain there until Gregory had an opportunity of consulting Desiderius, suggests that relations between pope and abbot were friendly, but not necessarily close or sustained.[138] Desiderius' political realism, and his probable memories of the abortive 'Crusading' plans of 1074, are not likely to have encouraged him to be associated directly with Gregory's grandiose military and diplomatic schemes. For, whatever Gregory himself may still have thought, his stance of 1080 was not one that was likely to be maintained for any length of time, or to point the way in his future dealings with his friends and foes.

b. *1081*

In the early months of 1081 that truth had still not dawned upon Gregory. He cherished sanguine hopes of drawing Robert Guiscard into his military plans in North and Central Italy. Probably early in February he tried to take advantage of Abbot Desiderius' good standing with the duke in order to discover—as he put it—how well disposed towards the Roman church the duke still was. In a letter he requested Desiderius to ascertain whether, if Gregory were forced to call a military expedition after Easter, Robert Guiscard would promise aid either personally or through his son. If no expedition took place, Gregory wished to know how many knights Robert Guiscard would be prepared to furnish for the pope's service in general (*in familiari militia sancti Petri*). Desiderius was also to sound the duke about whether he would devote Lent, when Norman knights customarily refrained from warfare, to military action led by Gregory himself or by his deputy, in order to subdue those vassals of the papal lands who were rebellious and to confirm the loyalty of the remainder. Gregory also asked Desiderius to

[137] *Regii Neapolitani archivi monumenta edita ac illustrata*, v (Naples, 1857), 89–90, no. 430; G. Fortunato, 'La badia di Monticchio', *Notizie storiche della Valle di Vitalba*, vi (Trani, 1904), 353–4, no. 1, referred to by Dormeier, *Montecassino*, p. 69 n. 280.

[138] *Reg.* viii. 15, pp. 535–6.

remind Robert Guiscard to restrain his nephew Robert of Loritello from the invasion of papal lands.[139] Clearly Gregory's mind was still set upon his plans of 1080. His letter seems to have been written in vain, for, apart from a brief notice in the Beneventan Annals that, perhaps early in 1081, Robert Guiscard made an expedition to Tivoli, which he may have intended as a gesture of help for Gregory,[140] there is no record either of action by Desiderius or of tangible response from Robert Guiscard. As in 1074, so in 1080–1 papal plans for direct military campaigns proved abortive.

In the course of 1081 Gregory's ability to command military support in pursuit of his objectives in Germany and in the papal lands was further eroded. Robert Guiscard became increasingly preoccupied with his Byzantine ambitions. In April, when he was making preparations at Brindisi, his envoy Ralph returned from Constantinople, denouncing the *soi-disant* Emperor Michael as an impostor and reporting on the seizure of the Byzantine throne by Alexius Comnenus (emperor 1081–1118).[141] Robert Guiscard was determined to press ahead with his designs before Alexius could consolidate his victory. After charging the guardians of his son Roger not to deny the papacy any aid that they could bring, in May he crossed the Adriatic; during the summer the Normans captured Corfu, Vonitza, and Valona, and laid siege to Durazzo.[142] By thus leaving Italy Robert Guiscard once again demonstrated how little he could be counted upon to help the papacy at Gregory's behest and convenience.

Moreover, the winter of 1080/1 witnessed the frustration of Gregory's hopes in Germany and Tuscany. On 15 October 1080 the anti-king Rudolf of Swabia had been killed at the battle of Hohenmolsen. In an age for which the outcome of battle declared the judgement of God, it was a damaging indication that Gregory's cause was not so securely that of righteousness and divine favour, or so sure of victory, as he had proclaimed. It proved hard to find a new anti-king in Germany, and Hermann of Salm, elected in August 1081, was a poor substitute for Rudolf. Also on 15 October 1080 Gregory's ally Countess Matilda of Tuscany had suffered a severe defeat at Volta, near

[139] Ibid. ix. 4, pp. 577–9; cf. William of Apulia, iv. 66–8, p. 206.
[140] *Annales Beneventani, a.* 1080, *MGH SS* iii. 181; cf. *Chron. Cas.* iii. 58, p. 438.
[141] Anna Comnena, 1. 15. 1–6, ed. Leib, i. 53–6.
[142] Ibid. 1. 14. 1, 4, and 3. 12, ed. Leib, i. 51, 53, 138–42; William of Apulia, iv. 177–284, pp. 214–16.

Mantua, in a battle against Henry's Lombard allies.[143] Gregory did not immediately appreciate the extent of these setbacks. He ended his letter of February 1081 to Abbot Desiderius with the remark that he had no sure tidings from north of the Alps, except that all who came from thence affirmed that Henry's circumstances had never been less fortunate![144]

Events were soon to dispel this illusion. For early in May 1081 Gregory learnt that Henry was at Ravenna on his way to Rome with a small German and Lombard force which he hoped to enlarge as he passed through the Exarchate and the march of Fermo. He planned to arrive before Rome at about Pentecost (23 May). Gregory sought Robert Guiscard's aid, but the duke's own overseas plans were too far advanced to be set aside.[145] Gregory also wrote to Abbot Desiderius, addressing him as *amande frater*, in order to inform him of what was afoot, and proclaiming confidence that Henry could not claim such requisitions (*fotrum*) from his Italian subjects as would enable him to reach Rome. Gregory said that he counted upon Desiderius' loyalty to himself and to the Roman church. He also referred to his own firm stand in face of the threats and promises that Henry had been making, saying that Henry and the archbishop of Ravenna had been tempting him with lavish promises of obedience and service.[146]

It is, indeed, more than likely that Henry, whom the hermit Bernard of Menthon had warned of the perils of military action while he was still *en route* from Germany,[147] was willing to enter into a dialogue with Gregory with a view if possible to settling the differences between them by diplomacy rather than by force. This would involve a practical resolution of the problems of *sacerdotium* and *regnum*, and a mutual and public recognition by Gregory and Henry that each was fitted for the papal and the imperial dignity. No doubt, after the events of the past five years Henry would have preferred to destroy Gregory. But especially since the attempt on his life by Cencius at Christmastide 1075 Gregory had to a remarkable degree possessed the

[143] Meyer von Knonau, *Jahrbücher*, iii. 314–17, 337–40, 415–18. For the significance of Rudolf of Swabia's fate in eleventh-century eyes, see esp. Henry IV, *Ep.* 17, ed. C. Erdmann, *Ausgew. Quell.* xii. 80, lines 10–15.

[144] *Reg.* ix. 4, p. 579.

[145] Anna Comnena, 1. 13. 10, ed. Leib, i. 51.

[146] *Reg.* ix. 11, (May 1081), pp. 588-9.

[147] *Alia vita sancti Bernardi Menthonensis*, i. 8, *AA SS Boll.*, Jul. ii. 1084.

loyalty of the citizens of Rome.[148] To gain his ends with the papacy and the imperial title alike, Henry needed their goodwill. A reconciliation with Gregory, whom they still so strongly supported, might yet prove the surest way. On the other hand, after the defeats of Rudolf of Swabia and Matilda of Tuscany, and in view of the manifest unreliability of his Norman allies, Gregory had no less reason to consider a settlement with Henry. It should be remembered that Gregory and his partisans at no time designated a German anti-king as a prospective emperor, so that the way was always open for Gregory to offer imperial coronation to a penitent Henry. In the light of this as of Henry's own limited commitment at Brixen to Guibert of Ravenna, Gregory's letter to Abbot Desiderius of May 1081 suggests that Henry had protested himself willing, if Gregory would countenance reconciliation, to offer in return concessions which may have included recognition of Gregory as pope and the abandoning of Guibert's claim to the apostolic see. Such an interpretation finds confirmation in the strongly Henrician *Liber de unitate ecclesiae conservanda*, written by an anonymous monk of Hersfeld. He recorded that in 1081 Henry went to Rome seeking to recover Hildebrand's favour and to incline him to mercy, but only if that were impossible to substitute another pope who would love and propagate peace.[149]

Henry's preparedness to treat with Gregory was probably increased by the failure of an attempt, as part of his preparations for his Italian expedition, to secure Robert Guiscard's alliance. The value to Henry of Norman goodwill is self-evident: an alliance would add to the number of Henry's advocates with Gregory if events developed by negotiation, but if there were conflict it would at least neutralize Gregory's chosen allies and at best lead to the encirclement of the papacy by German and Norman forces. Both Anna Comnena and William of Apulia described at length Henry's approach and its failure, while Gregory showed that he was aware of it. In his letter of May to Abbot Desiderius he transmitted intelligence received through Countess Matilda of Tuscany that Henry had made an agreement (*placitum*) with Robert Guiscard that the king's son Conrad would marry a daughter of the duke, who would hold of the

[148] For details and the sources, see Meyer von Knonau, *Jahrbücher*, ii. 586–90.

[149] ii. 7, 17, *MGH Libelli*, ii. 217–18, 232; see also Bruno, *Saxonicum bellum*, cap. 126, ed. E. Lohmann, *Ausgew. Quell.* xii. 394.

king the march of Fermo. Such a plan suggests that Henry recalled the answer that, according to Amatus, Robert Guiscard had returned to Henry's approach in the winter of 1075/6, and that Henry sought to provide the duke with a new fief to be held of himself. Gregory recognized the consequential danger at Rome: if the Roman citizens thought that Robert Guiscard was defaulting in the help that he had promised the papacy at Ceprano they would readily believe that such a plan for a German–Norman alliance was afoot and lose confidence in Gregory's authority. So while expressing confidence in the Romans' loyalty and service Gregory urged Desiderius to inquire into the duke's actions and to take appropriate steps; he himself was to come to Gregory as quickly as possible. It is not known how Desiderius reacted. But Robert Guiscard, for his part, was careful to enter into no commitment to Henry; and he kept in touch with Gregory.[150]

When, despite Gregory's expectations, Henry reached Rome on 21 May he found that the Romans were wholly unwilling to receive him, and he had to remain outside the city.[151] Henry issued a hastily drafted Manifesto addressed to the clergy and people of Rome in which he bade for their goodwill and sought their sponsorship for the imperial crown. He referred only obliquely to Gregory's alleged crimes, and not at all to Guibert of Ravenna or to the supersession of Gregory by Guibert. He ended his Manifesto by urging that a peaceful and agreed solution be found to current discords:

> We tell you the truth in all faithfulness: it is entirely our will and determination to visit you peaceably so far as in us lies. Then we plan to take counsel, first and foremost with all of you and then with our other faithful subjects, so that the longstanding discord between *sacerdotium* and *regnum* may be done away with, and everything may return to peace and harmony in Christ's name.[152]

150 Anna Comnena, 1. 13. 10, ed. Leib, i. 51; William of Apulia, iv. 169–84, pp. 212–14; *Reg.* ix. 11.

151 Gregory referred to the Romans' loyalty in *Reg.* ix. 11, while Henry's Manifesto of 1082 recognized it retrospectively: 'Sed longe aliter, ac sperabamus, vos inveniebamus, quia, quos putavimus amicos, sensimus inimicos, cum pro mera iustitia ad vos veniremus, ut pacem inter regnum et sacerdotium vestro consilio et canonica auctoritate componeremus': *Ep.* 17, *Ausgew. Quell.* xii. 78. This is borne out by *Chron. Cas.* iii. 49, p. 429; Benzo of Alba, vi, praef., p. 656; Bonizo of Sutri, ix, p. 613.

152 *Ep.* 16, *Ausgew. Quell.* xii. 74–6; Henry's silence about Guibert both now and in 1082–3 may have proceeded from a realization of Roman scruples about the prior choice of someone not a Roman cardinal-priest or -deacon: see below, pp. 189–90.

As was prudent in view of the Normans' loyalty to Gregory, Henry kept his options open on the issue of the papacy, neither condemning Gregory nor championing Guibert, but placing his own imperial coronation in the centre of the picture. However, he made no impression on the Romans, whose commitment to Gregory remained unwavering. His expedition had in any case arrived at Rome too late in the year to accomplish anything before the dangerous summer heat, and he returned to Germany having accomplished nothing.

During the rest of 1081 his position did not improve, while Gregory's became rather more favourable. This was mainly because, for all his military success across the Adriatic, Robert Guiscard had increasingly to face the reality of Alexius Comnenus' skill as a ruler. Not only did he consolidate his own power, but he also took energetic steps to counter Robert Guiscard. In the summer of 1081 he made an armistice with his eastern enemies, the Seldjuk Turks, and even solicited their aid as mercenaries against the Normans. He also negotiated at length with Henry IV with a view to tying down Robert Guiscard in the west, promising Henry 144,000 gold pieces and a hundred cloths of purple silk, with a further 216,000 gold pieces to follow when Henry next came to Italy. He fomented revolts against Robert Guiscard in South Italy and sought the support of Archbishop Hildebrand of Capua. He improved his situation in the Adriatic by a treaty with Venice which gave him naval support in return for commercial concessions.[153] All this diplomatic pressure indirectly told in Gregory's favour: it compelled Robert Guiscard to give more attention to Italian affairs, and also to Henry IV as the dangerous ally of his Byzantine enemy. Thus, after his hard-fought victory near Durazzo on 18 October, which in effect gave him control of Illyria, Robert Guiscard notified Gregory of his success; Gregory replied with a letter reminding him of his debt to St. Peter and of his duty to defend St. Peter's interests.[154] Henry IV, for his part, was encouraged by Alexius Comnenus' alliance, but his best interest lay in negotiation under as much diplomatic pressure as he could bring to bear. For the vast financial subvention that Alexius Comnenus

[153] Anna Comnena, 3. 10–11 and 4. 2. 2–3, ed. Leib, i. 132–8, 146–7; Dölger, *Regesten*, nos. 1067–70.

[154] *Reg.* ix. 17, pp. 597–8. For the battle, William of Apulia, iv. 366–435, pp. 224–6; cf. *Chron. Cas.* iii. 49, p. 429.

promised could as well be used to purchase Roman support in negotiation with Gregory as in warfare against him. So long as the Romans remained loyal to Gregory this consideration would remain the key to events.

Little is known of Abbot Desiderius' activities in the latter part of 1081, save that on 1 December he was at Dragonara, in Northern Apulia. In the presence of Cardinal-deacon Bernard of Pavia and others he renounced his rights over Santa Maria di Tremiti and agreed to the election and papal consecration of its abbot. If a new abbot were to be elected before his death Desiderius reserved the right to accompany the abbot-elect to the pope for consecration.[155] Only to this extent could Desiderius secure the interests of Montecassino at Tremiti, and he was forced to abandon most of its claims. But the tone of his relations with Gregory VII was more amicable than in any of their earlier dealings over Tremiti. Pope and abbot were clearly in sympathetic contact, and were able to reach a compromise solution which had not been attainable before. It set the matter at rest for the remainder of their lifetimes, and is thus a testimony to the improvement in relations between them since the mid-1070s.

c. *1082: events at Rome*

In 1082 Henry returned to Italy at a much earlier stage of the year; therefore he was able to spend more time both near Rome itself and elsewhere in Central Italy. He also brought a larger army. His new Manifesto was fuller and more carefully prepared than had been that of the previous year.[156] Naming Hildebrand, it arraigned him as one who constituted a stumbling block to peace and justice, and who denied to the sword of the temporal ruler its proper place in the divine order of the world. It especially pilloried Gregory's recourse to temporal warfare as an instrument of his rule. As in 1081, Henry presented his demands in the form of an appeal to the Roman clergy and people. He urged them to compel Hildebrand to stand to justice for his crimes, whether at Rome or elsewhere. In effect Henry now treated Gregory as Gregory had treated him in the years after

[155] See *Codice diplomatico del monastero di Tremiti* (as Ch. II n. 54), pp. 250–3, no. 84; cf. above, pp. 123, 135.

[156] *Ep.* 17, *Ausgew. Quell.* xii. 76–82; see Köhncke's comments, *Wibert*, pp. 48–9. For the similarity between this Manifesto and the full text of the Oppenheim *Promissio*, which may be a propaganda document of this time, see below, Appendix II.

Canossa—as a ruler whose authority was in suspense until final sentence should be passed either for or against him; and it was with the Romans that the final word must rest. So, forcibly though his charges against Hildebrand were expressed, in the Manifesto of 1082 Hildebrand's crimes were still treated as being *sub judice* and as a stumbling-block in the church that might be removed in one of two opposite ways—either by his repentance or by his deposition:

Tell him that he can come and make satisfaction to the church. He need fear no one but God: let him take oaths, let him take hostages, from us, in confidence that he can come to us and return to you—whether he is to remain in the apostolic see or whether he is to be deposed.

With repeated emphasis the Manifesto asserted that Hildebrand's record might yet be set straight and that he might be found to merit recognition as pope; only when all steps to this end had failed should he be deposed:

Behold! if God wills we shall come to Rome at the time appointed. If [Hildebrand] pleases let the matter be settled there; if he would rather come and meet us with our envoys, we agree to this, too. You yourselves also—as many of you as so wish—come, hear, judge! If he can and should be pope we shall obey him; but if not, according to your sentence and ours let provision be made of someone else who would fit the church's needs.

As in 1081 there was no mention of Guibert's election at Brixen or, indeed, of his existence; even if Hildebrand were to be replaced it was not stated or implied that it would be by him. What mattered was that Henry should receive from the Romans his just right of imperial coronation and that Hildebrand should no longer be allowed to oppress the church. The German king and the Roman clergy and people were together to order the Roman church freely, fully, and uncommitedly. Henry ended with this challenge to the Romans, who, it should be remembered, were still loyal to Gregory:

Let there be a discussion in the sight of the church: if it is right that you should have him as pope, defend him as a pope; do not defend him as a thief seeking places to hide. . . . Let him not be ashamed to humble himself in order to take away the universal stumbling-block of all the faithful, through whose universal obedience he should be exalted. . . . Behold! small and great complain of the stumbling-block that he has set, and beg for it to be taken away from them. Let him come with boldness: if his conscience be clean, he will indeed rejoice in the presence of all; when all are won over he will indeed have glory. . . . We are ready to do nothing against you but everything with you, if only we may find you not unmindful of our own good deeds.

Such was the Manifesto that Henry sent ahead of him. He did not lack inducements of a more tangible kind. Alexius Comnenus sent him the first instalment of the promised gold and silks, together with letters of encouragement.[157] But although he laid siege to Rome throughout Lent and ravaged the countryside round about, Henry again made little impact upon the Romans, to whom his Manifesto was addressed. Early in the summer he withdrew to North Italy, leaving Guibert at Tivoli to continue the harassment of the Romans and to attempt to undermine their loyalty to Gregory.[158]

Henry at this time occasioned only one, indirect, piece of damage to the fabric of Gregory's authority at Rome. In May there took place a meeting of higher clergy, including the bishops of the suburbicarian sees of Porto, Tusculum, Palestrina, and Segni. They condemned Gregory's attempt to raise funds for his resistance to Henry by mortgaging church property, affirming that church revenues should not be used for earthly warfare (*in militia seculari*) but only for the poor, for redeeming captives, and for the maintenance of divine service.[159] This protest cannot be interpreted as evidence of all-out opposition to Gregory or of positive support for Henry, since some of those who made it, like Bishop Bruno of Segni and Bonussenior, cardinal-priest of Santa Maria in Trastevere, remained faithful to Gregory until his death. Rather, its significance is twofold. First, the hostility at Rome to Gregory's use of church property for the financing of warfare shows that Henry's propaganda against

[157] Anna Comnena, 3. 10 and 5. 3. 1–2, ed. Leib, i. 132–6, ii. 13–14; Benzo of Alba, vi. 4, p. 664; *Vita Heinrici IV*, cap. 1, *Ausgew. Quell.* xii. 412–13; Dölger, *Regesten*, nos. 1077, 1080.

[158] Bonizo of Sutri, ix, pp. 613–14; Bernold, *a.* 1082, p. 437. Bonizo's allusion to the militant Alcimus (1 Macc. 7: 20–5) points the irony of Guibert's martial role in the light of Henry's arraignment of Gregory VII in his Manifesto.

[159] Z. Zafarana, 'Sul "conventus" del clero romano nel maggio 1082', *Studi medievali*, 3rd ser., vii (1966), 399–403; cf. Klewitz (as Ch. II n. 3), p. 38 n. 97. The question under discussion was: 'utrum bona ecclesiarum possent poni in pignore pro pecunia colligenda ad resistendum Wiberto archiepiscopo Ravennati Romanam sedem invadere conanti' (p. 402). Strong canonist support can be found for the *conventus*'s conclusion: Deusdedit, *Coll. can.* iii. 39–42 (37–40), 46 (44), pp. 285–6, 288–9. Of the participants named, only Peter, cardinal-priest of San Grisogono, at the time had a link with Montecassino: see above, p. 64; for Deusdedit and Abbot Desiderius, see above, p. 92. The background in the traditions of the early church is explained by A. H. M. Jones, 'Church Finance in the Fifth and Sixth Centuries', *Journal of Theological Studies*, NS xi (1960), 84–94.

the *scandalum* presented to the church by Gregory's military designs was shrewdly directed and propagated, and that it found an echo in Rome. Secondly, the meeting of May 1082 exhibited Gregory's militancy as being directed against Guibert of Ravenna; there was no reference to Henry himself. Other evidence confirms that the Romans regarded Guibert with particular animosity and that Gregorian partisans concentrated their propaganda upon him rather than upon the king.[160] In his approaches to the Romans Henry evidently did well in his own interest to keep Guibert's name and his election at Brixen out of the limelight, and to avoid a binding commitment to him as an alternative pope to Gregory. The Romans remained committed to Gregory and in 1082 all Henry's arguments, military might, and the supply of Byzantine money did nothing appreciably to shake their loyalty. Henry's best chance of recruiting Roman support and so of proceeding to imperial coronation may well have seemed to lie in a reconciliation with Gregory which would exclude Guibert and follow a mutual exculpation by Gregory and Henry.

While these events were taking place, the prospect of help for Gregory from the Apulian Normans became appreciably more favourable. Henry's more resolute action in Italy, together with his link with Alexius Comnenus and the resulting spectre of a Byzantine-supported rising in South Italy, continued to compel Robert Guiscard, however reluctantly, to give more of his attention to Italian affairs. Instead of pressing home the advantage that he gained by the fall of Durazzo to him on 21 February 1082 he decided to secure his rear in Italy. Leaving most of his army behind with Bohemond in charge, in April 1082 he landed at Otranto with a handful of followers. With a view to preventing a junction of Henry IV's forces with the Apulian rebels he headed for Rome. But it was soon clear that Henry had already turned northwards to confront Countess Matilda of Tuscany. So, during the remainder of 1082—and also for the whole of 1083—Robert Guiscard remained preoccupied in the south, with neither the immediate incentive nor the opportunity to intervene militarily in the papacy's favour. As was

[160] See Bonizo of Sutri, ix, pp. 613–14. Similarly, an early twelfth-century annotation of Donizo's *Vita Matildis* recorded the dispatch of treasure from the church at Canossa at the prompting of Countess Matilda and of Bishop Anselm II of Lucca 'pro defensione Romanae ecclesiae quae illo tempore persecutionem grandem habebat a Guiberto heresiarcha': *MGH SS* xii. 385 n. 14.

always the case after Ceprano, his commitment to it, though genuine, came low in his scale of priorities. Nevertheless, he was back in Italy. His presence would hereafter be a factor in the calculations of Gregory and Desiderius.[161]

d. *1082: events in South Italy*

Thus far events concerning Rome. Outside the city Henry's Italian expedition of 1082 deeply affected both the Normans and Montecassino. According to the Montecassino Chronicle, many of the Lombard inhabitants of South Italy (*omnes fere istarum partium homines*) reacted to Henry's presence at Rome by conspiring against 'the Normans', who therefore decided that the prudent course was one of reconciliation to Henry, since if he were to secure Rome and to command the resources of its neighbourhood he would be in a position to expel them from all their lands. The reference is unlikely to have been to more than those Normans who were subject to the volatile Prince Jordan of Capua; for Robert Guiscard is not known at this time to have had problems with the loyalty of his Lombard as distinct from his Norman subjects, and he cannot have welcomed Norman adherence to Henry, who was being helped by his own enemy Alexius Comnenus. The Chronicle goes on to relate how, after direct negotiations with Henry, 'the Normans' called in Desiderius, whom they uniquely trusted, to accompany them to the king; they were prompted, not only by considerations of their own security, but also by a desire arising from their fidelity to the Roman church to promote peace between pope and emperor. But when Gregory heard of their actions he excommunicated Henry and his adherents. 'The Normans' therefore turned from their previous love and service of Gregory to political and spiritual revulsion from him.[162] The reference

[161] For Robert Guiscard's return, see William of Apulia, iv. 458–527, pp. 228–33; Lupus Protospatarius, *a.* 1082, p. 61; Romuald of Salerno, pp. 194–5; Geoffrey Malaterra, iii. 34, pp. 77–8; *Annales Beneventani, a.* 1082, *MGH SS* iii. 182.

[162] *Chron. Cas.* iii. 50, pp. 430–1. At this point in the sole MS of Leo's continuators—Montecassino, Archivio capitolare, 450—a folio is missing and the opening part of the narrative of events in 1082 must be recovered from later versions—the fifteenth-century humanist recensions of Ambrogio Traversari and Agostino Patrizi, and the sixteenth-century printed text of Matthaeus Lauretus Hispanus: see Hoffmann (as Introd. n. 11), p. 142. However, the similarity of style and substance between the last sentence of the excerpts from Traversari and Lauretus on p. 430 makes it clear that, as from the words *Hoc audito omnes*, they refer to events in 1082, not 1083, and that they embody the beginning of the account resumed on

to a desire to promote peace between pope and emperor suggests that Henry's Manifesto of 1082 was known to the Capuan Normans, and that its propaganda for peace found an echo amongst them. It illustrates how prudent was Henry's show of preparedness to seek an agreement with Gregory.

Other evidence confirms and adds precision to the Chronicle's account. William of Apulia recorded that, because he feared the loss of his principality, Jordan did fealty to Henry, gave his son as a hostage, and supplied him with a large sum of money.[163] For the first time since Henry III's days a Norman prince had expressly recognized German lordship over South Italian lands. Gregory's letters show that he responded by excommunicating Jordan, *scienter periurus beato Petro et nobis*, on account of his fealty to Henry. He also wrote to Archbishop Hervey of Capua and to all the bishops of the Principate in order to confirm their loyalty and to enforce the excommunications that he had proclaimed. Gregory advised that the bishops should allow those who could not withstand pressure from those who had seceded to Henry to flee to the lands of the *gloriosus dux* Robert Guiscard (whose continuing loyalty he thus acknowledged), or of his brother Count Roger I of Sicily, or else to himself at Rome; but they were to encourage those who were of the necessary fortitude to stand their ground.[164]

From Desiderius' point of view Henry in 1082 thus once again brought about the state of affairs that he himself had always resisted and that in 1080 he seemed to have overcome—division between the Normans of Apulia and Capua. His own position was an unenviable one. Since Montecassino was situated so far to the north it was itself vulnerable to Henry when he was present with a military force in the environs of Rome. It was also vulnerable to Jordan of Capua, who had a record of proclivity to behave towards it with violence. Robert Guiscard had

p. 431. For the suggestion that this account is part of a much longer source, composed in the 1090s and used by Guido, see below, Appendix III.

[163] William of Apulia, v. 110–17, p. 242, cf. *Annales Beneventani, a.* 1080, *MGH SS* iii. 181; and Gaufredus Malaterra, iii. 35, p. 78. See Tirelli (as Ch. III n. 102), p. 862 n. 3.

[164] *Reg.* ix. 27, to Archbishop John of Naples, pp. 610–11; Bernold, *a.* 1084, p. 441, on which see Sander, *Der Kampf*, p. 122, Meyer von Knonau, *Jahrbücher*, iii. 452, Tirelli (as Ch. III n. 102), p. 990, and Deér (as Introd. n. 52), pp. 91–2, 135; *Reg.* ix. 26, to Archbishop Hervey of Capua and the other bishops of the Principate, p. 609.

made clear how low a priority he gave to helping Gregory by comparison with fighting the Byzantines, and also with quelling rebellion in South Italy. In any case until April he was across the Adriatic. So Desiderius' only feasible policy was, in the short term, to ward off Henry's extremer threats and demands as best he could by prudent diplomacy. In the long term he must work for a reconciliation between Jordan and Robert Guiscard in Gregory's obedience according to the pattern of 1059 and 1080, and—in the light of Henry's Manifesto of 1082 and of Gregory's still firm support from the citizens of Rome—seek a mutual appeasement of Gregory and Henry.

One thing emerges clearly from contemporary charters: Desiderius ended the summer on good terms with both the Norman leaders.[165] For the rest, the principal evidence is a passage of the Chronicle which continues the tale of events from the account of 'the Normans' ' apostasy from Gregory.[166] It comes from a later source which sought to maximize Desiderius' commitment to ultra-Gregorian positions; but since it is a Cassinese source it may nevertheless, with whatever exaggeration, preserve valuable recollections of Desiderius' attitude and conduct. The further possibility must be borne in mind that, as well as being included in Guido's continuation, this source may have been tampered with by Peter the Deacon, with his contrary concern to emphasize historical links and exchanges of mutual benefit between Montecassino and the German rulers.

It emerges from this source that Henry was able to place Desiderius under pressure to follow his neighbour Jordan of Capua in submitting to his lordship, and that his actions provided what has been described as 'the earliest evidence of an emperor's making a demand upon a reluctant prelate for homage subsequent to his consecration'.[167] Using the counts of Marsia as an intermediary, Henry sent a letter summoning Desiderius to him. The abbot did not at once reply, upon the pretext that he did

[165] See the documents for the year 1082 in *Reg. Pet. Diac.*: no. 418, 24 Sept., in which Jordan of Capua gave Montecassino the church of San Rufo, Capua, see Inguanez (as Ch. I n. 35), i, pp. 55–6, no. 19, Loud, 'Calendar', pp. 124–5, no. 27, and *Chron. Cas.* iii. 47, 61, pp. 425, 441; and no. 601, Oct., in which Robert Guiscard made it gifts at Amalfi which included the church of San Biagio: Ménager, *Recueil*, pp. 133–6, no. 42.

[166] *Chron. Cas.* iii. 50, pp. 431–2; see below, Appendix III.

[167] M. Minninger, *Vom Clermont zum Wormser Konkordat. Die Auseinandersetzungen um den Lehnsnexus zwischen König und Episkopat* (Cologne and Vienna, 1978), 35–7.

not know what form of epistolary greeting he should employ. A second, more threatening, letter from Henry summoned him without fail to the imperial abbey of Farfa, to which Henry is known to have come on 17 March. Desiderius now answered by sending a letter having the greeting *debite fidelitatis obsequium*, which he judged sufficiently ambiguous to evade a fealty that he could not rightly concede. He explained that he could not come to Henry *propter Normannos*, by which presumably he meant from fear of incurring Robert Guiscard's disfavour. But he also developed themes which indicate that he may have been testing Henry's sincerity in his Manifesto of 1082: if perhaps Henry did desire peace with the pope, Desiderius would contrive some opportunity of coming to him; and at the end of his letter, to encourage Henry, he pointed out that neither *sacerdotium* nor *regnum* could find lasting peace in the midst of such dissension as was then raging. Henry reacted angrily against Desiderius, prohibiting his own envoys to Jordan of Capua from having dealings with him and ordering Jordan to harass him until he should come to Henry's presence. Desiderius reported all this to Gregory VII, seeking his advice; however, no answer came from the pope. Henry then sent further letters both to Desiderius and to his monks, ordering the abbot to keep Easter (24 April) with him; but Desiderius continued to temporize. When Jordan put him under pressure to accompany him to Henry, Desiderius explained his perplexity to his monks, showing how any of the possible courses of action would be harmful to Montecassino. In the end he determined, in imitation of figures like Pope Leo I and St. Benedict himself, who had met Arian rulers to secure their subjects' interest, to go and meet the king.

When Desiderius reached Albano, where Henry kept Easter, he steadfastly resisted demands, backed up by threats, that he do fealty or homage, or that he receive his abbey from the king's hands. He thereby put Montecassino at risk, for Henry reacted by charging Jordan to go to the abbey with royal agents to whom he was to make it subject. Jordan, however, turned some of Henry's wrath away by speaking well of Desiderius. When Jordan eventually brought Desiderius before the king the abbot so far relaxed his stand as to promise him friendship (*amicitia*) and to say that, *salvo ordine suo*, he would help him as best he could to secure the imperial crown. But this was the limit of concession. Desiderius would not receive his abbatial staff from the king, although he promised to reconsider the matter when he saw him wearing the imperial crown; if he then still felt unable to receive the staff he would resign his office.[168]

As presented in the Montecassino Chronicle these events suggest that in 1082 Desiderius proceeded circumspectly and not without advantage to himself and to his abbey. He never infringed his loyalty to Gregory VII or compromised the claims of the *sacerdotium* as he saw them. He firmly avoided the king's demands that he do fealty or homage. By the exercise of prudence and diplomatic skill he brought Henry to conciliate rather than coerce him. Perhaps with Henry's Manifesto in mind he declared himself willing to help Henry to secure imperial coronation, but with the all-important qualification *salvo ordine suo*. Since in 1082 Henry's imperial coronation at Gregory's hands was very much a possibility, Desiderius was wise to leave open the question of his receiving his abbatial staff from a reconciled ruler. He also kept Jordan of Capua's goodwill, while doing nothing to forfeit Robert Guiscard's. The intention of the Cassinese source to present Desiderius in the best possible light as an upholder of Gregorian principles must be allowed for. But against the background of all that is known about Cassinese ideas and Desiderius' own outlook and character, it has the ring of basic reliability in showing how Desiderius drew advantage from a difficult situation while not compromising himself in matters of principle. The only probably false detail of the dealings of Desiderius, Jordan, and Henry is that with which the account as it stands comes to an end: in return for a large sum of money Henry gave Jordan a charter sealed with a gold seal, confirming to him all the principality except for Montecassino and its lands, which Henry kept for himself and the Empire. It reads like an interpolation by Peter the Deacon in his concern to emphasize royal generosity to the Normans and to Montecassino.[169]

The source which underlies the Montecassino Chronicle at this point goes on further to explore Desiderius' attitude to the issue of *sacerdotium* and *regnum* as it was allegedly debated in 1082.[170] He is said to have engaged in frequent debates with

[168] It is important to bear in mind how late it was before lay investiture became a critical issue: Schieffer (as Introd. n. 89), esp. pp. 153–76. Gregory is unlikely to have pressed his decrees of 1078 and 1080 upon the South Italian Normans more energetically than upon the Anglo-Norman lands.

[169] See below, Appendix IV.

[170] *Chron. Cas.* iii. 50, p. 433.

bishops accompanying Henry about the rights of the apostolic see (*de honore apostolice sedis*). More important, he debated them with Cardinal Odo of Ostia, whose adherence to Gregory the source only somewhat reluctantly concedes (*qui etiam pape Gregorio favere videbatur*). The arguments by which, as it was alleged, Desiderius overcame Odo and his other rivals were made to turn upon the Election Decree of 1059, to which Odo appealed in support of the contention that no pope should be established in the Roman church without imperial consent and that if one were so established he would be no pope and should be anathematized. In refutation Desiderius adopted an extreme stance: no pope, he was made to say, nor any archbishop or archdeacon or cardinal, nor any man whatsoever, might rightly so proceed. The apostolic see was a mistress, not a slave or anyone's subject, but was set over all; there could be no grounds for selling it as if it were a servant. If in 1059 Pope Nicholas II had acted as Odo claimed—the account continued—he had behaved unjustly and most foolishly; nor might a king of the Germans ever again set up a pope of the Romans. Odo came back with the angry answer that, if this thesis were bruited north of the Alps, absolutely everyone would band together to oppose it. Desiderius replied uncompromisingly that even if the whole world united to speak thus, no one could hinder his own party from thinking as it did; even if the emperor's power should prevail in the church for a season it would never win his consent. The Chronicle also represented Desiderius as discussing such questions with Guibert of Ravenna, whom he severely reproved for entangling himself with the papacy. When Guibert could not justify himself he explained that he had acted unwillingly and under duress; otherwise Henry would have deposed him from the see of Ravenna.

These discussions as related in the Montecassino Chronicle give rise to serious difficulties. There is no reason to doubt Odo of Ostia's presence at Albano in 1082. His movements in that year are largely unattested, but he may have been there under commission from Gregory to sound Henry's preparedness to seek absolution on the basis that he hinted at in his Manifesto.[171] But their supposed dialogue bears the stamp of a later stage of the Investiture Contest. It has long been recognized that, like other passages in the Chronicle,[172] the treatment here

[171] Meyer von Knonau, *Jahrbücher*, iii. 443; Becker, *Urban II.*, i. 55, 57–9.

[172] See below, Appendix VII.

of Pope Nicholas II and the Election Decree betray the influence of Cardinal Deusdedit's *Libellus contra invasores et symoniacos et reliquos scismaticos*, which was written in stages during the 1090s and given its final form *c.*1097.[173] Desiderius' extremer alleged statements appear to mirror the concern of those years with the king's right to influence the disposal of spiritual offices.

It is also remarkable that the Chronicle should refer to the presence of 125 bishops at the Lent council of 1059. This number does not appear in, neither does it correspond to, any surviving text of the Election Decree, but occurs only in certain items of imperialist propaganda.[174] It is not clear whence it came into the Chronicle, and the possibility that it was in a now lost text known at Montecassino cannot be excluded. But, as Odo of Ostia was made to point out, Desiderius was present at the Lent council of 1059 and subscribed the Decree. A story giving an aberrant number of those attending is suspect, and Desiderius is unlikely in real life to have reacted with surprise and indignation to a ruling which had once had his acquiescence. Moreover, the story betrays a misunderstanding of what was the probable intention of the Election Decree so far as royal power is concerned. The clause about the emperor's rights has been best explained as turning upon his personal merit: in the light

[173] See his polemic against the Decree, i. 11–13, *MGH Libelli*, ii. 309–13, also his veiled but bitter reference in the Dedicatory Epistle to his *Coll. can.*, pp. 4–5: 'Preterea antiquum ordinem electionis seu consecrationis Romani pontificis et cleri eius huic operi inserere libuit. Nam quidem olim in dei et sanctorum patrum sanctionibus contemptum ad sui scilicet ostentationem et adscribendam sibi ventosam auctoritatem, quę nullis canonicis legibus stare potest, scripserunt sibi novam ordinationem eiusdem Romani pontificis, in qua quam nefanda quam deo inimica statuerunt, horreo scribere; qui legit intellegat.' See Krause, PWD, pp. 207–17.

[174] Krause, PWD, p. 244 n. 31. It appears three times: in the German bishops' renunciation of loyalty to Gregory at Worms (1076), Anhang A, *Ausgew. Quell.* xii. 474; in the decree of the council of Brixen (1080), Anhang C, pp. 478–80; and in the *Dicta cuiusdam de discordia papae et regis*, ed. K. Francke, *MGH Libelli*, i. 459–9, the date of which is *c.*1084. The last source notes that copies existed in the papal archives and in Henry's chancery. Hoffmann suggests that *Chron. Cas.* may refer to the Worms or Brixen documents: p. 433 n. 22. The strongest argument in favour of this would seem to be the similarity of language between *Chron. Cas.*: 'ut numquam papa in Romana ecclesia absque consensu imperatoris fieret', and the bishops' letter at Worms: '. . . ut nullus umquam papa fieret nisi . . . per consensum auctoritatemque regis'. But the similarity is not close, and *Chron. Cas.* appears to suppose that Odo produced a text of the Decree (*privilegium Nycolai pape . . . ostendisset*), presumably from the papal archives. The words '. . . sciret se non pro papa abendum esse atque anathematizandum' seem, however, to take up those peculiar to the imperialist text of the Decree: 'non papa sed sathanas, non apostolicus sed apostaticus ab omnibus habeatur et teneatur' (cap. 9).

of his past conduct the apostolic see was to establish at each election, through the cardinals, the ruler's suitability to be involved.[175] But imperialist propagandists—who, rather than papalists, cited the Decree during the eleventh century, even in its authentic form—related it to the emperor's objective right and authority: according to them it reserved for him such a role as the Emperor Henry III had fulfilled in 1046. At Albano the Chronicle represented Odo of Ostia as expressing such a view and as thereby prompting Desiderius' hard-line reply. Odo's preparedness when pope to make concessions in order to win back imperialists to the papacy makes it plausible that, in 1082, he should have taken a moderate line. But it is unlikely that he held the view attributed to him in the Chronicle; for it would have invalidated the elections of Gregory VII, Victor III, and himself, to none of which Henry consented. The Chronicle's story seems to reflect unhistorical and exaggerated attempts in the 1090s, based upon Deusdedit's views, to present Desiderius as a *ne plus ultra* papalist in his view of *sacerdotium* and *regnum*.

Yet the story may contain a kernel of truth. Deusdedit's hostility to the Election Decree was also expressed in the Dedicatory Epistle of his canon-law collection of 1087, which was addressed to Desiderius as Pope Victor III.[176] Only five years after the discussions at Albano a more than hostile view of the Decree could thus be presented to him, and in Deusdedit he was certainly willing to patronize a radical opponent of royal intervention in church affairs. The inference must be that, while he may not have shared Deusdedit's view, it was at least not wholly uncongenial to him. The account in the Chronicle of Desiderius' dealings with Archbishop Guibert of Ravenna is more immediately plausible. Guibert's admission that he had become involved only unwillingly in Henry's plans for the papacy is understandable in view of his precarious position at Henry's whim right up to his enthronement in 1084. He himself referred to his unwillingness in letters to Bishop Anselm II of Lucca and, later, to Archbishop Lanfranc of Canterbury.[177] However prepared

[175] cap. 6; see W. Stürner, 'Der Königsparagraph im Papstwahldekret von 1059', *SG* ix (1972), 39–52, esp. 45–6, in criticism of Krause, whose general thesis is not affected.

[176] See above, p. 99.

[177] Anselm of Lucca, *Epistola ad Wibertum, MGH SS* xii. 3–5; F. Liebermann, 'Lanfranc and the Antipope', *EHR* xvi (1901), 328–32, at 330.

Desiderius may have been to talk to Henry he would clearly have no truck with Guibert as a papal candidate; his own election to the papacy in opposition to him was to confirm that this was so.

The chapter of the Chronicle ends with a statement that Desiderius concluded his dealings with Henry by receiving from him a diploma confirming Montecassino's possessions, and that he returned to Montecassino by Henry's leave. The story of the diploma is told in terms similar to that of Prince Jordan's, and again there is no corroborative evidence of a satisfactory kind. It does not fit well with Desiderius' uneasy dealings with Henry at Albano, and must be deemed improbable.[178]

A further problem which arises from the course of Desiderius' dealings in 1082 with Henry IV is whether he thereby incurred and persisted in excommunication by Gregory.[179] That he did was asserted by Archbishop Hugh of Lyons in a letter to Countess Matilda of Tuscany which was probably written in April or May 1087.[180] It contains the statement, which the archbishop put into the mouth of the monk Guitmund when Desiderius' election to the papacy was under discussion in March 1087, that 'a notoriously guilty person (*infamem personam*) should not be elected or instituted as pope; for [Desiderius] undoubtedly incurred guilt (*infamia*) by sustaining Pope Gregory's excommunication for a whole year and more without canonical penance'. In an obscure sentence Hugh further alleged that, at Montecassino a short time before he wrote to the countess, Desiderius had openly discussed the matter with unbecoming levity: 'Would not anyone seem mad whose tongue wagged about a bishop-elect of Rome after his absolution by the most blessed Pope Gregory, having formerly been an excommunicate?'[181] There is nothing directly to prove or to disprove these statements; but a number of considerations tell against their justice.

First, Hugh's letter was written in haste and anger, and it found no favour or credence with Countess Matilda, who was in a better position than he to know the truth of the matter.[182] For in Tuscany she was well informed about Roman affairs,

178 See below, Appendix IV.

179 See esp. T. Leccisotti, 'L'incontro di Desiderio di Montecassino col re Enrico IV ad Albano', *SG* i (1947), 307–19, to which the following discussion is indebted.

180 Hugh of Flavigny, ii, pp. 466–8.

181 'Numquid non delirans videretur, si quis Romanum ęlectum post absolutionem a beatissimo papa Gregorio susceptam, excommunicatum garriret?': pp. 466–7.

182 See below, p. 207.

while Hugh had not been to the city for many years. It was therefore unlikely that he knew of Henry's Manifesto of 1082 or appreciated the complex problem that Henry posed by it to Gregory and his adherents and well-wishers. Having arrived in Rome just after Desiderius' election as pope on 24 May 1086, he himself behaved as a man who was utterly perplexed. He at first concurred in the election but, having followed Desiderius to Montecassino, he repented after hearing the abbot's own accounts of what Hugh called his *nefandissimos actus* in 1082: they had included promising Henry aid to secure the imperial crown, encouraging him to enter the lands of St. Peter, and himself incurring excommunication. In his letter Hugh seems to have been misconstruing negotiations which were probably not unknown to Gregory and which were intended to test Henry's willingness to abandon Guibert as the price of his absolution and coronation by Gregory. If so, Hugh offered a tendentious and ill-informed account of dealings which, as the Montecassino Chronicle indicates, were by no means to Desiderius' discredit or harmful to the Gregorian cause.[183]

Secondly, the source underlying the Montecassino Chronicle heavily underlined Desiderius' care at Albano to avoid excommunication by association with those already under papal sentence. During his journey and stay near Henry, many bishops and magnates, many of his friends, and the imperial chancellor Bishop Burchard of Lausanne met him, but he gave none of them the kiss of peace; nor did he pray, eat, or drink with them. When he reached Albano, despite Henry's threats he neither entered his presence nor sent envoys. Thus he avoided the infection of excommunication.[184] There may well here be a retrospective concern to discredit such stories as Archbishop Hugh had put into currency; but, as with much else in this source, there may be a basis of truth in its picture of Desiderius. Memories at Montecassino were still fairly fresh when it was written. In his surviving letters Gregory himself made no such reference to Desiderius' excommunication as he made to Jordan of Capua's.[185] In 1082 Desiderius did nothing with regard to Henry or to Jordan of Capua which placed him in such peril as his long association with the three-times excommunicated

[183] See above, pp. 157–9.
[184] *Chron. Cas.* iii. 50, p. 432.
[185] In *Reg.* ix. 27.

Robert Guiscard.[186] Such considerations reduce the plausibility of his excommunication in 1082.

A final piece of evidence that tends to discredit Archbishop Hugh's story is the so-called *Iudicium de regno et sacerdotio.*[187] Not only does this tract exhibit Desiderius in early December 1083 as hitherto having customarily been in Henrician eyes a leader of those who 'se posuerunt contra ius'; it also presents the monk Guitmund, who in Hugh's letter arraigned Desiderius as an *infamis persona*, in the role of his close associate. It is true that Guitmund was clearly a headstrong man who might have changed his view, and also that by December 1083 there was time for Desiderius to have secured release from a 'whole year and more' of excommunication incurred in the spring of 1082. Yet Guitmund's presence with him at the Cassinese house of Santa Maria in Pallara tells against the archbishop's story, as does the assertion of Desiderius' habitual fidelity to Gregory. Desiderius' excommunication must be judged to be not proven; in the light of what seem to have been his intentions and actions in 1082 it lacks plausibility. However, it cannot be absolutely disproven.

In many respects Desiderius' part remains an obscure one. His hastening to Amalfi in 1065 to prepare gifts for Henry when he appeared to be about to come to Italy, and his long adherence to Robert Guiscard while he was excommunicated, show that Montecassino's interests always bulked large in his calculations. It is likely that in 1082 he went to the limit of prudence in order to safeguard them when Henry was at hand. Yet he was also concerned, in a way that at this time suited Gregory's interests as well as Montecassino's, to reconcile the Norman leaders Robert Guiscard and Jordan of Capua. Given Robert Guiscard's power, wealth, and reliability from Montecassino's point of view, and also the duke's implacable hostility to Alexius Comnenus, who was Henry IV's ally and paymaster, Desiderius had a long-term interest to keep free of all possible entanglements with Henry and to keep communications open with the pope, whose cause against Henry his benefactor Robert Guiscard was bound to some extent to espouse. And since April the duke had

[186] So in 1127 the monks of Montecassino claimed to Pope Honorius II without challenge that 'Casinensis vero ecclesia numquam in heresim decidit, numquam contra sedem apostolicam sensit': *Chron. Cas.* iv. 95, p. 556.

[187] See below, Appendix V.

been in South Italy. So Desiderius seems throughout to have been careful to keep in touch with Gregory and to do nothing that would have harmed his cause.

e. *1083*

With the benefit of Byzantine money and other treasure Henry was able in 1083 to secure the initial military success that had eluded him in the two previous years. Having returned to Rome early in the year he frustrated Gregory's Lent council. After bitter fighting which started before Easter (9 April) he captured the Leonine city on 3 June. Although Gregory continued to control the bridges over the Tiber and the principal buildings of Rome, he was forced to take refuge in the Castel Sant'Angelo. With the onset of the dangerous summer heat Henry built and garrisoned a fortification at the Palatiolus, between St. Peter's and the Tiber, in order to secure his gains while he withdrew from the city with the bulk of his army. On the day before he left he made a gesture of recognition to Archbishop Guibert, which probably took the form of allowing him to preside at mass in St. Peter's on the apostle's vigil (28 June).[188] It was a warning to the Romans that Henry was now powerful in the city and meant to bring matters to a head. But with the Lateran still far from his grasp he could not, even had he so wished, have taken the decisive steps to complete Guibert's election as pope by the Romans and to proceed to his enthronement, thus facilitating his own imperial coronation. In any case he probably did not as yet wish to provoke a definitive and hardened schism.

Events in South Italy are likely to have made him reluctant to do so. In June 1083 Robert Guiscard overcame the main centre of resistance to him at Cannae, and went on to harry Jordan of Capua into turning from Henry and making peace with himself.[189] So the Normans were once again united against Henry's interests, and their unity must have strengthened the resolve of Abbot Desiderius and his monks to avoid any binding commitment to him. Gregory, as well as Henry, now received money and treasure which he could use to help his cause: Robert Guiscard sent the Romans 30,000 gold *solidi*, while

[188] Bernold, *a.* 1083, pp. 437–9, gives the fullest evidence for this year, but he anticipates events of 1084. See also *Reg.* ix. 35*a*, pp. 627–8; Frutolf of Michaelsberg, *a.* 1083, p. 96; *Annales Augustani, a.* 1083, *MGH SS* iii. 130.

[189] William of Apulia, iv. 528–35, v. 106–20, pp. 232–3, 242–3.

Countess Matilda of Tuscany arranged for the melting down and and dispatch of the treasure of the church of Canossa.[190] On the other hand, Henry's stronger military position at Rome, and especially his garrison at the Palatiolus, placed him in a better position than ever before to pursue negotiations.

In 1083 there is evidence for the first time of serious disaffection from Gregory amongst the citizens of Rome: the brief notice in Gregory's Register of his November council recorded that the *Romanum vulgus* were victims of weariness and hunger which sapped their morale and discipline,[191] and the negotiations of the year were to prove that all ranks of society were involved. These negotiations seem to have gone on continuously. For a period of a year and three months which included 1083 Bishop Benno of Osnabrück was at Rome by Henry's order to assist those who were—as the king and his party saw matters—seeking peace and concord; Benno's biographer wrote of his frequent journeys between Gregory and Henry.[192] Henry was evidently concerned to use his measure of military success and the uncertainty of Roman loyalty to Gregory in order to seek his ends by way of negotiation.

He made considerable progress in this endeavour. He was able to establish contact with the citizens of Rome, or at least with a group of them, who sent envoys to him.[193] During the summer and after Henry's setting up of his garrison at the Palatiolus, without the knowledge of Gregory or his close associates a group within the papal service itself made a sworn agreement that, within fifteen days of Henry's return, they would set a time-limit within which they would compel Gregory to crown him emperor. If Gregory were dead or had fled and declined to return to the city, they would with Henry's counsel canonically elect a new pope—no name was given—who would crown him.

[190] Donizo, *Vita Matildis*, ii. 300–4, *MGH SS* xii. 385; Lupus Protospatarius, *a.* 1083, p. 61; see the allegations about Gregory's lavish disbursement of money in the poem edited by E. Dümmler, *MGH Libelli*, i. 433–4, esp. stanzas 13–14. Giesebrecht showed that the poem relates to the capture of the Leonine city in 1083: see Meyer von Knonau, *Jahrbücher*, iii. 478 n. 13.

[191] *Reg.* ix. 35*a*, p. 628. Another factor was perhaps Gregory's curtailment 'postquam expendium guerre crevit' of the ancient ceremonies of the *cornomannia*, which included gifts of money to poor families: Benedictus Canonicus, *Liber politicus*, 7 (i–ii), *Le Liber censuum* (as Introd. n. 61), ii. 107–8, 171.

[192] *Vita Bennonis*, cap. 22, cf. 17–18, *MGH Script. rer. Germ.*, pp. 21–5, 30–1; *Annales Yburgenses*, cap. 28, *a.* 1083, *MGH SS* xvi. 437.

[193] Lupus Protospatarius, *a.* 1083, p. 61.

They would also secure the fealty of the Roman citizens.[194] Apart from these clandestine negotiations Gregory and Henry were in more open touch. This is clear, not only from the activities of Bishop Benno of Osnabrück, but also from the employment of Henry's godfather Abbot Hugh of Cluny, probably in the first week of July, to negotiate at Sutri between Gregory and Henry; the negotiations were serious, but without result.[195] Moreover, many Romans came to terms with Henry—partly, said the Swabian chronicler Bernold, through bribes, partly in answer to the king's many promises, and partly from war-weariness. With the sole exception of Prince Gisulf of Salerno, whom Bernold thus identified as a hard-line anti-Henrician, almost all the Romans agreed with Henry that Gregory should convene a council in mid-November, and that its decisions *de causa regni* should be final.[196] Henry swore that he would respect the security of all those who came to and went from the council.

During the summer Gregory dispatched both to France and to Germany his letter of summons to the November council.[197] Like Henry's Manifesto of 1082, to which it was in effect a papalist counterpart,[198] it studiously left open the course of future developments. It did not shut the door against a reconciliation with Henry. But its tone of fortitude and unswerving zeal for righteousness left no doubt of Gregory's preparedness if necessary to follow a course of unflinching resistance to him, whatever the consequences. The re-establishment of Christian unity and communion was his overriding purpose: '. . . supported by God's help, we desire to take counsel with you about how we may establish the peace of God and how we may recall those

[194] *Sacramentum*, below, Appendix V.

[195] Reynald of Vézelay, *Vita s. Hugonis abbatis Cluniacensis*, iv. 26, Migne, *PL* clix. 903–4; H. E. J. Cowdrey, 'Two Studies in Cluniac History', *SG* xi (1978), 29 n. 42. For the date, see H. Diener, 'Das Itinerar des Abtes Hugo von Cluny', *Neue Forschungen über Cluny und die Cluniacenser* (Freiburg, 1959), 368, 387. Henry's relative mildness is apparent in his dissociating himself from Bishop Ulrich of Brescia's seizure of Abbot Hugh. According to the Montecassino Chronicle, probably soon after this event Hugh visited the abbey and concluded a monastic union: iii. 51, pp. 433–4; cf. *I Necrologi cassinesi* (as Ch. I n. 118), 29 Apr., and p. 73. The two abbeys and their rulers were evidently now in closer sympathy than in 1072: see above, p. 29.

[196] So, too, Sigebert of Gembloux, *Chronica, a.* 1083, *MGH SS* vi. 364; and Frutolf of Michaelsberg, *a.* 1083, p. 96.

[197] *Epp. vag.*, pp. 122–5, no. 51. Bernold knew of this letter.

[198] So Sander, *Der Kampf*, p. 139.

in schism to travel the royal way to the bosom of their mother the church.' At about the time of the dispatch of this letter a turn of events at Rome strengthened Gregory's hand. Fever wiped out the garrison that Henry had left at the Palatiolus, including its captain Ulrich of Godesheim; Gregory's followers razed the fortification to the ground. It seemed to be a judgement of God against Henry, who also lost the leverage for negotiation that such a military enclave provided.

Henry responded vigorously but not altogether wisely. He dispatched Guibert to Ravenna;[199] this action seems to have rested upon a hope that there might yet be a reconciliation with Gregory that would be easier if Guibert were out of the way, especially since he had hitherto found so little acceptance amongst the Romans. But Henry also sought to compensate and to improve his chances at the council by keeping away from Rome those strong-minded Gregorians who might weight it against him. He had Bishop Odo of Ostia arrested as he returned from a legatine mission to himself.[200] On about 11 November he seized and plundered near Sutri the envoys of the German princes. He also impeded French and Italian bishops whose presence might not help him: Bernold named Archbishop Hugh of Lyons, Bishop Anselm II of Lucca, and Bishop Reynald of Como. Henry was employing a double-edged weapon; for, by violating his promise of safe conduct, he antagonized many people at Rome. There was no attendance of imperialistic churchmen. So, when the council met for three days on 20 November with Henry near at hand, it consisted mainly of bishops and abbots from South Italy and a few Frenchmen. It was too small and unrepresentative to take major decisions *de causa regni*. Its main event seems to have been an allocution by Gregory about the Christian faith and the fortitude that the times demanded.[201] According to Bernold, Gregory was only with difficulty restrained from again excommunicating Henry by name; instead, he excommunicated in general terms all who had obstructed those of his own party who had endeavoured to come to Rome.

Henry's coercive measures had served their purpose in so far

[199] Guibert's withdrawal to Ravenna is confirmed by charters of Dec. 1083 and Jan. 1084: H. Rubeus, *Historiarum Ravennatum libri decem* (Venice, 1589), 309.

[200] This finds confirmation in *Reg.* ix. 35*a*, and Bonizo of Sutri, ix, p. 614.

[201] *Reg.* ix. 35*a*. For Gregory's legislation, see below, Ch. IV n. 113.

as they hamstrung the council and warded off a definitive sentence against him. But they did nothing to advance him towards the imperial title. That he kept up a propaganda war is clear from the tract known as the *Iudicium de regno et sacerdotio*, which purports to record an occurrence at the Cassinese house in Rome of Santa Maria in Pallara on 3 December 1083, and therefore little more than a week after Gregory's November council.[202] It also provides important evidence for Cassinese support of Gregory's cause. According to it, Gregorian partisans who were in touch with the pope set up an ordeal by which to establish the divine judgement *de regno et sacerdotio*. The first-named of the group was Abbot Desiderius,[203] who figures as the centre of a Gregorian circle of *soi-disant* religious men who over a considerable period had resisted what was right in the struggle of *regnum* and *sacerdotium*. Despite all their endeavours, the verdict of the ordeal went repeatedly and decisively in Henry's favour. The historicity of the ordeal is questionable. The document about it reads like a propaganda broadsheet drawn up ostensibly for Henry's own eyes,[204] but in fact to commend his cause to the Romans after the disaster at the Palatiolus and Gregory's emotional allocution to the November council.[205]

Such propaganda seems to have done Henry's cause in Rome little good. Bernold retailed the stories that hearsay brought to him in Swabia. The synchronization of the November council and Henry's return to Rome was a critical moment for those Romans of Gregory's entourage who in the summer had been inclined to turn from him.[206] Under the terms of the still secret *Sacramentum* those bound by it must within fifteen days secure either Henry's coronation or Gregory's deposition. Gregory's support after the council was too great for them to be able to comply. So they disclosed the matter to him. Bernold indicates that he absolved them from their oath, while other Romans continued to negotiate with Henry, who replied with a mixture of threats and blandishments. With Rome so polarized in its

[202] Below, Appendix V. Hirsch, 'Desiderius', pp. 82–4, argued for 1082, but he took insufficient account of the contest for Roman loyalties that persisted after the Nov. council, 1083. For a discussion, see Klewitz (as Ch. II n. 3), pp. 40–3.

[203] So it is likely that he was at the Nov. council among the *abbates Campani* of *Reg.* ix. 35*a*.

[204] Lines 38–9.

[205] '. . . totum fere conventum in gemitus et lacrimis compulit': *Reg.* ix. 35*a*.

[206] Bernold's picture of Henry's movements is confirmed by the *Annales Beneventani*, *a.* 1084, *MGH SS* iii. 182.

loyalties it was unlikely that in 1084 matters would be settled otherwise than by force.

f. *1084–5*

Henry spent the winter of 1083/4 in the vicinity of Rome, and he is said to have kept Christmas at St. Peter's.[207] According to Bernold he now abandoned hope of securing imperial coronation at Gregory's hands on terms that he could accept, and he awaited Guibert's return from Ravenna in order to be crowned by him.[208] He continued to enjoy Byzantine financial help, which, although it was meant for warfare against Robert Guiscard, he disbursed amongst the lower classes at Rome. He did, however, campaign briefly in Apulia. Thereafter, at a juncture when, as he said in one of his own letters, he so despaired of gaining Rome that he was minded to return to Germany, the Romans themselves sent envoys inviting him to their city and promising their obedience.[209] For at about this time thirteen cardinals and a considerable part of the Roman aristocracy went over to him.[210] With Roman aid he had no difficulty in entering the city on 21 March, and in occupying the Lateran palace. He held a council at St. Peter's in which Gregory's deposition was proclaimed. On Palm Sunday (24 March), in the words of Henry's letter, 'our pope-elect Clement was raised to the apostolic see by acclamation of all the Romans, and on Easter Day [31 March], to the joy of the whole Roman people, we were ordained and consecrated emperor by Pope Clement with the consent of all the Romans'. Gregory was forced again to take refuge in the Castel Sant'Angelo.

Despite the defections and Henry's euphoric words, a considerable part of the Roman aristocracy adhered to Gregory, as did all save one of the cardinal-bishops, John II of Porto; Gregory was therefore able to keep control of the Tiber bridges and of many Roman strongholds.[211] With Rome thus still

[207] Frutolf of Michaelsberg, *a.* 1084, pp. 96–8.

[208] Bernold, *a.* 1084, pp. 439–41, which, despite chronological confusion, remains an important source; Bonizo of Sutri, ix, p. 614. The fullest modern treatment is Meyer von Knonau, *Jahrbücher*, iii. 521–67. For Byzantine help in 1084, see Dölger, *Regesten*, no. 1114.

[209] *Ep.* 18, to Bishop Thierry of Verdun, *Ausgew. Quell.* xii. 82–4; see also Benzo of Alba, vi. 6, vii. prol., pp. 666, 669.

[210] For the defections, Beno, i. 1, iii. 10, pp. 369–70, 394; see Kehr (as Ch. II n. 21), pp. 976–80.

[211] Bernold's testimony is confirmed by Bardo, cap. 22, p. 20; cf. Beno, loc. cit.

deeply divided there followed bitter fighting for mastery of it, and Gregory's followers claimed some success. He himself sent Abbot Jarento of Saint-Bénigne, Dijon, with some cardinals to seek Robert Guiscard's help. Since he had defeated the Apulian rebels Robert was in a position to respond. As a Henrician victory at Rome would threaten his ability to pursue his primary concern of winning lands across the Adriatic, he did so with a considerable force.[212] According to the Montecassino Chronicle, on hearing about this Desiderius—who seems to have left Rome during the winter—instantly sent a messenger to Rome, who was to announce both to the pope his deliverance (*liberatio*) and also to the emperor the coming of the duke. A possible interpretation of this cryptic sentence is that Desiderius feared that, if there were fighting at Rome, Robert Guiscard would be concerned to reduce the city and to ensure that it could not become in imperial hands a threat from the rear to his Illyrian operations. So he wished to bring about Henry's withdrawal in time to forestall bloodshed and desolation.

In fact Henry left the environs of the city only on 21 May, and Rome experienced the Normans' fury. The sources give different accounts of what happened. The Montecassino Chronicle is brief and reproduces a source which, though in some respects circumstantial, gave an artificial version of events: Robert Guiscard came by night to the Roman church of Sancti Quattuor Coronati to the east of the Colosseum; advised by the Roman consul Cencius, he adopted the stratagem of starting a fire in the city; while the citizens were preoccupied with extinguishing it he swiftly freed Gregory from the Castel Sant'Angelo and at once conveyed him to Montecassino; Desiderius thereafter supported Gregory together with an entourage of Roman bishops and cardinals until he died.[213] A different picture, which does not thus gloss over the savagery of the Norman sacking of Rome, emerges in both Bernold and—the most reliable of the sources for these events—Geoffrey Malaterra. They make it clear that, having rescued Gregory from the Castel Sant'Angelo, Robert Guiscard restored him to the Lateran. After encountering

[212] For events at Rome see, besides Bernold and Henry IV's letter, William of Apulia, iv. 527–66, pp. 232–4; Gaufredus Malaterra, iii. 34–7, pp. 77–80; Hugh of Flavigny, ii, pp. 462–3; Bonizo of Sutri, ix, pp. 614–15; Donizo, *Vita Matildis*, ii. 217–58, *MGH SS* xii. 384; Landulf Senior, *Historia Mediolanensis*, iii. 33, *MGH SS* viii. 100; Guy of Ferrara, i. 20, pp. 548–50.

[213] *Chron. Cas.* iii. 53, pp. 434–5; see below, Appendix III.

further Roman hostility the Normans ravaged and burnt much of the city. According to Geoffrey Malaterra they thereafter returned victorious to the Lateran. Bernold recorded that, with Gregory in their company, they set about the recovery of papal lands outside the city,[214] to which Gregory returned for St. Peter's Day (29 June).[215] Robert Guiscard was nevertheless unable to dislodge the antipope Clement III from Tivoli, to where, as in 1082, he had retired.[216] When, in July, the duke withdrew to the south, Gregory feared the citizens' wrath after the Norman ravaging of Rome, and accompanied him on his journey.

Clement, too, did not for long remain near Rome, where he could not count on Henry's effective support now that he had secured his desire of imperial coronation. He was at the Lateran early in November, and he is said to have celebrated Christmas in St. Peter's. But soon after Gregory's death on 25 May 1085 the still considerable Gregorian party at Rome forced him to withdraw to Ravenna, which he is not known again to have left until the spring of 1087.[217] Not until 1094 would either a pope or the antipope be able for any considerable period of time to establish himself in the city.

It is virtually certain that Gregory did, indeed, pass through Montecassino; for he travelled to Salerno by way of Benevento and it was on his route.[218] Historians have been misleading when they have represented Gregory's progress to Salerno with Robert Guiscard as a shameful journey to near-captivity, and his final months as a period of weakness and bitterness. Although allowance must be made for partisan prejudice, that was not the view of contemporaries, nor is it what the evidence suggests.

[214] There is confirmation in a letter of Matilda of Tuscany to Henry's German opponents; 'Sciatis domnum papam iam recuperasse Sutrium atque Nepe. Barrabas latro, id est Heinrici papa, iste quoque aufugit': Hugh of Flavigny, loc. cit.

[215] Perhaps this was when, according to Bernold, in the presence of Bishops Odo of Ostia and Peter of Albano (John II of Porto, who had seceded, clearly being an error), Gregory passed canonical sentence upon Guibert's consecrators.

[216] Bonizo of Sutri and Guy of Ferrara, as above.

[217] Clement's diploma of 4 Nov. 1084 for San Marcello *in via lata* was issued from the Lateran: *Monumenta ordinis Servorum sanctae Mariae*, edd. A. Morini and P. Soulier, ii (Brussels, 1898), 191, cited in *IP* i. 76, no. 16. For his presence in Rome at Christmas, see the unconfirmed evidence of *Annalista Saxo, a.* 1085, *MGH SS* vi. 721. Bernold noted his departure from Rome; for his return in 1087, see *Chron. Cas.* iii. 68, p. 450.

[218] *Annales Beneventani, a.* 1084, *MGH SS* iii. 182; Gaufredus Malaterra, iii. 37, p. 80; *Chron. Cas.* iii. 58, p. 438.

William of Apulia said that Robert Guiscard conducted Gregory to Salerno *magno honore*, while for Bernold he remained 'in defensione iusticiae usque ad mortem firmissimus'.[219] Robert Guiscard had the strongest motive for making Gregory's journey free, solemn, and dignified: he looked forward to the consecration of the new cathedral of St. Matthew at Salerno, which Gregory performed in July 1084, soon after his arrival.[220] A cowed or a humiliated pope would have added nothing to the dignity of such an occasion. Moreover, the ceremony was marked by a gesture of reconciliation between Robert Guiscard and Jordan of Capua, whose concord Archbishop Alfanus celebrated in a distich set up in the cathedral.[221] At Salerno Gregory could take encouragement from the renewed concord of his Norman vassals as well as from the devotion of Robert Guiscard himself.

On the other hand, the duke did not long delay before reverting to his overriding concern—his campaign across the Adriatic Sea against Byzantium. He was a septuagenarian with no time to lose. Moreover, since he had returned to Italy the Normans had suffered ill fortune in Thessaly, a Greek and Venetian fleet had taken Durazzo, and in October 1083 Castoria had also been lost. So in the autumn of 1084 he left Italy for the last time.[222] It was some compensation for Gregory that in July 1084 Countess Matilda of Tuscany won a notable victory over Henry IV's Italian allies at Sorbaria near Mantua.[223] Guy of Ferrara's allegation that Gregory sought to promote another military campaign at Rome is doubtful,[224] but it shows that his enemies thought of him as being still an active force. Certainly he himself had a considerable entourage, and he exercised papal authority with vigour. His chancery produced impressive privileges.[225] In 1084 at Salerno he held a council during which he anathematized

[219] Bernold, loc. cit.; William of Apulia, iv. 557, p. 234; cf. Hugh of Flavigny, ii, pp. 465–6, 470–1.

[220] William of Apulia, v. 122–4, p. 242; cf. the Norman view expressed in v. 255–67, p. 250.

[221] 'Dux et Iordanus dignus princeps Capuanus / Regnent aeternum cum gente colente Salernum': Lentini and Avagliano, *Carmi*, no. 53; cf. William of Apulia, p. 243 n. 2.

[222] William of Apulia, v. 121–53, pp. 242–4.

[223] Bernold, *a.* 1084, p. 441; Bardo, caps. 23–4, pp. 20–1.

[224] As Ch. III n. 212.

[225] Esp. the privileges for Santa Sophia, Benevento (11 Dec. 1084), and San Salvatore, Fucecchio (dioc. Lucca; 9 May 1085): Santifaller, *QF* i. 261–7, nos. 217–18.

Henry, Clement, and their supporters.[226] He never wrote a nobler or more moving letter than the last encyclical, which his legates carried far and wide—Odo of Ostia on an extensive mission in Germany, Peter of Albano and Gisulf of Salerno to France, and Abbot Jarento of Dijon to Portugal; and he followed it up by other letters explaining his case.[227] It has been convincingly argued that Gregory's alleged last words, 'Dilexi iustitiam et odivi iniquitatem, propterea morior in exilio', were not an expression of failure and embitterment; they were a confident, even a triumphant, affirmation that he shared the blessedness that Christ promised in the Beatitudes to those who suffer for righteousness' sake (*propter iustitiam*).[228]

By its record that Abbot Desiderius sustained Gregory throughout these final events, the Montecassino Chronicle points to their sympathetic association during Gregory's last months.[229] Desiderius was certainly with him in his final illness. According to the Montecassino Chronicle he was present on 23 May 1085 when Gregory made his declaration about who should succeed him.[230] Gregory's biographer Paul of Bernried corroborates that he was then at Salerno, saying that he came there in the pope's sickness in order that he might be with him to the end; although he added the not otherwise attested story that on the day of Gregory's death Desiderius was absent from Salerno, as Gregory had prophesied.[231]

[226] Bernold, loc. cit. This is the probable occasion of Gregory's passing against the defector Cardinal Atto the public excommunication to which Desiderius subscribed according to Hugh of Lyons: Hugh of Flavigny, ii, p. 467.

[227] *Epp. vag.*, pp. 128–35, no. 54. For its circulation, see Bernold, loc. cit., and Hugh of Flavigny, ii, p. 441. *Reg.* ix. 29, pp. 612–13, may be a letter of summons to this council, and *Epp. vag.*, pp. 135–7, no. 55, a sequel.

[228] P. E. Hübinger, *Die letzten Worte Papst Gregors VII.* (Opladen, 1973); see also Pope Urban II's assessment in his *Ep.* 240, Migne, *PL* cli. 507.

[229] iii. 53, p. 435. Cassinese respect for Gregory's fortitude is further apparent in the anecdote which follows, from another source, of a dove settling on his shoulder as he said mass, with its message 'ut constanter vigore sancti Spiritus ceptum opus peragat': *Chron. Cas.* iii. 54, pp. 435–6.

[230] iii. 65, p. 447.

[231] cap. 109, Watterich, i. 539. Since the printed text is poor it is worth citing the relevant sentences from Admont, Stiftsbibliothek, MS 24, twelfth cent., f. 142^r: 'Predixerat eidem Desiderio scilicet Victori pater sanctus quod non interfuturus esset migrationi ipsius, quamvis ob hoc infirmantem invisisset ut cum eo usque in finem perseveraret, et sanctas exequias cum ceteris fidelibus celebraret, multumque eum attonitum tristemque eum reddiderat. Cumque heret in admiratione quidnam impedimenti futurum esset, subito nuntiatur ei a Nortmannis facta circumvallacio cuiusdam castelli suo monasterio subiecti; et compulsus necessitate succurrendi suis, abeundi licentiam accepit. Sicque licet invitus explendi prophetię locum dedit.'

If the attempt be made to draw a conclusion from the small amount of evidence that emerges in the margin of the wider struggle between Gregory and Henry about the standpoint of Desiderius and Montecassino, it would appear that from 1080 the association between Desiderius and Gregory was closer than at any other time in Gregory's pontificate. Desiderius had always been concerned to maintain the security and prosperity of his own abbey and its lands. To this end he had consistently sought the friendship and the unity of the Norman rulers of South Italy—both the princes of Capua and the duke of Apulia and Calabria. The princes of Capua were important as Montecassino's close neighbours; although, particularly after the succession in 1078 of the volatile and unreliable Jordan, the political skill and greater wealth of Robert Guiscard made him the leader whom Desiderius was the more concerned to cultivate. For many years Robert Guiscard was at loggerheads with Gregory, who three times excommunicated him and sought to keep him and the princes of Capua divided. At no time did Desiderius place his loyalty to Gregory above his friendship with Robert Guiscard. Yet as a cardinal-priest of the Roman church he never lost touch with Gregory, and he at all times looked for a *rapprochement* between Gregory and the Normans, and for the harmony of the Normans with each other. In the late 1070s a common bond between Gregory and Robert Guiscard began to develop, particularly over Byzantine affairs. In 1080 Desiderius was able to assist in bringing about at Ceprano a renewal of the papal treaty of 1059 with the Norman leaders.

The year 1080 also witnessed the final breach between Gregory VII and Henry IV. Henry's repeated expeditions to Italy in the ensuing years and the beginning—though not until 1084 the making definitive—of the Guibertine Schism, as well as Robert Guiscard's military campaign against the Byzantine Empire and the drawing together of Germany and Byzantium against the Normans and the papacy, created a complex and shifting political situation. In it the struggle between Gregory and Henry was pursued in diplomatic and propagandist, no less than in military, terms. The prospect and then the reality of schism compelled Desiderius to take a clear and firmly Gregorian line, in some respects of an extreme character, on the issue of *sacerdotium* and *regnum*. Montecassino's long-standing commitment to reform on its own terms now merged with papal interests, and Desiderius' own standing as a cardinal-priest led him to give his support more and more to Gregory, so that Henry's propagandists, such as the Hersfeld anonymous, saw in him an opponent of Henry's interests at Rome. When the schism was made definitive and Gregory was brought by Robert Guiscard to Salerno, Montecassino placed its resources behind him as never before. The restoration of friendship between Robert Guiscard and Jordan of Capua, at least for the moment, also fulfilled Desiderius' aspirations for Norman unity. By 1085 Montecassino and its abbot were established as pillars of the Gregorian cause. In the next chapter it will be argued that they continued to be so as the Guibertine Schism proceeded, and especially until, with Pope Urban II, another major pontificate supervened.

IV

Abbot Desiderius as Pope Victor III

GREGORY VII's successor as pope was Abbot Desiderius of Montecassino.[1] The long process of his election as Pope Victor III is one of the most obscure subjects in the history of the medieval papacy. A first step towards understanding it is an appreciation of the situation after Gregory's death at Salerno on 25 May 1085. At that time, both at Rome and in the church at large the Guibertine and Gregorian parties were more evenly balanced than has always been recognized. The antipope Clement III retained a considerable following in the city, and revulsion from the Gregorian party after the Norman ravaging in 1084 no doubt remained strong.[2] Yet Clement's periods of residence at Rome were few and insecure. He returned there for the spring and early summer of 1087, and again in 1089 and 1091; but that was all until he died in 1100.[3] Soon after Gregory's death he withdrew to Ravenna; according to Bernold he was constrained to do so by the hostility of his opponents in the city.[4] He laboured under the disadvantage that after 1084, as before it, he attracted much greater condemnation than Henry IV, on the grounds that he was a schismatic and an invader of the apostolic see.[5] Henry himself returned to Germany in the summer of 1084 and stayed there until 1090: having secured imperial coronation he had got what he wanted at Rome, and Clement's supporters were unable to secure his position in the

[1] The fullest discussion of Desiderius as pope remains Hirsch, 'Desiderius', pp. 91–103. The relevant annals of Meyer von Knonau, *Jahrbücher*, iv, are indispensable. For the Normans, see Chalandon, *Domination*, ii. 285–94. A. Fliche gives a useful but too unfavourable picture in the studies listed above, Introd. n. 43; there is a survey in Becker, *Urban II.*, i. 78–80.

[2] The main evidence for Clement's following at Rome comes from charters. See Kehr (as Ch. II n. 21), pp. 973–4, 980–3; Hüls, *Kardinäle*, pp. 262–4.

[3] For 1087: Bernold, *a.* 1087, p. 446; *Chron. Cas.* iii. 68, p. 450. For 1089: *Codex Udalrici*, no. 73, Jaffé, *Bibl.* v. 145–52; Bernold, *a.* 1089, p. 450; *Monumenta ordinis Servorum sanctae Mariae* (as Ch. III n. 217), ii. 196, no. 2, *IP* i. 76, no. 17. For 1091: Bernold, *aa.* 1091–2, pp. 451, 453.

[4] Bernold, *a.* 1085, p. 444.

[5] See above, pp. 152–3, and below, Appendix VIII.

city without more military backing than Henry was now likely to provide. In such circumstances the defection to Guibert in 1084 of so many Roman clergy, and especially cardinal-priests, was by no means an unqualified strength to his cause. Some were employed at large as legates, and the attendance list at Clement's council in Ravenna during Lent 1086 is a reminder that others were in attendance upon him there and so were also taken away from Rome.[6] Henry's preoccupation with Germany and Clement's absence at Ravenna with an entourage of Roman clergy left a debilitating gap of leadership and authority amongst those in Rome who were most likely to resist the Gregorian party of the city.

On the other hand, it would be wrong to underestimate the number and strength of those in and around Rome who remained actually or potentially loyal to Gregory's cause and memory. Of the cardinal-bishops only John II of Porto had defected to Guibert. The strategically critical Castel Sant'Angelo remained in Gregorian hands throughout the years 1084 to 1088.[7] The region round the church of Santa Maria Nova, which included the Cassinese dependency of Santa Maria in Pallara, was certainly under Gregorian control early in 1085, and Montecassino's property at Tusculum ensured loyalty there as well.[8] The urban prefect Cencius, whose family the Frangipani had property round the Colosseum, remained active at Rome; he was in touch with Montecassino, from which Desiderius sent him a reliquary.[9] The history of Desiderius' election as pope was to show how many of the Roman cardinals and clergy who were loyal to Gregory remained at Rome with considerable lay support, and how effectively they kept in touch with their confrères who

[6] In 1085 three such leading figures as Hugh Candidus, cardinal-priest of San Clemente, John II, cardinal-bishop of Porto, and Peter, cardinal-priest of San Grisogono (Gregory's sometime chancellor), served as legates in Germany: *GP* ii/1, p. 33, no. *16; Hüls, *Kardinäle*, pp. 119, 159, 171. For the Ravenna synod, see *Ep.* 3, Migne, *PL* cxlviii. 830–1; the Roman cardinals named were Anastasius, cardinal-priest of Santa Anastasia, and Robert, cardinal-priest of San Marco: Hüls, *Kardinäle*, pp. 145–6, 185–6.

[7] Bernold, *a.* 1084, p. 441; Henrician Manifesto, below, Appendix VI.

[8] P. Fedele, 'Tabularium S. Mariae Novae ab. an. 982 ad an. 1200', *Arch. stor. Rom.* xxiii (1900), 250–1, no. 27, a charter concerning a house 'qui est subtus Pallaria', dated 15 Feb. 1085 and drawn up with the consent of the clergy of Santa Maria Nova. For Tusculum, R. Ambrosi de Magistris, *Storia de Anagni*, ii (Anagni, 1900), 61, no. 3, cited by Hüls, *Kardinäle*, p. 257.

[9] *Chron. Cas.* iii. 66, 68, pp. 449, 450; Bloch (as Introd. n. 34), pp. 212–18; Hüls, *Kardinäle*, pp. 266–7.

had gone with Gregory to Salerno, and thence to Montecassino.[10]

The state of Rome after the Norman devastation is vividly conveyed by the verses that Geoffrey Malaterra wrote in his Chronicle, with its picture of both sides demoralized and doubtful, and popular loyalties fickle and wavering.[11] Rome provided neither party with a firm base of power, yet it offered opportunities for intervention to anyone with a secure foothold outside the city. Here, the Gregorians had a clear advantage. For Ravenna was a long way away and lines of communication with it were threatened by Matilda of Tuscany's forces. The road from Montecassino was shorter and easier; communication by sea was also possible. Montecassino itself was rich and powerful, and support from the Normans, though less reliable, could in some measure be anticipated. The Gregorians had on balance a somewhat better chance of securing their ends at Rome than had the Guibertines.

In the church at large, too, both sides had strengths and weaknesses. Clement was energetic in propagating his cause throughout Europe.[12] He was perhaps not without success in South Italy, where the ambiguous neutrality of at least some of the inhabitants of Bari may be indicated by its annalist, who referred to Clement as pope.[13] In 1090 Clement wrote to the Metropolitan Basil of Reggio in the confidence that Henry IV would soon descend upon Italy; his letter is also a reminder of the threat that Byzantine intervention still presented to the Gregorian cause.[14] Death took its toll of the Gregorian party. The loss on 18 March 1086 of Bishop Anselm II of Lucca deprived it of a dedicated leader in North Italy. In the south, Archbishop Alfanus I of Salerno, Abbot Desiderius' lifelong friend, died on 8 October 1085.[15] Not long before, death had overtaken Robert Guiscard. He had captured Corfu, but on 17 July an epidemic that had ravaged his army claimed his life on the Ionian island of Cephalonia. He had intended his

[10] See below, pp. 185–6, 194.

[11] iii. 38, pp. 80–1.

[12] Kehr (as Ch. II n. 21), pp. 356–8.

[13] Lupus Protospatarius, *aa.* 1087, 1089, p. 62; but see below, Appendix IX.

[14] Pitra, *Anal. noviss.* i. 479–80; Holtzmann, *Beiträge*, pp. 98–9, no. 1. Elsewhere in South Italy the dating of charters by Alexius Comnenus' regnal years was not uncommon, e.g. la Cava, Archivio capitolare, MS C.3, of June 1086, and many as yet unpublished items there.

[15] Bernold, *a.* 1086, p. 444; A. Lentini, 'Alfano', *DBI* ii. 255.

inheritance to pass to Roger Borsa, his twenty-five-year-old son by his second wife Sichelgaita of Salerno; but Roger had to face the rivalry of Bohemond, his elder half-brother, who was Robert Guiscard's son by Alberada of Buonalbergo. Sichelgaita and Roger hastened to Italy and managed to contain the threat that Bohemond represented to them. But three Apulian diplomas of March 1086 show that Sichelgaita, to whom they referred as *Sikelgaita dux* before naming Roger, for some months exercised a *de facto* regency on her son's behalf. So, during the critical winter and spring that followed Gregory's death, there was political uncertainty in Apulia, which was mitigated rather than ended in May 1086 when, after an accommodation with Bohemond, Sichelgaita seems to have allowed Roger Borsa to be duke in his own right. From the papacy's point of view, the uncertainty that sprang from these events was compounded because Roger Borsa's claim to the duchy was supported by his uncle Count Roger I of Sicily, who had never shown a concern for papal interests and was unlikely to encourage Roger Borsa to do so.[16] All this uncertainty in Apulia was made worse by renewed division between the two Norman principalities of the mainland. For in 1085 Bohemond had fled to Jordan of Capua and sought his support against Roger Borsa.[17] Jordan, moreover, was left as the stronger of the mainland princes, and from the papacy's point of view his record was chequered.

Nevertheless there were some compensations. A consequence of these developments was that the Gregorian party outside Rome no longer had its headquarters at Salerno, a city of Norman leaders who gave priority to their own concerns in Byzantium and South Italy, but at Montecassino. Montecassino was powerful, and it was near to Capua, whose prince had every reason to fear the further intervention in Italy of a Henry IV

[16] For Sichelgaita, Roger, and Bohemond, see William of Apulia, iv. 185–9, 193–7, v. 223–8, 292–4, 343–9, 361–3, pp. 214–15, 248–9, 256–7; Gaufredus Malaterra, iii. 41–2, iv. 4, pp. 82, 87; Orderic Vitalis, vii. 7, viii. 7, ed. Chibnall, iv. 30–3, 168–9; Ménager, *Recueil*, pp. 169–80, nos. 46–51; for Count Roger of Sicily's policies and attitudes, see Gaufredus Malaterra, iii. 42, iv. 1–4, pp. 82–7; cf. H. E. J. Cowdrey, 'The Mahdia Campaign of 1087', *EHR* xcii (1977), 1–29, at 9. The background is analysed by R. B. Yewdale, *Bohemond I, Prince of Antioch* (Princeton, NJ, 1917), 25–7; and esp. Ménager, *Recueil*, pp. 164–8. Montecassino never had dependencies in Norman Sicily: L. T. White, *Latin Monasticism in Norman Sicily* (Cambridge, Mass., 1938), 57, 72.

[17] William of Apulia, v. 331–409, pp. 254–8; Gaufredus Malaterra, iii. 41–2, iv. 4, pp. 82, 87.

whose obedience he had lately accepted but then renounced. Above all, Desiderius' position as senior among the Roman cardinal-priests gave him a major responsibility in papal affairs. In Tuscany, too, Countess Matilda was gaining strength, and her successes raised the flagging morale of the Gregorians. In 1085 Bernold noted her zeal and resilience under pressure; in his eyes 1086 was for her something of an *annus mirabilis* of progress and victory.[18]

In the months after Gregory's death Italy, like Rome itself, thus presented a picture of instability and uncertainty. Nevertheless, the withdrawal to Ravenna of Clement III and the lack of clear Guibertine leadership in Rome, Henry IV's absence in Germany and the unlikelihood of his return, the continuing presence in Rome of an organized Gregorian party, the waxing fortunes of Countess Matilda of Tuscany, the availability at Montecassino of a secure and accessible base for those Gregorians who had left Rome in 1084, and the ease of communication between Montecassino and Rome, were all factors that gave hope to those who did not waver towards the antipope's cause.

i. POPE GREGORY VII'S FINAL TESTAMENT

An investigation of the problems that the succession to Gregory presented must also take account of the final testament which he left for the guidance of his followers. Two sources preserve it. The first is the group of Hildesheim letters in the Hanover letter collection.[19] The second is a small piece of parchment inserted into the autograph manuscript of Hugh of Flavigny's Chronicle.[20] It is itself in Hugh's hand and preserves only the beginning of the testament as recorded in the Hanover letter collection; it is introduced by the words 'Dixit Urbanus papa in quadam epistola sua'.[21] In the material common to both sources Gregory made two dispositions for the future:

(*a*) Asked by the Roman bishops and cardinals who were at

[18] *aa*. 1085–7, pp. 442–7.

[19] *Briefsammlungen der Zeit Heinrichs IV., MGH Briefe*, v. 75–6, no. 35. The collection survives in a sixteenth-century copy.

[20] The sheet is inserted between folios 130 and 131 of the MS—Berlin, Deutsche Staatsbibliothek, Phillipps 1870; it bears the folio number 130*b*: see *MGH SS* viii. 466.

[21] No corresponding letter of Urban is known, but his Register is lost. In letters of 1089 to German bishops he followed, with some mitigation, Gregory's severer rules about excommunicates: *Epp*. 15–16, Migne, *PL* cli. 297–9.

Salerno whom he wished to succeed him, he replied that they should elect whomever they could procure of the three prelates Bishop Anselm II of Lucca, Bishop Odo of Ostia, and Archbishop Hugh of Lyons; he gave their names in that order.

(*b*) He was similarly asked for his advice about those under sentence of excommunication. He excepted Henry *dictus rex*, Archbishop Guibert of Ravenna, and their leading helpers and counsellors, to whom he left open the way of return by due and canonical satisfaction at the bishops' and cardinals' discretion; otherwise he absolved and blessed all who acknowledged his spiritual power as vicar of St. Peter so to do.

In the Hanover letter collection only, two further items follow:

(*c*) Besides charging the bishops and cardinals about many things not specified, Gregory urged them to have no one as pope who was not canonically elected (*ut neminem habeatis Romanum pontificem nisi canonice electum et sanctorum patrum auctoritate ordinatum*).

(*d*) The memorandum ends with a simple record of Gregory's actual or alleged last words: 'Dilexi iustitiam et odivi iniquitatem, propterea morior in exilio.'[22]

It is not clear in what circumstances the record of the final testament was compiled. It seems to be a summary of deathbed dicta uttered over several days, written down soon afterwards at Salerno by someone in Gregory's entourage, perhaps one of his chaplains.[23]

So far as the first disposition is concerned, the report fairly soon became current that Gregory had named Abbot Desiderius of Montecassino to be his successor, whether instead of or in addition to the three bishops. The latter view finds expression in the Montecassino Chronicle, where the account of Desiderius' election as pope opens with the story that, on the third day before he died, Gregory answered the bishops' and cardinals' inquiry in Desiderius' presence; he recommended them if possible to elect Desiderius, but if impossible to choose one of the

[22] See above, p. 174.

[23] The words *eos* and *illis* in the third disposition seem to exclude the *episcopi et cardinales*. Gregory's chaplains are said to have transmitted Gregory's last words by Bardo, cap. 38, p. 24. It should be remembered that contemporary deathbed testaments and admonitions were solemn and protracted: see e.g., the records of Pope Leo IX's death: Watterich, i. 170–1; and of Abbot Hugh of Cluny's: Cowdrey (as Ch. III n. 195), pp. 101, 104–6, 172–5.

bishops.[24] Upon examination, however, the chapter of the Chronicle which deals with Desiderius' election appears to be a disordered conflation of some eight constituent Sections which are of different date and purport.[25] Section i, which records Gregory's designation of Desiderius, reads like a late redactional introduction which attempts to harmonize the mutually contradictory Sections that follow. The earliest Sections to be written know nothing of such a designation. That dealing with events immediately following Gregory's death (ii) is particularly hard to reconcile with it. It tells how Desiderius himself sought to expedite an election. He urged that letters should be sent to Countess Matilda of Tuscany summoning to Rome Gregory's three episcopal nominees, together with others whom she might deem suitable. There is no hint that Desiderius was himself a candidate, and it would be hard to explain his alacrity in promoting an election if he were—especially so unwillingly as in 1086 he proved to be. A further Section in the Chronicle (iii), which summarized the events of 1086, proceeded upon the assumption that a group of clergy and laity then for the first time canvassed his candidature. Only in a late stage of the growth of stories about the succession to Gregory VII (Section iv) did a reference appear to a *iudicium* by Gregory in which he designated Desiderius. The conclusion seems to be irresistible that only in 1086, and so perhaps after the death of Bishop Anselm II of Lucca, did a claim to this effect come into the picture at Montecassino, or anywhere start to circulate. Apart from the Montecassino Chronicle it is attested in Guy of Ferrara's *De scismate Hildebrandi*, written in that year.[26] Guy,

[24] *Chron. Cas.* iii. 65, p. 447.

[25] For a synopsis and discussion, see below, Appendix VII. Roman figures which follow refer to Sections as there defined.

[26] '. . . cum iam in ultimis ageret, abbate Montis Cassinensis ad apostolatus successionem impulso, diem clausit extremum': i. 20, p. 549. Apart from the order of names in his final testament, further evidence that Gregory may have intended Anselm II of Lucca to succeed him is provided by Bardo's story that he sent him his mitre as a deathbed gift, 'tanquam potestatem suam ligandi et solvendi sed et miracula, credo, faciendi': cap. 32, pp. 22–3. The story is repeated by Paul of Bernried, for whom the mitre was 'pontificalis insigne potestatis': cap. 111, Watterich, i. 540. (Such gifts, interpreted, however, as tokens of friendship, are not unexampled; e.g. Lanfranc, *Ep.* 3. ii, lines 51–5: *The Letters of Lanfranc Archbishop of Canterbury*, edd. and trans. H. Clover and M. Gibson (Oxford, 1979), 42.) Paul of Bernried, who wrote *c.*1137, said that Gregory's nominees were Desiderius, Odo of Ostia, and Hugh of Lyons; he omitted Anselm of Lucca, whose early death had evidently caused his name to be forgotten. He also knew the remaining clauses of Gregory's final testament: caps. 109–10, pp. 539–40. Writing in England about a decade earlier, William

however, gave other, unreliable information about Gregory's stay at Salerno.[27] He also showed no knowledge of Gregory's having named anyone save Desiderius. This suggests that the story of Desiderius' designation grew up apart from the Salerno tradition of Gregory's final testament, perhaps at Rome in circles of which Guy had knowledge. Such circles appear to have been little involved in electoral preparations before 1086, but may thereafter have sought to justify their sponsorship of Desiderius by propagating a story that Gregory had designated him.

Like the record of Gregory's last words, the opening disposition of Gregory's final testament has excited much debate among historians. It is remarkable that the second and third dispositions should have largely escaped consideration, for they are both of the utmost importance in understanding events after his death. The second, *de excommunicatis*, shows that whoever drafted the final testament was concerned to record a mildness on Gregory's part that harked back to his relative restraint and to his emphasis upon possible reconciliation during his dealings with Henry IV in 1082 and 1083. Gregory had not since then been so accommodating. He had scarcely been restrained from repeating his excommunication of Henry during the November council of 1083. According to Bernold's record of his legislation of 1084 at Salerno he had renewed a stern sentence of excommunication upon Guibert, Henry, and all their party. Bernold also related how in April 1085, no doubt acting upon instructions from Gregory at Salerno, Bishop Odo of Ostia legislated at Quedlinburg not only against schismatic bishops but also against all those ordained by them. He was stringent about the return of even the unjustly excommunicated to the communion of the church.[28] It is true that by papal authority Odo also gave Bishop Gebhard of Constance power to reconcile penitents, and his dealings with the wavering Bishop Udo of Hildesheim demonstrate his preparedness to apply the oil of mercy rather than the wine of severity.[29] But there is nothing in the measures of 1084

of Malmesbury gave only Desiderius and Odo of Ostia as Gregory's nominees: *Gesta regum*, iii. 266, ed. Stubbs, ii. 325; William was probably influenced by the course of subsequent events.

[27] See above, p. 173.

[28] Bernold, *aa.* 1084–5, pp. 441–3.

[29] Ibid., *a.* 1084, p. 441; *Die Hannoversche Briefsammlung*, no. 7, *MGH Briefe*, v. 25–7.

to anticipate the mildness of Gregory's final testament, according to which he pronounced absolution and blessing upon lesser men who acknowledged his spiritual power, while he also opened a path of reconciliation even to Henry, Guibert, and their principal supporters. No doubt Gregory had been mindful of the dying Christ, who forgave his adversaries, when in his final testament he harked back to talk of reconciliation.[30]

The third of Gregory's dispositions that were selected for citation was that no one should be received as pope save by way of canonical election and according to the *sanctorum patrum auctoritas*. The compiler who singled it out may have been aware that the proper form of a papal election would be a critical and vexed issue when finding a successor to Gregory. Nevertheless, he gave no hint whatever about what in Gregory's view the proper form should be.

Such were the most important of the guidelines that Gregory seems to have left behind when he died in the early summer of 1085 for those of his followers who were with him at Salerno.

ii. ABBOT DESIDERIUS AND THE PAPAL ELECTION: 1085

If the analysis of the constituent Sections of the Montecassino Chronicle's account of the election which is offered below in Appendix VII is on the right lines,[31] after Gregory's death initial steps to provide a successor were taken with alacrity.[32] It has already been argued that, at this stage, there was no question of Desiderius' candidature. Instead, Desiderius took a strong lead in promoting the election of some other person. In this connection, at Pentecost (8 June), and so only a fortnight after Gregory's death, he somewhere—perhaps at or near Montecassino—met two of Gregory's supporters who were travelling

[30] Hübinger (as Ch. III n. 229), pp. 58–62, 68–74.

[31] The principal source for Desiderius' election is *Chron. Cas.*: see below, Appendix VII. Further evidence comes from Archbishop Hugh of Lyons's two letters of 1087 to Countess Matilda of Tuscany. The earlier appears in Hugh of Flavigny, ii, pp. 466–8; the final sentence suggests that it was written at Salerno or la Cava in Apr. or May. The second is in d'Achery, *Spicil.* iii. 426–7, and dates from Oct.–Dec., by which time Hugh had returned home. For its date, see R. Lehmann, 'Über den die Excommunikation des Erzbischofs Hugo von Lyon durch Papst Victor III. betreffenden Brief des Ersteren an die Grafin Matilde', *Forschungen zur deutschen Geschichte*, viii (1868), 641–8. The two letters also appear in Migne, *PL* clvii. 511–16, nos. 8–9.

[32] Section ii.

from Rome: Bishop Hubald of Sabina and a certain Gratian.[33] Their advent from Rome is a reminder that many of Gregory's party were still to be found there, and an indication that they maintained contact with their brethren at Salerno by way of Montecassino. Desiderius told them of the discussion that he had had with Gregory about the papal succession (*de ecclesie ordinatione*). At the same time Prince Jordan of Capua and his uncle Count Rainulf of Caiazzo arrived, and Desiderius found them ready to serve the Roman church as required (*ad servitium et adiutorium Romane ecclesie . . . libentissime ad omnia paratos*).[34] Desiderius urged the cardinals (*cepit deinde cardinalibus vehementer insistere*) with all speed (*quantocius*) to deliberate about how to fill the papacy. They should write to Countess Matilda of Tuscany, asking her to invite Gregory's three episcopal nominees to come to Rome without delay (*sine tarditate*), together with such other persons as she deemed fit for the papal office.[35] In all this Desiderius acted as the executor of Gregory's dying wishes, not as a beneficiary of them. He evidently considered it feasible to hold a well-attended election at Rome, and the note of urgency in his actions is apparent.

Nothing more is known of events in 1085 regarding the succession to Gregory in South Italy or at Rome. But throughout the following winter Countess Matilda and Bishop Anselm of Lucca were at the centre of diplomatic activity. In his earlier letter to the countess, Archbishop Hugh of Lyons said that he had received letters from the Roman church and from Anselm; a letter survives from Anselm to Abbot Pontius of Fraxinetum summoning Hugh to Italy and to the rescue of the Roman church (*matrem suam visitare et liberare de manu mortis*).[36] Hugh also reported that he had received letters and verbal messages from the countess herself. But on 18 March 1086 Anselm died at

[33] Hubald is attested as cardinal-bishop of Sabina from 1063 to 1094: Klewitz, *Reformpapsttum*, p. 118; Hüls, *Kardinäle*, pp. 125–6. Gratian may be the person referred to in the *Iudicium de regno et sacerdotio*: below, Appendix V.

[34] i.e. as required by Jordan's oath of 1080, '. . . secundum quod monitus fuero a melioribus cardinalibus, clericis Romanis et laicis, adiuvabo ut papa eligatur et ordinetur ad honorem sancti Petri': Deusdedit, *Coll. can.* iii. 288–9, pp. 395–6.

[35] Desiderius may have held open the list of candidates because of Gregory's verbal instructions as he knew them, or from an awareness (i) that, in some men's opinion, a dying pope might canonically recommend but not impose a successor: see below, p. 190; (ii) that some at Rome held that Roman priests and deacons had a prior claim: see below, pp. 189–90; and (iii) that Countess Matilda's rising fortunes made it expedient to let her add names.

[36] Hugh of Flavigny, ii, pp. 443–4.

Mantua. The Gregorian cause lost one of its most resolute upholders, and the person who was best qualified to succeed Gregory in the papal office, if a heroic figure were looked for.

iii. ABBOT DESIDERIUS AND THE PAPAL ELECTION: 1086

The next critical date that is known is Pentecost (24 May) 1086, when Desiderius was unwillingly elected at Rome to the papal office.[37] Shortly beforehand, Prince Gisulf of Salerno had returned from France and joined the Gregorian churchmen who were with Desiderius.[38] It is not known when his fellow legate Bishop Odo of Ostia returned from Germany, although the silence of the sources about him renders it unlikely that he was at the Pentecost election. There had, indeed, been no trace of him since 24 August 1085, when, having journeyed from Cluny to Nantua, a Cluniac priory in the diocese of Lyons, he presided there at the translation of the relics of St. Maximus; he used the occasion to preach in eulogy of Gregory VII.[39] He is likely to have left Cluny long before Archbishop Hugh of Lyons was scandalized by the recitation there on 3 April 1086 of the Good Friday prayers for the emperor, for which he reproved Abbot Hugh. Indeed, the archbishop's wrath may have been excited as much by the abbot's customary disregard of his own metropolitan claims as by any inherent impropriety in the Cluniac observance. For there is no evidence that Gregory had ever suspended the Good Friday prayers for the emperor or that their discontinuance was seen by anyone except the extremist Archbishop Hugh as a corollary of Henry's excommunication and deposition in 1076 or 1080. On the other hand, Hugh of Lyons certainly used the incident after his return in 1087 unsuccessfully to assert his jurisdiction over Cluny, and his language implies that he may already have done so in 1086; at very least, he then tried unsuccessfully to assert his moral authority over it.[40] But

[37] *Chron. Cas.*, Section iii; Hugh of Lyons's first letter.

[38] *Chron. Cas.*, Section iii.

[39] *Historia translationis reliquiarum s. Maximi apud Nantuacum*, Migne, *PL* cli. 265–8, written while Urban was pope.

[40] Hugh's second letter to Countess Matilda, in which his purpose as regards the Cluniacs was to report to her their *supergressiones et iniurias* against himself. For his claim to jurisdiction, see Cowdrey (as Introd. n. 9), pp. 52–6. So far as the events of 1086 are concerned, it is not clear whether the archbishop's stand against the abbot

the episode no doubt added to his suspicion of the Cluniac Odo of Ostia, who had recently been at Cluny, and helped to put him in a querulous frame of mind when a Cluniac figure was involved.

At Rome itself, apart from the problems arising from the insecurity of the Gregorian party there and the division of its forces between the city and Montecassino, three factors may be identified which ensured that the electoral process in 1086 would be very difficult. The first is the prevailing conflict of views about what was canonically acceptable in a papal election and so in fulfilling the third disposition of Gregory's final testament. The acuteness of this debate and the intensity of the feelings that it aroused are clear from the preface of Deusdedit's *Collectio canonum.*[41] In the body of his collection he illustrates how far current opinion at Rome was from accepting in its original form the Election Decree of 1059, which had in any case not been followed in the two intervening papal elections of 1061 and 1073.[42] He did not cite the Decree itself but only Pope Nicholas II's canons about papal elections from the Lateran councils of 1059 and 1060, which themselves gave a much-edited form of the Decree. Deusdedit assigned no place whatsoever to the cardinal-bishops or to the temporal power. His

was a juridical as well as a moral one. When saying that the prayer for the emperor was suspended (*interposita est*), Archbishop Hugh may refer to a provincial edict of his own, or he may indicate the moral corollary as he saw matters of Henry's deposition. Hugh's phrase about holding the abbot to account (*eumdem ad rationem posui*[*ss*]*emus*) may imply that he asserted jurisdiction. An indication that he did so is his complaint that the abbot refused to do penance when he was allegedly reduced to silence about the matter (*neque tamen debita poenitentia errorem cognitum emendavit*). Furthermore, the archbishop's statement that upon his tumultuous return to Cluny in 1087 the abbot held out Pope Victor III's letter notifying Cluny of his (the archbishop's) excommunication at Benevento 'ut sub praetentione litterarum nostras iniurias retineret', may suggest that in the archbishop's eyes there had been a wrongful refusal of jurisdiction by Abbot Hugh in 1086. In the sequel the archbishop certainly asserted his jurisdiction but with little result: 'Adhibito ergo nobis confratrum et coepiscoporum nostrorum consilio, et per eorum manum inter nos et abbatem colloquio constituo, cum intelligeret nos aliter cum illo concordiam non habituros, nisi culpa cognita praefatam orationem interponeret, iudicium nobiscum subire praetensis multis occasionibus recusavit, episcoporum tamen qui aderant studiis discordia nostra aliquantulum modificata est, et per inducias usque ad praefinitum terminum mitigata.'

[41] Cited above, Ch. III n. 173. For the confused state of contemporary ideas about episcopal and papal elections, see R. L. Benson, *The Bishop-elect. A Study in Medieval Ecclesiastical Office* (Princeton, NJ, 1968), 23–45; and for liturgical arrangements, E. Eichmann, *Weihe und Krönung des Papstes im Mittelalter* (Munich, 1951), 33–5.

[42] Krause, PWD, pp. 149–69.

guiding principle was that an election should be in the hands of the Roman *cardinales* in the restricted sense of the priests and deacons of the Roman church, whom the remaining *clerici religiosi* were to support. In this way a papal election should be exclusively the work of the Roman church; for a pope forced upon an unwilling church was not an *apostolicus* but an *apostaticus.*[43]

Deusdedit's choice of canonical material, so far as it bears upon the election of 1086–7, emphasized the following points. Like every bishop, the Roman pontiff should be elected by the clergy, desired and acknowledged by the people, and consecrated by the provinical bishops—thus fulfilling the requirement that *docendus non sequendus populus.*[44] The place of a papal election should normally be Rome, where the pope should be consecrated and enthroned in St. Peter's, conducted to the Lateran *patriarchium*, and there honoured. But in case of necessity an election might take place elsewhere than in Rome. In either event no outsider to the Roman clergy might interfere.[45] Lay princes and magnates were particularly excluded. They might be invited obediently to help in putting into effect an otherwise regular election. But there was no place for the emperor in the electoral process, and the intervention of the *princeps* nullified an election; although, according to the *Pactum Hludowici Pii* of 817, after his consecration a pope should send a legate to the Frankish king in order to establish a bond of friendship and love.[46] No less objectionable than royal interventions were disorderly elections over which the *turba* of lay citizens had control.[47] As regards the eligibility of candidates,

[43] *Coll. can.* i. 168–9 (137–8), p. 107; cf. *MGH Const.* i. 547, 551, nos. 384, cap. 1, and 386, cap. 4. Similar material occurs in contemporary collections: Anselm of Lucca, *Collectio canonum*, vi. 12–13, ed. F. Thaner (Innsbruck, 1906), 272–3; Bonizo of Sutri, *Liber de vita christiana*, iv. 87, ed. E. Perels (Berlin, 1930), 156, cf. *Liber ad amicum*, vi, pp. 593–4. Their main authority is the decree of Pope Stephen III (769): *MGH Conc.* ii. 85–6, no. 14. Anselm of Lucca's acceptance of this view may have made him reluctant to succeed Gregory in 1085–6.

[44] Deusdedit, *Coll. can.* i. 120 (97), 244 (116), pp. 86, 141–2.

[45] Ibid. i. 169 (138), 256–7 (207–8), 320 (244), ii. 113 (96), pp. 107, 146–7, 187, 240–1. For the last of these, see Eichmann (as Ch. IV n. 41), pp. 9–11. In it, by omitting the words *nam episcopus esse non poterit* from the list of those eligible, Deusdedit tacitly accommodated the custom whereby a number of eleventh-century popes who were already bishops retained their previous sees: see Goez (as Ch. II n. 41).

[46] Deusdedit, *Coll. can.* ii. 100 (83), cf. p. 14, lines 1–2, iii. 280, iv. 13 (11), 18 (16), pp. 228, 385–9, 406, 409–10.

[47] Ibid. iv. 20 (18), p. 410.

the first and if possible the definitive choice of the canonical electors should be the best of the cardinal-priests or -deacons of the Roman church itself. Only in urgent necessity might a clerk of another church be elected, and even so no one might be forced upon an unwilling church.[48] No bishop might even on his deathbed infringe the freedom of the electors by appointing or designating his own successor; although Deusdedit allowed that a dying pope might recommend names (*Ut imminente suo transitu idem pontifex* [*Romanus*] *de suo successore decernat*).[49]

For those holding such views the difficulties in 1086–7 spring readily to the eye. Gregory's final testament, of which Desiderius of Montecassino as senior cardinal-priest seems to have seen himself to be the executor, was a document that they could only with much qualification approve or implement. It was not in itself objectionable that Gregory should have recommended names of three possible successors. But it was difficult that the names were not those of Roman priests and deacons, who in their view should first be considered, but of bishops: for although Odo of Ostia—the second whom Gregory named—was a cardinal-bishop, Deusdedit gave cardinal-bishops no prior claim; while Anselm of Lucca and Hugh of Lyons ruled churches far away from Rome. Gregory's recommendations could, therefore, be entertained only after it was agreed that there was no eligible Roman priest or deacon. And there was another problem. Canon law as expounded by Deusdedit was impatient of what seems to have been Archbishop Hugh of Lyons's view of papal elections. As the problem of jurisdiction over Cluny illustrates, he was ever the champion of the rights of metropolitans and of the episcopate. According to one eleventh-century view, as an order in the universal church the episcopate should play its part in papal elections. Hugh gave it expression in his first letter to Countess Matilda.[50] It may be doubted whether Hugh

[48] Deusdedit, *Coll. can.* iv. 20 (18), p. 13, lines 29–30, p. 15, lines 6–7, i. 111–12 (92–3), 118 (96), 233 (186), ii. 161 (131), pp. 84, 86, 135–6, 268.

[49] Ibid., p. 14, lines 30–3, i. 49 (39), 131 (107), 135 (110), pp. 58, 90–1, 92. Cf. William of Malmesbury's view (as Ch. I n. 168).

[50] The claims of the episcopate were advanced in the *De ordinando pontifice, MGH Libelli*, i. 11; they survived into the twelfth century: Cowdrey (as Ch. III n. 195), p. 220. To Desiderius' election in 1086, for which he arrived too late, Archbishop Hugh of Lyons said that he and others at first 'assensum praebuimus' but later learned 'quam intolerabiliter Deum in ipsius electione offenderimus'; the first person plural implies a claim to participate in an election which was explicit in 1087: 'Ego et abbas Massiliensis atque archiepiscopus Aquensis apud Salernum commorantes, ab

was well informed about the Roman view, or whether Roman canonists like Deusdedit were familiar with Hugh's. But they were manifestly incompatible, and a meeting between those who held them would be fertile ground for misunderstanding and recrimination.

A second factor ensuring difficulties in 1086–7 was the problem of the excommunicate Guibertine leaders and rank-and-file, in view of Gregory's apparent change of front from a hard line at his Salerno council of 1084 to the milder dispositions of his final testament. In this as in other matters both Desiderius and Odo of Ostia appear to have set out to honour the final testament. As regards Desiderius, this appears to be the background of Archbishop Hugh of Lyons's first letter to Countess Matilda. In it Hugh represented Desiderius as advocating what seemed to his own hard-line mind an unthinkable mildness towards Henry and his party. On coming to Montecassino after Pentecost 1086 he had been shocked to hear Desiderius say that he had in his latter years pledged himself to help Henry gain the imperial crown. He had proceeded to claim credit for counselling the king to enter papal lands and pass through them to Rome, to boast about his own need of absolution for associating with Henry, and to speak of the blessedness of Cardinal Atto of Milan, who had died impenitent after defecting from Gregory in 1084.[51] Perhaps the most plausible explanation of Hugh's tirade is that it garbles debates in which Desiderius justified Gregory's prolonged preparedness in the 1080s to countenance negotiations with Henry, and in which, following the second disposition of Gregory's final testament, Desiderius also justified the notion of pardoning and blessing such lesser Guibertines as Atto. Archbishop Hugh's habitual violence of reaction and his ignorance of the situation at Rome in the 1080s would go far to explain his incomprehension of what he heard, especially if, as is likely, he had hitherto heard nothing of Gregory's final testament. As for Odo of Ostia's position as regards the final testament, Hugh of Flavigny's version of it, which was

episcopo Ostiensi et principe Salernitano et Cenciano Romano ex parte vicarii et Romanae aecclesiae invitati, ut communi consilio Romanum pontificem eligeremus, veniendo obedivimus': first letter to Countess Matilda.

[51] In 1072 Atto had been the Patarene candidate for the see of Milan, but he had not secured acceptance and withdrew to Rome. He became cardinal-priest of San Marco and compiled a canon-law collection: Hüls, *Kardinäle*, p. 185.

incorporated in one of Odo's letters, shows that he accepted it.[52] As pope he claimed to be Gregory's disciple in spirit and in deed,[53] and his own conciliatoriness towards Guibertines indicates the continuing influence of the testament upon his policy.[54]

Such mildness in Gregory's executors may not have been to the liking of other Gregorians and their allies besides Hugh of Lyons, for Gregory's deathbed dispositions had their echoes at Rome and in South Italy. A Henrician Manifesto suggests that Henry's partisans there were swift to represent its moderation as evidence of weakness.[55] To counter such propaganda many Romans may have favoured an intransigent stance. This view may have been shared by some at least of the Normans; for Jordan of Capua, in particular, had reason to dread Henry's vengeance after his return to the Gregorian camp. Thus, in 1086 many were concerned to see the struggle against Henry and the Guibertines continue, and to have a pope who would not readily mitigate or cease from it. It is understandable that their eyes should turn towards Desiderius as being if not the ideal, nevertheless the best available, choice. Montecassino itself had a tradition of hostility to royal pretensions, apparent in such literature as Amatus' *Liber in honore beati Petri apostoli*. The depiction of Desiderius in one of the sources of the Montecassino Chronicle as their resolute opponent, while Odo of Ostia was dangerously compromising,[56] may reflect the ideas of the mid-1080s as well as those of the turn of the century. Unlike Odo, too, Desiderius commanded vast material resources; as a neighbour, Prince Jordan of Capua could influence him more

[52] See above, pp. 181–2.

[53] 'De me porro ita in omnibus confidite, et credite sicut de beatissimo patre nostro papa Gregorio; cuius ex toto sequi vestigia cupiens, omnia quae respuit respuo, quae damnavit damno, quae dilexit prorsus amplector, quae vero rata et catholica duxerit confirmo et approbo, et ad postremum in utramque partem qualiter ipse sensit in omnibus omnino sentio atque consentio': *Ep.* 1, 13 Mar. 1088, Migne, *PL* cli. 283–4. The final words seem to refer to Urban's two-clause version of Gregory's final testament as in Hugh of Flavigny; it may have circulated with this letter. If so, Gregory's third disposition may have been omitted as no longer relevant after Urban's election. Such a profession as Urban's may have become standard: see Paschal II's *Gesta dampnationis privilegii* (1112), *MGH Const.* i. 571, no. 399.

[54] For examples, see H. E. J. Cowdrey, 'The Papacy, the Patarenes and the Church of Milan', *TRHS*, 5th ser., xviii (1968), 25–48, esp. 45–8; 'The Succession of the Archbishops of Milan in the Time of Pope Urban II', *EHR* lxxxiii (1968), 285–94; (as Ch. IV n. 16), *EHR* xcii (1977), 1–29, esp. 19–20.

[55] See below, Appendix VI.

[56] See above, p. 159.

readily than he could influence Odo of Ostia. So Desiderius tended to unite the interests of those Romans who, like Deusdedit, looked first of all for the election of a cardinal-priest or -deacon, with those in South Italy who feared a too ready reconciliation of the schismatics. But ultra-Gregorians like Hugh of Lyons were hostile to both candidates—to Odo as a temporizer and to Desiderius as the executor of Gregory's final testament; and they felt so strongly about the matter that any means would serve in order to frustrate the election of either of them.

A third factor in the situation in 1086–7 conveniently gave Hugh of Lyons troubled waters in which to fish. It was the behaviour of the Apulian Normans, Duke Roger and his mother Sichelgaita. They cannot in any case have found it easy to accept the enhanced standing of Prince Jordan of Capua, who was now the Norman leader to whom Gregory VII's partisans primarily looked, or to forgive his support of Bohemond. Hugh of Lyons's first letter to Countess Matilda shows how uneasy was their relationship with him even in 1087.[57] Nor can they have relished the place in Gregorian counsels of their kinsman and enemy Prince Gisulf of Salerno. Hostility developed in 1086 about the succession to the see of Salerno. After the death of Archbishop Alfanus I, Roger and his mother favoured another Alfanus, *custos* of the church of San Massimo, Salerno.[58] Apart from the tendentious calumnies of Archbishop Hugh of Lyons in his first letter to Countess Matilda, Alfanus appears to have been a suitable candidate who afterwards ruled his church satisfactorily and won the good opinion of Pope Urban II.[59] But Prince Gisulf of Salerno bitterly opposed his candidature. Roger and Sichelgaita were affronted when the Roman bishops and cardinals deferred to Gisulf by refusing to sanction his consecration. They vented their wrath by releasing and dispatching to Rome the imperial prefect Wezilo, whom Robert Guiscard had captured in 1084, and who now proceeded to fight bitterly there for the Guibertine cause until he perished in battle three

[57] Thus, in it Duke Roger came to the council of Capua 'quibusdam circumventionibus a Iordano principe iuveniliter illectus', and Archbishop Hugh was clearly taken aback by the agreement of the prince and the duke on Palm Sunday to encourage Desiderius to accept the papal office. Hugh also seems to have tried to dissuade Roger from going to Capua.

[58] For Alfanus II, see Ughelli–Coleti, viii. 391–2.

[59] Hugh wrote of his *manifestissima ambitio*. For Urban II's good opinion, see Pflugk-Harttung, *Acta*, ii. 49–50, 164–5, nos. 184, 198; *Epp.* 240, 300, Migne, *PL* cli. 507–8, 547–8.

years later.[60] The Apulian leaders were calling into question their own commitment to the Gregorian papacy, as well as the continuance in its service of the always fragile unity of Apulia and Capua. As often in Gregory's lifetime, so in the crisis of 1086–7 the papacy could not count upon united and effective Norman help.

These three factors must be kept in mind when considering the steps taken in 1086 to fill the papal throne. For the reconstruction of the events of the spring, when it was pressed upon Desiderius, who then absolutely declined to accept election, the relevant chapters of the Montecassino Chronicle appear to offer not a single narrative, but three distinct and parallel accounts (ii, iv, v).[61] Because of these and other repetitions, it is important that the historian should guard against exaggerating Desiderius' doubts and hesitations merely because the story is repeated several times. It is also important to establish the true sequence of events.

The longest and most complete of the three accounts which are initially involved when studying the events of 1086—iii—provides a framework of dates and episodes. It places the initiative for a papal election firmly at Rome rather than at Montecassino, in a convention there of bishops and cardinals drawn from various localities but including few if any from Gregorian circles at Montecassino and elsewhere in South Italy. It assembled at about Easter (5 April) and invited Desiderius, together with the Roman bishops and cardinals who were with him at Montecassino, to hasten to Rome where they would join them and Prince Gisulf of Salerno, who had just returned from across the Alps, in electing a new pope. This account expressly denies that anyone at all had as yet named Desiderius as *papabile* (*cum iam nulla de eo mentio ab aliquo fierat*). Instead,

[60] *Chron. Cas.* iii. 67, Section v. For the prefect Wezilo, see P. F. Kehr, 'Due documenti pontifici illustranti la storia di Roma negli ultimi anni del secolo xi', *Arch. stor. Rom.* xxiii (1900), 277–80. The identification with Wezilo is to be preferred to that with the *Petrus urbis praefectus* of the Guibertine party referred to in a charter of 5 Feb. 1088, written at Rome in the monastery of San Basilio: *Il regesto di Farfa di Gregorio di Catino*, edd. J. Giorgi and U. Balzani, v (Rome, 1892), 116, no. 1115; cf. L. Halphen, *Études sur l'administration de Rome au moyen âge*, Bibliothèque de l'École des hautes études, 166 (Paris, 1907), 151, and H. Hoffmann, in *MGH SS* xxxiv. 449 n. 2. The Chronicle's designation *prefectus imperatoris* is more appropriate for Wezilo; the military context points to him; and it is hard to see why Peter should have been with Duke Roger, whereas Wezilo was his father's captive.

[61] In this and the following paragraphs Roman figures refer to Sections as described below, Appendix VII.

when he arrived at Rome on Pentecost Eve (23 May) it was he who took the initiative in seeking the election of another, suitable person. However, in the evening the whole Gregorian party assembled in the church of Santa Lucia near the Septizonium, at the foot of the Palatine, and unanimously called for Desiderius to become pope. He steadfastly refused and the assembly broke up. On the morning of Pentecost itself he remained adamant. So the *presbiteri et cardinales episcopi* declared themselves willing to elect whomever Desiderius should name. Having consulted Cencius, the Roman city prefect, Desiderius named Gregory VII's second choice in his final testament—Bishop Odo of Ostia. He further agreed to maintain the pope-elect at Montecassino until times should improve. But then an unnamed cardinal (*quidam de cardinalibus*) suddenly and persistently vetoed Odo's election as being contrary to the canons. So, at last, Desiderius was borne tumultuously to the church of Santa Lucia and there elected, being given the name Victor. Since this happened against his will he assumed only the red mantle while refusing the white.[62]

This Section is of value in dating the Easter and Pentecost assemblies at Rome. Its presentation of Desiderius' candidature for the papacy as being canvassed for the first time in 1086 reinforces the Chronicle's evidence in Section ii for the events of 1085. By not mentioning Prince Jordan of Capua or other Normans it is in harmony with three other Sections (v, vi, vii), all of which represent Jordan as becoming concerned with the election only later in 1086, when it was intended to bring Desiderius back to Rome; it is improbable that he was in Rome at Easter or Pentecost.[63] There is every likelihood that Section iii is correct in indicating that the clergy and laity of the Gregorian party at Rome itself were at the centre of events at this stage; indeed, there is independent evidence of the concurrence of the Roman nobility.[64] The story of Desiderius' collaboration with

[62] For papal vesture, see Eichmann (as Ch. IV n. 41), pp. 33–5; Benson (as Ch. IV n. 41), pp. 152–3.

[63] So Chalandon, *Domination*, i. 292. There is no evidence for Jordan's whereabouts between Easter and Pentecost 1086. He had been in Capua in Nov., Dec., and Jan.: Montecassino, Archivio capitolare, caps. XII, no. 31, caps. XIII, no. 11, see G. A. Loud, 'Five Unpublished Charters of the Norman Princes of Capua', *Benedictina*, xxvii (1980), 161–76, at 172–3; la Cava, Archivio capitolare, MS B.36. See Loud, 'Calendar', pp. 125–6, nos. 32–3, 35.

[64] Lupus Protospatarius commented that Desiderius became pope 'consensu quorundam nobilium Romanorum': *a.* 1087, p. 62.

the prefect Cencius finds confirmation in the discovery of an inscribed reliquary containing relics of St. Matthew which Desiderius sent him, and which was placed in the main altar of the church of SS Cosma e Damiano in the Forum Romanum near the Frangipani fortress on the Via Sacra.[65]

Desiderius' counter-proposal that Bishop Odo of Ostia should be elected in his stead is also inherently probable. In 1085 Desiderius had already shown himself anxious to implement Gregory's final testament. With Bishop Anselm of Lucca no longer alive Odo was almost inevitably the next choice from Gregory's list: Archbishop Hugh of Lyons had not yet arrived at Rome; he had been for too long away from the city and its affairs; and he was too headstrong and ill-advised in his actions to be preferred to the prudent and proven Odo, cardinal-bishop of Ostia since 1080. The veto of Odo by *quidam de cardinalibus* is harder to evaluate. Against the plausibility of a veto it can be argued that in 1088 there was no decisive objection to him and that there is unlikely to have been one so recently as in 1086. But such an argument ignores how objectionable Odo's nomination in 1086 was if the law of Deusdedit's *Collectio canonum* were invoked.[66] According to it Roman cardinal-priests and -deacons must be considered before anyone else might come into the picture; given the personal character and the material resources of Desiderius, then the senior cardinal-priest, many at Rome may have seen him as the proper choice. But in 1088 there may have seemed to be at hand no such priority candidate. Many priests and deacons had seceded to the antipope, and it is hard to discern a similarly suitable figure amongst those who remained. Even from Deusdedit's standpoint it may, therefore, have seemed admissible to proceed in default to Odo of Ostia's election.

It may be regarded as morally certain that, at Pentecost 1086, Desiderius' candidature was for the first time proposed; that it was put forward by the Gregorians at Rome; that he made a counter-proposal of Bishop Odo of Ostia which was

[65] The relics may have been some of those given to Desiderius by Sichelgaita after Robert Guiscard's death. A later inscription indicates that Desiderius himself brought them from Salerno to Montecassino. He may have done so before the issue of the see of Salerno became acute: *Chron. Cas.* iii. 58, pp. 439–40; Bloch (as Introd. n. 34), pp. 212–17.

[66] It is tempting to suggest that the unnamed cardinal was Deusdedit, but there is no positive evidence for his identity.

vetoed on canonical grounds; and that he was himself tumultuously elected with the title Victor III. Nor is the fact of Desiderius' own refusal to accept his election open to serious doubt.[67]

Section iii is most open to question in what it says about the manner and consequences of Desiderius' refusal of the papacy at Pentecost in the church of Santa Lucia. The impression of abruptness and negativity seems to be the result of the author's deliberate attempt to lead up to his version of the events of 1087 (viii) by minimizing the tumultuousness of the events, which was itself canonically objectionable, by suppressing the contemporary political manœuvres of the Apulian Normans, and by insisting that Victor was elected *iuxta morem ecclesie*. From another Section—iv—whose author seems to have known iii and to have deliberately modified its picture of events, a more active Desiderius begins by contrast to emerge. Section iv rested his candidature upon Gregory's advice but also said that although Desiderius adamantly refused the papacy he nevertheless promised the Roman church his continuing aid by all other means at his command. In a further, perhaps somewhat earlier, account of events, Section v suggests a clear reason for Desiderius' refusal of the papacy at Pentecost 1086. It was the release and treacherous dispatch to Rome by Roger of Apulia and his mother Sichelgaita of the imperial prefect Wezilo; they acted in retaliation for the Roman refusal to consecrate Archbishop Alfanus II of Salerno.[68] By a date which is not precisely given, Wezilo succeeded by bribery in assembling a hostile force in the Capitol and in so harassing Desiderius that after four days—presumably counting from his election, and so on 27 May—he was forced to leave Rome for Ardea and after a further three days to go on to Terracina. It was there that, according to this Section, he divested himself of the papal insignia and, refusing any longer to wear them, returned to Montecassino. This account makes it clear that in the spring of 1086 Desiderius' unwillingness to accept the papal office was not arbitrary or the

[67] Cf. *Ann. Cas., a.* 1086, pp. 1422–3.

[68] There is nothing to suggest that Sichelgaita and Roger were at Rome. Charters help to establish their activities in the first half of 1086, and especially their presence in May at Salerno: Jan./Apr., Ménager, *Recueil*, pp. 173–5, no. 48 (Salerno); Mar., ibid., pp. 169–72, nos. 46–7 (no indication of place); May, ibid., pp. 175–80, nos. 49–51 (no. 51 was drawn up at Salerno, to which it refers as *hanc . . . Salernitanam civitatem*).

consequence of weakness, but that it had much to do with the hostile intrigues of the Apulian Normans.

Having returned to Montecassino, he seems to have led a life that was the reverse of uneventful or supine. No fewer than three of the constituent Sections of the Montecassino Chronicle as it now stands tell of attempts to take him back to Rome and enthrone him. The attempts occurred before the full summer heat. According to the early Section (v) that recorded the episode of the imperial prefect, the Roman cardinals and bishops now prevailed upon Prince Jordan of Capua to bring a large army to establish Desiderius at Rome; but Desiderius dissuaded him from proceeding. Another Section (vii) has it that Desiderius actually set out and reached the Roman Campagna. But he returned to Montecassino when he suspected that the expedition was a plot to make him pope under duress, instead of an uncommitted attempt to settle the question of the papacy by the united power of Prince Jordan, Count Rainulf of Caiazzo, and the Roman bishops. This indicates that Desiderius was demanding at least the degree of unity and collaboration amongst his Roman and Norman allies that had been apparent when he took energetic action in 1085 (ii). A further Section (vi) also records that Desiderius set out with Jordan, and that he returned rather than allowing himself to be made pope under constraint. But after his return to Montecassino he undertook a widespread and not unsuccessful recruiting campaign amongst Normans, Lombards, and others, to provide for the service of the Roman church. As regards Sections vi and vii, it is important further to bear in mind that in August Duke Roger and his entourage were absent in Palermo, where Count Roger I had been the duke's supporter since Robert Guiscard's death in 1085.[69] While Duke Roger was annoyed about the problem of the see of Salerno and especially while he was absent in Sicily Desiderius could not hope to work for the concerted support of the Capuan and Apulian Normans that he always desired. He was unlikely to feel that he had the military and diplomatic strength to proceed to firm steps regarding Rome and the papacy, especially with the imperial prefect Wezilo active in the city. But this by no means rules out the possibility that he was busy in other directions.

Distorted and tendentious though Archbishop Hugh of

[69] Ménager, *Recueil*, pp. 181–6, nos. 52–4.

Lyons's first letter to Countess Matilda may be, it bears out the picture of considerable activity on Desiderius' part. It may have been Desiderius himself who persuaded Hugh, subsequent to his arrival at Rome soon after Pentecost 1086 and his initial assent to Desiderius' election,[70] to remain in Italy against his original intention (*contra officii mei propositum*). It was certainly Desiderius who arranged for him to travel south and to join him at Montecassino, where, as he wrote, *ipsius ducatu pervenimus*. Hugh testifies to colloquies that Desiderius was holding there with the Roman bishops and cardinals, as it would seem in an attempt to justify Gregory's diplomacy of the 1080s and the mild provisions of his final testament. Hugh shows that Desiderius remained in touch by letter with Countess Matilda of Tuscany, using as his messengers certain of the cardinals.[71] While maintaining his refusal to acknowledge his own election to the papacy on the grounds of its tumultuous character, according to Hugh he was active in promoting a new election and in proposing fresh names that included Bishop Hermann of Metz.[72] If it is true that, as Hugh states, Desiderius renewed Hugh's commission as a standing papal legate, he also gave some attention to the wider government of the church.[73] When Hugh turned to describe Desiderius' convening of the council of Capua in 1087 it was with ample justification that he wrote as if the past year had been one of great, if in his eyes of wholly profitless, activity on Desiderius' part.[74]

The picture which emerges from all the evidence is of a Desiderius who was adamant in his refusal to become pope under any kind of compulsion; although in the Montecassino Chronicle as it stands his refusal gains exaggerated prominence by reason

[70] This remark tends to confirm Section iv's testimony that Desiderius rejected his election only after leaving Rome, rather than (as in Section iii) while still there.

[71] Hugh mentions two cardinals, using the initials *He.* and *B. He.* may be Bishop Hermann of Brescia, cardinal-priest of Santi Quattuor Coronati, and *B.*, Bonussenior, cardinal-priest of Santa Maria in Trastevere and later bishop of Reggio (Emilia): see Ganzer, *Kardinalat*, pp. 41 n. 6, 49; Hüls, *Kardinäle*, pp. 188–9, 202.

[72] Hermann of Metz was an exile from his see and in good standing with leading Gregorians, especially Countess Matilda: *Liber de unitate ecclesiae conservanda*, ii. 19, 30, 36, *MGH Libelli*, ii. 236, 256–7, 263–4; Meyer von Knonau, *Jahrbücher*, iv. 36–41.

[73] As also in the unreliable record of Victor III's council at Benevento: *Chron. Cas.* iii. 72, p. 454.

[74] 'Nunc vero, cum iam tandem post tantum laborem inaniter insumptum respirare videbamur, et ęlectionem totiens refutatam, et aecclesiae redditam . . . in proximo libere facere sperabamus. . . .'

of its reiteration in no fewer than five constituent Sections (iii-vii). But short of assuming the papal office Desiderius did much to serve the interests of the Roman church as he saw them. It must be remembered that the eleventh century was not so accustomed as the twelfth to popes who, because of difficulties at Rome, exercised the papal office from a distance. Since Roman and Norman loyalties were alike uncertain and divided, and since Guibertine hostility made the pope dependent upon external support, Desiderius may well have acted in the best interests of the Gregorian party by remaining aloof at Montecassino and building up its unity and strength from there, until Rome could be made subject to its effective authority.

Of other relevant events in 1086 the surviving evidence makes it impossible to say more. It is not clear whether Desiderius and his circle took part in any preparations of that year for the triumphs of 1087, which were to be so fortunate for the Gregorian papacy—the bringing of St. Nicholas' relics from Myra to Bari, and the expedition of Pisan and Genoese forces, with Roman and Amalfitan help, to sack the city of Mahdia in North Africa. There is no certainty that the translation of St. Nicholas was premeditated by an anti-Guibertine city faction; in all probability it was not.[75] But Countess Matilda, with whom Desiderius was in touch, is morally certain to have been aware of the planning of the Mahdia campaign, which may already have encouraged the Gregorians.[76] On the other hand, the divisions in their ranks and in those of their supposed allies also deepened. Archbishop Hugh of Lyons left Montecassino to take up residence at Salerno with Duke Roger of Apulia; he was accompanied by the like-minded Abbot Richard of Saint-Victor, Marseilles, and Archbishop Peter of Aix-en-Provence.[77] Hugh and his faction thus allied themselves with a Norman leader who was currently opposed to Desiderius and to the Roman bishops and cardinals who refused consecration to Archbishop Alfanus II of Salerno and who, more compromisingly, had sent the

[75] See below, Appendix IX.

[76] Cowdrey (as Ch. IV n. 16), *EHR* cxii (1977), 17-18.

[77] For Richard, himself cardinal-priest of an unknown title in the Roman church, see Ganzer, *Kardinalat*, pp. 32-6; Hüls, *Kardinäle*, pp. 217-18. Archbishop Peter of Aix (1082-1101) was a sometime monk of Saint-Victor, Marseilles: M.-H. Laurent, 'Chanoines et réforme à Aix-en-Provence au XIe siècle', *SG* iv (1952), 171-90, at 181-2. In Oct. 1086 the names of Hugh and Richard appear as witnesses to a spurious charter of Duke Roger of Apulia for la Cava: Ménager, *Recueil*, pp. 191-7, no. 56.

imperial prefect Wezilo back to Rome, where he was a thorn in their side. In view of these divisions, the year 1086 is likely to have ended with Desiderius and his associates still in a state of uncertainty about how best to proceed.

iv. ABBOT DESIDERIUS AND THE PAPAL ELECTION: 1087

The sources—mainly the Montecassino Chronicle (viii) and Archbishop Hugh of Lyons's two letters to Countess Matilda of Tuscany—indicate that in the course of Lent 1087 the question of the papacy sprang to life again somewhat suddenly, and this time at Capua. It may be presumed that the antipope Clement III's return to Rome combined with the military activity of the imperial prefect Wezilo to make it inadvisable for the Gregorians to plan an assembly there, as they would no doubt have preferred. But whereas the Roman proceedings of a year earlier had not been attended by the Normans, in 1087, when the scene shifted to his capital city, Prince Jordan was present; to Hugh of Lyons's displeasure he induced Duke Roger of Apulia also to attend with a large Apulian following. So, from the outset at least, a façade of Norman unity and collaboration was restored; it dismayed Hugh of Lyons, but Desiderius could hope to make it a reality and to put it to good use.

Certain features of the assembly at Capua are common ground to both the principal sources. They agree about Desiderius' leading role, which for Archbishop Hugh took the form of convening it but for the Montecassino Chronicle of presiding over it. They agree, too, about the prominence of the Gregorians from Rome—bishops and cardinals, and also lay figures like the urban prefect Cencius and Prince Gisulf of Salerno. According to both narrations the Normans of Apulia as well as of Capua were present. But the differences between the two sources are much more striking than the similarities, and it is necessary to establish what kernel of truth there may be in each of them.

The account in the Chronicle is summary, and clear in its own terms. It dates the council of Capua firmly to mid-Lent, and therefore to *c.* 7 March.[78] Desiderius presided in the capacity

[78] *mediante quadragesima*; cf. *mediante Maio* for the middle of May: iii. 23, p. 390. In a Section where dates are generally reliable this should be accepted: below, Appendix III.

of pope-elect, and—contrary to probability as well as to the testimony of Archbishop Hugh's two letters[79]—there was no discussion of the election in any shape or form.[80] It was only after the council ended, and then unexpectedly and without foreknowledge on Desiderius' part (*post finem concilii rursus insperate et nichil eo de his suspicante*), that the clergy and laity raised the issue most pressingly, whereupon his reaction was to remain for two days undecided. Only at length—the word *tandem* is repeated as though for emphasis—did concerted pressure from the prince of Capua and the duke of Apulia, supported by the other Gregorian clergy and laity, lead Desiderius on Palm Sunday (21 March) to confirm his election of 1086 by resuming the papal insignia (*preteritam electionem crucis et purpure resumptione firmavit*). Following on from Section iii, the picture is one of Desiderius accepting on Palm Sunday 1087 a canonically sufficient election that had already taken place in Rome at Pentecost 1086. This election had remained effective, although he himself had in the meanwhile refused to act upon it.

Archbishop Hugh of Lyons wrote to Countess Matilda at greater length, and in very different terms, about what he called the setting in order (*recuperatio*) of Desiderius' election. Far from constituting the decisive and definitive election which at Capua Desiderius as pope-elect was now brought to accept, the proceedings of Pentecost 1086 had in his eyes been rendered null and void. At the time they had indeed constituted an election. But viewed retrospectively from a year later three factors had subsequently nullified them. First, it had emerged—at

[79] Of the first as cited above, Ch. IV n. 50. In the second Hugh wrote, 'Et nos quidem licet de recuperatione electionis domni abbatis Montis Cassini a quibusdam sanctae ecclesiae Romanae episcopis et cardinalibus presbiteris dissenserimus, unde aliquibus illorum cur nobis aliter videretur, etiam apud Capuam palam rationes reddidimus'; the word *palam* probably but not certainly indicates publicity during the council.

[80] The only business other than the papal election of which there is record is the statement that, apparently at the council, Archdeacon Sichenolf subscribed a charter relating to a nunnery at Isernia: Ughelli–Coleti, vi. 325. Chalandon drew attention to a charter of Duke Roger, dated May 1087, for Abbot William of Sant'Angelo, Mileto, which was witnessed amongst others by Archbishop Alcerius of Palermo and Bishops Walter of Malvito, Constantinus of Venosa, Paschasius of Bisignano, and Rubbertus of Fiorentino, and also Abbots Berengarius of Venosa, William of Mileto, and Flandrinus of Troia: *Domination*, i. 294, citing Rome, Archivio del Pontificio collegio greco, MS A. X; now printed in Ménager, *Recueil*, pp. 212–15, no. 60. No place of issue is given. The date is a little late to warrant Chalandon's suggestion that the prelates concerned 'avaient sans doute assisté au concile'; but their number illustrates Roger's current involvement in church affairs.

least for Hugh and those who thought like him—that the choice of Desiderius was hateful to God (*quam intolerabiliter Deum in ipsius electione offenderimus*), because of the *nefandissimi actus* on Henry IV's behalf which had brought about his year-long excommunication. Secondly, by in effect intensifying an interpretation of Desiderius' conduct in the latter part of 1086 which Section iii in the Montecassino Chronicle played down but to which Sections iv, v, and vi gave colour, Hugh insisted that Desiderius had himself repeatedly and decisively disowned his election and had sought to secure the candidature of other men. Thirdly, according to Archbishop Hugh, Desiderius had himself objected to the tumultuousness of the proceedings at Pentecost 1086, which was a canonical obstacle to their validity.[81] So the election that Desiderius had so often rejected had been put back into the church's hands (*electionem totiens refutatam, et aecclesiae redditam*). The council of Capua had, therefore, assembled not to activate a former election but to carry out a fresh one. This was the purpose for which Desiderius summoned it, and he did so not as pope-elect but as ex-officio papal vicar in South Italy.[82] If Archbishop Hugh thus differed from the Montecassino Chronicle about the purpose of events at Capua, he also did so about their duration. In the Chronicle, discussions regarding the election were relatively long-drawn-out, extending over some ten or twelve days from just after the council of Capua until Palm Sunday. Hugh, who gave no date for the council, so foreshortened events that its proceedings seem to be compressed into Palm Sunday and its eve.

It is hard to assess the truth of these matters, although it is doubtful whether either account is intrinsically to be preferred: the account in the Chronicle is likely to have been written a decade and more after the events and to reflect a Cassinese view of what was fitting to have occurred; while Archbishop Hugh's account did not impress Countess Matilda and was coloured by

[81] '. . . in quot et quibus locis electionem suam non secundum Deum, sed tumultuarie factam asseverans, publice refutaverit, et numquam se adquievisse, vel in perpetuum adquieturum, sub terribili attestatione affirmaverit; quasve personas electionem reddendo aecclesiae idoneas eligi in Romanum pontificem dixerit . . . vobis magna ex parte manifesta sunt.' For tumultuous election, see above, p. 189.

[82] Neither the terms of the grant of a papal vicariate to Desiderius nor Cassinese traditions about the ex-officio rights of an abbot extend to any power so far outside the monastic order as the convening of a council of major and general importance: *Chron. Cas.* iii. 12, iv. 49, pp. 374, 516; cf. Pope Zacharias' bull of 18 Feb. 748 as falsified by Peter the Deacon: *IP* viii. 121–2, no. 22.

his own constitutional ideas about papal elections. However, other sources, not entirely connected with Montecassino, shared the basic conviction of the Chronicle that Desiderius was elected pope in 1086 and that at Capua in 1087 this election was activated; that this was the official papal view as publicized in Victor III's own letters in the summer of 1087 to the church at large is clear from Archbishop Hugh's second letter to Countess Matilda.[83] In view of the precise dates given in the Chronicle, Hugh's foreshortening of the time-scale must be suspect. On the other hand his testimony that the papal election was discussed during rather than after the council of Capua seems likely to be true.

The sources agree that Desiderius accepted the election as pope on Palm Sunday. The Chronicle says so only summarily, and it is from Archbishop Hugh's first letter that an attempt must be made to see how matters are likely then to have developed. As at Rome in 1086, there was a confrontation between differing views on the conduct of papal elections, which was now exacerbated by Hugh's presence and by his purpose to be, not pope, but a pope-maker. On one side of the constitutional difference were most of the Roman bishops and cardinals, many at least of whom acted upon a view that resembled Deusdedit's. They engaged Prince Jordan of Capua's support.[84] In their eyes Desiderius had been canonically elected pope at Pentecost 1086; the problem was that of giving effect to an already settled election by bringing the pope-elect to the point of accepting consecration. On the other side Archbishop Hugh was concerned to promote a fresh election, not to confirm an existing one. He believed that metropolitans had rights in papal elections like those of suffragans in archiepiscopal elections, and he meant to exercise them. Thus, he claimed that Bishop Odo of Ostia, Prince Gisulf of Salerno, and the Roman prefect Cencius, had summoned him from Salerno together with the cardinal-priest Abbot Richard and Archbishop Peter of Aix, who was metropolitan of the *provincia Narbonensis secunda*, 'ut communi consilio Romanum pontificem eligeremus'. On top of this difference there remained the wrangle over the see of Salerno.

[83] The view that Desiderius was elected in 1086 and in 1087 needed only consecration underlies as well *Ann. Cas., aa.* 1086–7, pp. 1422–5; and *Annales Cavenses, aa.* 1086–7, *MGH SS* iii. 190.

[84] As is clear from Hugh's remark that at Capua Desiderius sought to contrive his own election through 'fautores suos episcopos et principem'.

Prince Gisulf had always resisted the consecration of Alfanus II, which the Normans of Apulia desired. Strangely, in view of his own stay at Salerno, Archbishop Hugh of Lyons was also opposed to it; and at Capua Bishop Odo of Ostia at first took up a stand against it.

Hugh of Lyons indicates that by the eve of Palm Sunday Desiderius had acceded to his sponsors' wish that he should accept the papacy. But he still faced the implacable hostility of Hugh himself and of his French companions, whose opposition some Roman figures like Odo of Ostia and the monk Guitmund at first shared. This opposition prompted Desiderius once more to refuse to be pope and to license the election of whomsoever else those present might favour. Guitmund added to the confusion by alleging that Desiderius had sustained Gregory VII's excommunication for more than a year. Thereupon those who had been assembled dispersed into separate groups; by now it was late at night.

Hugh's account indicates that thereafter the outstanding questions were resolved in a manner contrary to his own wishes by quiet negotiation. First, Hugh and those who thought like him were excluded from further discussion; but Desiderius kept with him Duke Roger of Apulia and also the key figure of Odo of Ostia, as well as other Roman bishops and cardinals. Next the question of Archbishop Alfanus II of Salerno was dealt with. Despite Odo of Ostia's strong objection Desiderius during the night negotiated privately about it with Duke Roger. He conceded that Alfanus should be consecrated next day (Palm Sunday); in return the duke agreed to support Desiderius as pope.[85] This opened the way for the duke of Apulia and the prince of Capua to come into line together behind him. Fortified by the Norman unity that was always his central political consideration, Desiderius now could and did finally accept the papal office. Hugh of Lyons sourly commented that he did so after Sunday lunch and the Normans' siesta; he was under the influence of drink (*vino optinente superiora*), and also it was his reward for permitting Alfanus' *nefandissima consecratio*. To

[85] The Apulian Normans' need to retain control of the see of Salerno is underlined by events at Amalfi in 1088, when Prince Gisulf of Salerno established himself there. Gregory VII had never conceded Norman claims to it: see above, p. 139; and in 1088 Pope Urban II referred to Gisulf as 'karissimus filius noster Salernitanus princeps et Amalphitanus dux': P. Ewald, 'Die Papstbriefe der Brittischen Sammlung', i, *NA* v (1880), 275–414, at 356, no. 15. See Schwarz (as Ch. I n. 94), pp. 64, 250–1.

Hugh's disgust, lest another should usurp his right to consecrate the new pope Odo of Ostia accepted the *fait accompli*: 'conversus est in die belli' was his savage reproach.[86]

There his account breaks off. The Montecassino Chronicle records how, with the outstanding questions thus resolved, with united Norman support, and in the expectation of military aid from Countess Matilda of Tuscany,[87] Desiderius/Victor returned to Montecassino and there kept Easter (28 March). Soon afterwards, he set out by land for Rome escorted by Jordan of Capua and Gisulf of Salerno;[88] the latter was evidently not alienated by the consecration of Alfanus II but, like Odo of Ostia, had made the best of the situation. Victor crossed the Tiber near Ostia and, although seriously ill, he camped outside the Leonine city which Guibert's party held. His Norman allies were able to capture St. Peter's, and on the Sunday after Ascension Day (9 May) he was consecrated by four bishops, who included Odo of Ostia and the Gregorian stalwart Peter of Albano.[89] The account in the Chronicle concludes by recording that Victor stayed in Rome for about eight days and then returned to Montecassino. Other sources, particularly those of Guibertine sympathies but also Hugh of Flavigny, who shared Hugh of Lyons's estimate of Desiderius, referred to a severe dysentery which struck him during the mass after his consecration. For his opponents, Guibertine and extreme Gregorian alike, it represented a divine judgement against the event.[90]

[86] Citing Ps. 77: 9 (Vg.).

[87] *Chron. Cas.* iii. 69, p. 451, shows how speedily Matilda came to Rome.

[88] Roger of Apulia no doubt was preoccupied with the balance of power in the south between Bohemond and himself. In May/Dec. 1086 and in June 1087 they together subscribed charters: Ménager, *Recueil*, pp. 197–8, 215–19, nos. 57, 61; cf. pp. 203–12, no. 59 (falsification). But by Sept./Oct. they were again at war: Lupus Protospatarius, *a.* 1087, p. 62; cf. Yewdale (as Ch. IV n. 9), p. 27, Ménager, *Recueil*, pp. 167–8.

[89] Bernold, *a.* 1087, p. 446. See G. Miccoli, *Pietro Igneo. Studi sull'età gregoriana* (Rome, 1963), 130–1; Hüls, *Kardinäle*, pp. 90–1. *Chron. Cas.* iii. 68, p. 450, adds Bishops John III of Tusculum and John III of Porto: cf. Hüls, *Kardinäle*, pp. 120–1, 139–40. John III of Porto had been quickly appointed by the Gregorian party in opposition to the defector John II—a further sign of its vitality.

[90] *Chron. Cas.* refers to Desiderius' sickness only after Easter 1087: iii. 68, p. 450; but for Bernold he was 'iam plurimis annis infirmus, et in eadem infirmitate ordinatus': *a.* 1087, p. 447. Other accounts of his illness are: *Annales Augustani, a.* 1087, *MGH SS* iii. 132; *Liber de unitate ecclesiae conservanda*, ii. 17, 40, *MGH Libelli*, ii. 232–4, 270; Frutolf of Michaelsberg, *a.* 1085, pp. 102–3; Sigebert of Gembloux, *Chronicon, a.* 1086, *MGH SS* vi. 365; *Annales Brunwilarenses, a.* 1083, *MGH SS* xvi. 725; Orderic Vitalis, viii. 7, ed. Chibnall, iv. 166; William of Malmesbury, iii. 266, ed.

V. ABBOT DESIDERIUS AS POPE VICTOR III

Despite Desiderius' sickness the four months of his pontificate as Pope Victor III that now followed were, like the preceding two years, far from being inactive or uneventful. Countess Matilda of Tuscany evidently paid not the slightest heed to Archbishop Hugh of Lyons's complaints in his first letter but took action in Victor's favour. The Montecassino Chronicle records that, soon after he arrived back at Montecassino, she sent envoys from Rome, where she had established herself, and urgently requested that they meet. Despite the illness, for which she was duly solicitous, his response was to return to Rome by sea, apparently without any Norman escort. Together with others of his party Matilda and her army received him cordially, and he spent eight days at St. Peter's. After celebrating mass there on St. Barnabas' Day (11 June) he followed the countess's forces through Trastevere and into Rome. He secured control of a great deal of the city and its environs, so that for a time he had the loyalty of all Trastevere and of most of the Roman nobility and people, with control of the Castel Sant'Angelo, St. Peter's, and the cities of Ostia and Porto. He himself took up residence upon the Isola in the Tiber. But on the eve of St. Peter's day (28 June) a summons to arms as if by imperial command called out the Guibertine forces to mount a counter-attack. They recovered most of their losses but not St. Peter's. Victor's forces withdrew to Trastevere and to the Castel Sant' Angelo. On the patronal festival (29 June) neither side could hold divine service in St. Peter's, although Clement sang mass in the nearby church of Santa Maria *in turribus*. Victor was, however, able to celebrate mass in St. Peter's on 30 June before securing full control on 1 July; Clement III again withdrew from the Leonine city.[91]

Stubbs, ii. 326; Otto of Freising, *Chronicon*, vii. 1, ed. A. Hofmeister and W. Lammers, *Ausgew. Quell.* xvi. 500. For most sources Desiderius was taken ill at his consecration mass, but for Orderic Vitalis at Pentecost. According to Hugh of Flavigny, after his illness Desiderius belatedly repented, returned to Montecassino, and was there buried not as pope but as abbot: ii, p. 468.

[91] *Chron. Cas.* iii. 69, p. 451; Bernold, *a.* 1087, p. 446. Many reference books state that while at Rome in 1087 Victor placed the relics of Pope Leo IX over an altar in St. Peter's on account of the miracles that they had effected: see, e.g., J. Choux, 'Leone IX', *Bibliotheca sanctorum*, vii (1966), 1293–1301, at 1301. But it is not clear upon what evidence this is based.

It may not have been until after the middle of July that Victor left Rome.[92] When he did so he returned to Montecassino with a company of Roman bishops and cardinals. On the way he dedicated the church of the Cassinese dependency of San Nicola in Pica, to the west of Montecassino.[93] In late August he went to Benevento and held a council which bishops from Apulia, Calabria, and the Principate attended. During it he became gravely ill. Three days after it ended he returned in haste to Montecassino, where he died on 16 September.[94]

For a sick man it had been a full, eventful, and not unsuccessful four months. Moreover, there is evidence to suggest that he made an impact in North Italy, Germany, and France, and perhaps further afield. As is the case with the popes who followed him, no Register of his correspondence has survived.[95] But Bishop Bruno of Segni—himself an exponent of high-Gregorian ideas—served him as *bibliothecarius* of the Roman church.[96] Having regard to the unsettled nature of the times, the output of his chancery seems to have been substantial. Bernold testifies that, immediately after his assumption of the papal office, Victor dispatched notices of it to many destinations, thus fulfilling a canonical obligation. Bernold also referred to his renewal of Gregory VII's judgements upon Henry IV and his supporters;[97] this may relate to the circulation of the decrees of the council of Benevento which the Montecassino Chronicle says were disseminated through east and west.[98] It is hard to assess the work of this council, since the Chronicle's version of its decrees is a later, artificial compilation.[99] But it was important as marking the resumption of a series of papal councils at Benevento,[100] and it is likely to have passed decrees on many of

[92] See his privilege for Montier-en-Der, below, p. 209.

[93] *Chron. Cas.* iii. 72, pp. 453–5.

[94] Ibid.; *Annales Beneventani, a.* 1087, *MGH SS* iii. 182; *Annales Cavenses, a.* 1087, *MGH SS* iii. 190.

[95] It is uncertain whether the existence of a Register of Victor III is indicated in *Chron. Cas.* iv, prol., p. 459.

[96] His name appears in the Ravello charter cited below, p. 209; see Santifaller, 'Saggio', pp. 207, 435–6.

[97] *a.* 1087, p. 446; also Hugh of Lyons's second letter to Countess Matilda of Tuscany.

[98] *Chron. Cas.* iii. 72, p. 455.

[99] See below, Appendix VIII.

[100] There was a papal council at Benevento in 1059 (Nicholas II). Urban II continued the series in 1091; there were further councils in 1108 and 1113 (Paschal II).

the subjects that the Chronicle alleges.[101] Archbishop Hugh of Lyons's second letter to Countess Matilda confirms the circulation at least of its sentences against himself and his coterie; for upon his return to Burgundy Hugh of Cluny confronted him with Victor's letters embodying them. In a wider context Peter the Deacon wrote of many letters that passed from Victor to King Philip I of France as well as to Abbot Hugh of Cluny.[102] Leaving aside items that are certainly or probably spurious,[103] three letters or privileges of his survive intact or are specifically referred to: he confirmed the immunity of the abbey of Montier-en-Der (dioc. Châlons-sur-Marne) and placed it under the protection of the apostolic see;[104] he confirmed the possessions of the new see of Ravello near Amalfi, which he established;[105] and probably from him is a letter to a Byzantine empress (*gloriosae et dilectae filiae A. imperatrici augustae*) requesting the lightening of tolls levied by Byzantine officials on pilgrims to the Holy Sepulchre and an end to the harassment of such pilgrims by the seizure of their horses.[106] Other known

[101] As is suggested by Hugh of Lyons's second letter to Countess Matilda, and by the comment in the *Liber pontificalis* that Victor resisted Guibert as did Gregory VII and Urban II: March, *Liber pontificalis*, p. 135.

[102] *DVI*, cap. 18, Migne, *PL* clxxiii. 1029. For the suggestion that the *dilectum fratrem nostrum domnum Rotgerum sanctae ecclesiae apostolicae sedis cardinalem subdiaconum* of Hugh of Lyons's second letter to Countess Matilda of Tuscany may have been Victor III's legate whom he sent to France after the synod of Benevento, see D. Stiernon, 'Le cardinal-diacre Roger et les archevêques Rangier et Roger de Reggio Calabria', *Rivista di storia della chiesa in Italia*, xix (1965), 1–20, at 8–10; cf. Hüls, *Kardinäle*, p. 253. For an addition to the *Chronicon Beccense* referring to the subdeacon Hubert as an envoy to England of both Gregory VII and Victor III, and for comment, see *Councils and Synods with Other Documents Relating to the English Church*, i/2, edd. D. Whitelock, M. Brett, and C. N. L. Brooke (Oxford, 1981), 627 n. 4.

[103] These include Victor's supposed letter to the bishops of Sardinia: Pflugk-Harttung, *Acta*, ii. 140–1, no. 174; *IP* x. 381, no. †32, 406, no. †43.

[104] *Anal. iur. pont.* x (1869), 421, no. 59; Pflugk-Harttung, *Acta*, i. 26, no. 29 (wrongly ascribed to Victor II). The date is 14 July 1087.

[105] *Ep.* ii, Migne, *PL* cxlix. 962–4; cf. Ughelli–Coleti, viii. 199; *IP* viii. 401–3, nos. *1–3; Schwarz (as Ch. I n. 94), pp. 62–3. Victor's bull was issued at Capua, and indicates that he travelled there in July/Aug. 1087, no doubt *en route* to or from Benevento.

[106] *Ep.* i, Migne, *PL* cxlix. 961–2. Riant considered this letter to be from Pope Victor II to the Empress Theodora, who reigned alone from 12 Jan. 1055 to 22 Aug. 1056, the initial *A.* being an abbreviation of *Augusta*. It may be argued in support that in 1087 pilgrimage to the Holy Land through Byzantine territory was more restricted than in the 1050s, and Byzantium had no control over pilgrims to the Holy Places; there was no empress correspondingly named in 1087; and the Emperor Alexius Comnenus was still excommunicate; P. Riant, 'Inventaire critique des lettres historiques des croisades', *Archives de l'orient latin*, i (1881), 50–3, no. 17; Riant's

acta of Victor are his personal consecration of a Norman, Bonushomo, to be archbishop of Siponto;[107] his entrusting of the impoverished church of Trevi to the oversight of Bishop Peter of Anagni;[108] his adjudgement to Archbishop Roffrid of Benevento of the *parochiatus* of Biccari;[109] and his commissioning of Cardinal Peter of Albano to make subdeacon a later, unnamed abbot of San Lorenzo, Aversa.[110]

Victor seems to have taken further steps on behalf of the Gregorian party in Germany and North Italy. According to Bernold of St. Blasien he upheld the authority of Bishop Gebhard of Constance, whom Bishop Odo of Ostia had consecrated in 1084.[111] It was perhaps owing to Victor that the Brescian monk Hermann, who under Gregory VII had become cardinal-priest of Santi Quattro Coronati, became bishop of Brescia; if so, this further illustrates Victor's collaboration with Countess Matilda of Tuscany.[112]

He was active, too, in the affairs of Montecassino. Presiding in chapter there just before his death, he prohibited his successors from selling or alienating any of its lands, churches, vills, or other possessions; he ruled that none of its monks should make a charter or deed without the abbot's knowledge; and he laid down that subject monasteries should contribute to the

dating is adopted in JL 4342. But B. Leib argued that the letter was addressed by Victor III to Anna Dalassena, Alexius Comnenus' mother, during a time of regency. He criticized Riant for envisaging pilgrims at Jerusalem rather than *en route* through imperial territory: *Rome, Kiev et Byzanz à la fin du XIe siècle* (Paris, 1924), 87–8; cf. Chalandon, *Les Comnènes*, i. 57, 272. Several considerations tend to support Leib. A German pilgrimage of 1086, led by Bishop Pibo of Toul, Count Conrad of Lützelburg, and many German *principes*, went to Jerusalem and returned through Constantinople: *Gesta episcoporum Tullensium*, cap. 48, *MGH SS* viii. 647, cf. Meyer von Knonau, *Jahrbücher*, iv. 21 n. 38. The long tradition of contact and cordiality between Montecassino and Byzantium must also be borne in mind. Apart from the Germans, Victor III may have written in support of pilgrims using the Egnatian Way; many of them may have used the hospice at Montecassino and familiarized him with their misfortunes.

[107] Ughelli-Coleti, viii. 824.

[108] Referred to by Urban in Pflugk-Harttung, *Acta*, ii. 141–2, no. 175 (23 Aug. 1088), where the cordial reference to Victor is to be noticed: '. . . et a Victore reverende memorie tertio, qui nos . . . novissimus in hoc sacerdotalis regimine precessit officii . . .'.

[109] *IP* ix. 61, no. *33, cf. no. *35; 228, nos. *4 and *5.

[110] G. Parente, *Origini e vicinde ecclesiastiche della città di Aversa*, i (Naples, 1857), 288, cited by Hüls, *Kardinäle*, pp. 90–1.

[111] *Pro Gebhardo episcopo Constantiniensi epistola apologetica, MGH Libelli*, ii. 111.

[112] See Ganzer, *Kardinalat*, pp. 40–3.

victualling of the mother house by providing annual *prandia*.[113] Until three days before he died Victor retained the abbacy of Montecassino as well as the papal office;[114] but in chapter on 14 or 15 September he requested the monks, with the confirmation of the Roman bishops who were present, to elect their prior, Oderisius, to be abbot in his stead.[115]

The picture that emerges from these *acta* of Victor as an at least ordinarily energetic pope is confirmed by the positive reactions that he stimulated in friend and foe alike. Cardinal Deusdedit regarded him sufficiently highly to dedicate to him his *Collectio canonum*, while the Cassinese monk Gerold dedicated a hagiographical work to him.[116] That so many and such widely spread enemies, both Guibertine and extreme Gregorian, saw in his dysentery at mass on the day of his consecration an evidence of divine judgement against him suggests that they regarded him as a man of consequence.[117] The Guibertine cardinals thought him worth branding as a public apostate, and they severely condemned his electors and consecrators.[118] Perhaps the most striking evidence of his impact as pope is the hostility expressed in the *Liber de unitate ecclesiae conservanda*. The anonymous Hersfeld monk who wrote it referred bitterly to Victor under the sobriquet of Sergius. As Clement III's rival he was a *hereticus* who was the associate of Gregory VII and Odo of Ostia. He had been intruded into the papacy after Henry IV's departure from Italy and ordained by the zeal of the Hildebrandine party. His dysentery was an appropriate repetition of the penalty that of old had struck the heresiarch Arius. It bore witness that he had been intruded into the papacy in order to revive the fires once kindled by Hildebrand and to perpetuate his schism.[119] The author's acerbity seems in part to stem from

[113] *Chron. Cas.* iii. 73, p. 455; Dormeier, *Montecassino*, pp. 250–2, no. 5, cf. pp. 4–6. In the first of his rulings Victor may have had in mind Gregory VII's legislation to secure monastic property at his Nov. council of 1083, which Urban II confirmed at his council of Melfi (1089). If so, it illustrates continuity of work amongst the three popes. See the letter written by the sometime Cassinese monk John, cardinal-deacon of Santa Maria in Cosmedin and papal chancellor (*c.* 1088–1118), to Abbot Guy I of Molesme (1110–32): Mansi, xx. 726; cf. Hüls, *Kardinäle*, pp. 231–2, Dormeier, *Montecassino*, pp. 26, 59.

[114] For eleventh-century practice, see Goez (as Ch. II n. 41), esp. pp. 29, 39–40, 56.

[115] *Chron. Cas.* iii. 73, iv. 1, pp. 455–6, 467; cf. *Ann. Cas., a.* 1087, pp. 1424–5.

[116] See above, pp. 25, 99.

[117] See above, p. 206.

[118] No. vi, *MGH Libelli*, ii. 407–8.

[119] ii. 17, 40, *MGH Libelli*, ii. 232–3, 269–70. The choice of the sobriquet Sergius is unexplained; perhaps it was for its Byzantine associations.

a sense of betrayal that a monastic tradition at Montecassino which had once exhibited the conservatism of the *Diversorum patrum sententiae* should now have truck with the party of Hildebrand, the author of schism and the destroyer of the good old law of the church.[120] Just as the Hersfeld anonymous testified to Victor's impact by vilifying him, so the Gregorian Bernold applauded him and saw in his death a source of joy to Guibert and his party.[121]

In the longer term, his reign was remembered for the wider enterprises with which his name came to be associated. It was noticed that the relics of St. Nicholas came to Bari on 9 May 1087, and so on the very day of his consecration at Rome.[122] Two years later, in October 1089, Pope Urban II fully harnessed the cult of St. Nicholas to the Gregorian cause by personally consecrating his shrine at Bari and by departing from custom and ordaining Archbishop Elia of Bari bishop in his own local cathedral.[123] In this way Victor had his place at the full emergence of one of the most powerful and papally sponsored cultuses of the Middle Ages. Another momentous enterprise was the Pisan and Genoese expedition to Mahdia, which triumphantly sacked the city in early August 1087, and so in Victor's reign, when it gave a portion of the spoils to St. Peter at Rome.[124] The successes at Bari and Mahdia—two events within Victor's brief pontificate—invested the Gregorian papacy with the laurels of victory. At Bari writers were quick to equate the Greek name Nicholas with its Latin equivalent *victoria populi*; while at Pisa a triumphal song lauded the deeds of an expedition carried out by a Gregorian and anti-imperialist populace which included a pilgrimage to the Rome of Victor III.[125] There is no evidence that in 1087 contemporaries linked these exploits with Victor's papal name. But when some fifty years later Paul of Bernried wrote his life of Gregory VII it had come to stand for the

[120] See above, pp. 98–102. [121] *a.* 1087, p. 447.

[122] *Chron. Cas.* iii. 68, pp. 450–1; *Annales Cavenses, a.* 1087, *MGH SS* iii. 190. See F. Nitti di Vito, 'La traslazione delle reliquie di San Nicholà', *Iapigia*, viii (1937), 295–411, at 303, and *La ripresa gregoriana*, p. 161. In 1105 Pope Paschal II recalled that St. Nicholas' relics came to Bari 'praedecessoris nostri sanctae memoriae Victoris III temporibus': *Ep.* 167, Migne, *PL* clxiii. 178–9.

[123] See below, Appendix IX.

[124] See Cowdrey (as Ch. IV n. 16), *EHR* xcii. 1–29; also G. Scalia, 'Il carme pisano sull'impresa contro i Saraceni del 1087', *Studi di filologia romanza offerti a Silvio Pellegrino* (Padua, 1971), 565–625.

[125] For Pisa, see the source indicated in the last note; for Bari, below, Appendix IX.

victory of Gregory's cause. Paul spoke of alleged victories in Germany during Victor's reign, and not of events at Bari and Mahdia.[126] Yet his play upon the name Victor is a reminder that, with growing emphasis as years went by, Gregorian writers regarded Victor III's reign as a victorious link between those of Gregory VII and Urban II. The Montecassino Chronicle testifies to the link by recording Victor's deathbed recommendation of Odo of Ostia as a successor whom the Gregorians should strive to uphold in continuing all that he himself had done.[127]

In reviewing Desiderius/Victor's life between Gregory VII's death on 25 May 1085 and his own on 16 September 1087 it is impossible at any stage, right up to his deathbed, to condemn him for inactivity; not even his enemies like Archbishop Hugh of Lyons accused him of that. Nor was he half-hearted in his service of the Gregorian cause. His recorded attitudes and actions during this time yield no trace of his having favoured or served imperial interests. He seems, instead, to have regarded himself as an executor of Gregory's final testament. He sought to secure for the Gregorian party a strong enough basis of unity and power for it to challenge the Guibertines to good effect. Only when such a basis had been established would he accept the papal office. His attitude was often prudent and calculating rather than heroic or inspiring; it was not one that an ultra-Gregorian figure such as Hugh of Lyons could readily if at all comprehend. But it was attuned to the facts of current politics in Rome and South Italy, and it led to his eventual acceptance by most of Gregory's followers as his duly elected and worthy successor. His four months of activity in the papal office were not the torpid and colourless interlude that historians have too often seen. They were strenuous months which formed a genuine bridge between the reigns of Gregory and of Urban II. Victor III as an inactive and an ineffective pope belongs to the myths of history.

[126] cap. 109, Watterich, i. 539. The text of the Admont MS (as above, Ch. II n. 231) is: '. . . interim suasit eligi vicinum Desiderium, licet brevissimum victurum, non tamen absque typo victorie appellandum. Nam in diebus eius, qui quattuor artati sunt mensibus, famosam victoriam dedit dominus apostolicę sedis propugnatoribus de adversariis ipsius . . .': f. 142[r].

[127] 'Accipite eum et in Romanam ecclesiam ordinate meamque vicem in omnibus, quousque id facere possitis, habete': *Chron. Cas.* iii. 73, p. 456.

V

After 1087

FOR the purpose of the present study three themes in the relations between Montecassino and the papacy after Victor III's death are of especial significance: the abbey's tendency increasingly to identify itself with the more conservatively Gregorian elements in the Roman curia; the crisis of Cassinese affairs in the third and fourth decades of the twelfth century, when Montecassino's imperial connections found emphasis in the work of Peter the Deacon; and, in the intervening years, the vicissitudes of Victor III's reputation and official image as a true member of the succession of reforming popes.[1]

i. MONTECASSINO'S IDENTIFICATION WITH CONSERVATIVELY GREGORIAN ELEMENTS IN THE ROMAN CURIA

a. *The election of Pope Urban II*

Desiderius' chosen successor as abbot of Montecassino, Oderisius I, played a leading part in the election of Urban II and so cemented the bond between Montecassino and the papacy. The election was carefully contrived to meet the requirements and to claim the assent of as many as possible of Gregory VII's partisans, both at Rome and in the church at large.[2] It took place at Terracina, on the southern border of the Roman Campagna, between 8 and 12 March 1088. Very little is known about the course of events since Victor's death some six months before. The Montecassino Chronicle spoke of the gloom and despair that fell upon the Gregorian party (*tristitia ingens et desperatio cunctos nostre partis invasit*). It thereby showed

[1] The fullest account of the long-term developments discussed in this chapter remains Schmale, *Schisma*.

[2] The sources for Urban's election are his *Epp.* 1–2, Migne, *PL* cli. 283–5, and *Chron. Cas.* iv. 2, pp. 467–8. They are detailed, and show remarkable agreement. For modern discussions, see esp. Meyer von Knonau, *Jahrbücher*, iv. 192–7; Becker, *Urban II.*, i. 91–6; C. Servatius, *Paschalis II. (1099–1118). Studien zu seiner Person und seiner Politik* (Stuttgart, 1979), 15–16.

where it believed the abbey's loyalty to have been placed, and implied that high hopes had rested upon Victor. The Roman bishops were widely dispersed;[3] therefore, numerous messages were sent to them from the Romans, from the German Gregorians (*ultramontani*), and from Countess Matilda of Tuscany, pressing them to promote a new election.[4] When the bishops assembled, together with Abbot Oderisius—who thus assumed the kind of role that Desiderius had apparently played in the summer of 1085—they summoned the faithful Roman clergy and laity, and also the bishops and abbots of the Campagna, the Principate, and Apulia, to meet at Terracina during the first week of Lent (5–11 March). The Chronicle gives the timetable according to which events developed: on 8 March those concerned with the election assembled; on 9 March they met in the cathedral, agreed to hold an election, and began the canonical three-day fast; on Sunday 12 March Bishop Odo of Ostia was proposed, acclaimed, and enthroned.

It is clear from the Montecassino Chronicle and from Urban II's letters which he dispatched immediately after the election that no effort was spared to secure the genuine and public unanimity of all the electors. Equal care was taken to associate with the election whether directly or indirectly as wide as possible a cross-section of Gregorians in the church at large. To relieve the tensions within the Roman church that had bedevilled the electoral proceedings of 1086–7, each grade of the Roman church was accorded its separate means of signifying its consent; never before had all the cardinals been drawn so closely together in a single transaction of business. Every one of the cardinal-bishops was present, and on 12 March it was three of their number—those of Porto, Tusculum, and Albano—who as *caput eiusdem concilii* proposed that Odo of Ostia should be pope.[5]

[3] Early in 1088 Odo of Ostia was with Prince Jordan of Capua at the institution of an abbot of Casamari: P. Rondininus, *Monasterii Sanctae Mariae et Sanctorum Iohannis et Pauli de Casaemario brevis historia* (Rome, 1707), 93, cited by Hoffmann (as Introd. n. 52), p. 167.

[4] Archbishop Hugh of Lyons wrote his second letter to Countess Matilda in order to urge her to promote the election of someone committed to Gregorian principles as he saw them, and to use him as her agent. He also alluded to his approaches by letter to Roman bishops and cardinal-priests. There is no evidence that notice was taken of him. He was not, of course, at Terracina.

[5] Urban named those present, apart from himself, as Hubald of Sabina, John III of Tusculum, Peter of Albano, Bruno of Segni, and John III of Porto. The see of Palestrina seems to have been vacant: Migne, *PL* cli. 283B, 285A.

Abbot Oderisius of Montecassino was the representative spokesman (*legatus*) of the Roman deacons, Cardinal Rainer of San Clemente—the future Pope Paschal II—that of the priests, and the Roman prefect Benedict that of the laity, in adding the consent of each group to the bishops' proposal. Roman clergy and laity who could not be present were requested to send written submissions about whom they were willing to see elected. Thus, no steps were omitted to secure the express adherence of every interest at Rome, and to exclude every hint of tumult or uncertainty. In a wider field, while no concessions were made to such extreme claims to participation in an election as those which Archbishop Hugh of Lyons had advanced on behalf of metropolitans, many interests other than Roman ones were represented at Terracina. They included envoys of the German Gregorians (*ultramontani*), of Countess Matilda of Tuscany, and of the South Italian bishops and abbots; although, despite the position which papal measures since the Election Decree of 1059 had accorded them, the Norman princes seem to have been absent.[6] South Italian prelates were required to submit verbal or written undertakings that they would accept whatever the assembly might decide.

So far as it could be contrived, therefore, Urban could claim that he was elected by the unanimous and universal consent of catholics, both present and absent.[7] But a no less insistent theme of the election was that he carried authority because he was the designated successor of both Gregory VII and Victor III. According to the Montecassino Chronicle, on 9 March Bishop John III of Tusculum prepared for the election by solemnly rehearsing the guidance that the two popes had offered with regard to the succession.[8] Urban himself was repeatedly to claim that his election had proceeded according to the two popes' admonitions.[9] He presented himself to the church as

[6] Urban later claimed that his entry into Rome on 3 July 1089 was brought about 'sine omni Nortmannorum ope': Kehr (as Ch. IV n. 60), pp. 277–8. In Mar. Roger was at Salerno: la Cava, Archivio capitolare, MS C.17; MS C.19 suggests that he was still there in June and July.

[7] '. . . omnium tam praesentium quam et absentium praedictorum fidelium consensu'; '. . . de unanimi et universali catholicorum consensu ad Romanam ecclesiam ac Romani pontificalis culmen electos'; '. . . expetente nos atque cogente universa catholicorum . . . ecclesia': *Epp.* 1, 3, 4, Migne, *PL* cli. 283C, 286A, 287A.

[8] '. . . retulit per ordinem omnia, que de ordinatione ecclesie vel papa Gregorius antea vel postmodum papa Victor statuerant.'

[9] The electors acted 'auctoritatem atque imperium sanctae memoriae praedeces-

heir to them both, making Victor III the link between Gregory and himself in a unanimous and honourable papal tradition.

Urban's election was thus a skilfully contrived occasion.[10] It established him in an unbroken succession of reform popes of whom Victor III was regarded as one. Because of the part played by the Gregorians at Montecassino as well as by Abbot Oderisius in convening the assembly at Terracina, and because of the abbot's prominence as spokesman of the cardinal-deacons, it further consolidated the bonds between Montecassino and the papacy which had been greatly strengthened by the course of events since Gregory VII's journey to the south in 1084. And it left no doubt of the official papal evaluation of Victor III, the Cassinese pope, as a prime upholder of the Gregorian cause against its Guibertine adversaries.

b. *Abbot Oderisius I and Pope Urban II*

Urban II prepared the way for continued co-operation between Montecassino and the papacy by raising Abbot Oderisius to the rank of cardinal-priest and by himself consecrating him abbot. There seems nevertheless to have been a certain reserve in Urban's early dealings with the abbey, which may have been connected with his deliberate avoidance of Norman help in seeking to recover his position at Rome. But as time went on Montecassino contributed to the papal service more extensively than had been the case under Gregory VII. Urban increasingly showed it favour in his charters and in judgements on its behalf.[11]

Given its topographical position, it was of considerable assistance to Urban with regard to the First Crusade. Embodied in the Montecassino Chronicle is a narrative account of the Crusade up to its arrival before Antioch, which may have been incorporated from Leo of Ostia's lost *Historia peregrinorum*.[12]

sorum meorum Gregorii et Victoris habere se super hoc asserentes'; again, 'praesertim cum praedecessores meos viros omni veneratione dignos, Gregorium scilicet atque Victorem, hoc sibi divine praecipisse asserunt'; Urban was elected 'praecedente quoque gemina dominorum praedecessorum nostrorum Gregorii atque Vitellii [*sic*] inevitabili praeceptione', and 'dominorum meorum antecessorum gemina preceptione artatus': *Epp.* 1, 2, 4, Migne, *PL* cli. 283C, 285B, 287A; Ramackers (as Ch. II n. 92).

[10] The rights of bishops and priests for long remained controversial: e.g. Anacletus II, *Ep.* 9, Migne, *PL* clxxix. 699–700, and the Anacletan Pandulf's address in March, *Liber pontificalis*, p. 167.

[11] See above, pp. xl, 68–9.

[12] *Chron. Cas.* iv. 11, pp. 475–81. This chapter stands in close but undetermined relationship to the history of the First Crusade in Montecassino, Archivio capitolare,

It laid emphasis upon the providential purpose of the expedition, and told how the army led by Count Robert of Flanders, Duke Robert of Normandy, and Hugh of Vermandois, was commended to St. Benedict's protection at Montecassino as it made its way from Rome to Bari and thence across the Adriatic to Byzantium. Abbot Oderisius later helped Urban's Crusade by exchanging letters with the Emperor Alexius Comnenus; his purpose was to facilitate the orderly and peaceful passage of the Crusading army through the emperor's lands. A correspondence of 1097 was followed in 1098 by a further letter from Alexius; he made a gift to the abbey and was received into its confraternity.[13] Oderisius also wrote after 1099 to the Crusading leaders in the Holy Land, Godfrey of Bouillon and the Norman Bohemond, urging them to refrain from warfare against Alexius Comnenus.[14] The amicable contact that Montecassino thus maintained with Byzantium not only helped the Crusade but was also in harmony with Urban's attempts from the outset of his pontificate to restore good relations between Eastern and Western Christendom. He pursued them partly in order to foster the unity of the churches, and partly to deny to Henry IV of Germany the financial and political advantages that his good relations with Alexius had brought him in the years 1082-4.

In Oderisius' reign Henry himself presented Montecassino with few problems. Having received imperial coronation at the hands of the antipope Clement III, his principal reason for concerning himself with Rome or South Italy had disappeared, and he was preoccupied with German and North Italian affairs.[15] Oderisius was therefore spared any such crisis as Desiderius had to face in 1082 by his confrontation with Henry. He was able to maintain and develop a relatively easy and straightforward

MS 300, first edited by J. Mabillon under the title *Historia belli sacri: Museum Italicum*, i/2 (Paris, 1724), 130-236. For Leo of Ostia, see above, pp. xvii-xviii, 26. For the question of authorship, see esp. Meyvaert and Devos (as Ch. I n. 113), pp. 217-23; Hoffmann, *MGH SS* xxxiv, pp. xxviii-xxx.

[13] *Reg. Pet. Diac.*, nos. 146-7; *Chron. Cas.* iv. 17, p. 485; Trinchera, *Syllabus*, pp. 78-9, nos. 61-2; H. Hagenmeyer, *Die Kreuzzugsbriefe aus den Jahren 1022-1100* (Innsbruck, 1901), 140-1, 152-3, nos. 5, 11; Dölger, *Regesten*, nos. 1207-8. Alexius Comnenus' first letter contains the earliest reference to Crusaders as *peregrini*.

[14] *Chron. Cas.* iv. 17, pp. 485-6.

[15] On Urban and Henry, see A. Becker, 'Urban II. und die deutsche Kirche', *Investiturstreit und Reichsverfassung*, ed. J. Fleckenstein, Vorträge und Forschungen, 17 (Sigmaringen, 1973), 241-75, esp. 268-9.

amity with the papacy of Urban II upon a basis of mutual interest and untroubled by fears of conflicting loyalty.[16]

c. *Bruno of Segni and Pope Paschal II*

In the first decade of the twelfth century, relations between Montecassino and the papacy are most signally illustrated by the career and attitudes of Bruno of Segni, who was abbot from 1107 to 1111.[17] Bruno had been closely associated with Gregory VII. He controverted Berengar at the Lent council of 1079 at Rome,[18] and thereafter he was often in the pope's company; although, somewhat surprisingly, he was a member of the *conventus* of Roman clergy who in 1082 resisted Gregory's plans to use the revenues of the Roman churches in his struggle against Guibert of Ravenna.[19] Bruno was also an associate of Cardinal-bishop Peter of Albano.[20] As well as Gregory VII, Peter was instrumental in commending Bruno to the church of Segni for election as its bishop, probably in 1079.[21] In 1081 or 1082, despite his attitude in the Roman *conventus* he was subjected to imprisonment by the Henrician element at Segni.[22] Under Victor III he was *bibliothecarius et cancellarius* of the apostolic see, and he was a close counsellor of Urban II; like his patron Peter of Albano, Bruno illustrates the not inconsiderable element of continuity in the papal service that ran through the pontificates of Gregory, Victor, and Urban. Bruno gave Urban

[16] *Chron. Cas.* iv. 18, p. 486, included an account of Oderisius' contact with Henry IV through a monk named George. He announced his succession as abbot to Henry and promised fealty and service. But this account of a proposed royal confirmation of Montecassino's North Italian possessions in the presence of the emperor, his son Henry, and Countess Matilda of Tuscany, is clearly unhistorical, and perhaps a later attempt by Peter the Deacon to establish a tradition of Cassinese loyalty to the German monarchy.

[17] The principal sources for Bruno's life are *Chron. Cas.* iv. 31–42, pp. 496–511, and the anonymous *Vita* written 1178/82, in *AA SS Boll.*, July, iv. 478–84. For modern studies, see esp. Gigalski (as Ch. I n. 126); Ganzer, *Kardinalat*, pp. 57–62; R. Grégoire, *Bruno de Segni, exégète mediéval et théologien monastique* (Spoleto, 1965); Wattenbach-Holtzmann, iii. 874–6; H. Hoffmann, 'Bruno di Segni, santo', *DBI* xiv (1972), 644–7; Hüls, *Kardinäle*, pp. 129–30. For the significance of such saints' Lives as the anonymous *Vita*, see Toubert, *Latium*, pp. 74–5, 807–29.

[18] *Vita Brunonis*, cap. 6, pp. 479–80; Bruno of Segni, *Expositio in Leviticum*, cap. 7, Migne, *PL* clxiv. 404.

[19] See above, p. 152.

[20] *Vita Brunonis*, caps. 6–10, pp. 479–80. See Miccoli (as Ch. III n. 89), pp. 49–50, 75–6; Toubert, *Latium*, pp. 814–15.

[21] *Vita Brunonis*, caps. 7–12, pp. 479–80.

[22] See the Prologue to his Commentary on Isaiah, in A. M. Amelli, *S. Bruno di Segni, Gregorio VII ed Enrico IV in Roma (1081–3)* (Montecassino, 1903), 8–9.

long and faithful aid, accompanying him on his French itinerary of 1095–6 when he preached the Crusade at Clermont. He assisted Urban in the consecration of Abbot Hugh of Semur's third church at Cluny.

After a severe illness that he contracted in 1102 while he was in Apulia with Pope Paschal II, Bruno expressed the wish to enter a monastery. Paschal at first resisted, but eventually allowed him to enter Montecassino, although at the request of the people of Segni he retained his see.[23] To safeguard his usefulness to the papal curia and to the church of Segni, Abbot Oderisius agreed that he might have forty days' annual leave to attend to their service.[24] By 1104 he was more deeply involved at Rome; two years later he visited France as papal legate in company with Bohemond of Antioch, and sought to recruit for service in the east.[25]

In 1107 Bruno was elected abbot of Montecassino. He at first enjoyed the continuing confidence of Pope Paschal II, who in 1108 is said by the Montecassino Chronicle to have declared him worthy to be his successor as pope.[26] He was with Paschal at the synod of Benevento, which strongly condemned lay investiture.[27] But Bruno sharply opposed Paschal's acceptance of the Emperor Henry V's terms in the treaty of Ponte Mammolo of 11 April 1111, when the pope conceded the lay investiture of bishops after canonical election but before consecration.[28] Thereupon Paschal compelled him to resign his abbacy, using the pretext that it was irregular for him to be both abbot and bishop. He withdrew to his see of Segni, where he remained until his death in 1123.[29] He became partly reconciled to Paschal II, but he never again took part in papal business.[30]

[23] *Vita Brunonis*, caps. 19–21, p. 482.

[24] *Chron. Cas.* iv. 31, pp. 496–8.

[25] Suger, *Vie de Louis VI le Gros*, cap. 9, ed. H. Waquet (Paris, 1964), 46–50. For Bruno as legate, see T. Schieffer, *Die päpstlichen Legaten in Frankreich vom Vertrag von Meersen (870) bis zum Schisma von 1130*, Historische Studien, 263 (Berlin, 1935), 175–8.

[26] *Chron. Cas.* iv. 31, p. 498.

[27] Ibid. iv. 33, p. 499.

[28] For Bruno's reactions, see his letters, *Brunonis episcopi Signini Epistolae quatuor*, ed. E. Sackur, *MGH Libelli*, ii. 563–5.

[29] *Vita Brunonis*, caps. 25–7, 30, pp. 483–4; *Chron. Cas.* iv. 42, pp. 510–11; see Servatius (as Ch. V n. 2), pp. 300–2. Bruno's departure from Montecassino is not sufficiently accounted for by the sources. He may have become *persona non grata* to Lombards inside and outside the abbey, since in and after 1111 many rallied to Henry V against the Normans: *Chron. Cas.* iv. 40, p. 507; Fulk of Benevento, *a.* 1113, p. 163.

[30] He was present at the Lateran councils of 1112 and 1116: *MGH Const.* i. 370–3, no. 399; *Chron. Cas.* iv. 45, p. 513; Ekkehard of Aura, *Chronicon*, *a.* 1116, *Ausgew. Quell.* xv. 318–23.

Bruno's career illustrates how a strongly Gregorian figure of, in general, extreme and rigid views which were formed in the days of Gregory VII could find a place at Montecassino early in the twelfth century and rise to be its abbot. His presence there helps to explain the comparable attitude that colours some parts of the Montecassino Chronicle, especially those parts concerned with Desiderius' conduct in the 1080s as abbot, and then as Pope Victor III. But it also serves to reveal how fragile relations between Montecassino and the papacy could easily become.

ii. THE CRISIS OF CASSINESE AFFAIRS IN THE 1120s AND 1130s

a. *The onset of crisis*

The reign of the next abbot, Gerard (1111–23), seems nevertheless to have been for Montecassino, at least predominantly, a period of peace and equipoise.[31] Gerard was canonically and freely elected by the monks and consecrated by Paschal himself. Paschal visited Montecassino in 1115 and 1117, on the second occasion because of the Emperor Henry V's Roman expedition; Calixtus II also came in 1120. These visits consolidated the mutual familiarity and usefulness of the abbey and the papacy.

There can be little doubt, however, that during the early 1120s a time of endemic internal stress set in at Montecassino. One factor seems to have been the dying off of the *decani* whom Abbot Desiderius had appointed.[32] But even during his reign the abbey's sources of spiritual renewal seem to have been limited; although its many points of contact with the rigorous standards of the eremitical life seem then to have served for some as an incentive to excellence. It is probably symptomatic that during the early twelfth century references in Cassinese literature to eremitism as a source of current inspiration became few and far between.[33] But at just this time there were gathering

[31] For Gerard, see *Chron. Cas.* iv. 43–77, pp. 512–42.

[32] For Montecassino and the monastic crisis, see Schmale, *Schisma*, pp. 169–74, 205–6, 258; Hoffmann (as Introd. n. 13), esp. pp. 74–104. It is probably correct to discount the strictures on Cassinese monasticism in the *Vita Brunonis*, caps. 24–5, p. 483. But *Chron. Cas.* noted complaints about the austerity of Abbot Otto (1106–7) and divisions during abbatial elections: iv. 26, 29, pp. 492, 494–5; see also iv. 94, pp. 554–5.

[33] Alberic the younger's visionary literature is largely derivative: see above, p. 36.

strength to the north of the Alps newer monastic movements such as the Carthusians, Cistercians, and orders of regular canons such as the Premonstratensians, which had deep roots in the eleventh-century aspiration, so widespread especially in Italy, for a more austere, apostolic, and eremitical way of life. Cluny itself under Abbot Peter the Venerable (1122–56) became deeply affected by it.[34] At Montecassino monastic life was not quickened or renewed by any such influences, nor did it experience any such time of testing as Cluny underwent in Peter the Venerable's early years, or as St. Bernard of Clairvaux proposed in his letters and treatises. It remained set in eleventh-century ways when those ways were losing their vitality and relevance to contemporary needs.

Such a drift towards internal stagnation reacted adversely upon its external relationships. For the papacy, too, was undergoing change. After 1123 the key figure in the papal curia was the Frenchman Haimeric, who was papal chancellor until his death in 1141. In his time the papacy became more and more identified and connected with the personalities, outlook, and loyalties of the newer reform movements across the Alps. The older, Roman and South Italian connections of the papacy were eroded in favour of more international and forward-looking relationships with figures such as St. Bernard. Montecassino therefore tended to become spiritually and ecclesiastically isolated. Political developments compounded this isolation. After the antipope Clement III's death in 1100 the schism of the papacy was for all practical purposes at an end, and the Gregorian papacy became less dependent upon Montecassino's support against its rival. With the Concordat of Worms in 1122, the struggles of papacy and Empire were also abated; and in 1125 Henry V's death marked the end of Salian rule in Germany. The Roman curia had less need of Montecassino and the Normans as sources of aid and refuge in face of German opposition. On the contrary, Montecassino's Norman neighbours and patrons became more menacing because they were more united than they had been when they were divided amongst the three powers of Capua, Apulia, and Sicily.[35] In 1127 the weak Duke

[34] For Cluny and eremitism, see G. Constable, 'Cluny, Cîteaux, la Chartreuse: San Bernardo e la diversità delle forme di vita religiosa nel XII secolo', *Studi su S. Bernardo di Chiaravalle* (Rome, 1975), 93–114, repr. *Cluniac Studies* (London, 1980), no. XI.

[35] See esp. Bernhardi, *Lothar*, pp. 274–80; Caspar, *Roger II.*, pp. 74–81; Schmale, *Schisma*, pp. 81–2; Hoffmann (as Introd. n. 13), pp. 87–8.

William of Apulia died childless, leaving Count Roger II of Sicily as his heir. In 1128 Honorius II was constrained to invest him with the duchy of Apulia. Roger was well set upon the way to the establishment of a Norman kingdom. With the progress of the Normans towards political unity under a king, the papacy increasingly saw in them a source of danger rather than of help. Therefore, after the overcoming of the Guibertine schism and the elimination of the German threat, Montecassino tended to lose its traditional position as a mediator between the papacy and its would-be Norman allies. Papal interests seemed instead to call for a Montecassino which was directly dependent upon Rome and which might act as a bastion against a growing Norman menace.

The crisis in Montecassino's fortunes that resulted became apparent during and after the abbacy of Oderisius II (1123-6),[36] and especially with the accession to the papacy, after an election managed by the chancellor Haimeric, of Honorius II (1124-30). Even before his election, when he was Cardinal-bishop Lambert of Ostia, Honorius was aggrieved because Oderisius would not allow him and his clerks the lodging at Santa Maria in Pallara that his Cassinese predecessor at Ostia, Leo, had enjoyed.[37] As pope he was further offended by Oderisius' unwillingness to give the Roman church his abbey's financial support, especially for a campaign against the counts of Ceccano; there followed a time of discord and ill will.[38] After a conflict regarding marcher lands between the papal states and the *terra sancti Benedicti* Honorius accused Oderisius before a lay audience of behaving like a soldier, not an abbot.[39] In 1126 he compelled his monks to depose him, and he tried to force upon them his own candidate. They sought to uphold their independence by electing as abbot Nicholas of Tusculum (1126-7); but Honorius sought to impose his own choice of Seniorect, and sent Gregory, cardinal-priest of Santi Apostoli, to see that he had his way. The monks remained internally divided, and in 1127 Honorius was able to depose Nicholas. Seniorect (1127-37) was thereupon elected under the eye of Cardinal Matthew of Albano. When Honorius came to Montecassino in order to consecrate him, the monks resented the

[36] *Chron. Cas.* iv. 78-88, pp. 542-50. For his problems, see Hoffmann (as Introd. n. 13), pp. 74-104.

[37] *Chron. Cas.* iv. 81, p. 545.

[38] Ibid. iv. 83, p. 546.

[39] Ibid. iv. 86, pp. 547-8.

stringency of the pope's demands for fealty to Rome.[40] By these developments, and especially the last of them, the papacy's new policy towards Montecassino, which was directed towards seeking its straiter dependence and obedience, was placed beyond doubt.

b. *The Anacletan Schism*

Pope Honorius II died in 1130, at a time when the threat presented to the papacy by Roger II of Sicily's successes had become apparent. At Rome the chancellor Haimeric was mainly responsible for the election to the papacy, in hasty and high-handed circumstances by a minority of cardinals, of Innocent II (1130–43). In the city Innocent mainly owed his success to the Frangipani and to those cardinals, mostly of non-Roman and non-South-Italian provenance, who had been appointed under Honorius II; further afield his supporters were to be found amongst the newer-style religious orders and reformers. In opposition to Innocent and with a greater show of canonical propriety, a majority of the older cardinals who were of Roman and South Italian affiliations elected Cardinal Peter Pierleoni as the antipope Anacletus II. A schism thus opened at the centre of the reform papacy itself, which arose both from Roman factional politics and from contrasting views about ecclesiastical reform. Anacletus enjoyed greater favour in Rome than did Innocent, and he was also accepted by much of the South Italian church; more important in political terms, he was recognized by Roger II of Sicily. In 1130 Anacletus invested Roger with Sicily, Calabria, and Apulia, and on Christmas Day crowned him king of a hereditary kingdom.[41] It was a remarkable reassertion of older papal hopes with regard to the Normans. In the church at large, however, thanks largely to the zeal of St. Bernard of Clairvaux Innocent was recognized not only in France but also in Germany by Lothar of Supplinburg (1125–37), whom he crowned emperor in the Lateran in 1133 during Lothar's first Italian expedition. The Anacletan Schism inevitably led to conflict between Lothar and Roger II, which came to its climax in Lothar's second Italian expedition of 1136–7.

[40] *Chron. Cas.* iv. 89–95, pp. 550–6.

[41] For the course of events, see esp. Bernhardi, *Lothar*, pp. 288–334; Chalandon, *Domination*, ii. 1–97; Bloch (as Introd. n. 4), pp. 159–74. For the sources, see Deér (as Ch. III n. 118), pp. 62–6, no. xvii. 1–6.

Montecassino was inevitably drawn into these events. For most of the 1130s its position was complicated by the resistance of Prince Robert of Capua and Count Rainulf of Alife to Roger II's bid to unite the Norman lands. But together with Roger's manifest power, the bonds between Montecassino and Anacletus' party in Rome ensured that, despite the circumstances of Abbot Seniorect's election and endemic divisions amongst its monks, Montecassino for long adhered to the Anacletan cause.[42] It is unfortunate, but significant of later embarrassment at this adherence, that the Montecassino Chronicle provides only the scantiest evidence for the years from 1128 to 1135.[43] But thereafter the ready pen of Peter the Deacon has left a copious if tendentious record. Thus, much is known about Lothar's dealings in 1137.

When Lothar entered Italy Seniorect's loyalties began to swing towards the emperor, perhaps in response to a direct approach from him.[44] However, the abbot died on 4 February 1137, and in a bitterly contested election the monks, with Roger II's approval, chose as his successor the Anacletan Reynald of Tuscany.[45] Upon hearing of this Lothar commissioned his son-in-law, Duke Henry the Proud of Bavaria, to bring Montecassino to heel. Accompanied by Pope Innocent II, Duke Henry camped near the abbey in May but was not able to subdue it. Further campaigning in the south induced discontent in the German host. It was against such a background that in July Lothar and Innocent spent some days at Lagopesole, near Venosa, where they sought to hold an inquiry into Montecassino's loyalties during the Anacletan Schism. Lothar and Innocent differed as regards the abbey's culpability and its obligations to pope and emperor; in the end Abbot Reynald and each of his

[42] *Chron. Cas.* iv. 97, pp. 557–8; Anacletus' supporters included not only the former Abbot Oderisius II of Montecassino, who was still a cardinal, but also Amicus, cardinal-priest of SS Achilleo e Nereo, abbot of San Vincento al Volturno, and a former *decanus* at Montecassino: Schmale, *Schisma*, pp. 33, 62, 78, 205–6; Ganzer, *Kardinalat*, pp. 75–9; Hüls, *Kardinäle*, pp. 193–4, 221–2. For the preservation at Montecassino of Anacletus' letters, see P. F. Palumbo, 'La cancellaria di Anacleto II', *Scritti di paleografia e diplomatica in onore di Vincenzo Federici* (Florence, 1944), 81–131, esp. 81–4.

[43] *Chron. Cas.* iv. 96–7, pp. 556–8. Smidt almost certainly correctly considered this section to be the first part of Peter the Deacon's own continuation of the Chronicle: as Introd. n. 16.

[44] For Lothar's letters, see *Chron. Cas.* iv. 107, pp. 568–9, and *MGH Dipl. LIII*, no. 121*b–c*, with Hoffmann's comments at *MGH SS* xxxiv. 568 n. 2.

[45] *Chron. Cas.* iv. 103–4, pp. 564–6.

monks were compelled to swear fidelity to Innocent. In September Lothar returned to Montecassino as he prepared finally to withdraw to Germany. In the course of prolonged and strained negotiations Lothar conducted an inquiry into Reynald's election and subsequent conduct, and procured his deposition. Despite Innocent II's objections to the means adopted he caused Abbot Wibald of Stablo to be elected in his place.[46] On 22 September at Aquino Lothar issued his privilege for Montecassino, in which he referred to it as an imperial abbey.[47]

Like Lothar's other actions in the south during his Italian expedition, his dispositions at Montecassino did not for long survive his departure and death on 4 December 1137 as he crossed the Alps. Roger II of Sicily was able speedily to retrieve his position; Anacletus' death on 25 January 1138 and Roger's capture of Innocent on 22 July 1139 prepared the ground for Innocent to recognize Roger as king.[48] In the autumn of 1137 Abbot Reynald was able to recover much support near Montecassino. Wibald of Stablo felt compelled to negotiate with Roger, who peremptorily replied that he would never recognize an abbot of the emperor's making, and that if he laid hands upon him he would hang him. Wibald took the hint and on 2 November returned to Germany.[49] Montecassino returned to Roger II's obedience; but at his hands, as at those of others of its neighbours, it was repeatedly to suffer serious losses of treasure and resources.[50] The Anacletan Schism and its consequences were a reminder to Montecassino of its vulnerability to political vicissitudes and of its need to have the goodwill of temporal powers as well as of the papacy. Yet the Schism left it out of sympathy with the papacy that emerged, without lasting benefit from Lothar's intervention, and vulnerable to the will of Roger II.

[46] *Chron. Cas.* iv. 119–24, pp. 593–600. Bernard of Clairvaux was present and took part in the proceedings.

[47] *MGH Dipl. LIII*, no. 120; *Chron. Cas.* iv. 125, pp. 600–1.

[48] Fulk of Benevento, *a.* 1139, pp. 245–6.

[49] *Chron. Cas.* iv. 127, pp. 603–4.

[50] Serious losses began when Abbot Nicholas of Tusculum allied himself to Count Robert of Capua: *Chron. Cas.* iv. 90, pp. 551–2. For depredations under Roger II, see *Ann. Cas., aa.* 1139, 1140, 1143, pp. 309–10; *Chron. Cas.* iv. 99, p. 561. See Leccisotti (as Introd. n. 23), pp. 186–7.

c. *Peter the Deacon*

Montecassino's early twelfth-century changes of fortune supply the backcloth for the career of its most significant literary figure of the century—Peter the Deacon. Peter engaged in ceaseless literary activity and produced more than eighty works, many of which survive in Montecassino, Archivio capitolare, MSS 257 and 361. With good reason he has been said to have had a pathological personality.[51] His overriding concerns were a self-centred desire to magnify his own importance and reputation, as well as those of Montecassino through the centuries. Wherever evidence was lacking he brought plentiful resources of fantasy and invention to fabricate a past that suited his designs. In one educated at Montecassino it is remarkable that he should apparently have never mastered the Beneventan script.[52]

Apart from his labours on the Montecassino Chronicle and the *Registrum Petri Diaconi*[53] Peter wrote much hagiography. Much of it dealt with the abbey's early days and is little more than a tissue of fantasy and invention.[54] Much of his work was derivative; for example, his *De locis sanctis* was a valueless rehash of Bede and of the *Peregrinatio Silviae*. His much more useful *De viris illustribus Cassiniensibus* was based upon Isidore of Seville, while his *De ortu et vita iustorum Cassinensis monasterii* set the tone of his hagiographical extravaganzas; he borrowed heavily from Leo of Ostia's work in the Chronicle and from Abbot Desiderius' *Dialogues*. He also wrote much theological, homiletic, and exegetical work. His writings contain little that is by any stretch of the imagination of spiritual or religious value.[55] In form and in substance alike his writings cast a melancholy light upon the state of the abbey whose leading literary figure he was.

The antecedents of his political loyalties are not easy to determine. As a young man his exile at Atina seems to have resulted from loyalty to Oderisius II, an old-fashioned figure whose outlook harked back to Montecassino's great days in the

[51] By H. Bloch, 'Peter the Deacon', *New Catholic Encyclopaedia*, xi. 216.

[52] Meyvaert (as Introd. n. 18).

[53] See above, pp. xix–xx.

[54] On these works, see Caspar, *Petrus Diaconus*, pp. 47–104, 128–48.

[55] e.g. the debate which Peter represented himself as conducting with an anonymous Cistercian (*monachus Cistellensis*) failed to go beneath the surface of monastic issues: *Altercatio pro cenobio Casinensi*, Caspar, *Petrus Diaconus*, pp. 263–78, *Chron. Cas.* iv. 113–14, pp. 586–8.

late eleventh century. But Peter disclosed no clear awareness of what was at stake in the Anacletan Schism, seeing nothing save his abbey's narrow advantage, to which all else was subordinated. However, the family of Tusculum to which he claimed to belong and with which he sought to be identified rallied to the Emperor Henry V in 1111 and 1117, as to Lothar in 1137.[56] In his writings Peter always showed himself susceptible to imperial ideas based upon Roman tradition. At Lagopesole he accorded Lothar every respect, and he claimed that the emperor wanted him for the imperial service;[57] it was his hand that drafted his imperial charter.[58] Peter stands as an extreme example of the deference to imperial authority which became an element of Cassinese life in the fourth decade of the twelfth century and which, as in his editing of the Montecassino Chronicle, Peter was anxious to read back into an earlier age. Judged by the best standards of Benedictine monasticism, Peter's career demonstrates how shallow-rooted and short-lived was Montecassino's monastic achievement during its golden age.

iii. POPE VICTOR III'S POSTHUMOUS REPUTATION AND IMAGE

It was before the years of serious crisis at Montecassino that Victor III's reputation at Rome came to be such that he found so prominent a place in the frescos of Pope Calixtus II's audience chamber in the Lateran Palace, and during the crisis that under the conservatively-minded Anacletus II he was depicted in the oratory of St. Nicholas as being fully within the succession of reforming popes.[59] It is not easy to trace through the events that have been sketched in this chapter the vicissitudes of Victor's reputation from his death in 1087 until he found so apparently secure a place in the iconography of reform. But it is clear that, at the outset, it owed much to Urban II's repeated insistence during his early years as pope that he followed in Victor's

[56] Hoffmann (as Introd. n. 13), pp. 33–4, 39; P. Partner, *The Lands of St. Peter* (London, 1972), 142–72.

[57] *Altercatio pro cenobio Cassinensi*, ed. Caspar, *Petrus Diaconus*, pp. 248–80, cf. pp. 183–7, *Chron. Cas.* iv. 97, 107–14, 125, pp. 558, 568–90, 600.

[58] *MGH Dipl. LIII*, no. 120; cf. Caspar, pp. 187–94, 239–47. Peter also dedicated to Lothar his *Expositio in Regulam sancti Benedicti* (as Ch. I n. 123); Meyvaert (as Ch. I n. 123), pp. 130–48.

[59] See above, pp. xii–xiii.

steps no less than in Gregory VII's.[60] There is little evidence for the further development of his reputation either at Rome or at Montecassino until the writing of the accounts of his pontificate that are included in the Montecassino Chronicle. They are exceedingly difficult to date with any degree of accuracy. But the fabrication of Victor's bellicose allocution to the council of Benevento, which perhaps dates from the late 1090s, shows how he was by then being built up at Montecassino as an extreme opponent of the Guibertine cause.[61] A similar tendency is apparent in the long passages which display Victor in conflict with the antipope Clement III as St. Peter had striven with Simon Magus.[62] The propagandists at Montecassino made their borrowings from Deusdedit's *Adversus symoniacos* at a sufficient distance from the cardinal to have misunderstood his treatment of Victor's pontificate.[63] In view of the strongly anti-Guibertine and anti-imperial tone of this material, it might be tempting to assign it to the abbacy of Bruno of Segni, the old-guard Gregorian who resisted Pope Paschal II for his capitulation of 1111 to the Emperor Henry V. Bruno's own position is made clear by four letters which he wrote in or about February 1111, and in which he roundly condemned Guibert as a heresiarch who was rightly banished with his followers from the church.[64] He and Henry IV were enmeshed in the 'heresy' of investiture, so that his establishment as antipope was a work of the devil.[65] But there is good reason for not accepting the hypothesis of Bruno's influence in accentuating Victor's posthumous reputation as a Gregorian. He omitted Victor's name from his enumeration of recent popes in whose tradition he was persisting;[66] it was almost as if he wished to set himself at a distance from him. Uncharacteristically of Cassinese writers, he laid emphasis in his letters upon the fact that catholics and Guibertines execrated simony alike and in similar terms; only with regard to investiture was there an unbridgeable difference

60 See above, pp. 216–17.

61 *Chron. Cas.* iii. 72, pp. 453–5.

62 Ibid. iii. 70, p. 452.

63 See below, Appendix VIII.

64 As Ch. V n. 28. The first two letters, to Cardinal-bishop Peter of Porto and to Pope Paschal II, are copied into early folios of Montecassino, Archivio capitolare, MS 522, for which see above, p. 95.

65 *Epp.* 1, 3, 4.

66 'Et ego quidem quod dixi hoc dico et in Gregorii et Urbani sententia firmissime maneo': *Ep.* 3.

between them.[67] Upon this issue alone did Guibertines represent the servitude of the church, but catholics its liberty.[68] Nor did Bruno in his other works condemn simony in terms of the legends about Simon Magus upon which Deusdedit and Cassinese writers alike drew in their presentation of Victor III.[69]

Accordingly, it is impossible to say more than that, at Montecassino, the material incorporated in the Chronicle as it now stands appears to represent the standpoint with regard to Victor as pope of at least a party of the monks at the turn of the eleventh and twelfth centuries. At Rome during the second decade of the twelfth century, as in the writings of Bruno of Segni, Victor III tended to drop out as a link between Gregory VII and Urban II.[70] The Lateran frescos, and especially Anacletus', therefore seem to mark a revival of his reputation there. Its motive was perhaps to provide a counterweight to ideas characteristic of the newer religious orders. As they appealed to the life of the primitive church and of the early days of Christian monasticism, so the Anacletans sought to show the identity of the reform popes with their namesakes of an earlier age, and to exhibit the recent history of the papacy as a genuine *renovatio* of its models. Urban II's evaluation of Victor thus came into its own once more.

[67] 'Haec autem heresis, quae est de investitura, ideo Guiberti et Enrici specialiter esse dicitur, quoniam ad hoc Guibertus ab Enrico rege, immo ab ipso diabolo, papa ordinatus est, ut rex per eum optinere potuisset quod sibi a parentibus suis relictum esse dicebat, investituram scilicet et aecclesiarum ordinationes. Hoc enim erat quod ipse quaerebat, hoc erat quod per Guibertum se obtinere sperabat, hoc erat in quo ipsi a nobis maxime differebant. In aliis enim non multum a nobis differre videbantur. Dampnabant enim et ipsi symonaicos, et alia vitia aspernabantur, sicut et nos': *Ep.* 4, cf. *Ep.* 2.

[68] 'Sed ipsi servitutem, nos aecclesiae libertatem quaerebamus': *Ep.* 4.

[69] See Bruno's discussions in his *Libellus de symonaicis*, ed. E. Sackur, *MGH Libelli*, ii. 543–62.

[70] See the *Gesta dampnationis pravilegii* and the *Breviarium gestorum* of the Lateran council of 1112: *MGH Const.* i. 571–3, nos. 399, 400.

VI
Conclusion

UPON such an interpretation of the Lateran frescos, it may be concluded that, if the assessment of the career of Desiderius of Montecassino as abbot and as pope which has been given is basically correct, he was by no means undeserving of a place in their iconography. Their propaganda was tendentious; but it was an exaggeration rather than an invention or a radical distortion of Desiderius' words and deeds over a lifetime during which his work at Montecassino and at Rome was of a piece, and must be appraised accordingly.

The cardinal fact about Montecassino in its golden age is that, to a remarkable degree, it was in a position to determine its own way of life and pattern of external associations. The monastic revival which gathered strength there between the reigns of Abbots Aligernus and Richer, but which was at its height under Abbot Desiderius with results lasting into the early twelfth century, made it the outstanding ecclesiastical institution in Italy to the south of Rome. When Desiderius extended the *terra sancti Benedicti* so that it reached the sea, when he rebuilt and enriched the abbey itself, and when it became a community of some two hundred monks, many of whom were outstanding for their learning and practical skills, both Lombards and Normans looked to it for the satisfaction of their religious aspirations. After the alliance with the Norman princes that Desiderius lost no time in concluding, Montecassino found in them, and particularly in Robert Guiscard, guarantors and protectors upon whom it could normally rely.

As it built up its material and political position and enlarged its capacity to perform with exceptional impressiveness the round of monastic observance, work, and hospitality, it also promoted the search for religious renewal that was being widely extended in contemporary Italian society. It sought to encourage and nourish the Christian life in other monasteries, and no less in a large number of urban and rural churches. It strove against the contemporary abuses of simony and of clerical and lay unchastity. By fostering the observance of canon law in local churches it sought to promote an ordered, observant, and pastorally effective ecclesiastical life. In all this it acted without the direct or continual guidance of papal Rome, but was caught up in the resurgence of local church life, both monastic and secular, that characterized all parts of Italy during the eleventh century.

Nevertheless, as Abbot Desiderius' *Dialogues* illustrate, at Montecassino as elsewhere the pontificate of Leo IX was and remained epoch-making as itself a fountain-head of renewal and reform which demonstrated its revitalizing power at Rome and in other parts of Western Christendom. Leo left to the church an indelible memory of a uniquely vigorous and saintly pope who could draw together the objectives of the apostolic see and the zeal of its friends, both near and far. In Desiderius' time, Montecassino showed a capacity to develop and to extend its horizons, particularly in the area of canon law, where it seems to have progressed from codes of local and pastoral significance, through the conservative and rigid ideas of the *Diversorum patrum sententiae*, until it showed affinity with the stringent opposition to royal power over the church and the emphasis upon papal prerogatives of the *Collectio canonum* that Deusdedit dedicated to Desiderius as Pope Victor III. The Guibertine Schism, and especially its hardening between 1084 and 1100, compelled all who were thus minded to take a stand for the papacy as Gregory VII left it. When the evidence for Desiderius' election and conduct as pope is set in order and understood in the light of Montecassino's tendency since the late 1070s to grow towards the Gregorian papacy so long as it could carry the Normans of South Italy with it, there are good reasons for concluding that, although Desiderius in his last years was probably a sick man, he was willing and able to be first Gregory VII's executor and then his successor in the difficult circumstances that followed his death at Salerno. In the brief four months of his full exercise of papal power his activity was constructive and considerable.

If the standard of conformity to the aims and interests of the reform papacy by which Montecassino and Abbot Desiderius are to be judged were that of a cut-and-dried papal reform programme or series of programmes formulated and imposed from above, it would perhaps still be difficult to make them fit convincingly. But as Deusdedit's *Collectio canonum* serves to illustrate, 'Gregorian' aims and ideas themselves developed late and often tentatively, while there were sharp conflicts of view even among those at Rome who remained loyal to Gregory VII; it is tempting to say of Gregory and his partisans, *tot homines quot sententiae*. The institutions of the reform papacy were no less slow than its ideas to assume definitive shape, and until the Guibertine Schism their development was retarded. Under the early reform popes and again from *c.*1078, Montecassino's contribution to the papal service was far from negligible. But it was during the crisis years of 1084–7 that Desiderius was able to bring some of the energy and resourcefulness that he had devoted to building up Montecassino and extending its influence in South Italy, to the service of the beleaguered papacy itself; and he was also able gradually to win a considerable amount of political support for what he did. Under Urban II and Paschal II Cassinese monks were again recruited for tasks at Rome.

As the eventual successor of Gregory VII Desiderius/Victor seemed to many, both friend and foe, to be indeed his heir. By beginning where he left off, Urban II was able at length to rehabilitate the fortunes of the Gregorian papacy, and in his great endeavour of the First Crusade he had assistance from Abbot Oderisius I.

Although writers of the 1090s and afterwards exaggerated when they built up Desiderius/Victor as a strenuous and extreme Gregorian in his opposition to the antipope Clement III, so that a legend about him developed which could verge upon the grotesque, the records of his pontificate show that there was a basis of truth in what they wrote. Apart from the brevity of his reign, however, two considerations ensured that his deeds could not serve fully to establish him as a reforming figure with the stature in the papal office of either Gregory VII or Urban II. First, in retrospect, over a long lifetime he had never failed to prefer the interests of Montecassino whenever they had conflicted with those of the reform papacy, to which he had rallied only when they converged; and he retained to the end his habits of prudence and realism. Secondly, with regard to the brief duration of Montecassino's golden age and its eclipse in the years when Peter the Deacon stands as its representative figure, Montecassino under Desiderius failed to underpin its cultural and material wealth with the firm hold upon the spiritual and moral commitment to the Rule of St. Benedict which alone can give a monastic epoch or movement full credibility, if it stands within the Benedictine tradition.[1] In the years 1084–7 the Montecassino of Desiderius came to the reform papacy's rescue in its hour of direst need; and, as Pope Victor III, Desiderius was a genuine link between Gregory and Urban. But in the longer term Montecassino and its abbots could not offer the papacy the spiritual wisdom or the clarity of vision and purpose that might have helped to avoid the Anacletan Schism and the gradual attrition which led by 1130 to the end of the papal reform in its 'Gregorian' guise. It was Anacletus II, not Innocent II, who in the Lateran frescos finally and most graphically exhibited Desiderius/Victor as a hero of the papal reform. But it was Innocent and his party, not the Anacletans, who read aright the signs of the times through which they were living and to whom the future belonged. With the end of the reform papacy as it had emerged in the eleventh century the age of Abbot Desiderius of Montecassino was finally over.

[1] In venturing such a judgement an English historian cannot be unmindful of the final paragraph of Dom David Knowles, *The Religious Orders in England*, iii. *The Tudor Age* (Cambridge, 1959), 468.

Appendix I

Archbishop Guibert of Ravenna's Accession as the Antipope Clement III

SOURCES nearest in time to the events indicate that in 1080 Guibert's election at Brixen was played down as much as possible. His effective acclamation and enthronement as pope took place at Rome in 1084. It was not until this juncture that he assumed the title Clement III.

(i) *Evidence of official documents of, or closely associated with, Henry IV himself.* (*a*) Henry's diploma of 26 June 1080, i.e. of the day after the proceedings at Brixen, confirming the possessions of the church of Ravenna, was addressed 'Domno Uvigberto sanctae praedictae aecclesiae venerabili archiepiscopo nobisque dilectissimo et summae sedis electo apostolico': *MGH Dipl. HIV*, no. 322. (*b*) The Romans' oath to Henry in 1083 said that if he came to Rome within the time agreed the Romans would make Gregory crown him emperor; if through Gregory's fault this did not happen, 'nos papam eligemus cum tuo consilio secundum canones': below, Appendix V. (*c*) In his letter to Bishop Thierry of Verdun about events at Rome in 1084 Henry said: 'Quem Hildebrandum legali omnium cardinalium ac totius populi Romani iudicio scias abiectum, et electum papam nostrum Clementem in sede apostolica sublimatum omnium Romanorum acclamatione': *Ep.* 18, ed. Erdmann, *Ausgew. Quell.* xii. 84.

(ii) *Documents of Guibert as archbishop of Ravenna and as antipope.* Up to 24 March 1084 Guibert does not appear to have used the title Clement III. (*a*) In 1081 he began a charter for the church of Ravenna with the words 'Vuibertus servus servorum Dei sanctae Ravennatis ecclesiae archiepiscopus', and subscribed it 'Eg. Vui. Dei gratia Ravennas archiepiscopus'; Rubeus (as Ch. III, n. 199), pp. 307–8. (*b*) His confirmation of the possessions and privileges of the canons of Verona dated 2 March 1084 by JL 5319 is of later date: *Ep.* 1, Migne, *PL* cxlviii. 827–8; Köhncke, *Wibert*, p. 56. (*c*) After 24 March 1084 Clement used the style 'Clemens episcopus servus servorum Dei': for early examples, see Migne, *PL* cxlviii. 827–42; Morini and Soulier (as Ch. III, n. 217), pp. 191 ff. (not seen, but listed in *IP* i. 76, nos. 15–17; Rubeus, op. cit. 310–12). The phrase 'Clemens ego tertius presul Romanus' occurs in a letter of ? 1089 to Abbot Libo of Seltz dated in Clement's fourth year: P. Ewald, 'Acht päpstliche Priviligien', *NA* ii (1877), 219–20; on which see JL 5326. (*d*) A considerable number of charters from Ravenna between 1080 and 100 present a similar picture: *Monumenti Ravennati de' secoli di mezzo*, ed. M. Fantuzzi (Venice, 1802), xliv–xlv, pp. 91–3, and in the summaries that follow, cxxxvi. 16–20, p. 254, cxxxix. 1, p. 289, cxxxxii. 30–5, p. 312, cxxxxiii. 19, p. 332, cxxxxiv. 15, p. 345, cxxxxvi. 21–3, pp. 357–8, cxxxxviii. 60–2, p. 371, cxxxxix. 27, p. 383, clv. 14–16, p. 419.

(iii) *Evidence from the imperial abbey of Farfa*: Material in the *Liber largitorius vel notarius monasterii Pharphensis*, ed. G. Zucchetti, ii, Regesta chartarum Italiae (Rome, 1932), suggests that (*a*) it remained customary after 1080 to date charters in which a pope was named 'temporibus Gregorii VII papae': nos. 1213-16, cf. *Chronicon Farfense di Gregorio di Catino*, ed. U. Balzani, *Fonti stor. Italia*, xxxiii-xxxiv, ii. 92. No. 1217 (December 1080) is dated 'temporibus Clementis III papae', but the reference to Henry IV as *imperator* raises doubt about the dating clause; the opening reference to Clement III in no. 1218 (23 February 1084) may be editorial. But (*b*) from Guibert's enthronement at Rome the phrase 'temporibus Clementis III papae' is frequent in nos. 1219-1327. A number of Farfa's charters refer to 1084 as Clement's first year: *Il Regesto di Farfa* (as Ch. IV n. 60), pp. 92-3, 100, 104, 106-8, nos. 1097, 1100, 1104, 1106, 1107.

(iv) *Chronicles.* (*a*) The *Annales Augustani* record that in 1080 Guibert of Ravenna was set up (*superponitur*) against the excommunicate Gregory VII, whom German and Italian bishops had presumptuously repudiated. In 1083 Henry entered Rome and established in the apostolic see Guibert, who had been *dudum superpositum.* In 1084 the Romans at length unjustly rejected Gregory and installed Guibert, who was again described as *superpositum.*[1] He was given the name Clement (*Clementis nomine imposito*): *MGH SS* iii. 130-1. (*b*) Frutolf of Michaelsberg wrote that, at Brixen, a meeting of bishops and magnates adjudged that, although he was absent, Gregory should be expelled from the apostolic see. They chose Guibert to replace him. In 1084 Roman envoys asked Henry to return to Rome. Because Hildebrand, whom the Romans rejected, had fled, he brought Guibert into the city. Guibert received the papal office from many bishops and took the name Clement; he was then enthroned: *aa.* 1080, 1084, pp. 96-8. (*c*) The *Annales Yburgenses* record that Henry expelled Hildebrand and set up Guibert of Ravenna in his place *electione cunctorum*, and that 'mox consecratus, Clemens est nominatus': *a.* 1084, *MGH SS* xvi. 438. (*d*) Benzo of Alba said that on 24 March 1084 Henry 'imposuit ei nomen Clemens': Prol., *MGH SS* xi. 669. (*e*) The *Breve Chronicon Northmannicum* records that Henry 'constituerat Papam Guibertum archiepiscopum Ravennatensem, et fecit schisma in Ecclesia': *c.*1084, Cuozzo (as Ch. III n. 104), p. 172.

(v) *Polemical literature*: The nearly contemporary *Dicta cuiusdam de discordia papae et regis* (Brussels MS) state that in 1084 Henry IV '. . . iuxta maiorum consuetudinem Clementem, Ravennatis prius episcopum . . . papam constituit et de manu eius coronam imperialem . . . suscepit': *MGH Libelli*, i. 460.

For fuller surveys of the evidence, see Köhncke, *Wibert*, pp. 38-41, Sander; *Der Kampf*, pp. 21-4; and Meyer von Knonau, *Jahrbücher*, iii. 286-301.

[1] The verb *superponere* is used of Henry's elevation of Guibert in his letter of 1106 to King Philip I of France: *Ep.* 39, ed. Erdmann, *Ausgew. Quell.* xii. 122-31, at 128, line 32.

Appendix II

The Oppenheim *Promissio*

HENRY IV's Manifesto of 1082 (*Ep.* 17, ed. Erdmann, *Ausgew. Quell.* xii. 76-82) recalls in substance and in vocabulary the full text of the so-called Oppenheim *Promissio* of October 1076: Anhang B, ibid. 474-6. It has for long been a matter of scholarly debate whether the full text of the *Promissio* was as prepared in the negotiations between the king and the princes at Tribur-Oppenheim, or whether Henry later added the last sentence: for the debate, see especially the studies by A. Brackmann, C. Erdmann, and J. Haller, in *Canossa als Wende*, ed. H. Kämpf, Wege der Forschung, 12 (Darmstadt, 1963). It should be remembered that the text of the *Promissio* survives only in letter-collections: Hanover, Niedersächsische Landesbibliothek, MS XI. 671, sixteenth century, and two twelfth-century MSS of the Codex Udalrici, Zwettl, Stiftsarchiv, 283, and Vienna, Österreichische Nationalbibliothek, 398. The resolution of questions about the *Promissio*'s date and integrity must therefore be settled in terms of internal evidence and historical probability. Whereas there is no reason to doubt that the two opening sentences of the *Promissio* were drafted at Tribur-Oppenheim, it has always been difficult to reconcile the accusing tone in which the pope is addressed in the final sentence with Henry's abject position at that juncture, or with the course of events which culminated at Canossa. But the proposal of a mutual exculpation by pope and king would arise naturally from Henry's stronger position in 1082. Moreover, the parallels of language, argument, and motive between the final sentence of the *Promissio* and the Manifesto of 1082 are striking:

Promissio	Manifesto
Condecet autem et sanctitatem tuam ea, que de te vulgata scandalum ecclesię pariunt, non dissimulare, sed remoto a publica conscientia et hoc scrupulo, universalem tam ecclesię quam regni tranquillitatem per tuam sapientiam stabiliri (p. 476, lines 7-10).	Pro hac erumna compescenda sepius vocavit eum ęcclesia, ut de imposito sibi crimine se purgaret et ęcclesiam de scandalo liberaret (p. 78, lines 20-1). Non pudeat illum pro communi omnium fidelium auferendo scandalo humiliari, quorum communi obędientia debet exaltari. . . . Ecce pusilli et magni de eius scandalo clamant, et ut auferatur ab eis, rogant (p. 80, line 32-p. 82, line 4).

Furthermore, the idea of ending through mutual concessions the discord between church and kingdom had already been canvassed at the end of Henry's Manifesto of 1081:

> . . . hęc nostra omnino voluntas et sententia est, ut vos, quod in nobis est, pacifice invisamus ac deinde, collato omnium vestrum in primis aliorumque fidelium nostrorum consilio, diuturna discordia regni et sacerdotii de medio tollatur et omnia ad pacem et unitatem in Christi nomine revocentur (*Ep.* 16, *Ausgew. Quell.* xii. 76, lines 12–17).

The extended text of the *Promissio* makes excellent sense as a royal propaganda document of 1082, when the king or his followers may have added a final clause to the text which had opened the way to Canossa. Its intention would have been to remind Gregory of his former reconciliation to Henry and to advertise it to the Roman people as a precedent, while taking account of the king's own stronger position at the head of his army outside the gates of Rome. As such it is a logical sequel to the Manifesto of 1081 and a companion-piece to that of 1082. The latter year provides a likely *Sitz im Leben* for it.

It is at least deserving of consideration as possibly yet another broadsheet, like those edited below, Appendices V and VI, of an age which was prolific of such documents.

Appendix III

Evidence for a Continuous Source underlying Parts of the Continuation of the Montecassino Chronicle

CERTAIN chapters of the Continuation of the Montecassino Chronicle show similarities of vocabulary and outlook, and also a continuity of theme, which indicate that they may have formed part of a continuous source that Guido used. Unfortunately, the chapters in question begin at a point where the sole early MS—Montecassino, Archivio capitolare, 450—lacks a folio: see Hoffmann (as Introd. n. 11), p. 142. However the lost material can in part be supplied from humanist revisions of the second-recension text by Ambrogio Traversari (who probably worked on it between 1429 and 1453) and Agostino Patrizi (working *c.* 1470/80), and the printed edition of Matthaeus Lauretus Hispanus, *Chronicon antiquum sacri monasterii Casinensis* (Naples, 1616): *MGH SS* xxxiv, pp. xxxii–xxxiii, 426–30.

The attempt to reconstruct a source must take into account the following chapters:

(i) The material common to Traversari, Lauretus, and Patrizi, in iii. 49, pp. 428–9: the genesis of the quarrel between Gregory VII and Henry IV (1076–81).

(ii) The material common to Traversari and Lauretus in iii. 50, p. 430, except the opening sentence, which concerns the year 1083. The words *Hoc audito* introduce a different narrative, and material in common between p. 430, lines 9–10, 23–24, and the resumption of the text of MS 450 on p. 431, lines 1–2, shows that the narrative continues for the remainder of iii. 50, pp. 431–3, save that p. 432, line 33–p. 433, line 1, and p. 433, lines 27–9, may be later interpolations of Peter the Deacon: see below, Appendix IV. The whole of this material concerns Henry IV's Italian expedition of 1082.

(iii) The first sentence of the material common to Traversari and Lauretus, and the excerpt from Patrizi, in iii. 50, p. 430: Henry's Italian expedition of 1083.

(iv) iii. 53, pp. 434–5: Henry IV's Italian dealings of 1084, with no reference to Guibert's installation as antipope or to Henry's imperial coronation, but with a notice of Gregory's departure from Rome and death in 1085.

(v) iii. 66, pp. 448–9: Desiderius's election at Rome as Pope Victor III (April–May 1086), after a year during which the apostolic see lacked a pastor.

(vi) iii. 68–9, pp. 450–2, with the probable exception of p. 450, line 33–p. 451, line 1, and p. 451, line 33–p. 452, line 6: Victor III accepts his election as pope and is installed at Rome (March–June 1087).

(vii) iii. 72, p. 453, lines 1–3: Victor III returns to Montecassino (summer 1087).

(viii) iv. 2, pp. 467–8: the election of Urban II at Terracina (March 1088).

As thus arranged, these chapters tell a broadly but not completely continuous story, and they bear the imprint of a clear and positive interpretation of persons and events. So far as the texts of Traversari and Lauretus make a judgement possible, the beginning of the antagonism between pope and emperor—a title here consistently given to Henry—lay in the events of 1076 and 1077, during which Henry made his momentous journey to Italy and Canossa; the story proceeds to take in the events of 1080. There follows a consecutive treatment of Henry's further Italian expeditions of 1081, 1082, and 1083–4. The account of 1082 highlights, through Desiderius' debate with Cardinal Odo of Ostia, an extreme view of the liberty of the apostolic see and of a papal election; it also uses Desiderius to exhibit Guibert of Ravenna in an unfavourable light. A feature of the treatment of the events of 1084 is the almost complete passing over of the devastation at Rome caused by Robert Guiscard's Normans. It goes on to represent Gregory as having thereafter been supported by Montecassino rather than by the Normans, right up to the time of his death:

> [Robert Guiscard] papam Gregorium ad hoc monasterium usque deduxit; quem apostolicum noster abbas usque ad ipsius exitum cum episcopis et cardinalibus, qui eum secuti fuerant, sustentavit (ii. 53, p. 435).

Such a presentation of events recurs, in similar language, in the narrative of 1086, when the electors

> quesierunt ab eo [Desiderius], ut ipsum pontificem, quem eligerent, in Casinensi monasterio reciperet eumque, donec ecclesia tranquillaretur, cum suis omnibus sustentaret, sicut et de supradicto papa Gregorio fecerat (iii. 66, p. 449).

The source as a whole takes a distinctive view of Desiderius' election to the papacy (cf. above, pp. 194–7, 201–4). In 1086 he was definitively elected pope at Rome and thereupon took the name Victor. The election procedure depended on the clergy and people of Rome, and Desiderius was elected against his will. Only at Capua in March 1087 did he himself accept election. Thereafter he returned by way of Montecassino to Rome. After a military campaign by Countess Matilda of Tuscany's forces he was able to evict Guibert from St. Peter's and to celebrate mass there on 1 July. If the account of Urban II's election at Terracina (iv. 2, pp. 467–9) also draws in part upon this source, it goes on to show how Urban, too, was elected in face of exceptional difficulties in a way that satisfied the claims and rights of the Roman church. The whole body of material has coherence as if drawn from a tract concerning the Emperor Henry IV's attacks on the Roman church and the manner of electing a Roman pontiff.

Other features also stand out. The first is a distinctive treatment of many of the leading figures in the ecclesiastical politics of the 1080s. Abbot Desiderius is exhibited as a strong, active, diplomatic, and resourceful leader. He was courageous in defending Montecassino before Henry IV, whose extremer demands for fealty he *forti animo contempnebat.* He resisted Cardinal Odo of Ostia to the face on the issue of imperial intervention in papal elections, and on the same issue he reduced Guibert of Ravenna to making the weakest of excuses (iii. 50, pp. 431–3). More than once he performed the role of intermediary between pope and emperor (iii. 50, 53, pp. 431, 435). In 1086 his refusal to accept election was not the result of personal weakness but of commitment to his monastic vocation and of sound political judgement (iii. 66, cf. above, pp. 195–7). Once he had accepted his election at Capua, despite his sickness he was the brave and triumphant leader of his cause—'pro sancte utilitate ecclesie omnibus se disposuerat vel extremis periculis obiectare'. On 1 July 1087 he celebrated mass in St. Peter's (iii. 68–9, pp. 450–1). Guibert of Ravenna, on the other hand, was made to look by comparison craven and defenceless (iii. 50, p. 433). Ignored by the source in 1084 (iii. 53, pp. 434–5), he was thereafter always *Guibertus eresiarcha* (iii. 66, 68–9, pp. 448, 450–1). For Odo of Ostia, whether as cardinal or as Pope Urban II, this source held no brief. In debate with Desiderius about papal elections he was temporizing as a supporter of Gregory VII—'qui etiam pape Gregorio favere videbatur'—and Desiderius 'tam illum quam omnes qui eum adiuvabant, palam convicit' (iii. 50, p. 433). When Desiderius first put forward his name for the papacy he received a word of praise (iii. 66, p. 449), but when Desiderius/Victor III went to Rome in 1087 he was mentioned only as his consecrator (iii. 68, p. 450). Even in the account of his own election at Terracina Odo was not personally commended as a churchman (iv. 2, pp. 467–8).

As regards the Normans, Robert Guiscard and Jordan of Capua were neither accorded prominence nor were they in any way unfavourably displayed. In 1084 Robert Guiscard was a deliberate and resolute defender of Gregory VII, although he was not said to have brought him to Salerno; Robert was, however, tacitly exonerated from responsibility for the sacking of Rome (iii. 53, pp. 434–5). His son's ambiguous political behaviour in 1086 (see above, pp. 193–4) was not alluded to. Similarly, Jordan's submission to Henry IV in 1082 was disguised beneath a general reference to *Normanni* (iii. 50, see above, pp. 154–5). Like Roger of Apulia, Jordan was not mentioned in connection with the events of 1086. In 1087 the two Norman leaders were involved at Capua but not in a prominent way (iii. 68, p. 450). Lay Norman attitudes to Urban II's election were wholly ignored. The extent to which the Normans were a factor in papal politics between 1084 and 1088 was throughout disguised or minimized.

Countess Matilda of Tuscany's part in events was acknowledged. She was active in Gregory's service at Canossa (iii. 49, p. 428). Her forces gave Victor III strong support at Rome in 1087 (iii. 69, p. 451), and she was among the promoters of Urban II's election in 1088 (iv. 2, pp. 467–8). Cencius I Frangipani, *consul Romanorum*, was accorded a prominent position in the leadership of the Roman party: in 1084 he proposed to Robert Guiscard the stratagem of lighting a fire at Rome (iii. 53, p. 435); in 1086 he counselled Desiderius to propose Odo of Ostia as a papal candidate (iii. 66, p. 449); and in 1087 he was prominent at the council of Capua

(iii. 68, p. 450). Prince Gisulf of Salerno was also highlighted as a leader of the Roman party: he helped to initiate discussion of the papacy in 1086 (iii. 66, p. 448), and in 1087 Jordan of Capua and he led Victor III to Rome (iii. 68, p. 450).

Congruously with such a depiction of Cencius and Gisulf, this source throughout gave prominence to the Roman *episcopi et cardinales* and laity, especially to those Gregorian elements that remained at Rome in 1084. Only some of the *episcopi et cardinales* followed Gregory to Montecassino (iii. 53, p. 435). It was those who had not gone with him who assembled at Rome in 1086 and initiated the new papal election that took place there (iii. 66, pp. 448–9). In 1087 a specifically Roman element was present at Capua; when Countess Matilda established herself at Rome she with *ceteris beati Petri fidelibus* there received Victor III (iii. 68–9, pp. 450–1). The record of Urban II's election at Terracina opened very similarly to Victor's at Rome, as if it were intended to underline their comparability and authenticity:

1086 (iii. 66, p. 448)

Iam fere annus in tali fluctuatione transierat, quo in apostolica sede nullus pastor erat . . . cum circa paschalem festivitatem *episcopi et cardinales Romane ecclesie de diversis partibus Romam convenientes* mandaverunt predicto abbati, ut unacum episcopis et cardinalibus Romanis, qui secum tunc morabantur, et cum Gisulfo Salernitano principe . . . ad eos quantocius pergerent, *quatinus de Romane ecclesie ordinatione simul tractarent.*

1088 (iv. 2, p. 467)

Predictis igitur episcopis circumquaque dispersis rursus frequentes nuntii crebrique legati tam Romanorum quam ultramontanorum et comitisse Matilde ad eosdem episcopos transmissi hortabantur pariter atque rogabant, *ut de Romane ecclesie ordinatione studerent, ut in unum convenientes* caput facere christianitati satagerent, . . . *facile et in proximo casuram et confundendam ecclesiam, nisi pastorem haberet.* Tandem itaque rursum undique coadunati unacum nostro abbate Oderisio miserunt litteras Romanis clericis et laicis sancti Petri fidelibus ut, quotquot ex eis possent, prima ebdomada quadragesime Terracinam venirent . . .

As in 1086 at about Easter bishops and cardinals of the Roman church asked Abbot Desiderius to come to them at Rome, bringing the Roman bishops and cardinals who were with him and with Prince Gisulf, 'quatinus de Romane ecclesie ordinatione simul tractarent', so in 1088, 'ut de Romane ecclesie ordinatione studerent', the bishops together with Abbot Oderisius sent letters to the Roman clergy and laity summoning them to Terracina in the first week of Lent. The bishops of Porto, Tusculum, and Albano were *caput eiusdem concilii* in approving the election of the bishop of Ostia; in 1087 the bishops of Ostia, Tusculum, Porto, and Albano had taken the lead in consecrating Victor III at Rome (iii. 68, iv. 2, pp. 450, 468).

A second characteristic of the source under discussion is its secure and detailed grasp of the topography of Rome and its environs. So far as the regions of the city are concerned, it contains references to the *porticus sancti Petri* (the Leonine city) (iii. 50, 68, pp. 430, 450), the *insula Rome* (the Isola Tibertina) (iii. 69, p. 451), and to Trastevere (ibid.). It mentions the *arx* (or *castellum*) *sancti Angeli* (iii. 53, 69, pp. 434-5, 451). Amongst churches, besides St. Peter's (iii. 68-9, pp. 450-1) there appear the *diaconia sancte Lucie, que est iusta Septesolis* (Santa Lucia near the Septizonium) (iii. 66, pp. 448-9), Santi Quattuor Coronati (iii. 53, p. 435), and Santa Maria *in turribus* (iii. 69, p. 451). In Rome's environs there are named Albano (iii. 50, p. 432), Ostia (iii. 68-9, pp. 450-1), Porto (iii. 69, p. 451), Civita Castellana (iii. 53, p. 435), and—further away—Farfa (iii. 50, p. 431). At Terracina it was noticed that the cathedral was dedicated to St. Peter and St. Cesarius (iv. 2, p. 468), and Canossa was a *munitissima arx* (iii. 49, p. 428). Victor's consecration of the church of San Nicola in Pica was recorded (iii. 72, p. 453).

Thirdly, this source reflects views similar to those propounded by Cardinal Deusdedit in his *Coll. can.* and *Libellus.* (In this respect it is comparable to material in *Chron. Cas.* iii. 70, 72, pp. 452-5, on which see below, Appendix VIII.) Both at iii. 50, p. 433, where Desiderius insisted as against Cardinal Odo of Ostia that 'nec umquam debet a nobis hoc aliquatenus consentiri, nec Deo volente amplius fiet, ut rex Alemannorum papam constituat Romanorum', and in the accounts of Victor III's and Urban II's elections, it is in line with Deusdedit's prescriptions for papal elections (see above, pp. 188-90). Desiderius' root-and-branch hostility to the Election Decree of 1059 recalls Deusdedit's dismissal of it as 'novam ordinationem . . . in qua quam nefanda quam Deo inimica statuerunt, horreo scribere' (see above, Ch. III n. 173) and his only less vituperative treatment in *Libellus* i. 5-13, pp. 303-13, where 'patet prefatum decretum nullius momenti esse nec umquam aliquid virium habuisse (p. 311). So, too, the *Coll. can.* required the elimination of the lay power in papal elections: i. 169 (138), p. 107, 320 (244), ii. 162, iv. 13 (12), 18-19, 22 (16-17, 20), pp. 107, 187, 268, 406, 409-10. Whether or not the author of the source owed a direct debt to Deusdedit, the comparability of their attitudes to the principles and practice of papal elections is clear. So, too, Desiderius' profession of immovability before wrongful demands —'Potest quidem imperator ad tempus, si tamen permiserit Deus, prevalere et vim ecclesiastice iustitie inferre, nostrum tamen consensum ad hoc numquam poterit inclinare' (iii. 50, p. 433)—is in line with Deusdedit's injunction that ecclesiastical rulers should be steadfast under persecution: *Coll. can.* iv. 198 (116), 214 (122), pp. 499-505, 515-18.

What may be inferred about the authorship and date of Guido's putative source? It was certainly the work of a Cassinese monk: Desiderius is *pater Desiderius* (iii. 50, p. 431), and both he and Oderisius I are referred to as *noster abbas* (iii. 53, iv. 2, pp. 435, 467). He seems to have been writing at Montecassino—*ad hoc monasterium* (iii. 53, 68, pp. 435, 451). He knew Rome very well, but was writing late enough—and also sufficiently far from Rome—for his playing down of the Norman sack of the city to have plausbility. But he wrote before Guido's work on the

Continuation of the Chronicle, in which his tract was used as one of several sources (see, e.g., below, Appendix VII). It is tempting to suggest as a possible author the elder Alberic (see above, pp. 24, 73), who died at some time before 1105. The Montecassino Chronicle lists among his writings (iii. 35, p. 411) a lost *Contra Heinricum imperatorem De electione Romani pontificis* (*sic*; in his edition Hoffman notes an apparently erased point after *imperatorem*). This title would well describe the source under discussion. Alberic spent much of his life at Montecassino, but he also knew Rome, where he was in 1078/9 (see above, pp. 94–5). If Peter the Deacon is correct in recording his burial 'in urbe Roma iuxta ecclesiam Sanctorum Quattuor Coronatorum' (*DVI*, cap. 21, Migne, *PL* clxxiii. 1033), he ended his life there. If the Guido to whom he dedicated part of his *Breviarium de dictamine* (as Ch. I n. 105), p. 29, was, as seems likely, Leo of Ostia's continuator, Alberic and Guido were associated fairly closely. Yet beyond suitability there is no evidence for associating the source with Alberic. A firm attribution to him cannot be made, although it is an interesting possibility.

Appendix IV

Henry IV's Supposed Diplomas of 1082 for Prince Jordan of Capua and for Montecassino

ACCORDING to *Chron. Cas.* iii. 50, pp. 432–3, which forms part of the putative source discussed above in Appendix III, in 1082 Henry IV gave diplomas to Prince Jordan of Capua and Abbot Desiderius of Montecassino:

> Post hec imperator accepto a principe magno quantitatis pretio per preceptum aurea bulla bullatum confirmavit totius Capuani principatus attinentias retento sibi et imperio monasterio Casinense cum universis rebus ac pertinentiis suis (cf. *MGH Dipl. HIV*, no. *502);
>
> Desiderius autem ab eodem imperatore preceptum aurea bulla bullatum de huius loci possessionibus accipiens et licentia redeundi ab imperatore impetrata ad hoc monasterium est reversus (cf. *MGH Dipl. HIV*, no. *503).

The stylistic similarity of these sentences is apparent. It is not, however, clear whether some or all of their subject-matter is a later interpolation into the source, whether in its original form or as used by Guido. In favour of their being interpolations, and perhaps of their insertion by Peter the Deacon, it may be argued that they fit a little uneasily into their context, and that Henry's granting of a diploma to Montecassino comes unexpectedly after their strained dealings. Moreover, no original or copy of either diploma survives.

Successive editors of Henry's diplomas have regarded these references differently. In 1952 D. von Gladiss (*MGH Dipl. HIV*, Anhang, no. xiv, p. 684) saw no case for their authenticity. In 1979 A. Gawlick retained some doubts regarding Jordan's diploma (ibid. 693), although Deér accepted it (as Introd. n. 52), pp. 35, 202; and Hoffmann noted that Desiderius dated charters by Jordan's regnal years, citing *Codex diplomaticus Cajetanus*, ii, pp. 37–9, 124–6, nos. 213, 253: *MGH SS* xxxiv. 432 n. 20. But Gawlick expressed no reservation about the Montecassino diploma, drawing attention to a reference to the *statuta . . . trium Heinricorum* in *MGH Dipl. LIII*, no. 120, and also to a theft from Montecassino of seven gold bulls between 1465 and 1471, through which Henry IV's diploma might have been lost. However, since Peter the Deacon drafted *Dipl. LIII*, no. 120, he may have been the originator of the phrase about three Henrys—II, III, and IV—who issued diplomas; it would be in line with his concern to claim continuous imperial support for Montecassino (cf. *Chron. Cas.* iv. 109, 112, pp. 576, 580–2, where he claimed the goodwill of five (*sic*) Henrys in a list of *imperatores* who issued diplomas and 'qui omnes Casinensem ecclesiam dilexerunt ac magnis muneribus ornaverunt') if he had invented the reference to a diploma in *Chron. Cas.* iii. 50 as well as the similarly-phrased reference to Jordan of Capua's. The existence and the authenticity of these two diplomas are highly doubtful.

For an ostensible, earlier diploma for Montecassino in Alberic's *Breviarium de dictamine*, see *MGH Dipl. HIV*, no. *500, and Rockinger (as Ch. I n. 105), pp. 39–40; but see also Bresslau (as Ch. II n. 77).

Appendix V

The *Iudicium de Regno et Sacerdotio*

MSS: Original: none. Copy: London, British Library, MS Arundel 390, f. 132[r], late eleventh cent. Printed: in a footnote to Hugh of Flavigny, ii, pp. 460–1; whence Migne, *PL* cliv. 331–2. The *Sacramentum* only in Watterich, i. 456 n. 2; *Monumenta Gregoriana*, Jaffé, *Bibl.* ii. 678 n. 5; *MGH Const.* i, p. 651, no. 442; *MGH Libelli*, i. 614 n. 4.

QUIDAM qui dicuntur religiosi et sanctissimi, sicuti hactenus soliti sunt facere, se posuerunt contra ius et temptaverunt Deum et fecerunt quod facere non debuerunt; ob hoc magnum dedecus habuerunt. Nam isti sunt illi qui fecerunt iudicium de regno et sacerdotio, sed Deus qui est misericordissimus et piisimus previdit quod iustum est. Nam abbas Cassini montis, et cancellarius qui cardinalis est de sancto Paulo,[a] et episcopus Portuensis cum aliis coepiscopis, et Bernhardus diaconus, et Wimundus monachus qui alio nomine Christianus nuncupatur, et Gratianus, qui omnes ex precepto pape fecerunt hanc legem quam audituri estis. Set prius dicam qui benedixit aquam scilicet quidam vir qui est nimis religiosus et nuncupatur Petrus Neopolitanus et est monachus, qui prius presbyter fecit triduanum ieiunium cum aliis clericis qui ibi fuerunt, et ipse presbyter sanctissimus celebravit missam. Peracta vero missa, abiit ad aquam cum supradictis et benedixit aquam. Misit vero puerum quendam in aqua ex parte regis, ut Deus discerneret veritatem, si ipse rex haberet iusticiam. Mox ergo ut puer missus est in aquam, abiit iusum in fundo aque. Ad hoc miraculum stupefacti fuerant omnes qui ibi aderant, et unus illorum nomine Wimundus qui Christianus nuncupatur cepit dicere contra Gratianum: 'Certe tu impressisti puerum ut iret iusum in fundo aque.' Sed ipse Gratianus cepit detestare et dicere quia 'Nunquam feci tale quid.' Tunc ipse Wimundus nomine cum iracundia abiit ad papam et dixit quoniam 'Gratianus impressit puerum ut iret in fundo aquę.' Papa ut audivit precepit illi Wimundo et dixit: 'Vade et dic illis ut iterum mittant puerum in aquam, ut videamus si verum est quod tu dicis.' Ad tale preceptum perrexit ipse Wimundus et dixit omnibus illis qui ibi aderant ex parte papę, ut alia vice misissent puerum in aquam. Et ipsi ex precepto papę miserunt iterum puerum in aquam, et abiit puerulus iusum in fundo aquę sicut prius. Post hęc eandem legem ipsi supradicti fecerunt propter papam et miserunt puerulum in aquam, qui cepit natare desuper. Miserunt et alia vice, qui supernatavit similiter. Ob hoc impulerunt subtus aquam ut iret in profundum aquę, sed Deus non permittebat. Nam habuerunt eum suffocare in aqua. Ad tale miraculum sunt stupefacti et nesciunt quid agere

[a] Paulo: *originally abbreviated to* Pa.; *the* a *is now almost rubbed away*

debeant. Sunt modo consiliati ac fidem inter se dederunt, si res ista in propatulo esset regi per aliquem hominem, ut nec unus illorum audeat dicere sine communi consilio et sine consilio pape. Nam ipse accepit fidem ab omnibus, ut nullus audeat dicere. Hoc factum est in Pallaria in monasterio sanctę Marię, que est capella ipsius abbatis Cassini montis. Hoc factum est ad confusionem illorum qui fecerunt et ad salutem vestri imperii, et fuit factum in dominica die post missam de adventu Domini.

SACRAMENTUM

Tibi dicimus, rex Heinrice, quia nos infra terminum illum quem tecum ponemus ad .xv. dies postquam Romam veneris, faciemus te coronare papam Gregorium si vivus est vel si forte de Roma non fugerit. Si autem mortuus fuerit vel si fugerit et reverti noluerit ad nostrum consilium ut te coronet infra constitutum terminum, nos papam eligemus cum tuo consilio secundum canones, et ipsum papam studebimus per bonam fidem ut te coronet, et nos studebimus per bonam fidem ut Romani faciant tibi fidelitatem. Hęc omnia observabimus tibi absque fraude et male ingenio, nisi quantum communi consilio nostro et tuo addatur vel minuatur.

Apart from Desiderius the *dramatis personae* of the document are as follows:

Peter, cardinal-priest of San Grisogono, apparently referred to as *cancellarius qui cardinalis est de sancto Paulo*. In fact Peter was *cardinalis de sancto Petro*, and had been a cardinal-priest since *c.*1070. Berengar of Tours named him, together with Bishop John II of Porto and Petrus Neopolitanus, in connection with the Roman councils of 1078 and 1079: Huyghens (as Ch. II n. 54), pp. 103, 108–9. In 1082 he was among the Roman clergy who protested against Gregory's use of church revenues for military ends: above, p. 152. He appears as papal *bibliothecarius* in documents dated at the Lateran on 24 November 1083: Santifaller, *QF*, pp. 254–7, nos. 213–14. In 1084 he seceded to the Guibertine party, and died after 1092. See also Santifaller, 'Saggio', pp. 183–9, 398–424, 426–36; Hüls, *Kardinäle*, pp. 170–2.

John II, cardinal-bishop of Porto. He was bishop from *c.*1057 until after 1089. Like Peter he protested against Gregory's use of church revenues in 1082, and seceded to the Guibertines in 1084. See Klewitz (as Ch. II n. 3) pp. 35–6; Hüls, *Kardinäle*, pp. 118–20.

Bernard, deacon. He was perhaps the Bernard who often appears in Gregory VII's Register between 1073 and 1078.

Guitmund, or *Christianus*, monk. He was a sometime monk of la Croix-Saint-Leufroi in Normandy; in 1077 he travelled in Germany with Cardinal-deacon Bernard and Abbot Bernard of Marseilles when they were Gregory VII's legates there. He wrote against Berengar of Tours. According to Archbishop Hugh of Lyons he criticized Abbot Desiderius in 1086: above, pp. 162, 164. In the time of Pope Urban II he was bishop of Aversa. On him see especially G. B. Ladner, 'Two Gregorian Letters on the Sources and Nature of Gregory VII's Reform Ideology', *SG* v (1956), 225–42; Orderic Vitalis, iv. 13, ed. Chibnall, ii. 270–81.

Gratian. He was perhaps the Gratian of *Chron. Cas.* iii. 65, p. 447. A Gratian is also referred to in Countess Matilda of Tuscany's *Donatio* of 1102 as having been present when, in Gregory VII's time, she gave her lands to the Roman church: *MGH Const.* i. 654, no. 444.

Petrus Neopolitanus. See above, p. 93.

For the circumstances of composition of the document, see above, pp. 168–9. The apparent error about the patriarchal basilica to which the papal chancellor Peter was attached as cardinal-priest of San Grisogono may indicate that it originated with Henry's own chancery rather than with a Roman partisan having local knowledge.

Appendix VI

A Henrician Manifesto Regarding Gregory VII's Last Acts

MSS: Original: none. Copy: London, British Library, MS Cotton Nero C.V, f. 1^{v}, late eleventh cent. Printed: in a footnote to Hugh of Flavigny, ii, pp. 470–1. The Manifesto was also known to Sigebert of Gembloux, who cited most of it in his *Chronica*, *a.* 1085, *MGH SS* vi. 365, q.v. for minor variant readings.

VOLUMUS vos scire qui aecclesiasticę cure solliciti estis, quod apostolicus Hiltebrandus nunc in extremis suis ad se vocavit unum de xii. cardinalibus quem multum diligebat pre cęteris, et confessus est omnipotenti Deo et sancto Petro ac toti aecclesię valde peccasse in pastorali cura quę ei ad regendum erat commissa, suadente diabolo contra humanum genus odium et iram incitasse. Postea vero sententiam quę in orbem terrarum effusa est, pro augmento christianitatis cepisse dicebat.[1] Tunc demum misit predictum confessorem suum ad imperatorem et ad totam aecclesiam, ut optarent illi indulgentiam, quia finem vitę suę aspiciebat, et tam cito induebat se angelicam vestem, et dimisit ac dissolvit vincula bannorum omnium suorum imperatori, et omni populo christiano, vivis et defunctis, clericis ac laicis, et iussit suos abire de domo Theoderici,[2] et amicos Heinrici ascendere. Teste Mogontino archiepiscopo.[3]

[1] An apparent reference to Gregory's second excommunication of Henry IV in 1080: *Reg.* vii. 14*a*, pp. 483–7.

[2] i.e. the Castel Sant'Angelo.

[3] Wezilo (1084–8); imperial chancellor. His death provides the *terminus ante quem* of the Manifesto. For his concern with Italian affairs, see Cowdrey (as Ch. IV n. 16), *EHR* xcii (1977), 14.

Appendix VII

Abbot Desiderius' Election as Pope according to the Montecassino Chronicle

THE account in the Montecassino Chronicle of Desiderius' election to the papacy (iii. 65–8, pp. 447–51) is part of the material now usually ascribed mainly to Guido. It was, however, not written as a single, coherent, and consecutive narrative of the years 1085, 1086, and 1087. Instead, it is a shapeless conflation of a number of sources which appear to have been written at different times. Those who composed or transmitted them seem to have had very differing perspectives of events. In the Chronicle as it stands the constituent sources are arranged in a sequence that confuses the chronology and is misleading because of much repetition of material. The purpose of this Appendix is to isolate and comment upon these sources. They are discussed in what is apparently the true order of the historical events to which they relate.

(i) cap. 65, p. 447, lines 1–15 (Anno autem . . . diebus tribus.): late May 1085. This Section is probably a general introduction written by Guido himself. It records the last days, death, and burial of Gregory VII. At its heart are Gregory's alleged dispositions about the succession, which he made on the third day before his death (23 May). It tells how, in Desiderius' presence, the Roman bishops and cardinals asked Gregory for direction (*quid . . . iuberet*). Whereas the records of Gregory's last testament in the Hanover letter collection and in Hugh of Flavigny make no mention of Desiderius but commend Bishop Anselm of Lucca, Bishop Odo of Ostia, and Archbishop Hugh of Lyons, in this Section, which if by Guido is a relatively late one, Gregory charged that if possible the bishops and cardinals of the Roman church should promote Desiderius to the papacy.[1] If he could not be persuaded they should turn to the

[1] For Gregory's last testament, see above, pp. 181–2. The Chronicle reflects, with adaptation, a version identical with, or very like, the first disposition:

Hanover letter collection	Chron. Cas. *iii. 65*
. . . convenerunt ad eum [Gregory] *episcopi et cardinales* Romani, *qui ibidem aderant*, rogantes atque postulantes, ut, quem sibi subrogari vellet successorem in pontificatum, eis ostenderet. At ille secum aliquantulum cogitans hęc illis verba dedit: '*Quemcumque horum trium, Lucensem* scilicet *episcopum* vel *Ostiensem aut archiepiscopum*	. . . Gregorius septimus papa . . . interrogatus . . . ab *episcopis et cardinalibus, qui* tunc unacum Desiderio *presentes erant*, quid post suum obitum de Romane sedis ordinatione iuberet, respondit, ut, si unquam aliquomodo possent, eundem Desiderium ad hoc officium promoverent. . . . Si vero hunc nullatenus flectere ad ista valerent, aut *archiepiscopum*

three bishops, who are named in the reverse order to that in Gregory's testament: the electors should choose whomever they could first procure. The need for haste was underlined by the words *quantocius festinarent.* This Section has the character of an *ex post facto* justification of what the succeeding ones are so presented as to record. Thus, it gives warrant for the election in May 1086 of Desiderius in preference to Odo of Ostia or Hugh of Lyons, Anselm of Lucca having died on 18 March 1086. It also accounts for Odo of Ostia's candidature in 1086 (as a candidate who was to hand) and in 1088; while the first of the reasons given for Gregory's naming of Desiderius (*quod primum presbiter cardinalis Romane tunc ecclesie esset*) probably reflects why Odo was objected to in 1086: he did not belong to the priests and deacons of the Roman church who should have preference if any of them were *papabile.*[2] The reversed order of Gregory's list of episcopal nominees may be influenced by Anselm of Lucca's death and perhaps, since Hugh of Lyons is named before him, by coolness towards Pope Urban II. The haste that Gregory enjoined is a feature of Section ii; Desiderius' reluctance, which Gregory is depicted as having foreseen (*si unquam aliquomodo possent*), is apparent in Sections iii–vi.

(ii) cap. 65, p. 447, line 27–p. 448, line 1 (Die pentecostes . . . tarditate venirent.): June 1085. This Section, which follows Section iv awkwardly, deals with events within days of Gregory's death. Not only does it display Desiderius as taking an urgent initiative to secure the prompt filling of the papacy, but it shows absolutely no awareness that Gregory had designated him to succeed. His initiative would be hard to explain if he himself were a candidate, especially a reluctant one. This Section seems to be based upon a Montecassino account of the immediate sequel to Gregory's death which was written there before the currency at the abbey of any story about his candidature. The earliest plans at Montecassino thus appear to have been in line with Gregory's final testament, although it was envisaged that some other suitable person besides his three nominees might possibly be elected.

(iii) cap. 66, pp. 448–9: April–May 1086. This, which is by far the longest of the constituent Sections, totally ignores the events of 1085 as described in Sections i and ii, but follows naturally after the narrative of iii. 53, p. 435. Attempts to replace Gregory began as upon a *tabula rasa* at Eastertide (*c.*5 April) 1086, when a number of Gregorian bishops and

Lugdunensem, habere poteritis, in pontificem eligite.'

Lugdunensem Ugonem aut Ottonem *Hostiensem aut Lucensem episcopum, quem* prius *ex eis habere possent, in papam eligere* post suum obitum quantocius festinarent.

[2] Cf. Deusdedit, *Coll. can.* i. 111–12 (92–3), 118 (96), 233 (186), ii. 161 (131), pp. 84, 86, 184–5, 268. The Chronicle here gives four reasons why Desiderius should be chosen: (i) that he was then a cardinal-priest of the Roman church; (ii) that he was a man of the utmost prudence; (iii) that he was outstanding for his religion; and (iv) that he was high in the friendship of surrounding princes. It is not clear whether the author intended them to be understood as being Gregory's reasons or his own commentary; in the context the latter seems more likely.

cardinals at Rome summoned Desiderius and the Romans who were with him to come to the city and take counsel for the vacant see. The implication is that hitherto neither Gregory nor anyone else had put Desiderius forward as a candidate. On the eve of Pentecost (23 May) Desiderius took the initiative by proposing an unprejudiced election (*instante Desiderio, ut pontificatus apex personarum earum iniungeretur alicui, que vel ipsis vel ei videbantur idonee*). It was the clergy and laity in Rome who thereupon unanimously pressed Desiderius to be pope and who met with his firm refusal. When at a new meeting on Whit Sunday he still refused, the Romans agreed to elect whomever he should name. After consulting the Roman consul Cencius he put forward Bishop Odo of Ostia; but an unidentified cardinal vetoed his election as uncanonical. So the Romans elected Desiderius against his will, naming him Victor, but he refused to assume office. This Section is almost certainly part of a larger and independent writing: see above, Appendix III. It is often precise about dates, persons, and places. Yet it leaves an impression of artificiality and distance, on account of its ambiguity about Gregory's whereabouts in the last days of his life, of its disregarding the events of 1085, of its ignoring the Normans, and of its exaggerated insistence upon the unanimity and coherent action of the Roman clergy and people.

(iv) cap. 65, p. 447, lines 15–27 (Et quoniam . . . esse spopondit.): undated. This much briefer Section is closely related to iii, with which it has extensive parallels in language and substance. These become clear when the relevant passages are juxtaposed:

iii	iv
Iam fere annus in tali fluctuatione transierat, quo *in apostolica sede nullus pastor erat, nullus dominici gregis curam gerebat et Guibertus eresiarcha oves Christi sanguine redemptas suis cum sequacibus laniabat*, cum circa paschalem festivitatem episcopi et cardinales Romane ecclesie de diversis partibus Romam convenientes mandaverunt	Et quoniam *Romana ecclesia pastore destituta remanserat et heretici atque scismatici more luporum illam nitebantur invadere,*
predicto abbati, ut unacum episcopis et cardinalibus Romanis, qui secum tunc morabantur . . . ad eos quantocius pergerent, *quatinus de Romane ecclesie ordinatione simul tractarent*. . . .	*Desiderius unacum episcopis et cardinalibus* nec non et laicis religiosis, qui actenus in catholica unitate et obedientia pape Gregorii fideliter perstiterant, cepit unaniter agere, *qualiter eam posset decentissime ordinare.*
Eo die, quo applicuit, in vigiliis pentecostes instante Desiderio, *ut pontificatus apex personarum earum iniungeretur alicui, que vel ipsis vel ei videbantur idonee*, rennuerunt prorsus omnis Romanus et clerus et populus consentire. Per totam autem ipsam diem	Miserunt ergo et *convenire fecerunt undique aptas huic officio personas,* quatinus ex eis unanimi consensu eam *personam* cum gratia et auxilio Dei eligerent, que *idonea* et apta tanto ordini esset.

multa frequentia, quotquot catholice parti favebant tam clerici quam laici ad eum convenientes, iam circa vesperam congregati sunt pariter omnes tam episcopi et cardinales	*Convenientes post hec ad predictum abbatem episcopi et cardinales*
quam et ceteri Romani ..., *ceperuntque omnes unanimiter Desiderium multis precibus obsecrare, ut Romanum pontificatum suscipere non recusaret, eumque obtestare per divina, per humana omnia, ut subveniret periclitanti ecclesie in naufragio constitute*, multotiens ad genua eius nonnullis lacrimantibus omnes pariter ruentes. Desiderius vero, qui iam dudum decreverat vitam suam in quiete transigere et qui magis optabat in divina peregrinatione suum tempus finire,	*ceperunt eum* super prefati pontificis iudicio *appellare, utque in tanta temporis necessitate periclitanti subveniret ecclesie papatum suscipiendo, instantissime flagitare.*
cepit omnimodis refutare et hoc se numquam consensurum firmiter repromittere.	*Ad hec ille papatum quidem se suscipere obstinatissima responsione recusavit*, aliis vero, quibus sciret et posset, modis ad Romane ecclesie servitium se paratum esse spopondit.

As well as being briefer than iii, iv gives no particular details of dates, places, and people; although it manifestly follows it in recording the same events. Like iii it knows nothing of the events of 1085. However, the effect of the abbreviation is to accentuate Desiderius' role. In contrast to iii, it refers to Gregory's *iudicium* about the succession, clearly intending to convey that he had named Desiderius. It is thus the earliest of the Montecassino sources to indicate that he did so. This fact, together with its character as a précis of the first part of iii, indicates that iv is later than and in part dependent upon it.

(v) cap. 67, pp. 449–50: May 1086–May 1087. This Section opens with an account of certain aspects of events at Rome in May 1086 about which iii and iv were silent, because they avoided any reference to the Normans: the intrigues of Duke Roger of Apulia and his mother Sichelgaita against Desiderius, which included their inciting the imperial prefect Wezilo, whom they had released, against the abbot. They sought by this means to harass the Roman bishops and cardinals, who, prompted by Sichelgaita's brother and enemy Prince Gisulf of Salerno, were unwilling to consecrate the new archbishop of Salerno, Alfanus II. The election at Pentecost is assumed but not referred to, although v describes Desiderius' reluctance in terms that echo iii but avoid phrases in iii with which iv has parallels:

iii

Desiderius vero, qui iam dudum decreverat vitam suam in quiete transigere et *qui magis optabat in divina peregrinatione suum tempus finire*, cepit omnimodis refutare et hoc se numquam consensurum firmiter repromittere. *Instare illi vehementer, perseveranter insistere*, ipse vehementius reniti, resistere perseverantius, dicens . . .

v

. . . idem electus . . . pontificatus insignia ita dimisit, ut eis ulterius uti nullo unquam modo persuaderi potuerit, *decernens potius omni vite sue tempore in divina peregrinatione vitam finire* quam tanti ordinis fascibus gravissimis colla submittere. *Insistebatur ei cotidie precibus lacrimisque creberrimis*, obiciebantur ecclesiarum magna discrimina . . .; sicque Casinum reversus est.

However, whereas iii locates in Rome Desiderius' refusal to don the papal vestments, v states that he had withdrawn from Rome by way of Ardea to Terracina. The circumstantial account of v may be of earlier origin and more reliable on this point than iii's. Unlike iii and iv, v goes on to describe Desiderius' year of persistence in his refusal to exercise papal authority. It also describes how, after May 1086, the Roman cardinals and bishops persuaded Jordan of Capua to endeavour to conduct Desiderius to Rome for consecration. The project came to nothing, partly because Desiderius argued against it and partly from fear of the summer heat.

(vi) cap. 65, p. 448, lines 1–9 (Quod illi . . . infirma transirent.): ? Summer 1086. If what is probably an editorial introductory phrase of four words is disregarded, this Section has sufficient matter in common with the last sentences of v to make it likely that they cover the same events:

v

Non tamen ob hoc cardinales et episcopi, qui cum eo erant, aliquatenus quiescentes *Iordano principi instare ceperunt, ut quantocius properaret et propter consecrationem eiusdem electi Romam cum eis pergeret*. Qui cum magno exercitu *ad hoc monasterium veniens* partim deortatione ipsius electi, *partim timore estatis ulterius progredi nolens reversus est.*

vi

[Quod illi facere neglegentes] *cum Iordano principe clam machinabantur eidem abbati pastoralem curam iniungere et suasionibus multis nitebantur eum quoquomodo Romam perducere* putantes violenter se id ei posse imponere. Quod ipse persentiens omnino rennuere et contradicere cepit sicque *ad hoc monasterium reversus* iterum Normannos et Langobardos et omnes, quotquot potuit, ortari ad Romane ecclesie servitium cepit . . . *Sed quia fervor estatis nimius erat, propterea tunc Romam ire distulerunt*, quousque se et calor estatis imminuerat et tempora infirma transirent.

However, vi gives a more active impression than v of Desiderius' role: having returned to Montecassino he successfully incited Normans, Lombards, and others to come to the service of the Roman church, intending to take positive action when the weather cooled and circumstances were propitious.

(vii) cap. 65, p. 448, lines 10–15 (Postquam vero . . . infecta remansit.): ? Summer 1086. This Section might refer to an abortive expedition to Rome in the summer of 1085, after the events of Section ii. But this would raise the difficulty that Sections iii and iv know nothing of an attempt to make Desiderius pope before May 1086. It is therefore more likely to provide a further account of Jordan's abortive summer expedition of 1086 as recorded in the second part of Section v. In view of common references to Jordan and to Count Rainulf of Caiazzo, Sections ii and vii may come from the same source.

(viii) cap. 68, pp. 450–1: March–May 1086. This Section, which covers Desiderius' acceptance in March of his election at Capua, his return to Montecassino, and his subsequent journey to Rome for consecration on 9 May, seems like Section iii to belong to the source described above in Appendix III.

Appendix VIII

Victor III's Pontificate in the Montecassino Chronicle

LIKE the story of his election as pope, that of Desiderius' pontificate as Victor III appears to be made up of Sections which are of differing date and origin; although there are now no parallel accounts of the same events. The Sections may be determined as follows:

(i) cap. 69, p. 451, lines 5–33 (Post exiguum . . . Victoris rediit.). This Section gives a detailed account of events at Rome during Victor's presence there from 4 June to 1 July 1087, when it breaks off. It includes precise indications of date. Its treatment is factual, awarding neither praise nor blame to his character and actions. It perhaps belongs to the source discussed above, Appendix III.

(ii) cap. 69, p. 451, line 33–p. 452, line 6 (Eo itidem . . . sollemniter celebrare.). To the first Section is appended an anecdote of St. Peter's appearing to pilgrims on their way to St. Benedict, i.e. to Montecassino. He told them that he was about to keep his feast-day (29 June) there because of the storms that were shaking his church at Rome. The monks of Montecassino accordingly decreed to keep St. Peter's Day with the same solemnity as St. Benedict's. The anecdote is of indeterminate but perhaps early date.

(iii) cap. 70, pp. 452–3. The tone of the Chronicle as it stands now changes abruptly. Reverting to the events of the 1080s, its chronology becomes absurd. Victor's pontificate is presented in terms of the struggle between St. Peter and Simon Magus. He is, therefore, given high praise as a man of strength while Guibert is denigrated and mocked as a new Simon Magus who shared the heresiarch's fate. As the following comparison shows, the Section is based upon Deusdedit, *Libellus*, ii. 11–12, pp. 328–30:

Libellus	Chron. Cas. *iii. 70*
11. Quae omnia rectissime de *Guiberto* Ravennati quondam episcopo et ab eo execratis accipiuntur;	*Guibert*us interius eresiarcha,
qui post prestita domino suo beatae memoriae septimo Gregorio papae fidelitatis sacramenta et obedientiam novem annis exhibitam eiusdem *apostolicum thronum invasit*, favente et cooperante sibi Henrico rege, quem seducendo in symoniacam heresim . . . profundius impulit	*qui post prestita domino suo beate memorie Gregorio septimo pape fidelitatis sacramenta et obedientiam novem annis exibitam apostolicum thronum invas*erat, cernens Victorem papam ab omnibus in maxima veneratione haberi,

et avertit *ab observatione iuramenti, quod apud Canusiam Tusciae oppidum* prebuerat eidem domino *papae* . . .

Facto itaque, *ut assolet, vario bellandi eventu*, licet is, quem sibi prefati proceres prefecerant, occubuisset, tamen postmodum *diutissime plurimis depredationibus et incendiis ac caedibus utrimque decertatum est. Tandem prefatus* tyrannus, induratus ut Farao, *relictis ad resistendum in Germania copiis, assumpto partim suo, partim conducticio sive gregario exercitu, Romam et suburbana eius depredationibus et incendiis ac caedibus, quibus valuit, quadriennio devastavit. Et tandem suo Simone magis pretio quam vi inthronizato, ab eodem imperialem coronam accepit.* Et paulo post cum eodem militari Normannorum manu ducis Roberti . . . turpissime fugatus abscessit; *et tam non faventibus, quam non communicantibus sibi* ac *suis complicibus et Romae et in omni* regno suo *saevissimam et diuturnam intulit persecutionem. Huius rei causa et ecclesiae paene totius* regni *desolatae, et christiana religio propemodum dissipata, et* XC *milia hominum et eo amplius in diversis regionibus, beato papa Guiberto cooperante, caesa sunt. Qui etiam pulsis catholicis episcopis et abbatibus sceleratos et idiotas singulis civitatibus et* xenodochiis *vel ecclesiis singulos, interdum autem binos vel annuos prelatos damnabili prioris* et *magistri sui Symonis mercimonio substituens, in depredationibus sanctorum locorum christianorum sibi non faventium, immo et faventium, dum non esset qui armato resisteret, longe lateque, voluntate quidem* non minus su[i]

Hynricum imperatorem solvens *ab observatione iuramenti, quod apud Canusiam Tuscie oppidum* olim *pape* Gregorio fecerat, Romam attraxit et cum eo expugnare catholicam ecclesiam cepit. Hi vero, qui ex parte pape Victoris in ultramontanis partibus erant, imperatorem Rome remorare cognoscentes contra eum rebellare disponunt. Contra quos Heynricus imperator adveniens *facto, ut assolet, vario bellandi eventu diutissime plurimis depredationibus et incendiis ac cedibus utrimque decertatum est. Tandem prephatus* imperator *relictis ad resistendum in Germania copiis, assumto partim suo, partim conductitio sive gregario exercitu Romam et suburbana eius depredationibus et incendiis ac cedibus, quibus valuit, quadriennio devastavit et tandem suo Simone magis pretio quam vi inthronizato ab eodem imperialem coronam accepit et tam non faventibus quam non communicantibus sibi suis*que *complicibus et Rome et in omni* Romano imperio *sevissimam et diuturnam intulit persecutionem. Huius rei causa et ecclesie pene totius* Romani imperii *desolate et cristiana religio propemodum dissipata et* viginti *milia hominum et eo amplius in diversis regionibus beato papa Guiberto cooperante cesa sunt. Qui etiam pulsis catholicis episcopis et abbatibus et aliis* ecclesiarum prepositis scientia pariter et religione pollentibus *sceleratos et idiotas singulis civitatibus et* cenobiis *vel ecclesiis singulos, interdum autem binos vel annuos prelatos dampnabili prioris magistri sui Simonis* magi *mercimonio substituens in depredationibus sanctorum locorum* et *christianorum sibi non faventium, immo et faventium,*

Neron[is], *sed minus possibilitate crassatus est.*

12. . . . *Idem vero Guibertus, qui multo rectius papa Demens, quam papa Clemens dici debuit, in oppidulo suo, quod Argentum dicitur, quasi ad sui munitionem excelsa turri fabricata prestolatur symoniacos angelos, cum quibus volando in putidissimas stigias paludes* corruat, fractis *cruribus, scilicet* rebus *suis, Deo* nobis *propitio*, iam propemodum *confractis et ad nihilum redactis; cui nemo apostolicam reverentiam sive obedientiam exhib*uit *preter* suum Neronem *et* sceleratos *complices eius, vel qui se illi propter avaritiam, quae idolorum servitus, vel perpetuo vel ad tempus pacto iusiurando vendiderunt: quorum plurimi, quibus perfidia claruerat, dum execranda sacrificia celebrat, ne interessent,* aufugiebant, *scientes eundem nulli Romanorum successisse pontificum, sed prescripto modo periurum et invasorem ac symoniacum* domino *Gregorio papae fuisse superiniectum. Nam catholici, qui fidem et religionem zelo Dei tuebantur*, obeunte beatae memoriae papa Gregorio, reverentissimum *Victor*em Romanae ecclesiae cardinalem archipresbyterum et Cassinensem abbatem substituerunt; eoque non multo post decedente, Urbanum, qui praesens habetur, virum *scientia et religione prestantissim*um.

dum non esset, qui armato resisteret, longe lateque voluntate quidem Neronis et Decii, *sed minus possibilitate crassatus est. Idem vero Guibertus, qui multo rectius papa Demens quam papa Clemens dici debuit, in oppidulo suo, quod Argenteum dicitur, quasi ad sui munitionem excelsa turri fabricata prestolabatur simoniacos angelos, cum quibus volando in putidissimas Stigias paludes ru*eret *scilicet cruribus suis Deo* per omnia pape Victori *propitio confractis et ad nichilum redactis. Cui nemo apostolicam reverentiam sive obedientiam exhib*ebat *preter* imperatorem *et complices eius, vel qui se illi propter avaritiam, que* est *idolorum servitus, vel perpetuo vel ad tempus pacto iusiurando vendiderunt; quorum plurimi, quibus* eius *perfidia claruerat, dum execranda sacrificia celebr*aret non *inter*erant *scientes eundem nulli Romanorum pontificum successisse, sed prescripto modo periurum et invasorem ac simoniacum pape Gregorio fuisse superiniectum. Nam catholici, qui fidem et religionem zelo Dei tuebantur,* pape *Victor*i *scientia et religione prestantissim*o adherebant.

Deusdedit's *Libellus* was not completed, in its second recension, until a date between 1097 and 1101.[1] The chapters cited above must belong to the final work, since much is made of the fall of Argenta, to the north-west of Ravenna, in late 1097 or early 1098.[2] The version in the Chronicle must be the later of the two, for it not only condenses Deusdedit's but also makes interpolations, many of which are unintelligent and make nonsense of a coherent original. While it is no less hostile than Deusdedit

[1] See above, pp. 99, 160.

[2] Bernold, *a.* 1098, p. 465; see Meyer von Knonau, *Jahrbücher*, v. 13–14.

to the imperial cause, the Chronicle softens much that was personally discreditable to Henry. Much is omitted about his perjury and loss of German support in 1079 and 1080; his most basely fleeing from Rome in 1084 is passed over; and nothing is said of his shameful defeats at the hands of the woman Countess Matilda of Tuscany. Deusdedit repeatedly calls Henry *tyrannus* but the Chronicle substitutes *imperator* and changes *regnum* into *imperium.* In sharp contrast there is no softening of Deusdedit's condemnation of Guibert. In both accounts he shared the *hubris* and the *nemesis* of Simon Magus, and the loss of Argenta was so presented as to demonstrate this fact. Perhaps the most striking feature of this Section of the Chronicle is the accentuation of Victor III. Whereas Deusdedit refers to him with respect but only in due historical course, the Chronicle three times introduces his name into the body of the narrative, ending with the anachronistic claim that the antipope's discomfiture up to 1097 redounded to his advantage! Deusdedit's final words in praise of Urban II are adapted in the Chronicle to eulogize Victor III. All this reflects a concern at Montecassino *c.*1100 to magnify Victor's achievement as pope. This Section of the Chronicle is an incompetent rehash of Deusdedit in order to promote this end.

(iv) cap. 71, p. 453. There follows a brief account of the Mahdia expedition of 1087. It exaggerates Victor's role and is coloured by memories of the First Crusade. See Cowdrey (as Ch. IV n. 16), *EHR* xcii. 1–29, esp. 17–18.

(v) cap. 72, p. 453, lines 17–19 (Prephatus autem . . . sollempniter dedicavit.). This is a very brief notice of Victor's return to Montecassino and dedication of the church of San Nicola in Pica. It is perhaps derived from the source discussed above, Appendix III.

(vi) cap. 72, p. 453, line 19–p. 455, line 24 (Mense autem . . . occidentem disseminaverunt.). After an editorial introduction, p. 453, lines 19–21 (Mense autem . . . presidens ait:), this Section has the form of an allocuation by Victor to his synod at Benevento, held *c.*29 August 1087. It is made up of a variety of elements, many of them being citations from other material. (The following analysis was made independently of Hoffman's in *MGH SS* xxxiv. 453–5 but subsequently compared with it.)

(*a*) p. 453, lines 21–6 (Novit dilectio . . . profunda submergi.). The introduction is an almost verbatim citation of the *Narratio* of the Election Decree of 1059: *MGH Const.* i. 539, no. 382, lines 11–16:

Election Decree	Chron. Cas. *iii.* 72
Novit beatitudo *vestra,* dilectissimi *fratres et coepiscopi,* inferiora quoque membra *non latuit* . . . haec *apostolica sedes, cui auctore Deo deservio, quot adversa pertulerit, quot denique per simoniacae haeresis trapezitas malleis crebrisque tunsionibus subiacuerit, adeo ut columna Dei viventis iam*iam	*Novit* dilectio *vestra,* car*issimi fratres et coepiscopi,* omni etiam orbi *non latuit,* sancta Romana et *apostolica sedes, cui Deo auctore deservio, quot adversa pertulerit, quot denique per simoniace here*seos *trapezitas malleis crebrisque tunsionibus subiacuerit, adeo ut columpna Dei viventis videretur iam*

paene videretur [*concussa*] *nutare et sagena summi piscatoris procellis intumescentibus cogeretur in naufragii profunda submergi.*	*pene concussa nutare et sagena summi piscatoris procellis intumescentibus cogeretur in naufragii profunda submergi.*

The phrase *carissimi fratres*, the emphasis upon the *sancta Romana . . . sedes*, and the universal reference (*omni etiam orbi*) may echo Gregory VII's last letters, esp. *Epp. vag.*, p. 134, no. 55. The reading 'iam pene *concussa* nutare' is characteristic of the imperial version, which may be that cited. But all surviving texts of the papal version are relatively late and seem to trace back to a single copy; the word *concussa* seems to have dropped out. So this may be a citation of a lost, earlier papal text that contained it.

(*b*) p. 453, line 26–p. 454, line 21 (Guibertus enim . . . vinculo innodamus.). Victor proceeds at once to a sentence of deposition from holy orders and excommunication against Guibert of Ravenna (Clement III). In a preamble he is condemned in the severest terms as an imitator and underling of Simon Magus (*Simonis magi munitus perfidia ipsiusque officina factus*). The sentence falls only upon Guibert and not on his supporters. Henry is referred to (as *imperator*), but he is Guibert's agent and no express penalty is visited upon him.

(*c*) p. 454, lines 21–37 (Nosti preterea . . . hereticus estimandus.). Victor next excommunicates Archbishop Hugh of Lyons and Abbot Richard of Saint-Victor, Marseilles. He accuses them of having been ambitious to succeed to the papacy and of having gone into schism when they were disappointed. The terms in which the sentence is expressed appear to be based upon Victor's own letters of 1087 (see p. 455, lines 23–4), for Hugh of Lyons's second letter to Countess Matilda of Tuscany (above, Ch. IV n. 31) cites them in similar language:

Hugh of Lyons	Chron. Cas. *iii. 72*
[Abbot Hugh of Cluny] obiecit nobis quasdem literas, quas dicebat a Papa Urbano [*recte* Victore] sibi directas, in quibus continebatur, ut tam ipse quam sancti fratres sui *a* communione nostra, et Ricardi Massiliensis *abstinere cur*arent. . . .	Unde vobis apostolica auctoritate precipimus, ut *ab* eis *abstinere cur*etis, nec illis omnino communicetis.
Inter alia autem unum impudentissime mentiuntur, quia a *communione Romanae ecclesiae* nos *sponte* nostra *seiun*ximus; . . .	*quia Romane ecclesie communione* sua *sponte seiun*cti sunt . . .[3]

[3] For the reading *Victore* in Hugh's letter, see Lehmann (as above, Ch. IV n. 31). Victor's sanctions against Abbot Richard were referred to by Pope Urban II in a letter of 1088 to King Alphonso VI of León-Castile in which he disallowed a sentence by Richard: 'quod ergo ille gessit, quem Victor papa sanctae memoriae tertius legatione privaverat, nos irritum iudicamus': *Ep.* 6, Migne, *PL* cli. 289–90.

(*d*) p. 454, line 38–p. 455, line 9 (Constituimus etiam . . . esse sciat.). Canons against lay investiture taken, with minor variant readings, from canons 1 and 2 of Gregory VII's Lent council of 1080: *Reg.* vii. 14*a*, p. 480. Some, but not all, of the variants occur in the citation by Deusdedit, *Coll. can.* iv. 96, pp. 442–3, and *Libellus*, i. 16, p. 315.

(*e*) p. 455, lines 9–11 (Nec mirum . . . anathema sit.'). An alleged ruling of the council of Nicaea (325) about simony: 'Qui dat et qui recipit, anathema sit.' The Section is based upon Deusdedit, *Libellus*, ii. 2, p. 318. There is no such ruling in the records of Nicaea, but Deusdedit, *Coll. can.* cites similar texts: iii. 45 (43) (from the council of Gangra, *c.*345), 55, pp. 287–8, 292.

(*f*) p. 455, lines 11–14 (Quando ergo . . . errare est.). A declaration that simoniacal clergy are to be avoided on pain of sharing their excommunication; their priestly standing is denied. This is like Deusdedit, *Coll. can.* iv. 94, p. 441, changed from the first to the second person plural; it is given as a comment upon the second canon of the council of Chalcedon (451). See also Guy of Arezzo, *Ad Heribertum archiepiscopum*, ed. F. Thaner, *MGH Libelli*, i. 6–7, where it occurs in the first person.

(*g*) p. 455, lines 14–22 (Penitentia vero . . . invisibiliter habent.). Penance and communion may be received only at catholic hands; spiritual communion is better than communion received from heretics. This is a slightly modified and extended version of Deusdedit, *Libellus*, ii. 8, iv. 11, pp. 326, 365, where he cited an unidentified *sententia* of St. John Chrysostom.

The dependence of this supposed allocution on Deusdedit is apparent, and it can scarcely have been put together in its present form until the *Libellus* had been begun. However, there are differences from it. Deusdedit, who hotly rejected the Election Decree from which the *Narratio* is in part derived,[4] would hardly have approved of it, and there is none of Deusdedit's animus against Henry IV, who appears as *imperator*. The allocuation cannot have been compiled under Deusdedit's direct supervision or inspiration. It seems to be another Cassinese work of the very early twelfth century.

(vii) cap. 73, pp. 455–6. A summary of Victor III's rulings about monastic observance at Montecassino, and an account of his death. This chapter is not likely to have belonged to the source discussed above in Appendix III, since it records Victor's designation of Odo of Ostia to succeed him as pope and the source studiously avoids referring to any such procedure of designation.

[4] See above, Ch. III n. 173.

Appendix IX

Events at Bari in 1086–7

THE course of events at Bari and the conflicts among its citizens in the years 1086 and 1087 present difficult problems which call for a full-scale reappraisal. Only a few, tentative comments can here be offered.[1]

The principal relevant sources are as follows:

(i) *Chronicles.* The principal chronicle is the annals for the years in question in Lupus Protospatarius: *MGH SS* v. 51–63.

(ii) *Hagiographical sources.* There are three principal Latin accounts of the coming of St. Nicholas' relics to Bari in 1087:

(*a*) An account by Nicephorus, a clerk of Bari who was a monk of la Cava and then of San Benedetto, Bari, BHL 6179 [hereafter Nicephorus]. It is edited by F. Nitti di Vito (as Ch. IV n. 122), pp. 336–56, from Vatican Library, MS lat. 5074, pp. 5^v–10^v, Eng. trans. in Jones (as n. 1), pp. 176–93. Written in 1088, it is by a contemporary who represented the standpoint of the circle of Abbot (later Archbishop) Elia.

(*b*) An account by John, archdeacon of Bari, BHL 6190, edited from Vatican Library, MS Reg. lat. 477, ff. 29–38, by Nitti di Vito, pp. 357–66 [hereafter John of Bari]. Written by 1089, it discloses the view of Archbishop Urso.[2] Accounts (*a*) and (*b*) are similar enough to make it likely that they draw upon a common source.

(*c*) A further account, also bearing the name of Nicephorus but differing from the earlier one, is usually but not very happily known, on account of certain topographical detail, as the 'Jerusalem Legend'. It is printed in *Anal. Boll.* iv (1885), 169–92. Its date and provenance call for further study, but it seems to be a late eleventh-century composition from Tours, although the MS in which it survives—Ghent, Bibliothèque municipale 289—is of thirteenth-century date.

Another account of the translation, in Old Slavonic, appears in the so-called Kiev Legend, the authorship of which is uncertain. The edition and Italian translation by Nitti di Vito, pp. 387–98, are superseded by

[1] The main discussions of the translations of St. Nicholas' relics are Leib (as Ch. IV n. 106), pp. 51–74; Nitti di Vito (as Ch. IV n. 122) and *La ripresa gregoriana*; A. Gambacorta, 'Culto e pellegrinaggi a San Nicolà di Bari fino alla prima Crociata', *Pellegrinaggi e culto dei santi fino alla prima Crociata*, Convegni del Centro di studi sulla spiritualità medievale, 4 (Todi, 1963), 485–502; Orderic Vitalis, vii. 12, ed. Chibnall, iv. 54–68, 353–4; P. J. Geary, *Furta sacra. Thefts of Relics in the Central Middle Ages* (Princeton, NJ, 1977), 115–27; C. W. Jones, *Saint Nicholas of Myra, Bari and Manhattan. Biography of a Legend* (Chicago and London, 1978), 172–216. A study by G. Cioffari is awaited.

[2] For John, see F. Babudri, 'Le note autobiografice di Giovanni arcidiacono Barese', *Archivio storico pugliese*, ii (1949), 134–46.

G. Cioffari, *La leggenda di Kiev. La traslazione delle reliquie di S. Nicola nel racconto di un annalista russo contemporaneo* (Bari, 1980). Cioffari prints facsimiles of photographs of the sixteenth-century Codex Rumjancev, which is in Moscow, together with Italian and English translations. The precise date of the Kiev Legend is unknown but early; it seems to have been completed before *c.*1120. Its sources were apparently various, but they may have included a Greek version of Nicephorus.

(iii) *Bari charters.* These survive in two archives: those of the cathedral, *Cod. dipl. Barese*, i, on which see also Nitti di Vito, pp. 320–3; and those of the basilica of San Nicolà, *Cod. dipl. Barese*, v. For Norman ducal charters, see Ménager, *Receuil.* The central event of the years 1086–7 was the bringing to Bari of the relics of St. Nicholas of Myra. It was the work of a party of sixty-two sailors, forty-two of them men of Bari, who arrived in Antioch on a normal mercantile expedition. They there heard rumours that a company of Venetian merchants intended to seize St. Nicholas' relics from Myra, which, like Antioch, was currently in Moslem hands. The men of Bari conceived the plan of forestalling the Venetians. They went to Myra and, on 20 April 1087, they took the relics and brought them back to Apulia, where, after a short stay at San Giorgio, they returned with them to Bari on 9 May. The relics added strength to a cult of St. Nicholas that was already current in South Italy. They found their resting-place, not in the cathedral, but in a specially founded basilica.[3] In 1089 Pope Urban II consecrated the shrine, which rapidly became a major pilgrimage centre of Christendom.

In his vast study, *La ripresa gregoriana di Bari (1085–1105) e i suoi riflessi nel mondo contemporaneo politico e religioso* (Trani, 1942), Nitti di Vito argued that these events represented the victory at Bari of a Gregorian party. It opposed a Guibertine establishment led by Archbishop Urso, which had its centre at the cathedral and depended upon the greater local landowners and merchants. An opposing faction of lesser people led by Abbot Elia of San Benedetto was responsible for the securing of the relics of St. Nicholas. In 1089 Elia succeeded Urso as archbishop, and Urban II's consecration of him set the seal upon a Gregorian victory.[4]

There may be a kernel of truth in this reading of the evidence. Yet the picture is less clear-cut than Nitti di Vito supposed. Three problems call for discussion in the present connection:

[3] See esp. Paschal II, *Ep.* 167 (18 Nov. 1105), Migne, *PL* clxiii. 178–9. An attempt was made to establish that the site had been given by, or through, Archbishop Urso: *Cod. dipl. Barese*, i. 59–61, no. 32; Ménager, *Recueil*, pp. 215–19, no. 61, *Cod. dipl. Barese*, v. 111–12, no. 64; and the documents listed by Nitti di Vito, art. cit. 321–4.

[4] According to Latin sources Urso died in 1089. For another possibility, see J. Prawer, 'The Autobiography of Obadyah the Norman, a Convert to Judaism at the Time of the First Crusade', *Studies in Medieval Jewish History and Literature*, ed. I. Twersky (Cambridge, Mass., 1979), 110–34, at 117–18. In art. cit. (Ch. IV n. 16), *EHR* xcii (1977), 19, I ill-advisedly followed Nitti di Vito's conclusions. On Urso and Elia, see also N. Kamp, 'Vescovi e diocesi dell'Italia meridionale nel passagio dalla dominazione bizantina allo Stato normanno', Rossetti, *Formi di potere*, pp. 379–97, at 391, 394.

(i) Was the capture of the relics from Myra to any extent planned at Bari before the merchants who effected it set off for the Levant? The Latin hagiographical sources are unanimous in suggesting that it was not, but that it was the unpremeditated action of merchants already in the east who sought to forestall the Venetians.[5] This has been doubted, because the Kiev Legend tells of advance planning after a vision of St. Nicholas experienced by a priest at Bari.[6] Moreover, such planning suits the hypothesis of a Gregorian attempt under Elia's leadership the better to use an already established cultus in order to secure victory over Urso's Guibertine party. However, the notion of a deliberate suppression of information by the Latin sources has no warrant or likelihood. The account in the Kiev Legend of advance planning reads like a later adaptation of a vision attributed in the Jerusalem Legend to a monk who had it after the relics had arrived.[7] Urso's own part in receiving the relics tells against an over-sharp picture of urban antagonism.[8] Apart from the Kiev Legend there is no hint of premeditation, and the probabilities are against it.[9] The evidence points to the seizure of the relics on the spur of the moment by merchants who were nevertheless more than glad to furnish Bari with a patron saint comparable to St. Andrew at Amalfi or St. Matthew at Salerno.

(ii) Did social divisions at Bari correspond to an ecclesiastical confrontation there of Gregorians and Guibertines? The Latin hagiographical sources leave no doubt of a social division between an upper-class faction at Bari seeking to claim St. Nicholas' relics for the *episcopium*, and a mercantile and lower-class faction demanding their separate custody by Abbot Elia.[10] But none of the sources relates this division to ecclesiastical alignments.[11] The only evidence for Guibertine sympathizers at Bari is Lupus Protospatarius' statement that Victor III acceded to the papacy in the days of Pope Clement, and in 1089 his surprising reference to Archbishop Elia 'qui venerat adhuc cum praedicto papa Clemente'.[12] But this is no more than the lightest of Guibertine colouring in the pages of a single annalist. In fact, ecclesiastical loyalties do not seem to have been sharply defined. Urso was certainly in touch with Sichelgaita of Apulia and her son

[5] Nicephorus, p. 337; John of Bari, pp. 359-60; Jerusalem Legend, caps. 8-11, pp. 172-4, 185.

[6] Ed. Cioffari, pp. 87-91, 136-7. Nitti di Vito's identification of the priest with Elia lacks support: *La ripresa gregoriana*, p. 234.

[7] cap. 37, p. 187.

[8] Nicephorus, pp. 349-50; John of Bari, pp. 357-8, 365-6; Jerusalem Legend, caps. 35-6, pp. 184-5.

[9] The claim of the Bari merchants when at Myra that the pope had sent them to bring back the relics was expressly a fiction to deceive their custodians: Nicephorus, p. 338; John of Bari, p. 61; Jerusalem Legend, cap. 15, p. 175.

[10] Nicephorus, pp. 337-9; John of Bari, pp. 365-6; Jerusalem Legend, caps. 35-6, pp. 185-6. On the resulting strife, see Nitti di Vito, *La ripresa gregoriana*, pp. 261-74.

[11] The sources simply regarded the securing of the relics as a popular victory epitomized by Nicholas' name: 'Nam Nikolaus graece, latine victoria resonat populorum': Nicephorus, p. 346; Jerusalem Legend, cap. 35, p. 186. John of Bari significantly omits such an interpretation.

[12] *aa.* 1087, 1089, p. 62; but cf. references to *papa Gregorius* and *papa Urbanus*: *aa.* 1084-99, pp. 61-3.

Roger Borsa when they were creating difficulties for Abbot Desiderius, for in March 1086 they gave Urso the Jewry at Bari, which had been part of Sichelgaita's dower.[13] But in 1090 Clement III wrote of the Normans' long-standing hostility to him.[14] As for Elia, he was no thorough-going Gregorian, as is made clear by his attitude to lay lordship in relation to ecclesiastical wealth.[15] Loyalties at Bari were far from settled: Urso appears to have been less a Guibertine than a waverer, while Elia was motivated by local politics no less than by wider considerations. The key to events at Bari lay within the city—perhaps in movements towards something resembling a commune—rather than in the wider conflict of Gregorians and Guibertines.[16]

(iii) What, then, was the significance of Pope Urban II's intervention at Bari? After his success at Melfi in reconciling the Normans to each other and to the apostolic see,[17] it served to consolidate his own supporters in South Italy. He took exceptional steps to claim the loyalty of Bari, both in the new basilica and at the cathedral, and so of the two parties in the city; for not only did he personally consecrate the *confessio* or shrine of St. Nicholas but also, as he said 'against the custom of the Roman and apostolic church', he consecrated Elia in his local cathedral and conferred the *pallium* upon him there rather than at Rome.[18] He used the upsurge of religious zeal and civic pride that followed the arrival of the relics to capture Bari for the Gregorian papacy. In that sense the reform papacy triumphed there. But the triumph seems to have been the sequel to the fortuitous acquisition of outstanding relics, rather than the well-prepared recapture of a city which under Urso had largely apostatized to Guibert but under Elia was reclaimed from him.

[13] *Cod. dipl. Barese*, i. 56–8, no. 30, Ménager, *Recueil*, pp. 171–2, no. 47.

[14] Letter to the Metropolitan Basil of Calabria: Pitra, *Anal. noviss.* i. 479–80; Holtzmann, *Beiträge*, pp. 98–9, no. 1. For the date, see *IP* x. 21, no. 14.

[15] *Cod. dipl. Barese*, v. 73–4, no. 42, cf. 279–81, no. 164. See F. Babudri, 'Sinossi critica dei traslatori nicolaiani di Bari', *Archivio storico pugliese*, iii (1950), 3–94; Dormeier, *Montecassino*, pp. 102–3.

[16] A commune is suggested by the interpretation of the name Nicholas as *victoria populi*: see above, n. 11. It is fairly clear from the circumstances of the founding of San Nicolà that the cult of St. Nicholas was directed against two objects. The setting up of a pilgrimage centre apart from the cathedral points to animus against an older ecclesiastical establishment, while the construction of the basilica on the site of the Byzantine catapan's court shows aversion to Byzantine authority: Nicephorus, pp. 347–8; John of Bari, p. 366; *Cod. dipl. Barese*, i. 59–61, no. 32, Ménager, *Recueil*, pp. 215–19, no. 61. See also F. Schettini, *La basilica di San Nicolà* (Bari, 1967), 35–41. But the cult was probably not, in its inception, positively pro-Norman. Although Robert Guiscard had captured Bari in 1071, Norman control of the city remained ineffective in 1087, and the sources provide no hint of Norman involvement in or awareness of the translation and its immediate sequel at Bari. Bohemond secured possession only in Aug. 1089: Yewdale (as Ch. IV n. 9), p. 28.

[17] Chalandon, *Domination*, i. 296–7; Becker, *Urban II.*, i. 117–19.

[18] *Cod. dipl. Barese*, i. 64–5, no. 34.

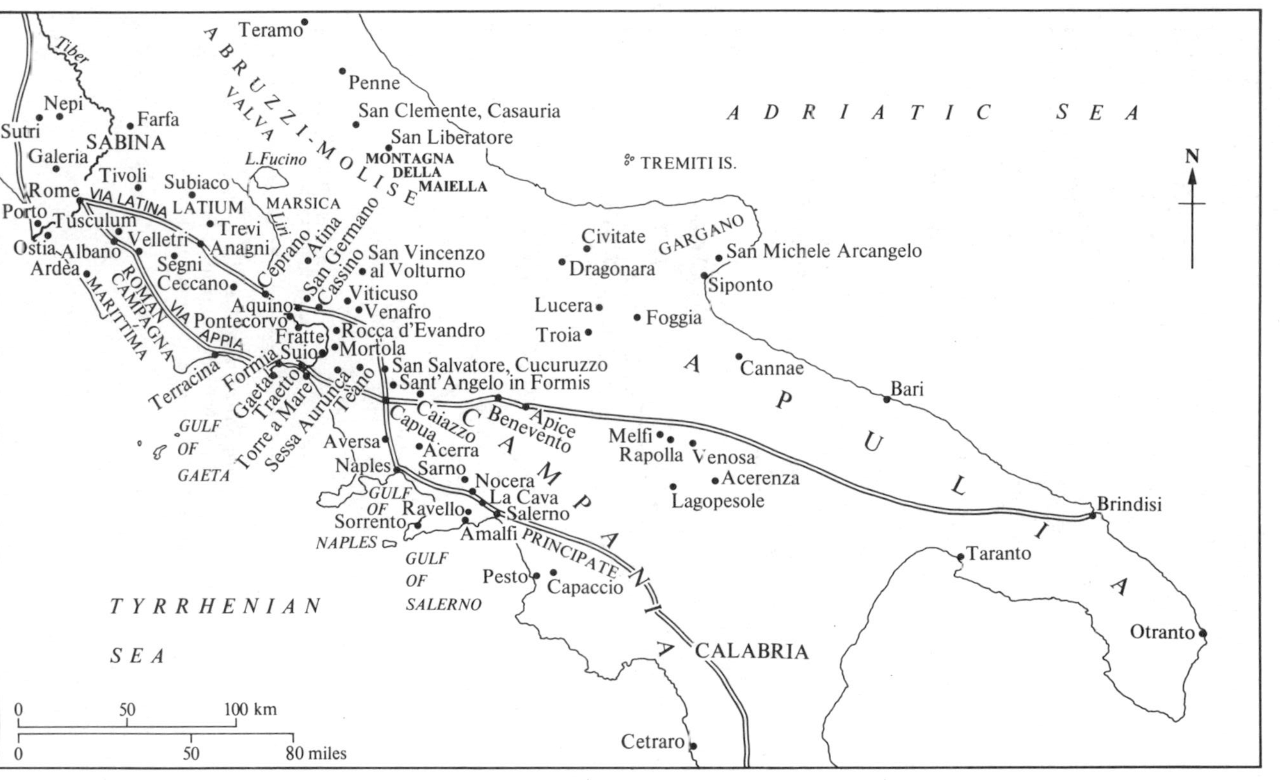

Map 1. South Italy

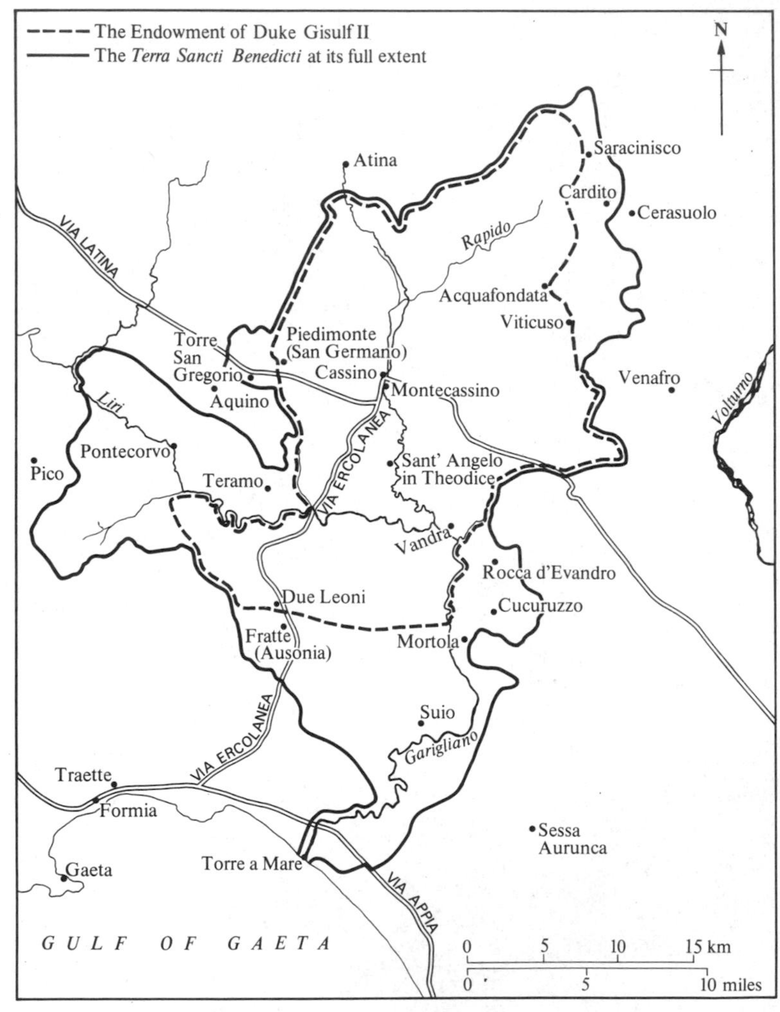

Map 2. *Terra Sancti Benedicti*
(Adapted with permission from the map at the end of Fabiani, '*Las terra di S. Benedetto, II*'.)

Select Bibliography

In some cases items mentioned in footnotes only once are excluded from this Bibliography. A few items not so mentioned have been included if they have helped materially to shape my view of the subject of this book. Abbreviations normally follow the recommendations of the *Repertorium fontium historiae medii aevi primum ab Augusto Potthast digestum*, new edn. by W. Holtzmann and R. Morghen, i, *Series collectionum* (Rome, 1962).

AA SS Boll.: *Acta sanctorum quotquot toto orbe coluntur* (Antwerp, Brussels, Tongerloo, 1643-).

Abh. Berlin: *Abhandlungen der* [*kgl.*] *preussischen* [*deutschen*] *Akademie der Wissenschaften zu Berlin, philosophisch-historische Klasse.*

ACOCELLA, N., *La traslazione di san Matteo* (Salerno, 1954).

— *Salerno medioevale ed altri saggi*, ed. A. Sparano (Naples, 1971).

Acta apostolorum apocrypha, post Constantinum Tischendorf denuo ediderunt R. A. Lipsius et M. Bonnet, 2 vols. (Leipzig, 1881-8).

AHP: *Archivum historiae pontificiae.*

ALBERIC OF MONTECASSINO: see LENTINI, A.

ALBERIGO, G., 'Le origini della dottrina sullo ius divinum del cardinalato (1053-87)', *Reformata reformanda. Festgabe für H. Jedin zum 17. Jun: 1965*, edd. E. Iserloh and K. Repgen, i (Münster, 1965), 39-58.

— *Cardinalato e collegialità. Studi sull'ecclesiologia tra l'xi e il xiv secolo*, Testi e ricerche di scienze religiose pubblicati a cura dell'istituto per le scienze religiose di Bologna, 5 (Florence, 1969).

— 'Regime sinodale e chiesa romana tra l'xi e il xii secolo', *Istituzioni ecclesiastiche*, i. 229-72.

ALFANUS OF SALERNO: see LENTINI, A.

AMANN, É., 'Victor III', *Dictionnaire de théologie catholique*, xv (1950), 2866-72.

Amatus: *Storia de' Normanni di Amato di Montecassino*, ed. V. de Bartholomaeis, *Font. stor. Italia*, xiii (Rome, 1935). See also LENTINI, A.

Anal. Boll.: *Analecta Bollandiana.*

Anal. iur. pont.: *Analecta iuris pontificii.*

Anna Comnena: ANNE COMNÈNE, *Alexiade*, ed. B. Leib, 4 vols. (Paris, 1937-76).

Annales Augustani, ed. G. H. Pertz, *MGH SS* iii (1839), 124-36.

Annales Barenses, ed. G. H. Pertz, *MGH SS* v (1844), 51-6.

Annales Beneventani, ed. G. H. Pertz, *MGH SS* iii (1839), 173-84; also O. BERTOLINI, 'Gli "Annales Beneventani" ', *Bull. Ist. stor. ital.* xlii (1923), 1-163.

Ann. Cas.: *Annales Casinenses*, ed. G. Smidt, *MGH SS* xxx/2 (1926-34), 1385-1449; for the Continuation (1098-1212), ed. G. H. Pertz: *MGH SS* xix (1866), 305-20.

Annales Cavenses, ed. G. H. Pertz, *MGH SS* iii (1839), 186-93.

Annales Ceccanenses, ed. G. H. Pertz, *MGH SS* xix (1866), 276-302.

Annales Romani, ed. L. Duchesne, *Reg. Pap. XIIIe s.*, ii (1889), 331–50.

Arch. Soc. rom.: *Archivio della* [*R.*] *Società romana di storia patria.*

ARNULF, *Gesta archiepiscoporum Mediolanensium*, edd. L. C. Bethmann and W. Wattenbach, *MGH SS* vii (1846), 6–31.

Ausgew. Quell.: *Ausgewählte Quellen zur deutschen Geschichte des Mittelalters*, ed. R. Buchner (Darmstadt and Berlin, 1955–).

AVAGLIANO, F., 'Monumenti del culto a San Pietro in Montecassino', *Benedictina*, xiv (1967), 57–76.

— 'Testi cassinesi per l'ufficio dei SS. Pietro e Paulo', *Benedictina*, xiv (1967), 161–202.

— 'Altri testi della liturgia cassinese per i SS. Pietro e Paulo', *Benedictina*, xv (1968), 19–43.

— 'I codici liturgici dell'archivio di Montecassino', *Benedictina*, xvii (1970), 300–25. See also LENTINI, A.

Bardo: BARDO, *Vita Anselmi episcopi Lucensis*, ed. R. Wilmans, *MGH SS* xii (1856), 1–35.

Becker, *Urban II.*: BECKER, A., *Papst Urban II. (1088–99)*, i, *MGH Schriften*, xix/1 (Stuttgart, 1964).

Beno: BENONIS ALIORUMQUE CARDINALIUM SCHISMATICORUM, *Contra Gregorium VII et Urbanum II scripta*, ed. K. Francke, *MGH Libelli*, ii (1892), 366–422.

BENSON, R. L., *The Bishop-elect. A Study in Medieval Ecclesiastical Office* (Princeton, NJ, 1968).

Benzo of Alba: BENZO OF ALBA, *Ad Heinricum IV imperatorem libri VII*, ed. G. H. Pertz, *MGH SS* xi (1854), 597–681.

Bernhardi, *Lothar*: BERNHARDI, W., *Lothar von Supplinburg*, Jahrbücher der deutschen Geschichte (Leipzig, 1879).

Bernold: BERNOLD, *Chronicon*, ed. G. Waitz, *MGH SS* v (1844), 385–467.

BERTOLINI, O., see *Annales Beneventani.*

BHL: *Bibliotheca hagiographica latina antiquae et mediae aetatis*, 2 vols. (Brussels, 1898–1901).

Bibl. casin.: *Bibliotheca casinensis*, 5 vols. (Montecassino, 1873–94). (Each vol. concludes with a separately paginated *Florilegium casinense*, = *Flor. casin.*)

BLOCH, H., 'Monte Cassino, Byzantium and the West in the Earlier Middle Ages', *DOP* iii. 163–224.

— 'The Schism of Anacletus II and the Glanfeuil Forgeries of Peter the Deacon of Monte Cassino', *Traditio*, viii (1952), 159–264.

— 'Monte Cassino, archabbey of', *New Catholic Encyclopedia*, ix (1967), 1080–3.

— 'Peter the Deacon of Monte Cassino', ibid. xi (1967), 215–16.

— 'Victor III, pope', ibid. xiv (1967), 647.

— 'Monte Cassino's Teachers and Library in the High Middle Ages', *La scuola nell'occidente latino dell'alto medioevo*, Settimane di studio del Centro italiano di studi sull'alto medioevo, 19 (Spoleto, 1972), 563–613.

Bonizo of Sutri: BONIZO OF SUTRI, *Liber ad amicum*, ed. E. Dümmler, *MGH Libelli*, i (1891), 571–620.

BORINO, G. B., 'Per la storia della riforma della chiesa nel sec. xi', *Arch. Soc. rom.* xxxviii (1915), 453–513.

— 'L'elezione e la deposizione di Gregorio VI', ibid. xxxix (1916), 141-252, 295-410.

BRESSLAU, H., *Handbuch der Urkundenlehre für Deutschland und Italien*, 2 vols. (2nd edn., Leipzig, 1912-31).

BRUGNOLI, G., 'Per il testo del *De rithmis* di Alberico di Montecassino', *Benedictina*, xiv (1967), 38-50.

BRUNO OF SEGNI, *Libellus de symoniacis*, ed. E. Sackur, *MGH Libelli*, ii (1892), 543-62.

— *Epistolae quatuor*, ed. E. Sackur, ibid. 563-5.

BUISSON, L., 'Formen normannischer Staatsbildung', *Studien zum mittelalterlichen Lehnswesen*, Vorträge und Forschungen, 5 (Sigmaringen, 1960), 94-184.

Bull. Ist. stor. ital.: *Bullettino dell'Istituto storico italiano e Archivio Muratoriano.*

CAHEN, C., *Le Régime féodal de l'Italie normande* (Paris, 1940).

CAPITANI, O., 'La riforma gregoriana e la lotta per le investiture nella recente storiografia', *Cultura e scuola*, ii (1962/3), 108-15.

— 'La figura del vescovo in alcune collezioni canoniche della seconda metà del secolo xi', *Vescovi e diocesi in Italia nel medioevo (sec. ix-xiii)*, Italia sacra, 5 (Rome, 1964), 161-91.

— 'Esiste un' "Età Gregoriana"? Considerazioni sulla tendenze di una storiografia medievistica', *Rivista di storia e letteratura religiosa*, i (1965), 454-81.

— *Immunità vescovili ad ecclesiologia in età 'pregregoriana' e 'gregoriana'* (Spoleto, 1966).

— 'Specific Motivations and Continuing Themes in the Norman Chronicles of South Italy in the Eleventh and Twelfth Centuries', *Normans in Sicily*, pp. 1-46.

CARBONARA, G., *Iussu Desiderii. Montecassino e l'architettura campano-abruzzese nell'undicesimo secolo* (Rome, 1979).

Caspar, *Roger II.*: CASPAR, E., *Roger II. (1101-54) und die Gründung der normannisch-sicilischen Monarchie* (Innsbruck, 1904).

Caspar, *Petrus Diaconus*: — *Petrus Diaconus und die Monte Cassineser Fälschungen: ein Beitrag zur Geschichte des italienischen Geisteslebens im Mittelalter* (Berlin, 1909).

— 'Studien zum Register Johanns VIII.', *NA* xxvi (1911), 79-156.

CASULA, F., 'Baresone di Torres', *DBI* vi (1964), 389-90.

CECCHELLI, C., 'Di alcune memorie benedettine in Roma', *Bull. Ist. stor. ital.* xlvii (1932), 83-158.

CHALANDON, F., *Les Comnènes*, i. *Essai sur la règne d'Alexis Comnène* (Paris, 1900).

Chalandon, *Domination*: — *Histoire de la domination normande en Italie et en Sicile*, 2 vols. (Paris, 1907).

CHARANIS, P., 'Byzantium, the West and the Origin of the First Crusade', *Byzantion*, xix (1949), 17-36.

Chron. Amalph.: *Chronicon Amalphitanum*, Schwarz, *Amalfi im frühen Mittelalter*, pp. 111-236.

Chronica sancti Benedicti Casinensis, MGH Script. rer. lang., pp. 468-88.

Chronicon breve Nortmannicum, Muratori, *RIS* v (1724), 278 (V)-(VI).

Chronicon Casauriense, Muratori, *RIS* ii/2 (1726), 776–1018.
Chron. Cas.: *Chronica monasterii Casinensis*, ed. W. Wattenbach, *MGH SS* vii (1846), 551–844; *Die Chronik von Montecassino (Chronica monasterii Casinensis)*, ed. H. Hoffmann, *MGH SS* xxiv (1980). [References throughout are to the latter edition.]
Chronicon Farfense di Gregorio di Catino, ed. U. Balzani, 2 vols., *Font. stor. Italia*, xxxiii–xxxiv (Rome, 1903).
Chronicon Salernitanum, ed. G. H. Pertz, *MGH SS* iii (1839), 470–559.
Chronicon Sublacense, ed. R. Morghen, *RIS*[2] (1927), xxiv/6.
Chronicon Vulturnense, ed. V. Frederici, *Font. stor. Italia*, lviii (Rome, 1925–40), lix (1925), lxx (1938), 3–121.
CILENTO, N., 'Sant'Angelo in Formis nel suo significato storico (1072–1087)', *Studi medievali*, iv (1963), 799–812.
— *Italia meridionale longobarda* (2nd edn., Milan and Naples, 1971).
CIOFFARI, G., *La leggenda di Kiev. La traslazione delle reliquie di S. Nicola nel racconto di un annalista russo contemporaneo* (Bari, 1980).
CLEMENTI, D., 'The Relations between the Papacy, the Western Roman Empire and the Emergent Kingdom of Sicily and South Italy, 1050–1156', *Bull. Ist. stor. ital.* lxxx (1968), 191–212.
Cod. dipl. Barese: *Codice diplomatico Barese*, 5 vols. (Bari, 1897–1902). i. *Le pergamene del duomo di Bari (952–1264)*, edd. G. B. Nitto di Rossi and F. Nitti di Vito (1897); v. *Le pergamene di san Nicolà di Bari, periodo normanno (1075–1194)*, ed. F. Nitti di Vito (1902).
Codex diplomaticus Cajetanus, 4 vols. (Montecassino, 1887–1960).
Codice diplomatico del monastero benedettino di S. Maria di Tremiti (1005–1237), ed. A. Petrucci, *Font. stor. Italia*, xcviii/1–3 (Rome, 1960).
CONANT, K. J., *A Brief Commentary on Early Mediaeval Church Architecture* (Baltimore, 1942).
— *Carolingian and Romanesque Architecture, 800–1200* (2nd integrated edn., Harmondsworth, 1978). See also WILLARD, H. M.
Corp. Bonn.: *Corpus scriptorum historiae Byzantinae*, 50 vols. (Bonn, 1828–97).
COWDREY, H. E. J., *The Cluniacs and the Gregorian Reform* (Oxford, 1970).
— 'The Mahdia Campaign of 1087', *EHR* xcii (1977), 1–29.
— 'Two Studies in Cluniac History, 1049–1126', *SG* xi (1978), 5–298.
— 'Pope Gregory VII's "Crusading" Plans of 1074', *Outremer. Studies in the History of the Crusading Kingdom of Jerusalem presented to Joshua Prawer*, edd. B. Z. Kedar, H. E. Mayer, and R. C. Smart (Jerusalem, 1982), 27–40.
CUOZZO, E., 'Il "Breve Chronicon Northmannicum" ', *Bull. Ist. stor. ital.* lxxxiii (1971), 131–232.
DA: *Deutsches Archiv für Erforschung des Mittelalters.*
d'Achery, *Spicil.*: D'ACHERY, L., *Spicilegium sive collectio veterum aliquot scriptorum qui in Galliae bibliothecis delituerant*, 3 vols. (new edn., Paris, 1723).
D'ALESSANDRO, V., '*Fidelitas Normannorum.* Note sulla fondazione dello stato normanno e sui rapporti col papato', *Annali della Facoltà di*

magistero dell'Università di Palermo, 1969, pp. 245–358, repr. *Storigrafia e politica*, pp. 99–220.
— 'Lettura di Amato di Montecassino', *Bull. Ist. stor. ital.* lxxxiii (1971), 119–30, repr. *Storigrafia e politica*, pp. 51–98.
— *Storigrafia e politica nell'Italia normanna* (Naples, 1978).
DAVRIL, A., 'La tradition cassinienne', and 'Conclusion générale', in 'Le culte et les reliques de Saint Benoît et de Sainte Scholastique', *Studia monastica*, xxi (1979), 377–408, 423–8.
DBI: *Dizionario biografico degli Italiani* (Rome, 1960–).
DÉCARREAUX, J., *Normands, papes et moines en Italie méridionale et en Sicile, XIe–XIIe siècle* (Paris, 1974).
DEÉR, J., *Das Papsttum und die süditalienischen Normannenstaaten (1053–1212)* (Göttingen, 1969).
— *Papsttum und Normannen. Untersuchungen zu ihren lehnsrechtlichen und kirchenpolitischen Beziehungen*, Studien und Quellen zur Welt Kaiser Friedrichs II., 1 (Cologne and Vienna, 1972).
DE GAIFFIER, B., 'Translations et miracles de S. Mennas par Léon d'Ostie et Pierre de Mont Cassin', *Anal. Boll.* lxii (1944), 5–32.
DELEHAYE, H., 'Saint Cassiodore', *Mélanges P. Fabre* (Paris, 1902), 40–50; repr. *Mélanges d'hagiographie grecque et latine, Subsidia hagiographica*, xlii (1966), 179–88.
DEL GUIDICE, G., *Codice diplomatico del regno di Carlo I. et II. d'Angiò*, i (Naples, 1863).
Del Re: DEL RE, G., *Cronisti e scrittori sincroni napoletani editi e inediti*, 2 vols. (Naples, 1845–68).
DEMUS, O., *Byzantine Art and the West* (New York, 1970).
—, *Romanesque Mural Painting* (New York, 1970).
De ordinando pontifice, auctor Gallicus, ed. E. Dümmler, *MGH Libelli*, i (1891), 8–14.
Desiderius, *Dial.*: DESIDERIUS OF MONTECASSINO, *Dialogi de miraculis sancti Benedicti*, edd. G. Schwartz and A. Hofmeister, *MGH SS* xxx/2 (1926–34), 1111–51.
Deusdedit, *Coll. can.*: see WULF VON GLANVELL, V.
Deusdedit, *Libellus*: DEUSDEDIT, *Libellus contra invasores et symoniacos et reliquos scismaticos*, ed. E. Sackur, *MGH Libelli*, ii (1892), 292–365.
DHGE: *Dictionnaire d'histoire et de géographie ecclésiastiques*, edd. A. Baudrillart, A. Vogt, and U. de Rouziès (Paris, 1909–).
DI MEO, A., *Annali critico-diplomatici del regno di Napoli*, 12 vols. (Naples, 1795–1819).
DINZELBACHER, P., 'Die Vision Alberichs und die Esdras-Apokryphe', *Stud. Mitt. OSB* lxxxvii (1976), 435–42.
Diversorum patrum sententie, sive Collectio in LXXIV titulos digesta, ed. J. Gilchrist, Monumenta iuris canonici, Series B: Corpus collectionum, 1 (Vatican City, 1973).
Dölger, *Regesten*: DÖLGER, F., *Regesten der Kaiserurkunden der oströmischen Reiches*, ii. *1025–1204* (Munich, 1925).
DONIZO, *Vita Matildis*, ed. L. Bethmann, *MGH SS* xii (1856), 351–409.
DOP: *Dumbarton Oaks Papers* (Cambridge, Mass., 1941–).

Dormeier, *Montecassino*: DORMEIER, H., *Montecassino und die Laien im 11. und 12. Jahrhundert, MGH Schriften*, xxvii (Stuttgart, 1979).
DOUGLAS, D. C., *The Norman Achievement* (London, 1972).
DVI: see Peter the Deacon, *DVI*.
EHR: *English Historical Review*.
EHRLE, F., 'Die Frangipani und der Untergang des Archivs und der Bibliothek der Päpste am Anfang des 13. Jahrhundert', *Mélanges offerts à M. Émile Chatelain* (Paris, 1910), 448–85.
EICHMANN, E., *Weihe und Krönung des Papstes im Mittelalter* (Munich, 1951).
ELZE, R., 'Die päpstliche Kapelle im 12. und 13. Jahrhundert', *ZRG KA* xxxvi (1950), 145–204; repr. *Päpste-Kaiser-Könige*, no. 20.
— 'Das *sacrum palatium Lateranense* im 10. und 11. Jahrhundert', *SG* iv (1952), 27–54; repr. *Päpste-Kaiser-Könige*, no. 1.
— *Päpste-Kaiser-Könige und die mittelalterliche Herrschaftssymbolik* (London, 1982).
ENGELS, O., 'Alberich von Montecassino und seiner Schüler Johannes von Gaeta', *Stud. Mitt. OSB* lxvi (1955), 35–50.
— 'Papst Gelasius II. (Johannes von Gaeta) als Hagiograph', *QFIAB* xxxv (1955), 1–45.
— 'Die Erasmuspassion des Papstes Gelasius II.', *Römisches Quartalschrift*, li (1956), 16–33.
— 'Die hagiographischen Texte Papst Gelasius II. in der Überlieferung der Eustachius-, Erasmus-, und Hypolistuslegende', *Historisches Jahrbuch*, lxxi (1956), 118–33.
Epp. vag.: see GREGORY VII.
ERDMANN, C., *Die Entstehung des Kreuzzugsgedankens* (Stuttgart, 1935); *The Origin of the Idea of Crusade*, Eng. trans. by M. W. Baldwin and W. Goffart (Princeton, NJ, 1977).
Fabianai, 'La terra di S. Benedetto': FABIANI, L., 'La terra di S. Benedetto: studio storico-giuridico sull'abbazia di Montecassino dell'viii al xiii secolo', i–ii (2nd edn.), *Misc. cassin.* xxxiii–xxxiv (1968); iii, *Misc. cassin.* xliii (1980).
FALKENHAUSEN, V. VON, *Untersuchungen über die byzantinische Herrschaft in Süditalien vom 9. bis ins 11. Jahrhundert* (Wiesbaden, 1967).
— 'I ceti dirigenti prenormanni al tempo della costituzione degli stati normanni nell'Italia meridionali e in Sicilia', Rossetti, *Forme di potere*, pp. 321–77.
FEDELE, P., 'Una chiesa del Palatino: S. Maria "in Pallara" ', *Arch. Soc. rom.* xxvi (1903), 343–73.
FLICHE, A., 'L'élection d'Urban II', *Le Moyen Âge*, 2ᵉ sér., xix (1915), 356–94.
— 'Le pontificat de Victor III', *Revue d'histoire ecclésiastique*, xx (1924), 387–412.
— *La Réforme grégorienne*, 3 vols. (Louvain and Paris, 1924–37).
— *La Réforme grégorienne et la reconquête chrétienne*, Histoire de l'église depuis les origines jusqu'à nos jours, edd. A. Fliche and V. Martin, 8 (Paris, 1946).

Flor. cassin.: see *Bibl. cassin.*
Font. stor. Italia: *Fonti per la storia d'Italia.*
FOURNIER, P., and LE BRAS, G., *Histoire des collections canoniques en occident depuis les Fausses Décretales jusqu'au Décret de Gratien*, 2 vols. (Paris, 1931-2).
Frutolf of Michaelsberg: FRUTOLF OF MICHAELSBERG, *Chronica (Frutolf und Ekkehards Chroniken und die anonyme Kaiserchronik)*, edd. F.-J. Schmale and I. Schmale-Ott, *Ausgew. Quell.* xv (1972).
FUHRMANN, H., 'Über den Reformgeist der 74-Titel Sammlung', *Festschrift für Hermann Heimpel zum 70. Geburtstag*, 2 vols. (Göttingen, 1972), ii. 1101-20.
— *Einfluss und Verbreitung der pseudoisidorischen Fälschungen*, 3 vols., *MGH Schriften*, xxiv/1-3 (Stuttgart, 1972-4).
Fulk of Benevento: FULK OF BENEVENTO, *Chronicon*, Del Re, i. 157-276.
FÜRST, C. G., *Cardinalis. Prolegomena zu einer Rechtsgeschichte des römischen Kardinalkollegiums* (Munich, 1967).
GALASSO, G., 'Social and Political Developments in the Eleventh and Twelfth Centuries', *Normans in Sicily*, pp. 47-63.
GALLO, A., *Aversa normanna* (Naples, 1938).
Ganzer, *Kardinalat*: GANZER, K., *Die Entwicklung des auswärtigen Kardinalats im hohen Mittelalter*, Bibliothek des Deutschen Historischen Instituts in Rom, 26 (Tübingen, 1963).
— 'Das römische Kardinalkollegium', *Istituzioni ecclesiastiche*, pp. 153-81.
GATTO, L., 'Ugo Maumouzet, conte di Manoppello, Normanno d'Abruzzo', *Studi . . . Morghen*, i. 355-73.
Gattula, *Historia*: GATTULA [GATTOLA], E., *Historia abbatiae Cassinensis* (Venice, 1733).
Gattula, *Accessiones*: — *Ad historiam abbatiae Cassinensis accessiones* (Venice, 1734).
Gaufredus Malaterra: GAUFREDUS MALATERRA, *De rebus gestis Rogerii Calabriae et Siciliae comitis et Roberti Guiscardi ducis fratris eius*, ed. E. Pontieri, *RIS*[2] (1925-8), v/1.
GAUSS, J., *Ost und West in der Kirchen- und Papstgeschichte des 11. Jahrhunderts* (Zurich, 1967).
GAY, J., *L'Italie meridionale et l'empire byzantine* (Paris, 1904).
GEOFFREY MALATERRA: see GAUFREDUS MALATERRA.
GIGALSKI, B., *Bruno, Bischof von Segni, Abt von Monte-Cassino (1049-1123): sein Leben und seine Schriften*, Kirchengeschichtliche Studien, 3 (Münster-in-Westfalen, 1898).
GOEZ, W., '*Papa qui et episcopus.* Zum Selbstverstandnis des Reformpapsttums im 11. Jahrhundert', *AHP* viii (1970), 27-59.
— *Grundzüge der Geschichte Italiens im Mittelalter und Renaissance* (Darmstadt, 1975).
GP: *Germania Pontificia*, ed. A. Brackmann, 3 vols. (Berlin, 1910-35).
GRÉGOIRE, H., *Bruno de Segni, exégète medièval et théologien monastique* (Spoleto, 1965).
— 'Le Mont-Cassin dans la réforme de l'église de 1049 à 1122', *Il*

monachesimo e la riforma ecclesiastica (1049–1122), Miscellanea del Centro di studi medioevali, 6 (Milan, 1971), 21–53.

GREGORIUS MAGNUS, *Dialogi*, ed. U. Moricca, *Font. stor. Italia*, lvii (Rome, 1924).

Gregory VII, *Epp. vag.*, or *Epp. vag.*: *The Epistolae vagantes of Pope Gregory VII*, ed. H. E. J. Cowdrey (Oxford, 1972).

Gregory VII, *Reg.*, or *Reg.*: *Gregorii VII Registrum*, ed. E. Caspar, *MGH Epist. sel.* ii (1920–3).

GUILLAUME, P., *Essai historique sur l'abbaye de Cava d'après des documents inédits* (Cava dei Terreni, 1877).

GUILLAUME DE POUILLE: see WILLIAM OF APULIA.

Guy of Ferrara: GUY OF FERRARA, *De scismate Hildebrandi*, ed. R. Wilmans, *MGH Libelli*, i (1891), 529–67.

HAGENMEYER, H., *Die Kreuzzugsbriefe aus den Jahren 1088–1100* (Innsbruck, 1901).

HAIDER, S., 'Zu den Anfängen der päpstlichen Kapelle', *MIÖG* lxxxvii (1979), 139–78.

HALLER, J., *Das Papsttum. Idee und Wirklichkeit*, ii (Darmstadt, 1962).

HALLINGER, K., *Gorze-Kluny. Studien zu den monastischen Lebensformen und Gegensätzen im Hochmittelalter*, Studia Anselmiana, 22–5 (Rome, 1950–1).

HEINEMANN, L. VON, *Geschichte der Normannen in Unteritalien und Sicilien*, i (Leipzig, 1894).

— *Normannische Herzogs- und Königsurkunden aus Unteritalien und Sicilien* (Tübingen, 1899).

HERBERHOLD, F., 'Die Angriff des Cadalus von Parma (Gegenpapst Honorius II.) auf Rom in den Jahren 1062 und 1063', *SG* ii (1947), 477–503.

HERMANN VON REICHENAU, *Chronicon*, edd. K. Nobbe and R. Buchner, *Quellen des 9. und 11. Jahrhunderts der Hambürgischen Kirche und des Reichs*, edd. W. Trillmich and R. Buchner, *Ausgew. Quell.* xi (1961), 628–707.

HERRMANN, K.-J., *Das Tusculanerpapsttum (1012–1046)*, Päpste und Papsttum, 4 (Stuttgart, 1973).

Hirsch, 'Desiderius': HIRSCH, F., 'Desiderius von Monte Cassino als Papst Victor III.', *Forschungen zur deutschen Geschichte*, vii (1867), 1–112.

HIRSCH, F., 'Die Auffassung des simonistischen und schismatischen Weihen im elften Jahrhundert, besonders bei Kardinal Deusdedit', *Archiv für katholisches Kirchenrecht*, lxxxvii (1907), 25–70.

— 'Kardinal Deusdedits Stellung zur Laieninvestitur', ibid., lxxviii (1908), 34–49.

— 'Die rechtliche Stellung der römischen Kirche und des Papstes nach Kardinal Deusdedit', ibid. lxxviii (1908), 595–624.

HOFFMANN, H., 'Der Kalendar des Leo Marsicanus', *DA* xxi (1965), 82–149.

— 'Das *Chronicon Vulturnense* und die Chronik von Montecassino', *DA* xxii (1966), 179–96.

— 'Die älteren Abtslisten von Montecassino', *QFIAB* xlvii (1967), 224–354.

— 'Die Anfänge der Normannen in Süditalien', *QFIAB* xlix (1969), 95-144.

— 'Petrus Diaconus, die Herrn von Tusculum und der Sturz Oderisius' II. von Montecassino', *DA* xxvii (1971), 1-109.

— 'Chronik und Urkunde in Montecassino', *QFIAB* li (1971), 93-206.

— 'Zur Abtslist von Subiaco', *QFIAB* lii (1972), 781-8.

— 'Bruno di Segni, santo', *DBI* xiv (1972), 644-7.

— 'Studien zur Chronik von Montecassino', *DA* xxix (1973), 59-162.

— 'Stylistische Tradition in der Klosterchronik von Montecassino', *MGH Mittelalterliche Textüberlieferung und ihre kritische Aufarbeitung*, pp. 29-41.

— 'Zum Register und zu den Briefen Papst Gregors VII.', *DA* xxxii (1976), 86-130.

— 'Der Kirchenstaat im Mittelalter', *QFIAB* lvii (1977), 1-45.

— 'Langobarden, Normannen, Päpste', *QFIAB* lviii (1978), 137-80.

— 'Zur Geschichte Montecassinos im 11. und 12. Jahrhundert', Dormeier, *Montecassino*, pp. 1-20. See also *Chron. Cas.*

HOFMEISTER, A., 'Maurus von Amalfi und die Elfbeinkassette von Farfa aus dem 11. Jahrhundert', *QFIAB* xxiv (1932/3), 278-83.

HOLTZMANN, W., 'Studien zur Orientpolitik des Papsttums und zur Entstehung des ersten Kreuzzuges', *Historisches Vierteljahrschrift*, xxii (1924), 167-99; repr. *Beiträge*, pp. 51-78.

— 'Die Unionsverhandlungen zwischen Kaiser Alexios I. und Papst Urban II. im Jahre 1089', *Byzantinische Zeitschrift*, xxviii (1928), 38-67; repr. *Beiträge*, pp. 79-105.

— 'Laurentius von Amalfi, ein Lehrer Hildebrands', *SG* i (1947), 207-36; repr. *Beiträge*, pp. 9-33.

Holtzmann, *Beiträge*: — *Beiträge zur Reichs- und Papstgeschichte des hohen Mittelalters*, Bonner historische Forschungen, 8 (Bonn, 1957).

HÜBINGER, P. E., *Die letzten Worte Papst Gregors VII.* (Opladen, 1973).

Hugh of Flavigny: HUGH OF FLAVIGNY, *Chronicon*, *MGH SS* viii (1848), 280-503.

HUGH OF VENOSA, *Vita quattuor priorum abbatum Cavensium*, ed. L. M. Cerasoli, *RIS*[2] (1941), vi/5.

Hüls, *Kardinäle*: HÜLS, R., *Kardinäle, Klerus und Kirchen Roms, 1049-1130*, Bibliothek des Deutschen Historischen Instituts in Rom, 48 (Tübingen, 1977).

— ' "Cardinalis sancti Petri" und "Cardinalis sancti Pauli" ', *QFIAB* lvii (1977), 332-8.

HUYGHENS, R. B. C., 'Bérenger de Tours, Lanfranc et Bernold de Constance', *Sacris erudiri*, xvi (1965), 355-403.

Inguanez, *Catalogus*: INGUANEZ, M., *Codicum Casinensium manuscriptorum catalogus*, 3 vols. (Montecassino, 1915-41).

— *Regesto di S. Angelo in Formis*, 2 vols. (Montecassino, 1925).

— 'Frammenti di un necrologio cassinese del secolo xi', *Misc. cassin.* xi (1932), 17-34.

— *I Necrologi Cassinesi*, i. *Il Necrologio del Cod. Cassinese 47, Font. stor. Italia*, lxxxiii (Rome, 1941).

INGUANEZ, M., 'Montecassino *camera imperiale*', *Atti del V congresso nazionale di studi romani*, iii (1942), 34–7.

— and WILLARD, H. M., *Alberici Casinensis Flores rhetorici*, *Misc. cassin.* xiv (1938). See also MIRRA, A.

IP: *Italia pontificia sive Repertorium privilegiarum et litterarum*, ed. P. F. Kehr, 10 vols. (Berlin, 1906–75).

Istituzioni ecclesiastiche: *Le istituzioni ecclesiastiche della 'societas christiana' dei secoli xi–xii*, 2 vols., Miscellanea del Centro di studi medioevali, 7–8 (Milan, 1974–7).

Jaffé, *Bibl.*: JAFFÉ, P., *Bibliotheca rerum Germanicarum*, 6 vols. (Berlin, 1864–73).

JEH: *Journal of Ecclesiastical History*.

JL: *Regesta pontificum Romanorum*, ed. P. Jaffé, 2 vols. (2nd edn. by W. Wattenbach with S. Loewenfeld, F. Kaltenbrunner, and P. Ewald, Leipzig, 1895–8).

JONES, C. W., *Saint Nicholas of Myra, Bari and Manhattan. Biography of a Legend* (Chicago and London, 1978).

JORANSON, E., 'The Inception of the Career of the Normans in Italy—Legend and History', *Speculum*, xxiii (1948), 353–96.

JORDAN, K., 'Das Eindringen des Lehnswesens in das Rechtsleben der römischen Kurie', *Archiv für Urkundenforschung*, xii (1932), 13–110 (separate repr. with supplementary notes, Darmstadt, 1971).

— 'Zur päpstlichen Finanzgeschichte im 11. und 12. Jahrhundert', *QFIAB* xxv (1933/4), 61–104.

— 'Die Entstehung der römischen Kurie', *ZRG KA* xxviii (1939), 97–152 (separate repr. with supplementary notes, Darmstadt, 1962).

— 'Die päpstliche Verwaltung im Zeitalter Gregors VII.', *SG* i (1947), 111–35.

— 'Die Stellung Wiberts von Ravenna in der Publizistik des Investiturstreites', *MIÖG* lxxii (1954), 155–64.

KAMP, N., 'Vescovi e diocesi nell'Italia meridionale nel passagio dalla dominazione bizantina allo Stato normanno', Rossetti, *Forme di potere*, pp. 379–97.

Kehr, 'Le bolle pontificie': KEHR, P. F., 'Le bolle pontificie anteriori al 1189 che si conservano nell'archivio di Montecassino', *Misc. cassin.* ii (1899).

— 'Due documenti pontifici illustranti la storia di Roma negli ultimi anni del secolo xi', *Arch. Soc. rom.* xxiii (1900), 277–83.

— 'Zur Geschichte Wiberts von Ravenna (Clemens III.)', *SB Berlin*, 1921, pp. 355–68, 973–88.

— 'Die Belehnung der süditalienischen Normannenfürsten durch die Päpste, 1059–1192', *Abh. Berlin*, 1934, no. 1. See also *IP*.

KITZINGER, E., 'The Gregorian Reform and the Visual Arts: a Problem of Method', *TRHS*, 5th ser., xxii (1972), 87–102.

KLEWITZ, H.-W., 'Studien über die Wiederherstellung der römischen Kirche in Süditalien durch das Reformpapsttum', *QFIAB* xxv (1933/4), 105–57; repr. *Reformpapsttum*, pp. 135–205.

— 'Die Entstehung des Kardinalkollegiums', *ZRG KA* xxv (1936), 115–221; repr. *Reformpapsttum*, pp. 11–134.

— 'Petrus Diaconus und die Montecassineser Klosterchronik des Leos von Ostia', *Archiv für Urkundenforschung*, xiv (1936), 414–53; repr. *Ausgewählte Aufsätze*, pp. 425–64.

— 'Montecassino in Rom', *QFIAB* xxviii (1936/7), 36–47; repr. *Ausgewählte Aufsätze*, pp. 465–76.

— 'Das Ende des Reformpapsttums', *DA* iii (1939), 371–412; repr. *Reformpapsttum*, pp. 207–59.

Klewitz, *Reformpapsttum*: — *Reformpapsttum und Kardinalkolleg* (Darmstadt, 1957).

— *Ausgewählte Aufsätze*: — *Ausgewählte Aufsätze zur Kirchen- und Geistesgeschichte des Mittelalters*, ed. G. Tellenbach (Aalen, 1971).

Köhncke, *Wibert*: KÖHNCKE, O., *Wibert von Ravenna (Papst Clemens III.)* (Leipzig, 1888).

Krause, PWD: KRAUSE, H.-G., 'Das Papstwahldekret von 1059 und seine Rolle im Investiturstreit', *SG* vii (1960).

KRAUTHEIMER, R., *Rome: Portrait of a City* (Princeton, NJ, 1980).

KUTTNER, S., '*Cardinalis*: the History of a Canonical Concept', *Traditio*, iii (1945), 129–214; repr. *The History of Ideas and Doctrines of Canon Law in the Middle Ages* (London, 1980), no. IX, with additional note on pp. 14–18.

LADNER, G. B., 'I mosaici e gli affreschi ecclesiastico-politici nell'antico palazzo Lateranense', *Rivista di archeologia cristiana*, xii (1935), 265–92.

— *I ritratti dei papi nell'antichità e nel medioevo*, i (Vatican City, 1941).

Lampert of Hersfeld: LAMPERT VON HERSFELD, *Annales*, edd. O. Holder-Egger and W. D. Fritz, *Ausgew. Quell.* xiii (n.d.).

LAURENTIUS MONACHUS CASINENSIS ARCHIEPISCOPUS AMALFITANUS, *Opera*, ed. F. Newton, *MGH Quell. Geistesgesch.* vii (1973).

LAWN, B., *The Salernitan Questions* (Oxford, 1963).

LECCISOTTI, T., 'Le colonie cassinesi in Capitanata', i. Lesina, *Misc. cassin.* xiii (1937); ii. Il Gargano, ibid. xv (1938); iii. Ascoli Satriano, ibid. xix (1940); iv. Troia, ibid. xxix (1957).

— 'Due monaci cassinesi arcivescovi di Siponto', *Iapigia*, xiv (1943), 155–65.

— 'L'incontro di Desiderio di Montecassino col re Enrico IV ad Albano', *SG* i (1947), 307–19.

— *Montecassino, sein Leben und seine Ausbreitung* ([Montecassino], 1949).

— 'Le relazioni fra Montecassino e Tremiti e i possedimenti cassinesi a Foggia e Lucera', *Benedictina*, iii (1949), 203–15.

— *et al.*, 'Il sepolchro di S. Benedetto', *Misc. cassin.* xxvii (1951).

— 'A proposito di antiche consuetudini cassinesi', *Benedictina*, x (1956), 329–38.

— 'Aligerno', *DBI* ii (1960), 381–2.

— 'Ordo Casinensis II dictus Ordo officii', *Corpus consuetudinum monasticarum*, i (Siegburg, 1963), 93–176.

— 'Riflessi Matildici sull'arce Cassinesi', *Atti e memorie della Deputazione di storia patria per le antiche provincie Modenesi*, 9th ser., iii (1963), 233–43.

Leccisotti, *Regesti*: *Abbazia di Montecassino, I regesti dell'Archivio*, edd. T. Leccisotti and F. Avagliano, i (1964); ii (1965); iii (1966); iv (1968); vi (1972); vii (1972); viii (1973); ix (1974); x (1975); xi (1977) (Rome: Ministero dell'interno. Pubblicazioni degli Archivio di Stato). See also LEO OF OSTIA.

LEHMANN, R., 'Über den die Excommunication des Erzbischofs Hugo von Lyon durch Papst Victor III. betreffenden Brief des ersten an die Grafin Mathilde', *Forschungen zur deutschen Geschichte*, vii (1868), 641–8.

LEHMANN-BROCKHAUS, O., *Schriftsquellen zur Kunstgeschichte des 11. und 12. Jahrhunderts* (Berlin, 1938).

LEIB, B., *Rome, Kiev et Byzance à la fin du XIe siècle* (Paris, 1924). See also ANNA COMNENA.

Le Liber censuum de l'église romaine, edd. P. Fabre and L. Duchesne, 3 vols., *Reg. pap. XIIIe s.*, vi (Paris, 1889–52).

Le Liber pontificalis, ed. L. Duchesne, 3 vols., *Reg. pap. XIIIe s.*, iii (Paris, 1886–1957) (= *LP*).

LENTINI, A., 'L'omilia e la vita di s. Scholastica di Alberico cassinese', *Benedictina*, iii (1949), 217–38.

— 'La "Vita s. Dominici" di Alberico cassinese', *Benedictina*, v (1951), 55–77.

— 'Alberico di Montecassino nel quadro della riforma gregoriana', *SG* iv (1952), 55–109.

— 'Sulla *Passio s. Modesti* di Alberico cassinese', *Benedictina*, vi (1952), 231–5.

— 'Ricerche biografiche su Amato di Montecassino', *Benedictina*, xx (1955), 183–96.

— 'Gregorio VII nel *De gestis apostolorum* di Amato cassinese', *SG* v (1956), 281–9.

— 'Le odi di Alfano ai principi Gisulfo e Guido', *Aevum*, xxxi (1957), 230–40.

— 'Leo Ostiensi e Gauderico', *Benedictina*, xi (1957), 131–46.

— 'Rassegna delle poesie di Alfano da Salerno', *Bull. Ist. stor. ital.* lxix (1957), 213–42.

— 'Il ritmo "Cives caelestis patriae" e il "De duodecim lapidibus" di Amato', *Benedictina*, xii (1958), 15–26.

— 'Il poema di Amato su S. Pietro apostolo', 2 vols., *Misc. cassin.* xxx–xxxi (1958–9).

— 'Alberico di Montecassino', *DBI* i (1960), 643–5.

— 'Alfano', *DBI* ii (1960), 253–7.

— 'Amato di Montecassino', *DBI* ii (1960), 682–4.

— 'Il carme di Alfano su S. Pietro', *Benedictina*, xiv (1967), 27–37.

— 'Litanie di santi e orazioni salmiche in codici cassinesi del secolo xi', *Benedictina*, xvii (1970), 13–29.

— 'Note sui monaci-vescovi dei secoli x–xi', *Benedictina*, xxiii (1976), 9–13.

Lentini and Avagliano, *Carmi*: — and AVAGLIANO, F., 'I carmi di Alfano I, archivescovo di Salerno', *Misc. cassin.* xxxviii (1974).

Leo of Ostia, *Narratio*: LEO OF OSTIA, *Narratio celeberrime consecrationis et dedicationis ecclesiae Cassinensis*, ed. T. Leccisotti, *Misc. cassin.* xxxvi (1973), 215–25. See also *Chron. Cas.*; ORLANDI.

Liber de unitate ecclesiae conservanda, ed. W. Schwenkenbecher, *MGH Libelli*, ii (1892), 173–284.

Liber largitorius vel notarius monasterii Pharphensis, ed. G. Zucchetti, 2 vols., Regesta chartarum Italiae, 9/1–2 (Rome, 1913–22).

LOEW, E. A., see LOWE, E. A.

LOHRMANN, D., 'Die Jugendwerke des Johannes von Gaeta', *QFIAB* xlvii (1967), 355–445.

— *Das Register Papst Johannes' VIII. (872–882)*, Bibliothek des Deutschen Historischen Instituts in Rom, 30 (Tübingen, 1968).

LOKRANTZ, M., *L'opera poetica di s. Pier Damiani* (Stockholm, 1964).

LOUD, G. A., 'Church and Society in the Norman Principality of Capua, 1058–1197' (Univ. of Oxford D.Phil. thesis, 1978).

— 'Abbot Desiderius of Montecassino and the Gregorian Papacy', *JEH* xxx (1979), 305–26.

— 'Five Unpublished Charters of the Norman Princes of Capua', *Benedictina*, xxvi (1980), 161–76.

— 'The Norman Counts of Caiazzo and the Abbey of Montecassino', *Misc. cassin.* xliv (1981), 199–217.

— 'How "Norman" was the Norman Conquest of Southern Italy?' *Nottingham Medieval Studies*, xxv (1981), 13–34.

Loud, 'Calendar': — 'A Calendar of the Diplomas of the Norman Princes of Capua', *Papers of the British School at Rome*, xlix (1981), 99–143.

LOWE (= LOEW), E. A., 'Die ältesten Kalendarien aus Monte Cassino', *Quellen und Untersuchungen zur lateinischen Philologie des Mittelalters*, iii (Munich, 1908).

— *The Beneventan Script: a History of the South Italian Minuscule* (Oxford, 1914).

— *Scripta Beneventana*, 2 vols. (Oxford, 1929).

LP: see *Le Liber pontificalis.*

LUCCHESI, G., 'Clavis S. Petri Damiani', *Studi su S. Pier Damiani in onore del card. A. G. Cicognani* (2nd edn., Faenza, 1970), 1–215.

— 'Per una vita di San Pier Damiani', *San Pier Damiani nel ix centenario della morte (1072–1972)*, 4 vols. (Cesena, 1972–8), i. 13–179; ii. 13–160.

— 'I viaggi di S. Pier Damiani', *S. Pier Damiani. Atti del convegno di studi nel ix centenario della morte* (Faenza, 1973), 71–91.

— 'Il sermonario di S. Pier Damiani come monumento storico agiografico e liturgico', *SG* x (1975), 9–67.

LÜHE, W., *Hugo von Die und Lyon* (Breslau, 1898).

Lupus Protospatarius: LUPUS PROTOSPATARIUS, *Chronicon*, ed. G. H. Pertz, *MGH SS* v (1844), 51–63.

Mabillon, *Annales OSB*: MABILLON, J., *Annales ordinis sancti Benedicti*, 6 vols. (Paris, 1703–39).

MANCONE, A., 'Il Registrum Petri Diaconi', *Bullettino dell'Archivio palaeografico italiano*, new ser., ii–iii (1956/7), 99–126.

— 'Un diploma sconosciuto del principe Gisulfo di Salerno a favore di Montecassino', ibid. iv–v (1958/9), 95–9.

MANITIUS, M., *Geschichte der lateinischen Literatur des Mittelalters*, 3 vols. (Munich, 1911–31).
Mansi: *Sacrorum conciliorum nova et amplissima collectio*, ed. J. D. Mansi, 31 vols. (Florence and Venice, 1759–98).
March, *Liber pontificalis*: MARCH, J. M., *Liber pontificalis prout exstat in codice manuscripto Dertusensi* (Barcelona, 1925).
MATRONOLA, M., *Un testo inedito di Berengario di Tours e il concilio romano del 1079*, Orbis romanus, 6 (Milan, 1936).
MÉNAGER, L.-R., 'La "byzantinisation" religieuse de l'Italie méridionale (IXe–XIIe siècles) et la politique monastique des Normands d'Italie', *Revue d'histoire ecclésiastique*, liii (1958), 747–74; liv (1959), 5–40; repr. *Hommes et institutions de l'Italie normande* (London, 1981), no. I.
— 'Les fondations monastiques de Robert Guiscard, duc de Pouille et Calabre', *QFIAB* xxxix (1959), 1–116.
Ménager, *Recueil*: — *Recueil des actes des ducs normands d'Italie (1046–1127)*, i. *Les premiers ducs (1946–1087)*, Società di storia patria per la Puglia, 45 (Bari, 1981).
Meyer von Knonau, *Jahrbücher*: MEYER VON KNONAU, G., *Jahrbücher des deutschen Reiches unter Heinrich IV. und Heinrich V.*, 7 vols., Jahrbücher der deutschen Geschichte (Leipzig, 1898–1909).
MEYVAERT, P., 'Peter the Deacon and the Tomb of St. Benedict', *RB* lxv (1955), 3–70; repr. *Benedict, Gregory, Bede and Others*, no. I.
— 'The Autograph of Peter the Deacon', *Bulletin of the John Rylands Library*, xxxviii (1955/6), 114–38.
— 'Alberic of Monte Cassino or St. Peter Damian?', *RB* lxvii (1957), 175–81.
— 'Bérenger de Tours contre Albéric du Mont-Cassin', *RB* lxx (1960), 324–32.
— 'The Exegetical Treatises of Peter the Deacon and Eriugena's Latin Rendering of the *Ad Thalassium* of Maximus the Confessor', *Sacris Erudiri*, xiv (1963), 130–48; repr. *Benedict, Gregory, Bede and Others*, no. XIII.
— *Benedict, Gregory, Bede and Others* (London, 1977).
— and DEVOS, P., 'Trois énigmes cyrillo-méthodiennes de la "Légende italique" résolues grâce à un document inédit', *Anal. Boll.* lxxiii (1955), 375–461.
— and — 'Autour de Léon d'Ostie et de sa *Translatio s. Clementis*', *Anal. Boll.* lxxiv (1965), 189–240.
MGH: *Monumenta Germaniae historica.*
— *Briefe*: *Die Briefe der deutschen Kaiserzeit.*
— *Const.*: *Legum sectio IV: Constitutiones et acta publica imperatorum et regum.*
— *Dipl. Kar.*: *Diplomata Karolinorum. Die Urkunden der Karolinger.*
— *Dipl. reg. imp. Germ.*: *Diplomata regum et imperatorum Germaniae. Die Urkunden der deutschen Könige und Kaiser.* Referred to according to name: *Dipl. OI*: Otto I; *Dipl. OII*: Otto II; *Dipl. OIII*: Otto III; *Dipl. HII*: Henry II; *Dipl. CII*: Conrad II; *Dipl. HIII*: Henry III; *Dipl. HIV*: Henry IV; *Dipl. LIII*: Lothar III.

— *Epist. sel.*: *Epistolae selectae.*
— *Libelli*: *Libelli de lite imperatorum et pontificum saec. xi et xii conscripti.*
— *Mittelalterliche Textüberlieferungen und ihre kritische Aufarbeitung* (Munich, 1976).
— *Quell. Geistegesch.*: *Quellen zur Geistesgeschichte des Mittelalters.*
— *Schriften*: *Schriften der MGH.*
— *Script. rer. Germ.*: *Scriptores rerum Germanicarum in usum scholarum ex Monumentis Germaniae historicis separatim editi.*
— *Script. rer. Lang.*: *Scriptores rerum Langobardicarum et Italicarum saec. vi–ix.*
— *SS*: *Scriptores.*
MICCOLI, G., *Pietro Igneo. Studi sull'età gregoriana* (Rome, 1960).
— *Chiesa gregoriana* (Florence, 1966).
MICHAUD, 'Chambre apostolique', *Dictionnaire du droit canonique*, iii (1942), 388–403.
Migne, *PL*: MIGNE, J. P., *Patrologiae cursus completus, series latina.*
MINNINGER, M., *Von Clermont zum Wormser Konkordat. Die Auseinandersetzungen um den Lehnsnexus zwischen König und Episkopat* (Cologne and Vienna, 1978).
MIÖG: *Mitteilungen des Instituts für österreichische Geschichtsforschung.*
MIRRA, A., 'I versi di Guaiferio monaco di Montecassino nel sec. xi', *Bull. Ist. stor. ital.* xliv (1931), 93–107.
— 'Guaiferio monaco poeta a Montecassino nel secolo xi', ibid. xlvii (1932), 199–208.
— and INGUANEZ, M., 'La visione di Alberico', *Misc. cassin.* xi (1932), 33–103.
Misc. cassin.: *Miscellanea cassinese.*
MONTCLOS, J. DE, *Lanfranc et Bérenger. La controverse eucharistique du XIe siècle* (Louvain, 1971).
Muratori, *Antiq.*: *Antiquitates italicae medii aevi*, ed. L. A. Muratori, 17 vols. (Milan and Arezzo, 1738–80).
Muratori, *RIS*: *Rerum italicarum scriptores*, ed. L. A. Muratori, 25 vols. (Milan, 1723–51).
See also *RIS*².
NA: *Neues Archiv der Gesellschaft für ältere deutsche Geschichtskunde.*
NEWTON, F., 'The Desiderian Scriptorium at Monte Cassino: the Chronicle and Some Surviving Manuscripts', *DOP* xxx (1976), 35–54.
— 'Leo Marsicanus and the Dedicatory Text and Drawing in Monte Cassino 99', *Scriptorium*, xxxiii (1979), 181–205.
NITTI DI VITO, F., 'La traslazione delle reliquie di San Nicolà', *Iapigia*, viii (1937), 295–411.
Nitti di Vito, *La ripresa gregoriana*: — *La ripresa gregoriana di Bari (1085–1105) e i suoi riflessi nel mondo contemporaneo politico e religioso* (Trani, 1942). See also *Cod. dipl. Barese.*
NORDEN, W., *Das Papsttum und Byzanz* (Berlin, 1903).
Normans in Sicily: *The Normans in Sicily and South Italy*, Lincei Lectures, 1974 (Oxford, 1977).

Orderic Vitalis: *The Ecclesiastical History of Orderic Vitalis*, ed. M. Chibnall, 6 vols. (Oxford, 1969–80).

ORLANDI, G. [I.], '*Vita sancti Mennatis*: opera inedita di Leone Marsicano', *Istituto lombardo, Accademia di scienze e lettere: Rendiconti, Classe di lettere e scienze morali e storiche*, xcvii (1963), 467–90.

— *Iohannis Hymmonidis et Gauderici Veliterni, Leonis Ostiensis, Excerpta ex Clementinis recognitionibus a Tyrranio Rufino translatis*, Testi e documenti per lo studio dell'antichità, 24 (Milan, 1968).

OV: see RODGERS, R. H.

PALAZZINI, P., 'Frammenti di codici in Beneventana. Ammanuensi cassinesi a Fonte Avellana?', *Aevum*, xvii (1943), 254–8.

PALMAROCCHI, R., *L'abbazia di Montecassino e la conquista normanna* (Rome, 1913).

PANTONI, A., 'La basilica di Montecassino e quella di Salerno ai tempi di S. Gregorio VII', *Benedictina*, x (1956), 23–47.

— 'Documenti epigrafici sulla presenza di settentrionali a Montecassino nell'alto medioevo', *Benedictina*, xii (1958), 205–32.

— 'Descrizioni di Montecassino attraverso i secoli', *Benedictina*, xix (1972), 539–86.

— 'Le vicende della basilica di Montecassino attraverso la documentazione archeologica', *Misc. cassin.* xxxvi (1973).

PARTNER, P., 'Notes on the Lands of the Roman Church in the Early Middle Ages', *Papers of the British School at Rome*, xxxiv (1966), 67–78.

— *The Lands of St. Peter* (London, 1972).

PÁSZTOR, E., 'Riforma della chiesa nel secolo xi e l'origine del collegio dei cardinali', *Studi . . . Morghen*, ii. 609–25.

— 'San Pier Damiani, il cardinalato e la formazione della curia romana', *SG* x (1975), 319–39.

— 'La curia romana', *Istituzioni ecclesiastiche*, i. 490–504.

Paul of Bernried: PAUL OF BERNRIED, *Gregorii papae VII vita*, Watterich, i. 474–546.

PENCO, G., *Storia del monacesimo in Italia delle origini alla fine del medio evo*, i (Rome, 1961).

PETER DAMIANI, *Opera*, 2 vols., Migne, *PL* cxliv–cxlv.
See also PIERRE DAMIEN.

Peter the Deacon, *DVI*, or *DVI*: PETER THE DEACON, *De viris illustribus Casinensibus opusculus*, Migne, *PL* clxxiii. 1003–50.

Peter the Deacon, *OV*: see RODGERS, R. H.
See also *Chron. Cas.*; *Reg. Pet. Diac.*

Pflugk-Harttung, *Acta*: PFLUGK-HARTTUNG, J. VON, *Acta pontifica romanorum inedita*, 3 vols. (Tübingen and Stuttgart, 1881–6).

PIERRE DAMIEN, *Lettre sur la toute-puissance divine*, ed. A. Cantin, Sources chrétiennes, 191 (Paris, 1972).
See also PETER DAMIANI.

Pitra, *Anal. noviss.*: PITRA, J. B., *Analecta novissima Spicilegii Solesmensis altera continuatio*, 2 vols. (Paris, 1885–8).

PONTIERI, E., *I Normanni nell'Italia meridionale*, i. *La conquista* (Naples, [1971]).

Poupardin: POUPARDIN, R., *Les Institutions politiques et administratives des principautés lombardes de l'Italie méridionale (IXe au XIe siècles)* (Paris, 1907).

QFIAB: *Quellen und Forschungen aus italienischen Archiven und Bibliotheken.*

RABIKAUSKAS, P., 'Die römische Kurie in der päpstlichen Kanzlei', *Miscellanea historiae pontificum*, xx (Rome, 1958).

RABY, F. J. E., *A History of Christian Latin Poetry from the Beginnings to the End of the Middle Ages* (2nd edn., Oxford, 1953).

— *A History of Secular Latin Poetry in the Middle Ages*, 2 vols. (2nd edn., Oxford, 1957).

RB: *Revue bénédictine.*

Reg.: see Gregory VII, *Reg.*

Reg. pap. XIIIe s.: *Bibliothèque des Écoles françaises d'Athènes et de Rome*, 2ème série: *Registres et lettres des papes du XIIIe siècle*, 16 vols. (Paris, 1883-).

Reg. Pet. Diac.: *Registrum Petri Diaconi.*

REHM, B., 'Zur Entstehung der pseudoclementinischen Schriften', *Zeitschrift für neutestamentliche Wissenschaft*, xxxvii (1938), 77-184.

— 'Clemens Romanus II. (Ps. Clementinen)', *Reallexicon für Antike und Christentum*, iii (1957), 197-206.

REINDEL, K., 'Studium zur Überlieferung der Werke des Petrus Damiani', *DA* xv (1959), 23-102; xviii (1962), 314-417.

— 'Neue Literatur zu Petrus Damiani', *DA* xxxii (1976), 405-43.

Repertorium fontium historiae medii aevi primum ab Augusto Potthast digestum, new edn. by W. Holtzmann and R. Morghen (Rome, 1962-).

REUTER, W., *Die Gesinnung und die Massnahmen Gregors VII. in den Jahren 1080 bis 1085* (Greifswald, 1913).

*RIS*²: *Rerum italicarum scriptores: Continuatio*, 34 vols. (Città di Castello and Bologna, 1900-).

ROCKINGER, L., 'Briefsteller und Formelbücher des eilften bis vierzehnten Jahrhunderts', *Quellen und Erörterungen zur bayerischen und deutschen Geschichte*, ix (1863).

RODGERS, R. H., *Petri Diaconi: Ortus et vita iustorum cenobii Casinensis*, University of California Publications: Classical Studies, 10 (Berkeley, Los Angeles, and London, 1972) (= Peter the Deacon, *OV*, or *OV*).

Romuald of Salerno: ROMUALD OF SALERNO, *Chronicon*, ed. C. A. Garufi, *RIS*² (1900-35), vii.

Rossetti, *Forme di potere: Forme di potere e struttura sociale in Italia nel medioevo*, ed. G. Rossetti (Bologna, 1977).

RUBEUS, H., *Historiarum Ravennatum libri decem* (Venice, 1589).

SABA, A., 'Montecassino e la Sardegna medioevale', *Misc. cassin.* iv (1927).

SALVINI, R., 'Monuments of Norman Art in Sicily and South Italy', *Normans in Sicily*, pp. 64-92.

Sander, *Der Kampf*: SANDER, P., *Der Kampf Heinrichs IV. und Gregors VII.* (Berlin, 1893).

Santifaller, *QF*: *Quellen und Forschungen zum Urkunden- und Kanzleiwesen Papst Gregors VII.*, i. *Quellen: Urkunden, Regesten, Facsimilia*, ed. L. Santifaller, Studi e testi, 190 (Vatican City, 1957).

Santifaller, 'Saggio': SANTIFALLER, L., 'Saggio di un elenco di funzionari impiegati e scrittori della cancellaria pontificia dall'inizio all'anno 1099', *Bull. Ist. stor. ital.* lvi (1940), 1-858.

SB Berlin: *Sitzungsberichte der [kgl.] preussischen [deutschen] Akademie der Wissenschaften zu Berlin, philosophisch-historische Klasse.*

SCHETTINI, F., *La basilica di San Nicola* (Bari, 1967).

SCHIEFFER, R., *Die Entstehung des päpstlichen Investiturverbots für den deutschen König, MGH Schriften*, xxviii (Stuttgart, 1981).

SCHIPA, M., *Alfano I, archivescovo di Alerno. Studio critico-letterario* (Salerno, 1880).

Schmale, *Schisma*: SCHMALE, F.-J., *Studien zum Schisma des Jahres 1130* (Cologne and Graz, 1961).
See also Wattenbach–Holtzmann.

SCHMID, K., and WOLLASCH, J., 'Societas et fraternitas. Begründung eines kommentierten Quellenwerkes zur Erforschung der Personen und Personengruppen des Mittelalters', *Frühmittelalterliche Studien*, ix (1975), 1-48.

SCHMIDT, T., *Alexander II. und die römische Reformgruppe seiner Zeit*, Päpste und Papsttum, 11 (Stuttgart, 1977).

SCHMITZ, P., *Histoire de l'ordre de Saint Benoît*, 7 vols. (Maredsous, 1942-56.

SCHNEIDER, C., *Prophetisches Sacerdotium und heilsgeschichtliches Regnum im Dialog, 1073-1077. Zur Geschichte Gregors VII. und Heinrichs IV.*, Münstersche Mittelalter-Schriften, 9 (Munich, 1972).

SCHRAMM, P. E., *Kaiser, Rom und Renovatio* (2nd edn., Darmstadt, 1957).

SCHWARZ, U., *Amalfi im frühen Mittelalter (9.-11. Jahrhundert)*, Bibliothek des Deutschen Historischen Instituts in Rom, 49 (Tübingen, 1978).

SCHWARZMAIER, H.-M., 'Der *Liber vitae* von Subiaco', *QFIAB* xlviii (1968), 80-147.

— 'Das Kloster St. Georg in Lucca und der Ausgriff Montecassino in die Toscana', *QFIAB* xlix (1969), 148-85.

— *Lucca und das Reich bis zum Ende des 11. Jahrhunderts*, Bibliothek des Deutschen Historischen Instituts in Rom, 41 (Tübingen, 1972).

SERVATIUS, C., *Paschalis II. (1099-1118). Studien zu seiner Person und seiner Politik*, Päpste und Papsttum, 14 (Stuttgart, 1979).

SG: *Studi Gregoriani* (Rome, 1947-).

SMIDT, W., 'Über den Verfasser der drei letzten Redaktionen der Chronik Leos von Monte Cassino', *Papsttum und Kaisertum (Festschrift P. Kehr)* (Munich, 1926), 263-86.

— 'Guido von Monte Cassino und die "Fortsetzung" der Chronik Leos durch Petrus Diaconus', *Festschrift Albert Brackmann*, ed. L. Santifaller (Weimar, 1931), 293-323.

— 'Die vermeintliche und die wirkliche Urgestalt der Chronik Leos von Montecassino', *QFIAB* xxviii (1937/8), 286-97.

— 'Die "Historia Normannorum" von Amatus', *SG* iii (1948), 173-231.

SOUTHERN, R. W., 'Lanfranc of Bec and Berengar of Tours', *Studies in*

Medieval History Presented to Frederick Maurice Powicke, edd. R. W. Hunt, W. A. Pantin, and R. W. Southern (Oxford, 1948), 27–48.

Steindorff, *Jahrbücher*: STEINDORFF, E., *Jahrbücher des deutschen Reichs unter Heinrich III.*, Jahrbücher der deutschen Geschichte, 2 vols. (Leipzig, 1874–81).

Stud. Mitt. OSB: *Studien und Mitteilungen zur Geschichte des Benediktinerordens und seine Zweige.*

Studi . . . Morghen: *Studi sul medioevo cristiano offerti a Raffaello Morghen*, 2 vols., Istituto storico italiano per il medio evo, Studi storici, 83–92 (Rome, 1974).

STÜRNER, W., 'Der Königswahlparagraph im Papstwahldekret von 1059', *SG* ix (1972), 39–52.

SYDOW, J., 'Cluny und die Anfänge der apostolischen Kammer', *Stud. Mitt. OSB* lxiii (1951), 45–66.

— 'Untersuchungen zur kurialen Verwaltungsgeschichte im Zeitalter des Reformpapsttums', *DA* xi (1954/5), 18–73.

SZÖVÉRFFY, J., 'The Legends of St. Peter in Medieval Latin Hymns', *Traditio*, x (1954), 275–322.

— 'Der Investiturstreit und die Petrus-Hymnen des Mittelalters', *DA* xiii (1957), 228–40.

TELLENBACH, G., 'Der Sturz des Abtes Pontius von Cluny und seine geschichtliche Bedeutung', *QFIAB* xlii (1963), 13–55.

TIRELLI, V., 'Osservazioni sui rapporti tra sede apostolica, Capua e Napoli durante i pontificati di Gregorio VII e di Urban II', *Studi . . . Morghen*, ii. 961–1010.

Tosti, *Storia*: TOSTI, L., *Storia della badia di Monte Cassino*, 3 vols. (Naples, 1842–3).

TOUBERT, H., 'Le renouveau paléochrétien à Rome au début du XIIe siècle', *Cahiers archéologiques*, xx (1970), 99–154.

— ' "Rom et le Mont-Cassin": nouvelles remarques sur les fresques de l'église inférieure de Saint-Clément de Rome', *DOP* xxx (1976), 1–33.

Toubert, *Latium*: TOUBERT, P., *Les Structures du Latium médiéval*, 2 vols., Bibliothèque des Écoles françaises d'Athènes et de Rome, 221 (Rome, 1973).

TRAMONTANA, S., *I Normanni in Italia. Linee di ricerca sui primi insediamenti*, i. *Aspetti politici e militari* (Messina, 1970).

— *Mezzogiorno normanno e svevo* (Messina, 1972).

TRHS: *Transactions of the Royal Historical Society.*

Trinchera, *Syllabus*: TRINCHERA, F., *Syllabus Graecarum membranarum* (Naples, 1865).

Ughelli–Coleti: UGHELLI, F., *Italia sacra*, new edn. by N. Coleti, 10 vols. (Venice, 1717–22).

VEHSE, O., 'Benevent als territorium des Kirchenstaates bis zum Beginn der Avignonischen Epoche', *QFIAB* xxii (1930/1), 87–160.

WAIFERUS, *Historia inventionis corporis s. Secundini*, *AA SS Boll.* Feb. ii (1658), 531–5.

WALEY, D. P., *The Papal State in the Thirteenth Century* (London, 1961).

WALTER, C., 'Papal Political Imagery in the Lateran Palace', *Cahiers archéologiques*, xx (1970), 155–76; xxi (1971), 109–36.

Wattenbach-Holtzmann: WATTENBACH, W., and HOLTZMANN, R., *Deutschlands Geschichtsquellen im Mittelalter*, new edn. by F.-J. Schmale, 3 vols. (Darmstadt, 1967–71).

Watterich: WATTERICH, J. B. M., *Pontificum Romanorum qui fuerunt inde ab exeunte saeculo ix usque ad finem saeculi xiii vitae ab equalibus conscriptae*, 2 vols. (Leipzig, 1862).

WHITTON, D., 'Papal Policy in Rome, 1012–1124' (Univ. of Oxford D.Phil. thesis, 1979).

WILLARD, H. M., 'The *Fundicus*, a Port Facility of Montecassino in Medieval Amalfi', *Benedictina*, xix (1972), 253–61.

— 'Abbot Desiderius and the Ties between Montecassino and Amalfi in the Eleventh Century', *Misc. cassin.* xxxvii (1973).

— and CONANT, K. J., 'A Project for the Graphic Reconstruction of the Romanesque Abbey at Montecassino', *Speculum*, x (1935), 144–6. See also INGUANEZ, M.

William of Apulia: GUILLAUME DE POUILLE, *La Geste de Robert Guiscard*, ed. M. Mathieu, Istituto Siciliano di Studi bisantini e neoellenici, Testi e monumenti, 4 (Palermo, 1961).

William of Malmesbury: WILLIAM OF MALMESBURY, *Gesta regum Anglorum*, ed. W. Stubbs (London, Rolls Series, 1889).

WOLLEMBORG, L., 'L'abate Desiderio da Montecassino e i Normanni', *Samnium*, vii (1934), 5–34, 99–119.

— 'Il papato e la formazione dello stato normanno d'Italia (1016–1085)', *Samnium*, x (1937), 5–34, 117–46.

WÜHR, W., 'Die Wiedergeburt Montecassinos unter seinem ersten Reformabt Richer von Niederaltaich (†1055)', *SG* iii (1948), 369–450.

WULF VON GLANVELL, V., *Die Kanonessamlung des Kardinals Deusdedit*, i (Paderborn, 1905) (= Deusdedit, *Coll. can.*).

YEWDALE, R. B., *Bohemond I, Prince of Antioch* (Princeton, NJ, 1917).

ZAFARANA, Z., 'Sul "conventus" del clero romano nel maggio 1082', *Studi medievali*, 3rd ser., vii (1966), 399–403.

— 'Ricerche sul'*Liber de unitate ecclesiae conservanda*', ibid., vii (1966), 617–700.

ZEMA, D. B., 'The Houses of Tuscany and of Pierleoni in the Crisis of Rome in the Eleventh Century', *Traditio*, ii (1944), 155–75.

— 'Economic Reorganization of the Roman See during the Gregorian Reform', *SG* i (1947), 137–68.

ZRG KA: *Zeitschrift der Savigny-Stiftung für Rechtsgeschichte, kanonistische Abteilung.*

Index

Abbreviations a.: abbey; ab.: abbot; abp.: archbishop; adn.: archdeacon; ap.: antipope; b.: battle; bp.: bishop; c.: count; card.: cardinal; ch.: church; cs.: countess; d.: duke; da.: daughter; dn.: deacon; e.: eastern; emp.: emperor; emps.: empress; j.: judge; kg.: king; m.: monk; MC: Montecassino; mon.: monastery; mq.: marquis; p.: pope; pat.: patriarch; pr.: prince; pt.: priest; s.: son; St.: Saint; subdn.: subdeacon; t.: treaty; w.: western; wf.: wife

DATE DUE